Praise for *To Govern the Globe*

"*To Govern the Globe* is a brilliant distillation of 700 years of geopolitics, exposing how we arrived where we are, amid the worsening climate crisis and collapsing world orders. Al McCoy's eloquently written book is a call to action for us all, as time still remains to prevent an unprecedented cascade of catastrophes." —AMY GOODMAN, host of *Democracy Now!*

"In *To Govern The Globe*, Alfred McCoy deftly shows how successive world orders, seemingly entrenched and impossible to uproot, eventually decline. Periods of imperial decay, marked by unbridled greed, military overreach, and the spread of disease, can also give rise to revolutionary new perspectives. Where is the United States now, in the bloody, ultimately futile cycle of conquest and ruin? McCoy's provocative work generates probing questions about our global capacity for humanism and our collective chances for survival. With new cold wars looming between the US, Russia, and China, McCoy's writing is an indispensable guide for coping with the twin terrors of climate catastrophe and multiple pandemics." —KATHY KELLY, peace activist and co-coordinator of the Ban Killer Drones campaign

"A fascinating look at the rise and fall of empires and what it means for world orders. From colonial exploitation and capitalist ravaging of people and planet to arms-racing and warfare, Alfred McCoy offers a deep dive into how this history has led to the climate crisis—and the impacts it will have on our future." —RAY ACHESON, disarmament program director at the Women's International League for Peace and Freedom

"In an age where most scholars concentrate on a limited specialty, no one sees a bigger picture more brilliantly than Alfred McCoy. In this powerful, enlightening, and frightening book he gives us a magisterial view of the empires of the past—and of the force in our future that promises to dwarf them all." —ADAM HOCHSCHILD, author of *King Leopold's Ghost*

To Govern the Globe

World Orders and Catastrophic Change

Alfred W. McCoy

Haymarket Books
Chicago, Illinois

© 2021 Alfred McCoy

Published in 2021 by
Haymarket Books
PO Box 180165
Chicago, IL 60618
773-583-7884
info@haymarketbooks.org
www.haymarketbooks.org

Distributed to the trade in the US through Consortium Book Sales and
Distribution (www.cbsd.com) and internationally through Ingram Publisher
Services International (www.ingramcontent.com).

ISBN: 978-1-64259-578-9

Cover design by Eric Kerl.

Published with the generous support of Lannan Foundation and the Wallace
Action Fund.

Special discounts are available for bulk purchases by organizations and institutions. Please email info@haymarketbooks.org for more information.

Library of Congress Cataloging-in-Publication data is available.

10 9 8 7 6 5 4 3 2 1

*For my sister, Dace, and her husband, Sir Richard Ground,
who devoted their working lives to doing large things in
small places—he as chief justice of Bermuda and she as
founder of the National Trust for the Cayman Islands,
which saved a species, the blue iguana, from extinction*

Contents

Maps and Graphs

Foreword

Alfred McCoy rose to prominence as a historian during the Vietnam War era when he blew the lid off the CIA's role in heroin trafficking in Southeast Asia. Though McCoy is undoubtedly a brilliant scholar, that moniker hardly captures the true spirit of the immensely consequential and groundbreaking work he has given to us all.

For decades, McCoy has gone to where the history is unfolding, and, like an archeologist, has dug away to reveal stories that would otherwise go untold. McCoy was nearly killed by US-backed paramilitaries early in his career, and the CIA was so concerned about his revelations on drug trafficking that it tried to stop the publication of his book *The Politics of Heroin*. He was spied on by the FBI, audited by the IRS, and viewed as a threat by other three-letter agencies.

McCoy is one of the most eminent scholars in the world on the abuse of power and authority, on surveillance and repression, on the historical evolution of state-sanctioned torture in the United States and elsewhere, and, more recently, on the rapidly declining state of the US empire.

McCoy's latest book, *To Govern the Globe*, is a formidable work of scholarship spanning an incredible arc of world history. Yet it is a gripping and fast-paced read that manages to distill the complex history of the rise and fall of world empires into a narrative that is simultaneously exhilarating and terrifying. The book's scope is so massive that only a scholar of McCoy's skill could even consider attempting to capture it. McCoy's meticulous understanding of the past and present failures and excesses of empires gives him the rare credibility to offer a detailed, damning picture of the grim realities humankind faces as history transforms into our future. After reading *To Govern the Globe*, however, I must conclude that embedded within McCoy's book is a ray of hope demanding to be seen by us all before it's truly too late.

—Jeremy Scahill, August 2021

Author's Note

This book arose from the coincidence of two accidents, one imagined and the other all too real. During the first weeks of a sabbatical from the University of Wisconsin–Madison, I was much taken with the idea of a book that would analyze the rise and fall of empires through their geopolitics. For nearly a month, the project raced along at accelerating speed, hitting five, six, seven thousand words until, unexpectedly, it crashed into a conceptual wall, leaving a wreckage of factors and actors lying on my desk. I had tried, and failed, to explain the multifaceted phenomenon of empire through a monocausal argument.

To recover, I called my editor, Tom Engelhardt. Thanks to a few minutes of his oblique, Zen-like questions without answers, I plunged into weeks of thought that led, in February 2019, to a short essay for his online journal *TomDispatch* that contained the core argument for this book.

About the same time my initial book idea crashed, I had an actual accident, slipping on black ice in the middle of a harsh Wisconsin winter and shredding three of the four tendons in my right knee. When I awoke from surgery, I was in a locked leg brace that prevented me from driving, flying, or even walking more than a few steps. For nearly four months, all I could do was sit at the kitchen table, leg propped up, hands at the computer, reading and typing eighteen hours a day, seven days a week. By the time the leg brace came off at the start of summer, I had turned that short article into a first draft of this book.

After those four months of immobility, the Association for Asian Studies flew me to Bangkok, where I had the opportunity to try out the book's core argument, conceived in immaculate isolation, in a cavernous hotel ballroom full of regional experts. After that, I celebrated my mobility by continuing around the globe for some unconventional fieldwork, in order to liven up this narrative of world orders over the past six centuries—stopping at Angkor Wat for adjectives, an Oslo museum for visuals to describe Viking ships, Bruges to view the ceremonial fireplace celebrating the lineage of Emperor Charles V (with four statues of his grandparents, including Ferdinand and Isabella), and then on to London to stroll that city's streets and museums with family, collecting insights as we went. As Julys go, it was different and memorable. I continued writing even as I flew, and by the time I got back home in August that first draft was largely edited. Those few exciting months of insight and travel were followed by a full year of painstakingly dull editing, cutting, revising, and fact-checking.

The text that emerged is an ambitious work, and, by the same token, it is necessarily imperfect. During my fifty-year career as a historian, I have published dozens of books and hundreds of essays that required the reading of countless thousands of historical studies and documents. Yet all that work proved woefully inadequate for the challenges of this project. In covering the globe and spanning seven centuries, this study required a depth and breadth of historical knowledge beyond the ken of any individual historian—indeed beyond what anyone could ever learn in the span of a single lifetime.

Fortunately, I did not have to work alone. For nearly a century now, historians have refined the discipline's craft and expanded its coverage to allow us a nuanced understanding of the last millennium. I drew upon that rich corpus by reading several thousand articles and book extracts focused on centuries and continents beyond my narrow specialization as a historian of modern Southeast Asia. I came away impressed with both the magisterial sweep and granular focus of narrative history that makes it, in my view, the queen of social sciences. And I became convinced that our understanding of almost any contemporary problem, no matter how seemingly recondite or intractable, can be enriched by a historical perspective.

That belief in the exceptional analytic power of history underlies this study's attempt to use the past as a prism for understanding the present and speculating about the future. But a caveat is instantly in order. When the present has receded far enough to become the past, most historians can tell us not only what happened, but why it happened just that way. Even if other historians argue about those conclusions, as they are wont to do, they still have to admit that the work in question has offered insight or understanding. However, in using the past to predict the future, historians have accrued a lengthy record of projections that are risibly wrong. Mindful of that dismal record, as I track key trends from the past through the present and into the future, I have tried to avoid the most obvious pitfalls by hewing closely to the published climate science. I hope this approach may deepen our understanding of this profoundly shared experience.

With the prospect of irreversible global warming bearing down upon us with undeniable force, such conjecture seemed to me a chance well worth taking. Despite the risks of error, we still need a way to apply our extraordinarily rich historical knowledge to the future, to try to understand our difficult choices and their likely consequences. Nonetheless, my conclusions about the future are obviously and necessarily speculative.

Another caveat is also in order. This is a work that sweeps across seven centuries, a vast span of human history, and touches, in varying degrees, on the stories of ten modern empires, each of which has a dedicated cadre of specialists. I am a historian of just one of those empires and one of these periods. Clearly, specialists will find fault with some of this study's specifics. Indeed, I admit the likelihood of errors of fact or interpretation and apologize in advance for all of them. But in a larger sense, such failings are inherent in the nature of a work whose logic lies in its broad sweep through periods and empires in an effort to discern the deeper dynamics of change across centuries—which is, I would argue, the ultimate justification for the continued presence of the ancient discipline of history in the modern academy.

A final admission: although historians aspire to a timeless recounting of the past, we are all products of our own time, in some way recasting the past from the perspective of our present. In my case, writing at the cusp of a shift in Washington's global power has, I hope, sharpened my analytic focus, allowing me to sort through the confusion of an ongoing imperial decline and identify a more lasting form of global power called the world order. Writing at a time when climate change threatens our ordered world has allowed me to look back over the past seven hundred years to see parallel moments, when maelstroms of various sorts acted with similar force, creating or destroying earlier world orders.

In a generation or two, historians, writing from the perspective of another time, will no doubt see this past differently. But for now, with all its limitations, this book is my attempt to look back on the past to identify the deeper, underlying trends that have shaped the present and may well influence our future.

Alfred W. McCoy
Madison, Wisconsin

Chronology
World Orders, 1300 to 2300

Iberian Age

1300 Carbon dioxide (CO_2) in atmosphere is stable at 275 parts per million.

1347 Black Death pandemic reaches Europe, kills 60 percent of the population.

1415 Portugal ventures abroad, capturing port of Ceuta, North Africa, and massacring Muslims.

1441 Portugal's ships arrive from Western Sahara with first shipment of African slaves.

1453 Ottoman Empire occupies Constantinople, ending the Byzantine Empire.

1455 Papal bull gives Portugal right to conquer Africa and enslave Africans.

1456 Portugal builds its first fortified port (*feitoria*) at Arguin, Mauritania, West Africa.

1469 Marriage of Queen Isabella of Castile and Ferdinand of Aragon merges their kingdoms.

1488 Portuguese explorers reach the Cape of Good Hope.

1493 Christopher Columbus returns from his first voyage to the New World.

1494 Spain and Portugal sign the Treaty of Tordesillas, dividing the world beyond Europe.

1510 Portuguese fleet captures Goa, India, as capital for their Asian empire.

1511 In Santo Domingo, Spanish friar Antonio de Montesinos condemns enslavement of Amerindians.

1520 Spanish conquistador Hernán Cortés defeats Aztec Empire, occupies Mexico City.

1532 Spanish conquistador Francisco Pizarro captures the Inca emperor at Cajamarca, Peru.

1545 Spain opens the world's largest silver mine at Potosí, Bolivia.

1570 Christian Holy League armada destroys Ottoman fleet at Lepanto, Greece.

1578 Muslim forces slaughter Portugal's king, aristocracy, and army in Morocco.

1581 Seven United Provinces of the Netherlands declare independence from Spain.

1588 Spanish Armada loses half its forces in a failed invasion of England.

1602 Dutch East India Company is established as world's first major corporation.

1618 Thirty Years' War begins in Europe.

1648 Peace of Westphalia ends the Thirty Years' War.

1689 England's Bill of Rights protects basic liberties of all subjects.

1764 British East India Company defeats Mughal Empire at Buxar, northeast India.

1771 Richard Arkwright opens world's first textile mill at Derbyshire, England.

1784 Scottish engineer James Watt designs the steam engine.

1791 Slave revolt starts in the French colony of Haiti.

1793 Eli Whitney invents cotton gin, making slave-grown US cotton globally competitive.

1804 Napoleon crowned emperor of France.

1805 British navy defeats French-Spanish fleet at Cape Trafalgar, Spain.

British Imperial Era

1807 British Parliament outlaws the slave trade.

1813 Napoleon defeated at Battle of Leipzig in Germany, sent into exile.

1815 Congress of Vienna ends Napoleonic Wars, advocates abolition of the slave trade.

1833 Britain frees 775,000 slaves in West Indies; pays owners £20 million, ex-slaves nothing.

1857 Mutiny by Indian troops leads to end of East India Company and starts direct British rule.

1859 World's first commercial oil well drilled in Titusville, Pennsylvania.

1879 Henry Morton Stanley begins explorations to claim Congo for King Leopold of Belgium.

1880 CO_2 in atmosphere is at "preindustrial" baseline of 280 parts per million.

1882 Thomas Edison installs coal-fired electrical grid in lower Manhattan.

1885 Berlin Conference divides Africa among rival European empires.

1896 Physicist Svante Arrhenius predicts rising CO_2 emissions will warm Arctic climate.

1898 British forces use Maxim machine guns to slaughter 10,800 Muslim jihadists in Sudan.

1899 British begin defeat of Boer settlers in South Africa with mass incarceration of civilians.

1900 A dozen empires rule 146 colonies, covering 40 percent of the globe and one-third of humanity.

1906 Britain launches the HMS *Dreadnought*, the world's first battleship.

1914 World War I starts and is soon stalemated in murderous trench warfare.

1916 In the Battle of Jutland, British navy defeats German fleet and maintains food blockade.

1919 Victors in World War I expropriate the empires of their enemies at Versailles Peace Conference.

1927 Spanish defeat Berber rebels in North Africa with poison gas bombardment.

1935 US tests the B-17 Flying Fortress, the first effective long-range bomber aircraft.

1937 Italian leader Benito Mussolini conquers Ethiopia using mustard gas against troops and civilians.

1940 Nazi Germany occupies France, but loses the air war in the Battle of Britain.

1941 Japanese Imperial forces attack Hawaii, Philippines, and Malaya.

1943 Nazi Germany suffers massive defeat at Stalingrad, Soviet Union.

Washington's World Order

1944 Allied nations establish international economic order at Bretton Woods, New Hampshire.

1945 UN Charter adopted at San Francisco; Japan surrenders after US drops atomic bombs.

1947 US Central Intelligence Agency formed to fight Soviet Union in the Cold War.

1948 UN General Assembly approves Universal Declaration of Human Rights.

1949 US and Western Europe establish North Atlantic Treaty Organization.

1953 CIA-sponsored coup ousts Iran's elected prime minister, installs the Shah in power.

1954 US Navy launches the USS *Nautilus*, world's first nuclear-powered submarine.

1956 Britain and France invade Egypt's Suez Canal Zone, withdraw in defeat.

1958 CO_2 in atmosphere reaches 316 parts per million, up from 280 parts in 1880.

1960 Petroleum products (oil, natural gas) surpass coal as a main source of US energy supply.

1961 CIA's invasion of Cuba at the Bay of Pigs ends in humiliating defeat.

1962 France negotiates end to Algerian War, frees fourteen African nations.

1964 Washington begins escalation of its military involvement in the Vietnam War.

1965 US-backed general seizes power in Indonesia, murders a million suspected Communists.

1966 US launches world's first Defense Satellite Communications System.

1972 After 58,000 combat deaths, US withdraws forces from South Vietnam in defeat.

1973 Britain joins the European Union after freeing its last major colonies.

1979 CIA starts covert war against Soviet occupation of Afghanistan.

1989 Soviet forces withdraw from Afghanistan after unsustainable losses.

1991 After breakup of Soviet Union, US becomes world's sole superpower.

2001 US launches CIA covert operation to overthrow Taliban government in Afghanistan.

2002 China marks first year as member of the World Trade Organization.

2003 Washington invades Iraq and begins nine-year occupation.

2013 Beijing launches trillion-dollar Belt and Road Initiative to develop Eurasia.

2014 China begins dredging to form island military bases in South China Sea.

2015 World's nations adopt Paris accord to limit climate change.

2016 As populist, anti-globalization demagogues win office worldwide, Donald Trump is elected US presdent.

2017 US withdraws from Paris climate accord; Beijing hosts Belt and Road Forum.

2018 CO_2 in atmosphere reaches 410 parts per million.

2019 Beijing commissions the *Shandong*, its first China-built aircraft carrier.

2020 China completes world's second system of global telecommunications satellites.

2021 US withdraws unconditionally from Afghanistan as Taliban rebels capture the countryside and threaten cities.

Twenty-First Century and Beyond

2024 China finishes high-speed rail network with 24,000 miles of track.

2027 Beijing's investment in Belt and Road Initiative reaches $1.3 trillion.

2030 China's economic output reaches $36 trillion and is 40 percent larger than America's.

2034 For the first time in US history, people over age sixty-five outnumber children under eighteen.

2040 Average world temperature reaches 1.5°C above preindustrial levels.

2049 US social welfare spending on the elderly reaches 50 percent of federal budget.

2050 As CO_2 in atmosphere approaches 550 parts per million, rising sea level floods Shanghai, Saigon, Mumbai, and Bangkok.

2060 Average world temperature reaches 3.0°C above preindustrial levels.

2070 North China and northern India have heat waves fatal for those without air conditioning.

2100 Average world temperature reaches 5.0°C above preindustrial levels.

2200 Global warming raises sea level by as much as seven feet.

2300 Temperature of 9.0°C above preindustrial levels raises sea level by eighteen feet.

Chapter 1
Empires and World Orders

When the clock struck midnight on New Year's of 2050, there was little cause for celebration. There were, of course, the usual toasts and air kisses in the high-rise apartments and climate-controlled compounds of the comfortably affluent. But for most of humanity it was just another day of adversity bordering on misery—a desperate and often losing struggle to find food, water, shelter, and safety.

After storm surges had swept away coastal barriers erected at enormous cost, rising seas were flooding the downtowns of major cities that once housed more than 100 million people. The streets of Alexandria, Bangkok, Mumbai, Saigon, and Shanghai were flooded with several feet of standing seawater that fouled water mains, filled sewers, and shorted out power lines, rendering much of those cities uninhabitable. Low-lying regions like the Mekong Delta, the Nile Delta, and the coast of Bangladesh were sinking or had sunk beneath surging seas, displacing millions of farming families. Relentless waves were eating away at shorelines around the world, putting villages, towns, and cities at risk.[1]

Every summer, temperatures in tropical latitudes worldwide soared, often remaining well above 100°F (38°C) for weeks at a time. Farmlands in Africa and Asia were being lost to drought and desertification, making staple grains increasingly unaffordable for the world's poor. With the oceans still warming rapidly, coastal communities struggled to find the schools of fish that had once been their main source of protein. As 140 million climate change refugees in Africa, Latin America, and South Asia filled leaky boats or marched overland in their desperate search for food and shelter, affluent nations worldwide were shutting and walling their borders, leaving ships packed with people to founder at sea and pushing crowds back from those borders with tear gas and gunfire.[2]

Yet even these reluctant host countries were hardly immune from the pain. In the United States, there was insufferable heat, uncontrollable wild-fires, unpredictable weather, and unending hunger. Every summer, powerful hurricanes pummeled the East and Gulf Coasts, forcing insurance companies to cancel coverage for millions of homeowners. New York, Boston, and San Francisco built massive seawalls to survive the storm surges, but the federal government had abandoned Miami and New Orleans to the relentless rise of the tides.[3]

Blistering summer heat and devastating storms had reduced the harvests from the country's Midwestern and Southern breadbaskets by 10 to 20 percent, raising food prices and bringing ever more hunger to the nation's poor. Every year, cities across America suffered one or two months of sweltering 90-degree weather, with Los Angeles and Phoenix regularly enduring weeks of temperatures above 120°F (49°C). Massive wildfires devastated vast stretches of the West, destroying dozens of towns and thousands of homes every summer.[4]

Such widespread suffering will not come from some unforeseen disaster but from a simple and already well-understood imbalance in the basic elements that sustain human life—air, earth, fire, and water. As carbon dioxide emissions from fossil fuels climb to an unsustainable 550 parts per million in the atmosphere by 2050 and average world temperatures rise by as much as 4.2°F (2.3°C), climate change will degrade the quality of life in every country and continent on earth in ways that are hard to grasp. With seas warming, permafrost receding, and moist rain forests in Africa and the Amazon drying into savannah, the closing decades of the twenty-first century will bring even more adverse conditions.[5]

This dismal vision of life on earth at midcentury comes not from some flight of literary fantasy on my part, but from the published environmental science on global warming. Such data-dense reports have long predicted a troubled future for humanity. Although the impact of climate change on the current system of global governance is still uncertain, we can all see the troubling signs of environmental crisis right now in the world around us— severe summers, intense storms, increased flooding, and worsening wildfires.

The Fiery Summer of 2019–2020

Indeed, in the summer of 2019, the world was already on fire. As temperatures around the globe climbed to scorching records, devastating forest fires erupted on six continents. After California experienced what the state called the "deadliest and most destructive wildfires in its history in 2017 and 2018," the fire season of 2019 brought 7,860 blazes that burned 260,000 acres of woodlands. As fiery winds reached more than 100 miles per hour in Northern California and relative humidity dropped to a bone-dry 1 percent, utility companies suspended electrical service to avoid sparking more fires, plunging towns and cities into darkness. Climate change had already expanded the state's fire season by 75 days, so those wild fires were not a cyclical event, likely to abate anytime in the foreseeable future.[6]

Simultaneously in South America, the Amazon experienced its worst wildfires in eleven years. According to Brazil's space agency, the number of outbreaks increased by 30 percent to 89,178 fires, which devastated 2.4 million acres, an area larger than Yellowstone National Park. Since 2004, the Brazilian state of Pará alone had lost forest covering 15 million acres, an area about the size of Ireland or Sri Lanka, threatening the long-term survival of the vast Amazon rain forest.[7]

As the earth turned on its axis and summer came to the Southern Hemisphere, temperatures soared to a record 120°F (°49C) in Sydney, sparking a maelstrom of bushfires across Australia. In October, lightning struck Gospers Mountain in the state of New South Wales, igniting a fire that burned two million acres before it was contained. Dozens of similar mega-fires soon swept the country's heavily populated southeast, destroying sixteen million acres of forests over the next four months. Although the government mobilized three thousand army reservists to fight the flames, 34 people died, more than 2,700 homes were destroyed, and hundreds of millions of wild animals perished. Clouds of smoke darkened the skies above Canberra, Melbourne, and Sydney. They formed a giant plume the size of the United States that circled the globe, fouling the air above cities in New Zealand and as far away as South America.[8]

That December, while the world was still burning, the United Nations convened a climate conference in Madrid. Representatives from nearly two hundred nations met with a mandate to adopt strict emission controls that would keep any increase in the globe's average temperature below 1.5°C—the target the UN had set four years earlier in Paris to control climate change. "The decisions we make here will ultimately define whether we chose a path of hope or a path of surrender," said UN Secretary-General António

Guterres in his opening address. "We have the tools, we have the science, we have the resources. Let us show we also have the political will that people demand from us."[9]

Unfortunately, that political will was sadly lacking. Despite a desperate midnight effort to patch together an agreement on emissions goals, the conference ultimately (and unsurprisingly) failed because of opposition from the very few countries responsible for producing much of the world's greenhouse gases. Representatives of smaller nations, reported the *Washington Post*, accused Australia, Brazil, and the United States—the very places with those burning forests—"of obstructing key parts of the negotiations and undermining the spirit and goals" of the Paris climate accord.[10]

Not only did the diplomats representing those three countries cripple the conference, they also did so at the behest of politicians famous both for their full-throated opposition to environmental science and for a deep belief that climate change denial was the best way to defend national sovereignty and protect the world order that had long assured their prosperity.

Given that Australia produces 37 percent of the world's coal exports, its conservative government has a strong stake in the global economy's reliance on carbon fuels. Almost all of that coal goes to China, adding to the carbon dioxide emissions that make this Asian nation the world's leading source of greenhouse gases. Prime Minister Scott Morrison has long been an aggressive advocate for the Australian coal industry, famous for appearing before Parliament during one scorching heat wave brandishing a large black lump and saying soothingly, "This is coal. Don't be afraid, don't be scared." In December 2019, he denied any link between the inferno ravaging his land and climate change, saying: "There are some fires that have been started by just carelessness, others sadly have been the result of direct arson, many have been created by dry lightning strikes." Simultaneously, his deputy prime minister denounced environmental activists who tied the fires to climate change and the coal industry, calling those claims "the ravings of some pure, enlightened and woke capital-city greenies."[11]

While the Amazon burned, Brazil's populist president Jair Bolsonaro blamed environmentalists, saying, "Regarding the fires in the Amazon, I'm under the impression that [they] could have been set by the NGOs [non-governmental organizations], because they had asked for money." When Brazil's space agency released satellite data showing a sharp rise in the Amazon's deforestation, Bolsonaro called the report "a lie" and fired the physicist who headed the agency. Pope Francis condemned the "blind and destructive mentality" of those behind the devastation of the rain forest, but Bolsonaro shot back, saying: "Brazil is the virgin that every foreign pervert wants to get their hands on." Speaking at the UN General Assembly that September, he insisted that those forests were "practically untouched," attacked the "lying and sensational media" for fake news about the fires, and dismissed any idea that the Amazon rain forest is "a heritage of humankind."[12]

Still, Donald Trump outdid them both in his determined denial of climate science. Back in 2012, citizen Trump had tweeted: "The concept of global warming was created by and for the Chinese in order to make US manufacturing non-competitive." During the 2016 presidential campaign, candidate Trump called it a "hoax." In June 2017, newly inaugurated President Trump announced his withdrawal from the UN's Paris climate accord, claiming it "disadvantages the United States to the exclusive benefit of other countries." When his own administration released its *National Climate Assessment* in November 2018, including a grave warning about the dangers of rising greenhouse gases, Trump said, "I don't believe it." Lending real force to those words, his White House team doubled down on its demolition of every possible emissions control measure adopted by the previous administration.[13]

Speaking in January 2020 to world leaders in Davos, Switzerland, then-president Trump delivered a withering dismissal of climate activists. With a knowing smile, he told the corporate executives who filled the seats before him: "We must reject the perennial prophets of doom and their predictions of the apocalypse. . . . They are the heirs of yesterday's foolish fortune tellers. And I have them, and you have them, and we all have them. . . . They predicted an overpopulation crisis in the 1960s, mass starvation in the '70s, and an end of oil in the 1990s." Then, portraying himself as a staunch defender of the current world order, he added: "These alarmists always demand the same thing: absolute power to dominate, transform and control every aspect of our lives. We will never let radical socialists destroy our economy, wreck our country or eradicate our liberty."[14]

Trump's attack on climate science occurred while smoke from that incendiary summer's fires was still circling the earth, creating one of human history's cruelest ironies. In their determined denial of climate change, the leaders of Australia, Brazil, and the US were destroying the very world order they were seemingly so set on defending. Moreover, their populist rhetoric as well as their myopic insensitivity to the gravity of the historical moment were shared by a rising generation of political leaders worldwide.

In the US, both liberal and conservative political elites in the New York–Washington corridor of power have been on top of the world for so long that they can't remember how they got there. In 1945, following a catastrophic war that left some 70 million people dead and countless cities destroyed, Washington led the world in forming a new system of global governance, exemplified by the United Nations, that would not only assure US hegemony but also foster an era of unprecedented peace and prosperity. But as populism, nationalism, and anti-globalism came to dominate the country's public discourse around 2010, surprisingly few American leaders rose to defend their world order. When accelerating global warming began to weaken that international system, many seemed remarkably oblivious to the dangers of climate change, remaining largely silent after Trump's 2017 withdrawal from the UN climate accord. The opposition Democratic Party's candidates dutifully endorsed climate science during their 2020 presidential primary, but even they relegated its discussion to a single, soon-forgotten "town hall" meeting and remained focused on domestic issues for the rest of the campaign. Indeed, in February 2020, at one of the most watched Democratic primary debates, not a single question was asked about climate change. During the presidential debates that fall, moderators asked the first questions about climate change in 20 years, prompting Trump to blame California's disastrous wildfires not on global warming but on the state's failure to rake the forests. His Democratic challenger, Joe Biden, promised a $2 trillion plan to achieve net-zero emissions by the far-distant date of 2050, while somehow preserving a role for the oil and gas industry.[15]

For ordinary citizens trying to understand how such powerful forces might play out in the coming decades, the real question is not the future of US global hegemony but the fate of the world order that Washington built at the peak of its power after World War II. For the past 75 years, American global dominion had rested on a "delicate duality."[16] The raw realpolitik of overseas military bases, covert coups, and military interventions had been balanced by a surprisingly liberal world order—with sovereign states rich and poor meeting at the UN to debate problems like climate change, an international rule of law that muted armed conflict, a World Health

Organization that worked cooperatively to end epidemics, and a development effort led by the World Bank that lifted nearly half of humanity out of extreme poverty.[17] By 2020, however, Washington and the entire world faced a fundamental question: Can this liberal international system survive the ongoing erosion of US global power and the potentially catastrophic heating of the planet?

Despite the many challenges facing the country, America's foreign policy elites remained supremely confident that Washington's world order would survive even the eclipse of the country's global hegemony. Indeed, many of them staked their reputations on that debatable proposition. At a September 2018 meeting in Philadelphia, a veritable who's who of prominent American leaders, including Joe Biden, former national security adviser Susan Rice, and another ex–national security adviser, H.R. McMaster, concluded that "tectonic shifts in the global order and its institutions were possible but not yet imminent."[18] Amid a proliferation of populist autocrats worldwide and their attacks on the global economy, Princeton political scientist G. John Ikenberry remained confident that the American-made world order would endure because international issues such as climate change make its "protean vision of interdependence and cooperation . . . more important as the century unfolds."[19] Somewhat more cautiously, the long-serving president of the influential Council on Foreign Relations, Richard N. Haass, argued in a 2019 essay that the "post–Cold War order cannot be restored," but that Washington could still "regain its reputation as a benign actor" and thus save the world from "deeper disarray" or even "trends that spell catastrophe."[20]

Such experts seemed to be saying that the decline of US global power was, by itself, nothing special. After all, in the four thousand years since humanity's first empire formed in the Fertile Crescent, at least two hundred empires have risen, collided with other imperial powers, and in time collapsed.[21] In the past century alone, two dozen modern empires have fallen, and the world has prospered in their wake. The global order did not even seem to blink when the other superpower of the Cold War era, the Soviet empire, imploded in 1991, freeing its fifteen "republics" and seven "satellites" to become 22 newly capitalist nations. Washington took that epochal event largely in stride. There were no grand triumphal events in the tradition of ancient Rome, with manacled Russian captives and their plundered treasures paraded down Pennsylvania Avenue. Instead, a Manhattan real estate developer bought a twenty-foot concrete chunk of the Berlin Wall for display near Madison Avenue, which would soon be barely noticed by busy shoppers.[22]

So, if the decline of the planet's sole superpower is no more consequential than, say, the Soviet collapse, what, we might ask, will it take to change Washington's world order? Or thought of a bit differently, once US global power has faded, what sort of legacy will it leave and how long will that legacy last? To address such complex questions, it's necessary to turn to history. Admittedly, its analogies are always imperfect, yet the past remains our best means of understanding the present and our only viable guide to the future.

Apart from nations and above even empires, there is a less visible but more lasting level of global governance: the world order. Despite being overshadowed by the rise and decline of empires, it has played a surprisingly significant, if seldom emphasized, role in international relations for the past five centuries. Through the way they structure relations among nations and shape the cultures of the peoples who live within them, world orders can outlast the powerful empires that created them. Those global systems, in turn, have largely been shaped historically by how they treated just two key political issues: human rights and state sovereignty. For over five hundred years, changing definitions of those two seemingly small areas of human society have, in fact, produced seismic shifts in the global order and the conditions of life for much of humanity.

World orders are far more deeply integrated into society than we might imagine. Indeed, over the past five centuries, their uprooting has required a perfect storm of history's most powerful forces. Projecting that past into the future, climate change is now gathering sufficient destructive strength to cripple Washington's liberal world order and create an opening for Beijing's decidedly illiberal one. If ongoing carbon control measures fail to prevent the impending environmental maelstrom, then the eclipse of the current global system will undoubtedly have lasting, deleterious consequences for the planet and its peoples, leaving the legacy of Washington's world order with about the significance of that block of Berlin Wall concrete on Madison Avenue. To grasp the implications of these impending changes, we need to understand the character of world orders, particularly their surprisingly profound influence.

The Nature of World Orders

Despite their aura of awe-inspiring power, empires tend to be ephemeral creations of an individual conqueror like Alexander the Great or Napoleon Bonaparte that fade quickly after their death or defeat. By contrast, world orders are much more deeply rooted, resilient global systems created by a convergence of economic, ideological, and geopolitical forces. On the surface, they entail diplomatic agreement among the most powerful nations, which are usually those with formal empires or international influence. Lacking the sovereignty of nations and the raw power of empires, world orders are essentially broad agreements about relations among nation-states and their peoples, lending them an amorphous, even elusive quality.

At a deeper level, however, world orders entwine themselves in the cultures, commerce, and values of countless societies. They influence the languages people speak, the laws that order their lives, and the ways they work, worship, and even play. They are woven into the fabric of an entire civilization, with a consequent capacity to far outlive the empires that formed them. If the economic globalization of the past two centuries was a process, then the current world order is its ultimate product. World orders have much less visible power than empires, but they are more pervasive and persistent. To uproot such a deeply embedded global system takes an extraordinary event, even a catastrophe. Across the span of five continents and seven centuries, a series of calamities—from the devastating epidemics of 1350 through the coming climate crisis of 2050—has produced a relentless succession of rising empires and fading world orders.

If we focus on the last five centuries, new world orders seem to arise when a maelstrom of death or destruction coincides with some slower, yet deeper, social transformation to sweep away the old order. Since the start of the age of exploration in the fifteenth century, some 90 empires, major and minor, have come and gone.[23] In those same five hundred years, however, there have been just three world orders, all arising in the West—the Iberian age after 1494, the British imperial era from 1815, and the Washington world system from 1945 to perhaps something like 2030.

Each transition to a new world order has occurred when a massively destructive cataclysm has coincided with major social change. The rise of the Iberian age of exploration was preceded by a century of epidemics, known as the Black Death, that killed 60 percent of the populations of Europe and China, rupturing the constraints of the medieval social order. Similarly, the British imperial era emerged when the ravages of the Napoleonic Wars coincided with the dynamism of the industrial revolution, unleashing the power of coal-fired steam energy and imperial rule to change the face of the globe. After the unprecedented devastation of World War II, Washington's leadership in rebuilding and reordering a damaged planet established the current world system. By the middle decades of the present century if not before, global warming caused by fossil fuel emissions will likely equal or surpass those earlier catastrophes on a universal scale of "disaster magnitude," with the potential to precipitate the eclipse of Washington's world order and the ascent of Beijing's global system.[24]

Such world orders are not the mere imaginings of historians trying, decades or centuries later, to impose their own logic on a chaotic past. In each case, the great imperial powers of the moment tried to reorder their worlds for generations to come through formal agreements: the Treaty of Tordesillas in 1494, the Congress of Vienna in 1815, and the San Francisco Conference, which drafted the UN charter, in 1945. Should China succeed America as the world's preeminent power, future historians will likely look back at the Belt and Road Forum, which in 2017 brought representatives of 130 nations to Beijing, as the formal start of the Chinese era.

Only weeks after the navigator Christopher Columbus returned from the Americas in 1493, the pope awarded Spain all lands west of an imaginary line drawn down the middle of the Atlantic and affirmed Portugal's prior claim to lands and seas east of that line. Significantly, the Vatican granted both kingdoms the right to reduce all the peoples they conquered or captured within those global domains to perpetual slavery. To determine that line's precise location, those two Iberian powers met for months in a small Spanish city to negotiate the Treaty of Tordesillas. Not only did it (and related papal bulls) divide the world beyond Europe between those two kingdoms, but it also forged history's first global order by imposing a religious segregation between Christians and "pagans" that would persist for another three hundred years.

The succeeding British world order was shaped by both the Congress of Vienna in 1815, which would reapportion Europe after Napoleon's defeat, and the Berlin Conference of 1885, which would divide up all of Africa among the European powers on grounds of their supposed racial superiority.

As Britain's imperial age collapsed into two world wars, Washington's new world order took form in two major conferences: in 1944 at Bretton Woods, New Hampshire, where 44 Allied nations created an international finance system exemplified by the World Bank; and a year later at San Francisco, where 50 nations adopted the UN Charter.

Each of these treaties would shape their worlds in the most fundamental ways, articulating universal principles meant to define the nature of nations and the rights of all humans who lived within them. Over the span of half a millennium, this succession of hegemonic global orders also conducted what seems like a never-ending debate, largely within the Western intellectual tradition, over the nature of human rights and the limits of state sovereignty.

In dividing the world between two Catholic kings, the Treaty of Tordesillas and parallel papal decrees created an expansive form of state power that might be called imperial sovereignty. Not only could rising empires conquer whole continents, but they could also extend their territory to encompass entire oceans through the legal doctrine of a closed sea (*mare clausum*). Under this principle, Portugal gained dominion over the Indian Ocean while Spain claimed the Pacific. When the Protestant Dutch began exploring the Indian Ocean a century later, they rejected that principle to argue for "freedom of the seas"—a doctrine that the British later made foundational to their imperial age and that Washington extended to the skies and even to space. In a deliciously ironic twist, a rising China has recently shaken the current global order by reviving the Iberian principle of *mare clausum* to claim an adjacent sea as its sovereign territory.[25]

During the five centuries following Tordesillas, such expansive forms of state sovereignty would become intertwined with changing concepts of human rights. Each global hegemon has, in its time, visited some sort of outrage upon humanity, inspiring reformers to articulate higher standards for human rights and liberties. By encouraging the Catholic conquest of overseas territories, those fifteenth-century papal decrees used the distinction between Christian and pagan to legitimate both the enslavement of Amerindians and the human traffic in millions of Africans. Almost from the moment these abuses began, however, Spanish religious leaders like Bartolomé de Las Casas and Francisco de Vitoria condemned them as crimes, beginning a process that, through decades of political struggle, arrived at the realization that all humankind is one—thereby laying the conceptual foundation for both human rights and international law.

As the Protestant Reformation swept through Europe in the sixteenth century, the Dutch rebelled against the Spanish Empire to claim their own national independence under a constitution that articulated principles of religious freedom. A century later, the British Parliament ousted King James II, a Catholic sovereign who threatened their Protestant faith, and enacted the Bill of Rights of 1689, which articulated, for the first time, foundational principles of individual liberty. That same year, the philosopher John Locke published his influential *Two Treatises of Government* arguing that, under natural law, everyone had the right to life, liberty, and property. Yet both the Dutch and British Empires would reserve such liberties for themselves, leaving them free to carry Iberia's slave trade and its transgressions against indigenous sovereignty to new heights. After Britain's religious reformers fought for decades to resolve the contradiction between liberty at home and slavery abroad, the Royal Navy, starting in 1807, launched an 80-year campaign to eradicate the slave trade in the Atlantic and Indian Oceans. That largely successful effort thereby established a defining attribute of their emerging world order. But in the late nineteenth century, the colonial powers—the British foremost among them—used an invented hierarchy of civilized races and "lesser breeds" to justify their conquests in Africa and Asia, where they stripped their colonial subjects of civil rights and extracted from each of them months of unpaid labor.[26]

Formal resolution of these imperial contradictions would have to wait until 1945, when Washington led the world's nations in drafting the UN Charter that promised its peoples the freedom to form their own states and in approving another declaration three years later that assured them universal human rights. Clearly, the current international system, with 193 sovereign states meeting as equals at the UN, represents enormous progress beyond the imperial age, when a dozen empires ruled a third of humanity. Yet, in its pursuit of global power, Washington soon began to defy the international conventions that defined its own world order—contravening national sovereignty through covert CIA interventions and brutal wars around the globe, while violating human rights through the propagation of torture. Although the US embrace of human rights at first lent legitimacy to its international system, a succession of sanguinary conflicts and torture scandals in South Vietnam, Central America, and Iraq, among other places, would slowly corrode its international leadership.

The past five centuries have seen a clear continuity in the debate over human rights within a Western tradition, which suddenly donned a universal guise at the UN in 1948. The center of the world order might have shifted from Spain to Britain and to the US, but the continuous evolution of those underlying principles from one era to the next smoothed these imperial transitions. Now, as US global power starts to fade, an emerging Chinese world system is challenging that universal standard by subordinating human rights to a competing principle of unchecked national sovereignty. In an important divergence from the current international order, Beijing has asserted unlimited authority to suppress the rights of Tibetan, Uyghur, and other ethnic/religious minorities. Through repression at home and diplomatic pressure abroad, Beijing has been conducting what the international organization Human Rights Watch called "the most intense attack on the global system for enforcing human rights since that system began to emerge in the mid-20th century."[27] As the first non-Western global hegemon in five centuries, China values collective material security over individual liberty, confronting the international community with a potential rupture in its centuries-long discourse over human rights.

While there has, until recently, been an ideological continuity from one world order to the next, some marked differences are evident as well. Just as the British imperial system was far more pervasive than its Iberian predecessor, so Washington's world order went beyond both to become rigorously systematic and deeply embedded on a nearly global scale. The 1815 Congress of Vienna was an ephemeral gathering of two dozen diplomats whose influence faded within a decade. In contrast, the United Nations and its 193 member states have, for more than 75 years, sustained thousands of permanent staff with broad international responsibilities over almost every imaginable aspect of human society. Not only did the 1944 Bretton Woods Conference create the International Monetary Fund (IMF) and the World Bank, but it also led to the formation of the World Trade Organization (WTO), which today regulates commerce among 164 member states.

Beneath such broad organizing principles of sovereignty and human rights, the economy of each world order has been driven by a distinctive form of energy: first, massed human muscle power; then mastery of the winds; and, most recently, fossil fuels in the form of coal, oil, and natural gas. Empires are inherently predatory, plundering the planet for the raw resources needed to sustain their power, while leaving behind a trail of human suffering and environmental devastation. During the Iberian age, Spain and Portugal harnessed the winds to propel their ships anywhere on the globe, even as they abducted legions of slave laborers for the raw muscle power to work the mines and plantations of the New World. At approximately the midpoint of this era, two rising states perfected the use of wind and muscle power, as the Dutch refined the windmill and sailing ship while the British carried the transatlantic slave trade to its historic peak.

In the nineteenth century, as Britain's imperial era superseded the Iberian age, its industrial revolution developed the coal-fired steam engine to knit together the globe, propelling ironclad steamships across the oceans and steam locomotives along ribbons of steel that crisscrossed the continents. Then, as America supplanted Britain, its industry perfected the gasoline-fired internal combustion engine to drive automobiles across the country, aircraft around the world, and rockets into the exosphere.

At the dawn of the twenty-first century, as the globe began to suffocate from coal and oil emissions, rival hegemons in Beijing and Washington found themselves in a quandary. The US remained wedded to its entrenched carbon-fueled economy, resisting the shift to alternative energy sources at both national and international levels. In its breakneck race to become the world's leading economy, China, too, seemed trapped in a residual reliance on both coal-fired electricity and oil-powered transport, slowing its transition to renewable energy at home and abroad. With both the ascendant and the established hegemon mired in their carbon-fueled past, the future of the planet and its world orders was very much an open question.

In brief, each successive world order has been organized around not two but three defining attributes—the principle of sovereignty that delineated each state's territorial boundaries, the concept of human rights that governed all peoples within those boundaries, and a distinctive form of energy that drove the economy sustaining it all. And note that these factors do not simply lie alongside each other like drowsy sunbathers on a summer beach; rather, they interact dynamically, like acrobats linking arms, pyramiding upward and pulling apart. The British, for instance, used fossil fuels to drive their industrial revolution, which advanced human rights by freeing humankind from the need for the massed muscle power of slave labor. But they also presided over an imperial age that superseded the sovereignty of indigenous states in Asia and Africa, while extracting coerced labor from close to a quarter of humanity.

Each of these world orders has also exhibited a distinctive duality: an underlying tension between power and principle, between the ruthless realpolitik that empires have exercised and the lofty principles of human rights they have espoused. Not only did the Iberians develop the African slave trade, but they later discovered its antidote in the concept of human rights. Historians understand that imperial dominion has been a harsh experience for its subjects, but they often seem to believe that their own empire has been somehow exceptional—a little less brutal or a bit more benign than the rest. An exploration of the dualities in each world order will help us shed that delusion.[28]

Lacking the boundaries of a nation-state or the powerful, visible presence of an empire, world orders might seem intangible or even imagined. But they do in fact intrude, often quite profoundly, into the way most of humanity live their lives. And they usually prove much more resilient than the great empires that gave them birth. Nevertheless, because world orders are influenced in their rise and decline by the fortunes of the great powers that formed them, we need to briefly consider the character of modern empires.

Thinking about Empire

In both their formation and eclipse, world orders are entangled with the fates of empires. Rising empires sometimes have the power to form a new global system, while a deeply rooted world order can somehow survive the decline of the global hegemon that created it. The Iberian empires lost their preeminence by the early seventeenth century, but their global system persisted for another two centuries. The British Empire began its retreat nearly a century ago, but elements of its world order have continued seamlessly right to the present moment, thanks to its amicable transatlantic handoff of the imperial baton to the United States.

Clearly, an exploration of world orders requires an understanding of the term "empire," which has carried an ideological taint that long barred its serious study in the United States. Thanks to that aversion, many Americans, scholars and citizens alike, have remained unfamiliar with both the nature of empires and the complex dynamics of their rise and fall.

In the US for most of the twentieth century, the topic of empire remained an ideological minefield for historians. In the bitter aftermath of the Spanish-American War of 1898 and the bloody pacification of the Philippines, the term "imperialist" became a partisan epithet that Democratic progressives hurled at their Republican opponents. During the 40 years of the Cold War, Moscow used the Marxist-inflected "imperialist" to denigrate the United States. So, within the US, Washington might be considered a "world leader" or even a "great power," but never an empire. Its Cold War enemy, the Soviet Union, was the one with an empire—indeed, one that President Ronald Reagan even branded "an evil empire."[29] Since the US was supposedly an "exceptional" nation that somehow won world power while avoiding anything akin to imperialism, proper American historians could not and did not study the topic of empire during the Cold War.

In the aftermath of the 2001 terror attacks and the 2003 invasion of Iraq, the term lost its subversive taint, and policy specialists across the political spectrum began to ask whether or not America's global power was in decline.[30] At this critical moment when its hegemony was being challenged, the world's most powerful empire was arguably its least studied, denying citizens and scholars alike the analytic tools they needed to track their country's future.

Empire is one of the most venerable of all forms of human governance. In that cradle of humanity called the Fertile Crescent, civilization's key components appeared in relatively quick succession—agriculture around 8500 BCE; domesticated animals, 8000 BCE; bronze metallurgy, 4000 BCE; writing, 3200 BCE; and history's first transregional empire, founded by Sargon of Akkad, in 2300 BCE. In just six millennia, a relative blink in humanity's three hundred thousand years as a species, empire emerged as one of civilization's essential elements.[31]

In the four thousand years since the first empire appeared, the world has witnessed a continuous succession of some 200 of them, of which 70 were large or lasting.[32] From this perspective, for America to insist that its global military presence has been anything other than imperial is akin to saying its farmers did not engage in agriculture. Empires are not an aberration. They are not likely to be erased in the foreseeable future by technological change or reformed out of existence through international law.

At the risk of unduly simplifying a complex chronology, we can divide those four thousand years of imperial history into three distinct periods. During an initial classical phase lasting some two and a half millennia (from

2300 BCE to 400 CE), a relentless succession of rival empires—Assyria, Persia, Athens, Macedonia, Carthage, and Rome—warred over a relatively limited portion of the planet extending from the Mediterranean Sea to the Persian Gulf. Elsewhere during this period, other centers of imperial power appeared in China, India, Southeast Asia, and Mesoamerica, creating enduring civilizations in each of those regions.

Among the empires of this classical phase, Rome, along with China, would prove exceptional for its combination of imperial durability, diversity, and expansiveness. For more than four centuries, the Roman Empire encompassed 55 million people and two million square miles across parts of three continents, reaching from Britain to Babylonia.[33] Indicating the intimate relationship between empire and a broader social order, this system survived for so long, says historian Johan Galtung, because "so many individuals were 'romanized,' having Latin as their language and Roman mores as their *Weltanschauung* (world view)."[34]

Then, as mass migrations and social change broke the hold of those classical empires, the world entered a thousand-year interregnum lasting roughly from 400 to 1400 CE. Scattered about the globe, autonomous empires had little transcontinental contact. While the Maya, Angkor, Chinese, Byzantine, and Holy Roman Empires were dominant in their respective regions, they were usually limited in their territorial reach and short-lived when they overreached. Even the Umayyad Caliphate, whose conquests brought Islam to diverse peoples from northern India to southern Spain, lasted less than 90 years (661 to 750 CE) before breaking apart. Similarly, Mongol and Turkic horsemen, led respectively by Genghis Khan and Tamerlane, ranged widely across the steppes and sands of Eurasia from 1200 to 1400, conquering vast domains that quickly fragmented into regional imperial powers.[35] This middle millennium—with Angkor in its inland grandeur, the Maya in their forest fastness, and Byzantium ruling ever-shrinking territories astride the Bosporus Strait—can teach us many things, but, thanks to the isolation of each of them, relatively little about the nature of a world order.

In the most recent imperial age, which dates from the start of Portuguese exploration in 1420, Europe's overseas empires finally brought all the continents into sustained contact, allowing the formation of history's first true world order. By the 1930s, European colonies and ex-colonies covered 85 percent of the globe's land area, making imperialism a universal human experience.[36] As rival empires contended incessantly on land and sea for regional or global dominion, a succession of three resilient world orders emerged, each identified with the empires that created them—the Iberian, British, and American.

Born of war and conquest, empires are unstable, even volatile forms of governance that often exhibit contradictory attributes—they are constant yet changing, idealistic but barbaric, and powerful yet fragile. Take, for example, that central paradox of power and fragility. At their peak, the world's dominant empires seemed to possess insuperable power, manifest in their awesome weaponry. In 1570, Spain led a Christian armada of 203 ships, carrying 60,000 men and 1,800 guns, that destroyed a comparable Muslim fleet in the Mediterranean Sea.[37] In 1906, the British navy launched the world's first true battleship, the HMS *Dreadnought*, with rapid-firing guns that hurled 850-pound shells accurately to a range of twelve miles. A century later, in 2001, the US Navy ruled the seas with a dozen aircraft carriers such as the USS *Enterprise*—a veritable floating "garrison town" with six thousand sailors and 70 roaring jet aircraft—which were symbolic of military strength unmatched on the planet.[38] Yet even at such moments of awe-inspiring power, each of these empires was just decades away from decline, facing external challenges and internal changes that would bring an end to its dominion.

In addition to pressures from rival powers, empires also decline from internal weakness, when their ruling elites prove incapable of managing challenges. Throughout its nineteenth-century expansion, the British Empire was administered by elites well educated at the universities of Oxford or Cambridge and defended by naval officers rigorously trained for command. During Britain's piecemeal dissolution of its empire after World War II, however, leaders from its insular landed aristocracy, animated by a sense of racial superiority, presided over searing imperial debacles of decolonization in India, Kenya, and Egypt. Similarly, it was the US business, diplomatic, and military elites, all tempered by their respective professions, who managed the extraordinary expansion of Washington's global power right after World War II. Some seven decades later, however, economic change has fostered extreme income inequality inside the United States, creating a class of self-aggrandizing billionaires who have captured the Republican Party and the presidency, with consequent costs for its world system.[39] When a ruling political party retreats from rationality into delusional politics, that nation forfeits both its claim to and capacity for global leadership.

As coalitions of diverse nations and peoples, empires are arguably the most complex and varied of all governments, and have assumed different forms and suffered divergent fates throughout their four millennia of history. Many have lasted a decade or less; some a century or more; and a few an entire millennium. In something so disparate and diverse as an empire, no single factor, not even one so central as leadership, can provide a complete explanation for its fate. Yet, if there is one element that can help explain their rise and fall across time, that would probably be geopolitics.

The Uses of Geopolitics

During the past century, countless commentators have used the term "geopolitics" to explain the fate of nations and empires. But few have grasped the full meaning and fraught history embedded in this elusive concept. Geopolitics is essentially a method for the management of empire through the use of geography (air, land, and sea) to maximize military and economic advantage. Unlike conventional nations, whose peoples can be readily mobilized for self-defense, empires are, by dint of their extraterritorial reach and the perils inherent in the overseas deployment of armed forces, a surprisingly fragile form of government. They seem to require a strategic visionary who can merge landforms, seascapes, and societies into a sustainable global system, allowing such strengthened empires both extraordinary power and exceptional economic opportunity.

To minimize the hazards of military campaigns in unfamiliar terrain far from home—that is, to give an empire a fighting chance at survival against formidable odds—requires a resilient geopolitical architecture. Whether by inspired intuition or careful study, successful empire builders, from Roman leader Julius Caesar to American president Dwight Eisenhower, have often proved skilled strategists, acquiring allies and territories that they can knit together into a sustainable, defensible array. As empires decline, the same strategic architecture that assured their ascent can also prove fateful, as rival powers launch deft blows, often with novel military technologies, to breach a vulnerable point on an established hegemon's sprawling frontier. However else it might be used or abused, the most appropriate term for such grand imperial designs is "geopolitics."

The practice of geopolitics, even if from horseback, is as old as empire. Until the dawn of the twentieth century, it was the conquerors themselves—from Alexander the Great to Julius Caesar and Napoleon Bonaparte—who had the geopolitical vision that guided their relentless imperial expansion.

Ancient Athens demonstrates well the paramount role of geopolitics in shaping an empire's destiny. For two centuries, from roughly 500 to 300 BCE, Athens built a maritime empire that made it the dominant power in the eastern Mediterranean. Under the leadership of Themistocles, an imperial visionary, it fortified its port at Piraeus and assembled a fleet of some two hundred trireme galley ships, manned by seventeen thousand citizen rowers, just in time to defeat a massive Persian invasion in 480 BCE. Once fully formed, the Athenian navy swept enemy fleets from the Aegean Sea and established the Delian League, requiring Greek city-states dotting those islands to donate either ships or silver to maintain the hegemony of Athenian power.[40]

Over the next century, the trade and tribute that flowed into the port of Piraeus allowed an impressive cultural flowering of Athenian politics, democracy, philosophy, and arts. The writings of Aristotle and Socrates, the famed speeches of Demosthenes, the statecraft of Pericles, the histories of Herodotus and Thucydides, and dramas of Euripides and Sophocles all date from this extraordinary period.

By the fifth century BCE, however, the steady growth of Athens into the largest city in the Greek world, with an urban population of 65,000, made grain imports critical for its survival.[41] According to Demosthenes, Athens filled its food deficit for some 100,000 residents in its home region of Attica by importing about 26,400 metric tons of wheat annually, with fully half of that total arriving from Black Sea districts via the Bosporus Strait on more than a hundred merchant ships. That meant, however, that the city was vulnerable to starvation should an enemy close the narrow sea-lanes through the Bosporus and Dardanelles Straits that tied the Black Sea to the Aegean.[42]

This geopolitical weakness was exposed during the Peloponnesian War, when Athens fought a coalition of city-states led by Sparta, a conflict that dragged on from 431 to 404 BCE. After a quarter century of relentless combat on land and sea, the Spartan commander Lysander destroyed the Athenian navy in the Dardanelles and blocked grain shipments from the Black Sea, starving the city into submission through a long, cold, desperate winter. This crushing defeat broke the Delian League and ended Athens's reign over a prosperous maritime empire.[43]

Writing at the cusp of Greece's decline and Rome's rise, the ancient Greek historian Plutarch attributed the fates of these two empires to the character of their leaders. In his famous *Parallel Lives*, Plutarch tried to encompass the enormity of Julius Caesar's conquest of Gaul (all of modern France and Belgium) by listing numbers to show the scale of his triumph. In nine years of war, Caesar "took by storm more than eight hundred cities, subdued three hundred tribes, and fought pitched battles . . . with three million men, of whom he slew one million . . . and took as many more prisoners." The reason for such success, said Plutarch, lay in Caesar's character, for he inspired his troops by "willingly undergoing every danger," slept in the open to steel his body, and fought with daring in the front ranks alongside his legionnaires.[44]

But in his own account, Caesar himself reduced this story to its geopolitical essentials. "All Gaul is divided into three parts," he wrote in the famed first sentence of his military memoir *Gallic Wars*. "Of all these, the Belgae are the bravest, because . . . they are the nearest to the Germans, who dwell beyond the Rhine, with whom they are continually waging war; for which reason the Helvetii also surpass the rest of the Gauls in valor, as they contend with the Germans in almost daily battles." When nearly four hundred thousand of those formidable Helvetii marched out of their Alpine cantons to occupy Gallic lowlands in 58 BCE, he deployed geopolitics to defeat them—seizing strategic terrain, controlling grain supplies, and manipulating rival tribes. Instead of selling the vanquished Helvetii into slavery, as other Roman generals might have done, Caesar, mindful of his empire's geopolitical balance, returned them to their Alpine homelands with generous provisions, lest the Germans fill the void, crossing the Rhine and destabilizing Gaul's natural river frontier.[45]

The Modern Study of Geopolitics

In more modern times, as the world's industrial nations began competing for overseas empires around 1900, they turned to scholars for a grand geopolitical design to guide their imperial expansion. Through the extraordinary careers of just four scholar-officials who developed and deployed geopolitics during the twentieth century, we can see the surprising influence of this concept in shaping the fate of nations and empires. In the actual process of building empires, their ideas usually proved blunt instruments at best. But they also forged some sharp academic tools that allow us to cut through all the historical complexities to analyze the causes of imperial decline.

When Washington took its first steps onto the world stage in the 1890s, an American naval historian, Captain Alfred Thayer Mahan, argued that sea power was, through the exceptional mobility of warships, the key to national security and international influence. His writings inspired Washington's decision to build a blue-water navy and seize an empire of islands for naval bases stretching halfway around the globe, from Puerto Rico to Hawaii and the Philippines. Mahan's international influence was extraordinary. His view that modern wars turned on a concentration of capital ships for a "decisive battle" would shape the strategies of Germany in World War I and Japan in World War II.[46]

Little more than a decade after Mahan wrote his seminal studies of sea power, an English geographer, Sir Halford Mackinder, published a highly influential article that shifted the focus of geopolitics from sea to land. Writing in 1904, when the Trans-Siberian Railway was completing its 5,700-mile crawl from Moscow to Vladivostok, Mackinder argued that future rails would knit Eurasia into a unitary landmass that, along with Africa, he dubbed the tri-continental "world island." When that day came, Russia, in alliance with another land power like Germany, could expand across Eurasia's vast "heartland," allowing "the use of vast continental resources for fleet-building, and the empire of the world would be in sight."[47]

MACKINDER'S WORLD ISLAND
THE NATURAL SEATS OF POWER, 1904

At the end of World War I, the eruption of revolution in Russia gave Mackinder's sweeping, visionary ideas about Eurasia's "heartland" the aura of prophecy. As the Versailles Peace Conference opened in 1919, he turned that famous essay into a book, which contained his most memorable maxim: "Who rules East Europe commands the Heartland; Who rules the Heartland commands the World-Island; Who rules the World-Island commands the World."[48] In an ill-fated attempt to apply that grand strategy, the British government dispatched Mackinder to negotiate with the anti-Bolshevik forces still holding out in southern Russia. He returned to London with a foolhardy scheme for stopping the formation of the Soviet Union, which the cabinet quickly dismissed, allowing him to fade quietly into obscurity.[49] Were it not for the recurring appeal of his ideas in Nazi Germany and Cold War America, he would have been forgotten.

After the Versailles peace settlement at the end of World War I stripped Germany of its colonial empire and assigned foreign troops to occupy its Rhineland frontier, another influential geopolitical analyst named Karl Haushofer exchanged his general's epaulets for a geography professorship at the University of Munich. There he applied Mackinder's conception of the Eurasian "heartland" and developed the idea of *Lebensraum*, or living space, to assure that his fatherland would never again suffer the strategic blunders that had led to its humiliating defeat in 1918.[50]

While Mackinder himself was courting the powerful in postwar London, Haushofer was teaching geopolitics to top Nazis in Munich, first to his graduate assistant Rudolf Hess (later the deputy führer) and then to Adolf Hitler himself. While the Nazi leader was writing *Mein Kampf* inside Munich's Landsberg Prison in 1924, Haushofer spent five months, during weekly meetings, tutoring Hitler in geopolitics. In that manifesto, Hitler echoed Haushofer's ideas about *Lebensraum*, saying that Germany could only be fed "at the expense of Russia . . . to obtain by German sword sod for the German plow and daily bread for the nation." Haushofer was later rewarded with influential positions in the Third Reich for both himself and his son Albrecht, who advised top Nazi diplomats about the geopolitics of European conquest.[51]

In 1942, the führer dispatched a million men, ten thousand artillery pieces, and five hundred tanks to breach the Volga River at Stalingrad and capture that Russian "heartland" for *Lebensraum*. In the end, the Reich's forces suffered 850,000 casualties—killed, wounded, and captured—in a vain attempt to break through East Europe's "rimland" into Eurasia's "heartland" region.

A quarter century later, as the United States recoiled from its searing defeat in the Vietnam War, Zbigniew Brzezinski, an émigré Polish aristocrat and autodidact when it came to geopolitics, went from teaching international relations in New York City to serving President Jimmy Carter as national security adviser in Washington, DC. There his risky geopolitical gambits gained an attentive audience in the Carter White House when Moscow invaded Afghanistan in 1979.[52]

As an intellectual follower of Mackinder, Brzezinski would prove adept at applying the British don's famous dictum about the geopolitical connection between Eastern Europe and Eurasia's "heartland."[53] Wielding a multibillion-dollar CIA covert operation like a sharpened wedge, Brzezinski drove radical Islam from Afghanistan deep into Soviet Central Asia. That geopolitical gambit drew Moscow into a debilitating decade-long Afghan war, which weakened the Soviet Union sufficiently for Eastern Europe, three thousand miles away, to finally break free of its imperial grasp. Asked about the enormous human suffering his geopolitical strategy had inflicted on Afghanistan and the role of that chaos in the creation of a militant Islam hostile to the US, Brzezinski was coolly unapologetic. "What is most important to the history of the world?" he asked in 1998. "The Taliban or the collapse of the Soviet empire? Some stirred-up Moslems or the liberation of Central Europe and the end of the Cold War?"[54]

In retirement, Brzezinski resumed his study of Mackinder's theory, proving more balanced as an armchair analyst than he had been as presidential adviser. In his 1998 book *The Grand Chessboard*, Brzezinski warned, with considerable prescience, that US dominance over Eurasia remained "the central basis for global primacy" and the chief requisite for continuation of Washington's hegemony.[55]

As the twists in Brzezinski's career illustrate so clearly, the concept of geopolitics has proved more useful for those who prefer to analyze empires rather than build them. By separating the analysis of geopolitics from the dubious causes that have embraced it, such as imperialism and fascism, we can recover some useful insights about the forces that often shape the fate of empires and their world orders. If we combine Mahan's emphasis on naval strength as the means to control continents with Mackinder's focus on the "world island," we will find that a succession of leading empires—Portuguese, Dutch, British, US, and Chinese—have all tried to achieve global power by dominating that tri-continental landmass of Europe, Asia, and Africa. Indeed, Portugal's sixteenth-century chain of 50 fortified ports around Africa and across the Indian Ocean seems strikingly similar to China's current string of 40 commercial ports covering much of the same terrain. Of course, China's position has also been strengthened by a transcontinental grid of railroads and pipelines. Beneath the visible, much-discussed issues of trade and technology, this geopolitical strategy has become a battering ram for Beijing to break Washington's control over Eurasia and thereby challenge its global hegemony.

In the chapters that follow, we will apply the prism of geopolitics to reduce even long wars, whether the Thirty Years' War or World War II, to their strategic essentials in a single page or paragraph, sifting through and selecting from the myriad details that conventional military historians often use to fill entire books on a single battle. Just as military science teaches officers tactics for optimum deployment of troops for warfare, so geopolitics has often guided world leaders to array complex military, economic, and diplomatic forces for the exercise of global power. Whether its geopolitical design is won from horseback or planned in an academic office, every empire must form a defensible frontier, with strategic bastions, loyal allies, and secure lines of communication for efficient movement of weapons, provisions, and personnel. Ideally, all these components should intersect and overlap until they achieve a systemic integrity, a veritable synergy, whose sum is geopolitical power. In the real world, where empires are often created though a mix of pluck and luck, geopolitical flaws, whether embedded at the outset or evolving over time, can often determine an empire's fate.

Compounding these complexities, geopolitics itself is enormously elusive, making it difficult to distinguish between the banal and the brilliant. Geopolitics in the hands of a grand master can crush armies or conquer whole continents. But seemingly similar strategies can lead to searing defeat. Nearly two millennia after Caesar's conquest of Gaul, Napoleon sought a similar strategic balance by forging dozens of German ministates into his Confederation of the Rhine. Caesar's deft geopolitical balancing of Gaul and Germany on the fulcrum of the Rhine River survived for some four hundred years; Napoleon's similar attempt lasted all of seven. Telling the difference between the brilliant and the inept use of geopolitics, in the moment or even long after the fact, is challenging. So, in this analysis of the interplay of empires that shaped the succession of world orders, caution must be the watchword in the application of geopolitics to explain their rise and fall.

This historical narrative, spun out over the centuries, will focus on some essential dimensions of human history, doing its best to show how world orders form, function, and fail, leaving a legacy that shapes succeeding eras. Just as geopolitics guides our study of empires, so the ever-changing sources of energy will serve as the main theme in analyzing the succession of world orders. By exploring slavery as a form of energy that drove the world economy in the Iberian age, we will gain a deeper appreciation of the ambiguous legacy of fossil fuels, developed by Britain and perfected by America, in liberating humanity from such cruel bondage while simultaneously condemning it to suffer the adversity of climate change.

Using energy to explain slavery or geopolitics to analyze empires is an attempt at grappling with the daunting complexities of these global political systems. Such an effort is certainly not meant to celebrate their self-styled glories or even to condemn their many excesses, though just stating such details, as I have done below, carries its own clear censure. Probing the history of these hegemonic empires adds to our understanding of how each shaped the succeeding world order, leading us step-by-step to the threshold of the future. Hopefully, this approach will cast new light on the past five centuries of world history, while teaching us something about the underlying character of our own age and the unique challenges we face in carrying it forward into the future.

Statue of Friar Antonio de Montesinos by Antonio Castellanos (Credit: Alamy)

Chapter 2
The Iberian Age

In August 1960 on Lisbon's historic waterfront, Portugal staged an elaborate commemoration for a minor prince known as Henry the Navigator, who died in 1460. Led by the president of Brazil, a delegation of international dignitaries inaugurated the spectacular Monument to the Discoveries, which soars above the Tagus River to a breathtaking peak of 171 feet. At the apex of this massive concrete structure stands Prince Henry, larger than life, holding up a model sailing ship and pointing across the Atlantic toward "the roads of the sea."

Some two hundred miles south at the Sagres Peninsula, naval vessels from fourteen nations sailed in parade formation past the ruins of the prince's castle. Overhead thundered jet fighters from Britain, Spain, and the United States, paying tribute to the famous Sagres Academy, where Henry reputedly gathered the world's most brilliant cartographers and mathematicians to map those roads to exploration. After the jets' roar had faded and the ships had sailed away, more than three hundred historians attended an international conference in Lisbon to reflect on the remarkable role of that scholar prince in launching the Age of Discovery.[1]

But there was another date in the prince's biography that was of great historical consequence, yet little discussed during those days of celebration—1441, the year that marks the start of the modern struggle over human rights. That was the year one of Prince Henry's voyages of discovery reached a point on the African coast eight hundred miles south of Lisbon that the ship's crew would mistakenly name Rio Douro (river of gold). Instead of the gold they were searching for, however, they found an unexpected prize: twelve captive slaves, whom they likely seized from a Tuareg desert encampment. When they returned to Lisbon, docking just a few miles downriver from where that soaring monument now stands, the prince's response was not what one would have expected from such a celebrated figure.

"I see before my eyes," wrote the royal chronicler of Henry's reaction, "how great his joy must have been . . . not for the number of those captives, but the hope, oh Sainted Prince!, for others you could have in the future." Indeed, three years later, more of his ships returned, holds filled to capacity with 235 slaves seized in raids further down the African coast. When they docked, crowds gathered as Prince Henry, astride a strong horse, claimed his rightful share of the human cargo, the "royal fifth" of 46 slaves. The rest were divided into lots that separated families, with much weeping, says the court chronicler, as "mothers clung to their children and were whipped with little pity."[2] Nonetheless, that chronicler celebrated the enslavement of those Africans who once "only knew how to live in a bestial sloth," but now "turned themselves with a good will into the path of the true faith."[3]

Setting aside all the mythmaking, the prince did not, as his hagiographers have claimed, preside over innovations in navigation and naval architecture that made the age of exploration possible. There was no scholarly academy on that windy promontory at Sagres. No wise men. No intellectual innovation. Just a castle with stone ramparts and a decorative compass motif in its garden. But Henry did organize slaving expeditions, negotiate papal approval legitimating the trade in captive Africans, and, above all, develop the first sugar plantations, which made slavery profitable.[4]

On the other side of the Atlantic in October 1982, the presidents of Mexico and the Dominican Republic inaugurated a monument with a more somber message. Rising one hundred feet above the waterfront of Santo Domingo, a statue of the friar Antonio de Montesinos, gazing out across the Caribbean Sea, raises a giant bronze hand in an angry gesture to commemorate the impassioned sermon he gave here in 1511, denouncing Spanish abuse of the Amerindians. Flanked by the uniformed military of both nations, the president of Mexico pointed out that this had been "the first time a voice was raised in defense of human rights. Never before in the history of humanity had the victor questioned the basis of his victory." Indeed, that sermon marked the start of the Iberian world's long, painful appraisal of the dark underside of Prince Henry's legacy.[5]

In 1502, as the first ships carrying Spanish colonists and conquistadors to the New World approached Santo Domingo, their commander had told them: "You have arrived at a good moment. . . . There is to be a war against the Indians and we will be able to take many slaves." For the next ten years, those conquistadors swept the island of Hispaniola, enslaving the population and slaughtering any who resisted. In the process, they reduced the original population of 400,000 to just 60,000. By 1511, the result was so horrific that Father Montesinos, who had recently arrived with the New World's first contingent of Dominican friars, felt compelled to give an Advent sermon that would, in the end, echo across the Atlantic. Even now, over five hundred years later, it seems remarkable that this priest could have spoken with uncompromised honesty.[6]

"I am the voice of Christ in the desert of this island," Father Montesinos told the Spanish colonists in his congregation.

> All of you are in mortal sin and live and die in it due to the cruelty and tyranny which you practice with this innocent people. Tell me by what right and with what justice do you hold these Indians in such horrible servitude? With what authority have you waged such detestable war, bringing havoc and death never before seen on these people who were living peacefully on their lands? How can you keep them so exhausted and oppressed, without giving them food . . . by which you cause their deaths, or more accurately put, by which you murder them? All of this so you can daily acquire more gold. Are these not human beings? Do they not have rational spirits? Are you not obliged to love them as you love yourselves? Can you not hear this? Can you not feel this?[7]

That sermon marked the start of an intense debate over slavery and the human rights of Amerindians that was to roil Iberia's empires for the rest of the century. Seated in the congregation on that historic day was Diego Columbus, the viceroy of the Indies and son of the famed explorer, who was outraged. Father Montesinos was soon recalled to Spain, where he gained an audience with King Ferdinand. Disturbed by the priest's report, the king called a convocation in 1512 that drafted the Laws of Burgos, which recognized the rights of American Indians to own property, earn wages, and have access to Christian instruction. Under those laws, however, a Spanish conquistador was required to warn Amerindians, at first contact, that should they refuse to immediately accept the church as their lord and superior, "I will make war everywhere and . . . I will take your wives and children, and I will make them slaves." When those laws proved woefully inadequate, the king's grandson and heir Emperor Charles V enacted the New Laws of 1542, so strictly barring the enslavement of Amerindians that their enforcement sparked a revolt among Spanish colonists in Peru. The emperor also appointed Father Montesinos as Protector of the Indians in Venezuela, where in 1540, for doing his duty, he was murdered by a colonist.[8]

In this way, almost from its start, the Iberian world order developed a duality between harsh imperial rule, marked by slavery and slaughter, and lofty ideals of a common humanity. As Spain's conquistadors subdued the Caribbean with their steel swords, massacring indigenous peoples who had only wooden weapons, its Catholic priests recoiled from the cruelty and articulated strikingly modern principles of human rights. No world order so thoroughly violated human rights, and no other would agonize over those crimes with such a tortured conscience. By the end of its first century as a world power, Spain would try to balance the granting of protections to the Amerindians with the provision of sufficient labor for the mines and plantations of the New World through a cruel compromise: the African slave trade.[9]

From Prince Henry's first human cargoes in the 1440s, the traffic in African slaves would grow over the next four centuries into a vast commerce that carried ten to twelve million captives across the Atlantic in one of history's greatest and cruelest migrations. Not only did the Portuguese explorers start that inhumane traffic; they were also principals in a commerce that carried 52,000 African slaves to Spanish America between 1520 and 1595—making slavery one of the defining attributes of the Iberian age. That human traffic would increase markedly during Portugal's union with Spain from 1580 to 1640, when the Portuguese shipped 300,000 African slaves to Spanish America.[10]

If we were to paint world history with the broad brush of his hagiographers, then we might say that Prince Henry laid the foundations for a new way to govern the globe. As Portuguese and Spanish explorers found pathways across the world's waters to colonize parts of Asia, Africa, and the Americas in the fifteenth and sixteenth centuries, they formed an Iberian world order defined by an expansive view of sovereignty that justified imperial conquest and by a narrow vision of human rights that fostered mass enslavement.

That system still casts its shadow across our modern era. Born of the Black Death that swept Europe between 1350 and 1450, the Iberian world order would survive for three centuries before the British imperial era superseded it in 1815. Yet its invented hierarchy that claimed free Christians were superior to enslaved Africans launched a struggle over the nature of human rights that persists to this day. Similarly, the Vatican's sacral authority to resolve diplomatic disputes has yielded to the United Nations and the World Court, but the underlying principle of a universal jurisdiction that transcends national boundaries remains.

The Iberian age also presided over Europe's transition beyond an exclusive reliance on animal energy and waterpower. In the high medieval period, a typical European village of three hundred adults had only 15 horsepower in human labor, supplemented by 30 more from a herd of 60 draft animals, and 3 additional horsepower from a water wheel that milled its grain into flour. Water mills, used since ancient Rome, were a vital energy source, serving many purposes from boring gun barrels to grinding glass. The historian Marc Bloch argued that the disappearance of slavery from Europe by the tenth century coincided with the spread of waterpower and its "more efficient use of natural inanimate forces."[11]

The Iberian world order, however, gained its exceptional global reach by harnessing new forms of energy—massed muscle power that maximized the output of the human body and wind currents that propelled mills and ships. The windmill arrived in Europe from Persia in the twelfth century and spread rapidly, with 4,500 of them in England by the fourteenth century and 4,000 in Holland by the seventeenth century. By adopting a triangular sail, Portuguese ships like the famed *caravela de armada* doubled the capacity of sailing craft to tack close to the wind, making them master of the world's oceans. Compared to the water wheel's modest 3 horsepower, sailing craft circa 1600 were powerful machines producing 50 horsepower, and Holland's larger windmills could generate up to 60.[12]

For the next three centuries, sailing ships would carry millions of African slaves across the Atlantic for work in a new form of agriculture that was both exceptionally cruel and highly profitable: the sugar plantation. While the output of Europe's free yeoman farmers was constrained by the limits of an individual human body and the temperate climate's short six-month growing season, slave laborers massed on plantations in tropical latitudes were driven mercilessly year-round to extract unprecedented levels of productivity. In the sixteenth century, after developing the sugar plantation, or *fazenda*, as a new form of agribusiness on the islands of Madeira and São Tomé off the coast of Africa, the Portuguese brought the system to Brazil.

From there, it migrated to European colonies in the Caribbean—making that unique institution synonymous with the slave trade for nearly four centuries.[13] So profitable was the slave plantation and so persistent was its human traffic that this form of labor did not die from natural economic exhaustion. To extirpate it would require the full force of the British Empire and an American civil war.

In sum, the energy transition of the Iberian age was exemplified by two key artifacts—the caravel sailcraft that conquered the world's oceans and the *fazenda* slave plantation that massed human muscle for extraordinary profits and productivity.

The Cataclysm of the Black Death

The Iberian age emerged from the Black Death pandemic (ca. 1350–1450), which was nothing less than world history's greatest wave of mass mortality. In just four years, that pandemic of bubonic plague killed up to 60 percent of Europe's population, leaving some 50 million dead.[14] Though China's demographic statistics are less precise, mortality there was comparable, with the country's population falling from 123 million in 1200 to just 65 million by 1393. One chronicle records that nine out of ten people in China's Heibei Province died from the plague.[15] As lesser, yet still lethal, versions of the Black Death recurred over the next half century, world population fell by nearly 20 percent, from 440 million to just 350 million, and would not fully recover for another century.[16]

Starting in China, the plague spread across the grasslands of Central Asia, where the rise of the Mongol Empire had created conditions ideal for the transmission of the disease over once-impassible distances. After a millennium of sending mounted raiders to invade Europe from the east, Central Asia produced its most formidable leader in Genghis Khan, who was born a minor tribal chief and became a brilliant tactician. Starting in 1215 with their conquest of northern China, Mongol armies of mounted archers then headed west, penetrating Europe as far as the Danube River and capturing the great cities of the Middle East. Stretching for five thousand miles across Eurasia at its peak in 1280, the Mongol Empire stabilized Central Asia sufficiently for trade caravans to travel the Silk Road safely between China and Europe. A half century later, those caravan routes would carry rodents bearing the Black Death from China across the grassy steppes to the edge of Europe.[17]

When the plague arrived, Europe was already suffering from several decades of serious economic stagnation that left it vulnerable to disease. At the start of the fourteenth century, Europe's climate had turned bitterly cold and wet as Alpine glaciers advanced, and crops began to fail with fatal frequency—bringing a sudden end to several centuries of prosperity that had been marked by expanding agricultural production, a rising population that reached 75 million, and growing cities.[18] During this "Little Ice Age," the Baltic Sea froze over in 1303 and 1306. As grain yields fell by half, the continent suffered recurring bouts of famine, with its population falling by 10 to 25 percent.[19] By the time the plague struck in 1347, Europe had become a crowded continent, with the great bulk of its population struggling and often failing to produce sufficient food—conditions that made it particularly susceptible to the Black Death.[20]

The plague first reached Europe in 1347 when Mongol forces besieging the Black Sea port of Caffa in Crimea, then Genoa's easternmost trading outpost, were suddenly devastated by the disease. Before they withdrew, the Mongols reportedly used catapults to hurl suppurating corpses over the city walls. As the Genoese defenders succumbed, they fled homeward to Italy in a dozen ships carrying ailing crews and infected rats. By the time the fleet reached Messina, Sicily, in October, the sailors had "sickness clinging to their very bones."[21]

Over the next six years, the plague would spread across Europe from Mediterranean ports to northern Italy, France, and England before reaching the continent's periphery in Scotland, Scandinavia, and Poland. Despite rigorous public health measures, Venice, then Europe's most prosperous city, suffered 72,000 deaths among a population of 120,000. Florence lost half its 100,000 residents amid anarchy and mass flight. "How many grand palaces," wrote the poet Giovanni Boccaccio of his beloved Florence, "how many stately homes, how many splendid residences once full of retainers, of lords, of ladies, were now left desolate of all, even to the meanest servant!" Neighboring Siena experienced 88,000 deaths among 97,000 people, prompting a local notary to write: "This is the end of the world." In Avignon, in southern France, 62,000 deaths in just three months left seven thousand houses standing empty. In England, Winchester lost 8,000 in a population of 10,000; and the plague cut a similar swath through London.[22]

One of the infected merchant ships expelled from Italy sought refuge first in Marseilles and then in Spain, spreading the epidemic at each stop. Moving inland from the coasts via five separate points of infection, the Black Death reached about 35 percent of the Iberian Peninsula over a two-year period, ravaging populations already weakened by the privations of protracted warfare. In the south, it suddenly swept through the Castilian army that was besieging the Muslim Emirate of Granada in 1350. Its commander, King Alfonso XI, died of the disease on Good Friday, becoming the only European monarch to succumb.[23]

Had the Black Death been a singular disaster, Europe's population might have recovered within a generation. But this plague, argues medievalist Robert S. Gottfried, was unique among epidemics for "its deadly combination of virulence and frequency." Indeed, every five to twelve years from 1361 to 1494, new epidemics appeared in parts of Europe, each taking up to 20 percent of the population. Spain, for example, suffered eight bouts of plague, cutting the population of Catalonia and its port city Barcelona from 430,000 in 1365 to 278,000 in 1497. During the century following Europe's first infection, recurring plagues may have cost the continent up to 75 percent of its inhabitants, making them, said historian David Herlihy, "the most devastating natural disasters ever to strike Europe."[24]

In its relentless winnowing, that pandemic pummeled the old social order and catalyzed the continent's shift in dramatic new directions. At the most basic level, it caused lasting labor shortages that slashed revenues on feudal estates and forced aristocrats to seek alternative income through warfare, fostering a century of incessant conflict in France, Italy, and Spain.[25] To cope with the scarcity and high cost of labor, the plague's aftermath also witnessed what Herlihy has called a "period of impressive technological achievement"—including innovative agricultural techniques, labor-saving technologies like the printing press, and a "revolution in maritime transport" with larger sailing ships that needed smaller crews.[26] Through recurring population losses, the manorial system run by serfs disappeared from western and central Europe, replaced by independent yeoman farmers. The weakening of merchant guilds led to a more entrepreneurial form of commerce that, argues Gottfried, "propelled Iberian, English, and Dutch merchants to look for new markets and open trade from Europe to the rest of the world."[27]

That demographic disaster also had a profound geopolitical impact, securing Europe's vulnerable eastern frontier and freeing it to turn west and explore the oceans. For nearly a thousand years—from Attila the Hun's invasion of the Roman Empire in 447 CE through the Ottomans' defeat of a Byzantine army near Constantinople in 1302—Europe had succumbed to successive waves of "barbarian" armies riding out of the grasslands to the East. During the several centuries before 1300, the incursions of mounted warriors from Central Asia had reached a crescendo, writes historian William McNeill, "capped and climaxed by the Mongol storm." But when the pandemic devastated those nomadic peoples, it effectively destroyed steppe society, ending future threats to Europe from Central Asia and also curtailing the century-long "Mongol peace" across the region. The plague thus severed the main trade routes that had carried Asia's riches to Europe, encouraging the search for alternatives.[28]

In sum, the Black Death set the continent in motion, launching the transition to a new world order. In the Iberian Peninsula, this crisis of the medieval social system unleashed the gathering force of Europe's ongoing innovations in banking, warfare, and seamanship, sending navigators far into the Atlantic, where they searched for islands to settle and routes for direct trade with Asia. During the century that followed the end of the worst plagues in 1420, Iberian exploration would bring the continents into regular contact for the first time in history, and so allow for the formation of a world order to regulate their interactions.

Worlds Apart in 1400

Today it is difficult to imagine just how separate the continents were on the eve of European expansion in 1400. With a world population of just 350 million people, only 4 percent of the current total, vast expanses of the earth were occupied only by nomadic hunters and herders. Europe was populous and powerful, holding 20 percent of the world's people—double its present portion. With a similar share, China was the only other area with comparable demographic weight, although India was not far behind. Separated by unexplored oceans, endless deserts, and dense forests, the few settled areas on the planet with sufficient population to sustain a state were just starting to emerge from centuries of regional isolation, weaving the first slender threads of trade between Asia, Africa, and Europe.

In the process, the Mediterranean would become a crossroads for the cultures and commerce of those three continents. Stretching for 2,500 miles and protected from the Atlantic's storms, that sea had milder winds and many islands that made it sailable by small ships without maps or navigational instruments. The sea itself was a free zone beyond the control of any power, the site for the seizure of hundreds of ships in these years by pirates, both Christian and Muslim. There was, moreover, incessant localized warfare—among city-states on the Italian Peninsula, in the Adriatic Sea between commercial rivals Genoa and Venice, and in the Balkans between the Ottoman and Byzantine Empires.[29]

At the western end of the Mediterranean, the Iberian Peninsula was an area of both continuous warfare and cultural cross-fertilization between militant Christian crusaders in the north and a Muslim emirate in the south. Throughout the fourteenth century, the warrior societies in these northern Iberian kingdoms of Castile and Aragon would continue their violent campaigns against both rival Christian monarchs and Muslim Granada. In 1400, Iberia was still absorbed in this tempestuous Mediterranean world, and its turn to Atlantic exploration was still several decades away.[30]

The Mediterranean region was separated from most of Africa's peoples by the vastness of the Sahara's sands and scrub. But from the eleventh century on, Berber merchants led caravans across the desert from the West African goldfields in Ghana and Mali, supplying two-thirds of the bullion for late-medieval Europe. On the other side of that vast continent, a powerful Muslim sultanate ruled the Swahili coast from its port city at Kilwa in modern Tanzania, while the Shona kings further south in Zimbabwe controlled the copper and gold mines between the Limpopo and Zambezi Rivers.[31]

By 1400, Arab trade routes across the Indian Ocean linked Africa to rich kingdoms in India, Indonesia, and China. Much of northern India was in tumult after an invasion by Tamerlane's Turko-Mongol troops in 1398, but in the subcontinent's southwest the Vijayanagar Empire was presiding over a Hindu Golden Age with lively overseas trade.[32] Further east across the Bay of Bengal, a Malay sultanate on the Straits of Malacca with some 50,000 inhabitants controlled the spice trade from the islands farther east in Indonesia. To the north, the inland capital of Angkor's empire in present-day Cambodia was on the brink of a climate change–driven collapse that would soon transform that million-person city into an empty ruin, swallowed by jungle.[33] Across the rugged mountains that separated Southeast Asia from China, the new Ming dynasty had recently expelled its Mongol invaders, but had now retreated into a defensive crouch—expanding the Great Wall to bar more nomad invasions and turning away from the sea by extending the thousand-mile Grand Canal to its new capital at Beijing.[34]

Beyond these trade circuits, there were three continents still unknown to anyone beyond their own shores. By 1400, several centuries of trade, travel, invasion, and migration had brought the tri-continental landmass of Europe, Asia, and Africa into closer contact, but Australia and the Americas were surrounded by immense seas and thus remained undiscovered, except, of course, by those who lived there. Since Australia's aboriginals worked for subsistence, not trade, their remote continent would not be mapped for another four centuries.

Circa 1400, state formations had appeared in four main areas of the New World in the Americas. In the Andes, the Incas were just beginning a conquest that would soon make them lords of a mountain kingdom extending three thousand miles from present-day Ecuador to Chile. In the Yucatán Peninsula, the mighty Maya Empire at Chichén Itzá had recently broken up, replaced by a smaller capital at Mayapán with some fifteen thousand inhabitants. Farther north in the Valley of Mexico, numerous small city-states were engaged in incessant warfare from which would emerge, just 30 years later, the powerful Aztec Empire. In North America, the great Mississippian settlement of terraced plazas and temples, near present-day St. Louis, collapsed after 1300, leaving in its place the more localized tribal confederations—the Iroquois, Cherokee, Creek, Natchez, and others—that would someday confront the Europeans.[35]

Iberia Forges a World Order

In the decades after 1400, such regional isolation and tenuous trade contacts gave way to conquest and commerce that would, in little more than a century, knit the continents together into a new world order. As Tamerlane's horsemen swept across Central Asia and the Ottoman Turks captured the Byzantine Empire's capital at Constantinople in 1453, Iberia's kingdoms turned their explorations seaward for a century. Not only did Portugal and Spain extend their empires to four continents, but they also created the first world order worthy of the name, one commingling commerce, conquest, and religious conversion. Starting in 1420, Portuguese mariners, sailing in the light, lethal caravel warships that synthesized advances in navigation and naval warfare, pushed southward down the African coast. Over the next century, they would round Africa, seize control of the Indian Ocean, and build some 50 fortified ports from Brazil to Southeast Asia, allowing them to dominate much of world trade for most of the sixteenth century. Somewhat later, Spanish conquistadors followed Columbus across the Atlantic to subdue the Aztec and Inca kingdoms, laying claim to an overseas empire that covered much of what is now Latin America.

Maritime exploration by itself was nothing new. Indeed, ships from several societies had already crossed the world's widest and wildest oceans. For nearly four centuries, from 700 to 1050, Viking longships raided towns around Europe and ranged across the unexplored waters of the North Atlantic, establishing settlements in Iceland around 874, Greenland in 982, and Newfoundland briefly in 1001. One of their few surviving ships, built about 890 and buried in a funeral mound, has a stout 78-foot keel that frames a wide, shallow hull of flexible planks capable of skimming stormy Atlantic swells like an autumn leaf.[36]

While the Vikings were exploring the North Atlantic, Austronesian mariners used balancing outriggers to settle islands that covered half the globe's circumference. As early as 500 CE, those mariners had already crossed the Indian Ocean from Indonesia to settle in Madagascar and were navigating the Pacific by the stars and currents, reaching Hawaii around 900 and Easter Island circa 1200.[37] As the Portuguese were beginning to venture down the western coast of Africa, China sent its admiral Zheng He to explore Southeast Asia and the Indian Ocean. He made it as far as East Africa before the Ming dynasty decided instead to turn inward and ignore sea travel.[38] Many societies worldwide had a capacity for exploration, but until the Portuguese began their slow progress down the coast of Africa, none had combined commerce, capital, and sea power to create a maritime empire that could bring the continents into close, continuous contact.

Unlike past explorations for settlement, tribute, or plunder, Iberia's overseas expansion would prove to be a determined commercial enterprise driven by the quest for trade and profit. Returning from his first voyage to the Americas in March 1493, the Italian mariner Christopher Columbus, sailing on behalf of Spain, took refuge from a storm in Lisbon's harbor. The Portuguese king was so "disgusted and grieved" at the news of his discoveries that he ordered an armada fitted out to seize the new lands for himself. Upon learning of that threat, Spanish monarchs Ferdinand and Isabella sent an envoy to Lisbon and sought support from the Vatican for their new territorial claims. In response, Pope Alexander VI, Spanish-born and friendly toward Ferdinand, issued two decrees (*Inter Caetera* and *Eximiae Devotionis*) awarding the Spanish crown perpetual sovereignty over all lands "one hundred leagues towards the west and south from any of the islands commonly known as the Azores."[39]

In issuing those decrees, Alexander VI effectively diminished the extent of an earlier papal bull (*Romanus Pontifex*, 1455) that had given Portugal the exclusive right to "possess . . . islands, lands, harbors, and seas" in Africa and authority to "subdue all Muslims and pagans" and "reduce their persons to perpetual slavery."[40] Although the Vatican then served as Europe's de facto international court, these competing claims, supported by contradictory papal bulls, now required some direct diplomacy.

To determine just where the Vatican's line should lie, Spanish and Portuguese diplomats met for months in 1494 in the small Spanish city of Tordesillas. There the high-stakes negotiations moved the pope's dividing line somewhat to the west to run midway through the Atlantic, effectively splitting the non-Christian world between those two Iberian powers. Through this division, the Portuguese preserved their exclusive claim to the African coast. Brazil's bulge into the Atlantic meant it too fell within their domain, while Spain gained unchallenged dominion over the rest of North and South America. Once the Portuguese navigator Ferdinand Magellan's crew circumnavigated the globe for the first time in 1522, Spain and Portugal resolved the resulting tensions by eventually negotiating an additional dividing line through the Pacific.[41]

Through exploration and expansion, the Iberians used those papal decrees to infuse their emerging world order with two central principles. First, imperial sovereignty would be boundless, capable of encompassing non-Christian lands of every sort by conquest and the world's largest oceans by exploration. More fundamentally, in the conquest of alien lands, a Christian monarch was morally and legally empowered, by papal authority, to enslave all their peoples in perpetuity.

Portugal's Global Empire

At first blush, Portugal must have seemed an unlikely vessel for Europe's expansion. The kingdom took form as a relatively small state during the two centuries that its militant monastic orders, the Knights Templar and Order of Aviz, struggled against the Islamic occupation of the Iberian Peninsula.

Their crusade finally captured Lisbon in 1147 and drove the last Muslims out of the south in 1249, establishing Portugal as one of Europe's oldest nations. After the grand master of the Aviz religious order took the throne as Dom João I in 1385, the new king secured the country's independence by repelling a massive Castilian invasion. That victory established the Aviz dynasty, which would rule Portugal for the next two centuries.

Though politically stable, the new kingdom was one of Europe's poorest, ruling a country with erratic rainfall, rocky soils, a small population, and few forests for shipbuilding. The Black Death of 1350 had taken a terrible toll, and the population would require a full century to recover. At the start of its explorations, Portugal had less than a million people and its largest city, Lisbon, only 40,000 residents. Even at the peak of its imperial power in the sixteenth century, Portugal had just three hundred ships, most crewed by foreign sailors and built from tropical teakwood at Goa, its colonial capital on India's west coast.[42]

Though its navigators were skilled and its soldiers courageous, the kingdom's inherent poverty resulted in a commercial approach to exploration that was fundamentally parasitic. During its century-long crawl down the long west coast of Africa, its prime export would be slaves, prompting a determined diplomacy that effectively legalized this emerging human traffic. During its century of dominion over the Indian Ocean, Portugal would use its naval power to expropriate the existing trade of Asian merchants.

In turning to the sea as its only possible source of wealth, the Portuguese crown had several important advantages—adventurous commanders, innovations in navigation thanks to contact with Muslim society, and, paradoxically, a fanatical mission to defeat Islam. In 1415, King Dom João I led an expedition of two hundred ships and 20,000 men across the Strait of Gibraltar to seize the rich Muslim port of Ceuta, gateway to the Atlantic and terminus for the caravans that crossed the Sahara from the gold mines of West Africa. Exhibiting the religious fervor that would ultimately consume it, the Aviz dynasty's army sacked the old city, slaughtering half its Arab population and selling the other half into slavery. Fighting heroically at the king's side during the city's capture was his fourth son, Prince Henry, later known as the Navigator, the reputed progenitor of the Age of Discovery.[43] By capturing a key bastion astride such strategic straits, Portugal could then safely shift Iberian trade toward the Atlantic and venture down the coast of Africa.[44]

At the fulcrum between the seaborne commerce of the Atlantic and the Mediterranean, Portugal was well placed to benefit from a myriad of fifteenth-century innovations that made blue-water exploration possible. The first and most formidable problem to be solved was navigation. For at least a century, Mediterranean captains had been sailing open waters by measuring latitude from the stars and using the pole star or compass for direction. Atlantic sailors who strayed from the coast had the prevailing westerly winds to bring them back safely toward shore. But as Portuguese explorers pushed below the equator, the North Star disappeared, while the South Atlantic's prevailing winds and currents were both temperamental and unknown.

During the fifteenth century, Iberian navigators solved such problems through a mix of academic research and practical seamanship. The translation of Ptolemy's *Geographia* into Latin in 1409 listed the longitudes and latitudes known to the ancient world, creating a benchmark for additional tables. Drawing upon astronomers' refinements of Arab practices, Portuguese sailors came to use a simplified circular astrolabe or cross-staff to measure the angle (declination) between the sun or stars and the horizon to determine a ship's latitude in open waters. As a capstone to all this research, in 1478 the Spanish astronomer Abraham Zacuto published his "Great Book" in Hebrew with 64 detailed tables to accompany an improved maritime astrolabe. After Spain's expulsion of its Jewish population in 1492, he fled to Lisbon, where he became the court astronomer. There his work was published in Latin and used to train Portuguese navigators.[45] Between 1419 and 1460, with such innovations at hand, Lisbon's mariners launched their expeditions down the African coast to Cape Verde. In the course of these 35 voyages, they would discover, in 1427, the North Atlantic's subtropical gyre—a remarkable confluence of ocean currents. As the caravels turned homeward for Portugal off the African coast near the Canary Islands, they found that a northwest current swept them toward the Azores, in the mid-Atlantic, where another current carried them due east for a thousand miles, safely back to Lisbon.[46]

While improved navigation could guide Portuguese sailors across the open sea, they also needed better ships to survive such rugged waters. With wide hulls and square sails, the dominant Mediterranean *cocche* merchant ship was difficult to maneuver in the Atlantic's heavy seas, particularly when sailing directly into the wind. Drawing upon Arab and Italian designs, a new vessel appeared in the fourteenth century with a square foremast and triangular lateen sail aft for greater maneuverability. This design culminated in the creation of the Portuguese caravel, an agile 50-ton cargo ship with two lateen sails, and the heavier, 150-ton warship, the *caravela de armada*, with four masts. Along with their triangular sails' far greater suitability for upwind sailing, these new craft, like their Arab antecedents, had a shallow draft, ideal for beaching on foreign shores or exploring rivers.[47]

Above all, however, Portugal's superior shipboard artillery made its *caravela de armada* the most lethal weaponry of its age—indeed, the precursor of modern naval warfare. The first artillery had appeared in Europe around 1326, four centuries after China discovered gunpowder. By the 1430s, ponderous siege guns could fire 1,500 pound stone balls, reducing the strongest castle walls to rubble in a day.[48] In 1499, naval artillery became a decisive factor in the Battle of Zonchio, in Greece's Gulf of Corinth, when Ottoman ships carrying heavy cannon sank a Venetian ship, so unnerving the rest of the Christian fleet that it retreated in defeat.[49] By the 1530s, it was standard for Mediterranean war galleys to have five bow guns, including a massive, 5,000-pound cannon firing a 50-pound ball, flanked by pairs of lighter guns. Since shipboard artillery had an effective range of just two hundred yards, galley fleets could normally release just one volley before the ships closed for the hand-to-hand combat typical of Mediterranean naval warfare since ancient Rome.[50]

The Portuguese crown promoted innovations in shipboard artillery, strengthening the caravel's decks to support heavier guns in 1474 and later training teams of skilled gunners. Instead of five bow guns on the front deck, the caravel carried rows of cannon beneath its decks, allowing continuous lethal broadsides in the attack, while protecting gun crews when the ships closed for swordplay. Portuguese artillerymen were exceptionally skilled, and would later be prized as mercenaries by Asian monarchs in India and Southeast Asia.[51] With hulls made of planks nailed to stout frames, the Portuguese ships could also sustain repeated gun recoils in ways that lighter Asian vessels with sewn hulls could not.[52]

The shift from the oar-powered Mediterranean war galley to the wind-driven gunship revolutionized maritime commerce and combat. "Exchanging oarsmen for sails and warriors for guns," says historian Carlo Cipolla, "meant essentially the exchange of human power for inanimate power." By harnessing the enormous propulsive energy of wind, sailcraft could be built with deeper, more robust hulls and reinforced gun decks capable of massive firepower, as well as large holds with capacity for more cargo. "On the ocean," adds Cipolla, particularly the Atlantic with its strong westerly winds and long rollers, "galleys had no chances whatsoever. When they were not sunk by the guns of the great sailing ships they were easy prey to the fury of the elements."[53]

By 1500 the Portuguese *caravela de armada* had navigation instruments to cross the widest ocean, sails adequate for the strongest headwinds, a sturdy hull for guns and cargo, and lethal cannon that could destroy enemy fleets or breach the walls of port cities. As a result, a small flotilla of Portuguese caravels, manned by no more than a thousand soldiers and sailors, could defeat a far larger Asian armada by sailing through its formation with broadsides blazing, thus crippling their ships without ever closing for bloody hand-to-hand combat. Given such assets, Lisbon's empire not surprisingly grew to encompass half the globe through three distinct phases—first, its protracted exploration of five thousand miles of African coastline; then, a sweep across the Indian Ocean in a decade of warfare to seize fortified ports from the Persian Gulf to the Spice Islands of eastern Indonesia; and, finally, the maintenance of that dominion for a full century, until the Dutch and British supplanted them after 1600.

Around Africa

Over the span of 80 years and the reigns of five kings, Portugal's progress down the west coast of Africa was slowed to a fitful crawl by its obsessive pursuit of gold and slaves. After two of Prince Henry's squires, on a mission to raid Muslim ships, were blown off course in 1418 and accidentally discovered the Madeira Archipelago six hundred miles out in the Atlantic, the prince granted them rights to settle it. From that base, Prince Henry sent two expeditions to seize the Canary Islands from Spain; though repulsed, they carried off African residents, many of them Christian converts, as slaves. In response to their bishop's protests, Pope Eugene IV issued three stern papal bulls demanding the immediate manumission of these captives and the end to further Portuguese raids on the Spanish islands.[54]

The Portuguese crown also funded fifteen voyages along the African coast before one finally cleared Cape Bojador in the western Sahara in 1433.

Located just south of the Canaries and shrouded in myths about sea monsters, the cape was a formidable psychological and physical obstacle to further southern exploration. With dangerous shoals extending fifteen miles into the sea, strong currents, frequent fogs, and difficult prevailing winds, Arab geographers had called those waters the "green sea of darkness."[55]

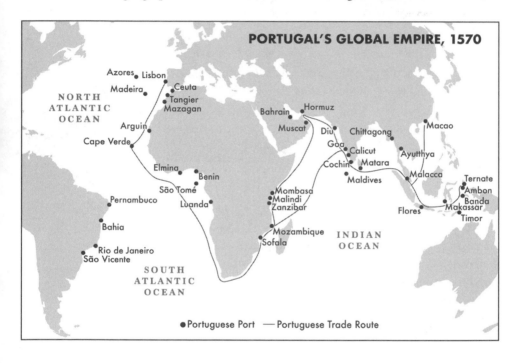

With that barrier finally breached, Prince Henry spent another decade sending more expeditions down a desolate thousand-mile stretch of the African coastline where the Sahara met the sea; in 1443 they first reached settled areas around the Cap d'Arguin, now a national park in modern Mauritania. There they became absorbed in slave raiding, slowing further exploration for decades.[56] By 1448, some 51 caravels had sailed beyond Cape Bojador, bringing back a total of 927 slaves. So lucrative was the traffic that, in 1456, Prince Henry built Portugal's first *feitoria*, or fortified port, at Arguin. By the time he died in 1460, his many expeditions had only advanced 1,500 miles, leaving most of the continent's western coast still unexplored.[57]

As his captains delivered the first African captives, Prince Henry, in a clever diplomatic artifice, petitioned the Vatican to elevate his explorations to a crusade, prompting Pope Eugene IV to issue a bull (*Dum Diversas*, 1452) that would legitimate "perpetual servitude" for all non-Christian captives.[58] Although the Roman Empire's legacy of widespread slavery had faded from Europe by the tenth century, the Justinian *Digest* of Roman law, which shaped medieval jurisprudence, advocated the enslavement rather than slaughter of war captives. While earlier papal bulls had granted Christian crusaders limited rights to enslave Muslim captives in the Holy Land, the pope now broadened that permission to allow for the perpetual slavery of all peoples beyond the known world.[59]

Just a few years after the Vatican's initial endorsement of the slave trade, Pope Nicholas V issued the decree *Romanus Pontifex* in 1454, a papal bull so broad that historian Charles Boxer called it "the charter of Portuguese imperialism." In this expansive document, the pope proclaimed: "We have lately heard, not without great joy and gratification . . . how our beloved son the noble personage Henry, prince of Portugal . . . as a Catholic and true soldier of Christ . . . has peopled with orthodox Christians certain solitary islands in the ocean sea . . . Thence also many Guineamen and other Negroes taken by force . . . have been . . . converted to the faith." In light of such deeds, the pope granted Portugal perpetual sovereignty over Africa's entire coast south of Cape Bojador, with the right "to invade, search out, capture, vanquish, and subdue all Saracens and pagans whatsoever and . . . to reduce their persons to perpetual slavery." So complete was the grant that Portugal's king arranged a solemn proclamation of this papal bull at Lisbon's Santa Maria Cathedral, reading it in both the original Latin and a Portuguese translation before representatives of the city's foreign communities.[60]

The decree came at a significant turning point in the history of the slave trade in Europe. Although common under the Roman Empire, slavery had slowly subsided until the church banned the enslavement of Christians in 992 CE. By the twelfth century, the practice had given way to serfdom in northern Europe, although the human traffic persisted around the Mediterranean, particularly in Spain where Christian and Muslim kingdoms used each other's war captives as slaves. Still, the traffic remained limited, and the conditions of slavery were carefully regulated under the thirteenth-century Spanish code of the Siete Partidas, which gave slaves the right to marry and provided terms for winning their freedom.[61]

During the fourteenth century, the Black Death left a distinct divide in labor practices across the heart of Europe. In England, France, and Germany, the scarcity of labor had encouraged a shift from serfdom to free wage labor. In the south, by contrast, Mediterranean societies experienced an increased demand for captive labor. Slaves from Greece and Crimea came to comprise a significant proportion of the local populations in Tuscany and Catalonia, which had suffered heavy losses from the plague.[62]

The Portuguese exploration of Africa, however, turned a traffic in dozens into a commerce of thousands and later tens of thousands. While Muslims had assigned their slaves diverse tasks from domestic duties to military service, the Portuguese now concentrated their African captives on sugar plantations, first on islands off the coast of Africa and later in Brazil. In the half century that followed the first African captives' arrival in Lisbon in 1441, Portuguese sea captains would enslave some 150,000 Africans, shipping them to the Azores and Madeira for farm work, and Spain, Italy, and Portugal itself, which were all seriously short of labor after decades of recurring plagues.[63] Not surprisingly, those captains dehumanized their African captives, describing them, in one 1508 travel account, as naked cannibals with teeth "filed and sharp as those of a dog" and "wild men, whom the ancients called satyrs."[64]

With royal support and papal sanction, Portugal's slave trade quickly became an organized commerce, and to manage it the crown established its *feitoria* trading posts at Arguin island in modern Mauritania (1456), at Elmina Castle in Ghana (1482), and on São Tomé Island, in the Gulf of Guinea (1493). For the next century, caravels sailing north from the *feitoria* at Elmina Castle also carried cargoes of gold dust to Lisbon that would be minted into Portugal's famed gold *cruzado* coinage.[65] The long-term Portuguese presence in West Africa meant that trade replaced raids, leading to complex negotiations with local kingdoms to secure a steady supply of gold and slaves.[66]

From its headquarters on the Lisbon waterfront, which included holding cells, the royal monopoly, called the Casa da Guiné, sent caravels fitted with chains and neck rings to Africa every year from 1510 to 1550, which brought back about two thousand slaves annually, many for reexport to Spain and the Americas. After Spain's King Charles V allowed direct slave imports into his American colonies in 1518, the Portuguese transatlantic trade grew rapidly. By 1650, 703,600 slaves had been sent to the Americas, largely to toil on Brazilian and Caribbean sugar plantations. This human traffic became a significant source of Portugal's revenues, bringing income nearly double that of the Elmina gold trade.[67]

Portugal first developed its new model for the slave plantation on two island colonies off the coast of Africa. As the ruler of Madeira, Prince Henry sent experts with sugarcane samples from Sicily and awarded a squire permission to build a grinding mill. Although the island's rugged landscape kept farms small, sugar production climbed to over 2,240 tons by 1500, propelled by the sweat labor of two thousand African slaves. Farther south on the more arable São Tomé Island, slaves built a flourishing sugar industry with exports rising to 25,000 tons by the end of the sixteenth century, making this fertile island the world's largest sugar producer. Each of the island's profitable *fazendas* had a workforce of 150 to 300 slaves and an efficient water-powered mill to crush the cane, thereby becoming a new template for tropical agribusiness that would flourish when it later spread across the Atlantic to Brazil and the Caribbean.[68]

The understanding that the plantation was central to the proliferation of sugar raises a far more fundamental question: Why, among all the plants on the planet, did cane sugar become so popular, in so much demand from consumers, and thus remain startlingly profitable? From the time an infant sucks its mother's milk, all humans develop a taste for sweetness. Our hunter-gatherer ancestors used sweetness as one key to distinguish between edible and inedible plants. Although humans started domesticating honeybees about nine thousand years ago, the taste of sucrose from sugarcane would remain unknown to Europeans until about 1100 CE, when Muslim conquerors first introduced the plant to the Mediterranean, particularly the islands of Crete, Cyprus, Malta, and Sicily. At first, when the supply was limited and the price still high, the seductive taste of sugar would remain an aristocratic privilege. But as sugar plantations spread to both sides the Atlantic and production increased rapidly in the seventeenth and eighteenth centuries, cane sugar became an affordable and adaptable staple in the European diet. It would be used in beverages like beer, as a sweetener to render porridge more palatable, as an ingredient in countless dishes, and, ultimately, for baked desserts like puddings, candies, and cakes. By the mid-eighteenth century, the British cup of tea sweetened with sugar had become, with its mix of caffeine and sucrose, a midday energizer that cut across the class divide, shared by everyone from affluent merchants to the poorest field hand. As its empire expanded in the nineteenth century, the most significant change in the British diet would, in fact, prove to be a fivefold increase in sugar consumption, which provided one-sixth of the country's calories—a success story unequaled by any other food in world history.[69]

In this way, the slave plantation became another defining element of the Iberian age, providing Europe's economy with a new, profitable form of agriculture. The human body is a relatively inefficient machine, capable of a sustained output of only half a horsepower during a ten-hour working day. Laboring on small plots during a six-month temperate growing season, Europe's yeoman farmers produced a grain harvest that was only 20 percent of that from China's rice paddies. And these yields, low as they were, would in fact decline during the three centuries of the Iberian age.[70]

By the end of the fifteenth century, however, Portuguese plantations off the coast of Africa had broken multiple barriers to productivity, effectively maximizing the potential of human muscle power—including a tropical locale for year-round farming, the massing of slave laborers on large landholdings for the concerted output of team labor, and the kind of coercion that enforced a relentless intensity of effort. Made to labor for nearly double the hours of British yeoman farmers, African slaves would have an average working life of just seven years on the plantations of Brazil and the Caribbean. In the 1630s, a Jesuit plantation manager in Bahia, Brazil, wrote that the high mortality among slaves required an annual 6 percent replacement rate. A Barbados planter reported the same rate of slave losses, saying that "he that hath but a hundred Negroes should buy half a dozen every year to keep up his flock." As long as the transatlantic human traffic could feed this voracious appetite for fresh slaves, plantations proved sustainable and highly profitable. Indeed, an econometric analysis of US agriculture in the early nineteenth century found the Southern slave plantation was 35 percent more efficient than a northern family farm.[71] By literally working massed teams of slaves to death, the tropical sugar plantation maximized the energy output of the human body, creating a cruel economic logic that would drive the relentless expansion of the slave trade for the next four hundred years.

Following a hiatus of several decades, serious exploration of the African coast resumed under the reign of King Dom João II, who dedicated much of his realm's resources to the effort. From bases in the Gulf of Guinea, Portuguese captains would complete their exploration of the continent's west coast all the way to its southern tip in just six years, a startling speed compared to the 55 years it had taken to cover the coast's northern half. Between 1482 and

1488, explorers sailed south along the African coast, planting stone pillars (*padrão*) on headlands from the Congo River to the Cape of Good Hope.[72]

Across the Indian Ocean

Compared to its fitful, century-long exploration of Africa's west coast, Portugal's conquest of the Indian Ocean proceeded with stunning speed. More than any city, country, or even continent, this ocean was the sixteenth century's greatest imperial prize. Spanning nearly five thousand miles at its widest point, the Indian Ocean in 1500 was bounded by some of the world's richest kingdoms. Suffering only seasonal cyclones, it was also free from the winter storms of the North Atlantic and the frequent typhoons of the Pacific. Even more important, its monsoons blew reliable trade winds in an annual southwest/northeast cycle, allowing Asian kingdoms to conduct much of their commerce by sea and Europeans to sail from South Africa to India and back. Of all the world's oceans, it was the most favorable for maritime trade.

The longest trade routes across the Indian Ocean carried precious and costly spices like nutmeg, cloves, and pepper from eastern Indonesia and South India through the Red Sea to Suez. From there, they would be transported across that peninsula for shipment on Venetian galleys across the Mediterranean to Europe. Around the Indian Ocean's sprawling shoreline, Gujarati Muslims, Hindu Tamils, and Malay Muslims all moved freely through prosperous port cities that were generally unfortified. More than any other comparable trade corridor, the Indian Ocean was an open sea.[73]

Despite its expanse of 27 million square miles (about 14 percent of the earth's surface), that vast ocean had a surprisingly small number of maritime choke points, making it susceptible to geopolitical dominion by an aggressive naval power. To change that open ocean into a closed sea, Portuguese captains would have to capture just four strategic points—the East African coast, the entrance to the Red Sea, the mouth of the Persian Gulf, and the Straits of Malacca. Guided by a clear strategic plan for just such a mission, they would do all this, with one key exception, in only a decade.

In July 1497, the navigator Vasco da Gama left Lisbon with four ships crewed by 170 men, made landfall in Sierra Leone, and then did something unprecedented. Instead of clinging to the coast like earlier explorers, his pilots steered due south into the open ocean, caught the South Atlantic's great gyre, and were carried by its currents for six thousand miles across the sea to the Cape of Good Hope. After picking up a skilled local pilot at Malindi in East Africa, the fleet crossed the Indian Ocean on prevailing monsoon winds, reaching Calicut on the Malabar Coast of South India in May 1498 and so becoming the first European mariners to complete the voyage to India. When da Gama's sailors touched shore at the thriving Indian port of Calicut, they were met by two Spanish-speaking Muslims from Tunisia, one of whom asked: "What the devil has brought you here?" The Portuguese replied, accurately enough: "We have come to seek Christians and spices." By the time da Gama's two surviving ships returned to Lisbon in August 1499, they had sailed 23,000 miles, much of it across open sea, and pioneered Portugal's trade route to the Indies.[74]

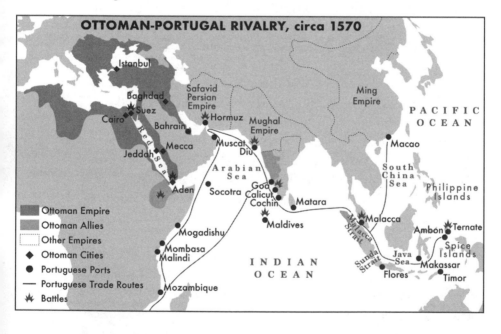

The windfall profits from these first cargoes of pepper and other spices inspired a redoubled effort by the Portuguese crown, which over the next six years dispatched annual expeditions—totaling 81 ships and seven thousand men—on the route da Gama had pioneered. One of these was carried westward by the South Atlantic's winds to skirt the coast of Brazil, affirming Portugal's claim and allowing a later colonization. On his next voyage to Asia in 1502, da Gama transformed himself from explorer to conqueror, determined to capture a permanent enclave on the Indian coast. Leaving Lisbon with a fleet of 20 armed ships and eight hundred men, da Gama would extract tribute in gold from the Muslim sultan at Kilwa, East Africa, before crossing to Calicut, the center of South India's lucrative pepper trade. After massacring four hundred Muslim "infidels" on a pilgrim ship offshore, he punished the city's Hindu king for rejecting his terms of trade by slaughtering hundreds of ordinary fishermen and bombarding the port, inflicting heavy damage on an unfortified city.[75]

When the Indian king quickly mobilized a flotilla of 80 ships to retaliate, da Gama demonstrated the lethal power of Portuguese warships. According to a contemporary Portuguese chronicle, he "ordered the caravels to come astern of the other in a line and to run under all the sail they could carry, firing their guns whenever they could." After passing through the Indian armada firing broadsides, the Portuguese ships "made haste to load again," turned, and attacked once more. With their big guns firing at the waterline to puncture the hulls and light guns aiming to topple the masts, the Portuguese fleet sank several Indian ships and damaged others. By contrast, the light guns on the Indian craft could do little harm. The Portuguese soldiers stayed below decks and suffered few casualties, but the carnage among the Indian troops massed on their open decks was horrific. Nonetheless, the Hindu king of Calicut, the zamorin, refused to submit. A lesser rajah down the coast at Cochin did allow the Portuguese to establish a trading post, but da Gama returned to Portugal having failed to build a fortified enclave, retiring in disgrace.[76]

The following year, King Manuel I (1469–1521), an ambitious administrator of the imperial enterprise, dispatched more ships, commanded by renowned navigator Afonso de Albuquerque, to establish a permanent base in India. Arriving there without mishap, the Portuguese found their ally, the Cochin rajah, in dire straits, driven out of his capital by an attack from the powerful Calicut king. After retaking Cochin and leaving behind a tiny garrison of 150 men and five ships with the difficult task of defending the rajah, Albuquerque set sail for Lisbon with a shipment of spices. Meanwhile, the garrison commander at Cochin, Captain-Major Duarte Pacheco Pereira, would prove himself to be, in the words of historian Roger Crowley, a "tactical genius, geographer, and experimental scientist." When Calicut's king laid siege to Cochin with an army of 60,000, Pacheco's small detachment led the rajah's force of 8,000 in repulsing repeated attacks and defeated the enemy fleet of 52 ships. By observing the relation between the phases of the moon and changing tides, Pacheco was able, during five months of warfare, to shift his sparse troops strategically around Cochin's shallow lagoon to blunt attacks by nominally superior forces. Frustrated by his repeated failures, the Calicut king finally sued for peace, allowing Pacheco to secure Portugal's first foothold in Asia before he returned in triumph to Lisbon with a rich cargo of pepper and spices.[77]

Duarte Pacheco Pereira, Portuguese explorer, circa 1520 (Credit: Alamy)

And so, with surprising speed, Portugal's Asian empire took form. With access to advice from experienced explorers such as Albuquerque and Pacheco, King Manuel and his royal council framed a surprisingly comprehensive geopolitical design for dominion over the Indian Ocean. In a *regimiento* decree issued at the start of the conquest, the king ordered his

Asian governor, first, to control the East African coast by occupying the ports at Kilwa and Mombasa; next, to build a fort at the mouth of the Red Sea to block all trade by the sultan of Egypt; and, finally, to establish fortified trading ports across the Indian Ocean from South India to the Straits of Malacca. Although most of those waters were still unexplored by the Portuguese, the king's orders had correctly identified three of the four maritime choke points for imposing a *mare clausum* when it came to the Indian Ocean's commerce.[78] That such a vast ocean could be so easily controlled was a paradox that would propel tiny Portugal to global power.

As his instruments for fulfilling those plans, the king was well served by a few gifted governors and small contingents of determined troops. Brutalized in the long wars against Muslims in Morocco, Portuguese soldiers, according to historians B.W. Diffie and G.D. Winius, showed determination and discipline in battle. Undeterred by superior numbers, they fought ferociously even when wounded, and exulted in the slaughter of their enemies. While Spanish conquistadors readily massacred masses of Aztec and Incan troops who lacked horses, steel, or gunpowder, the Portuguese usually faced Asian armies and navies with greater numbers and comparable weapons. Whenever opportunity allowed, the Portuguese acted upon their deep animus against Muslims, murdering those they encountered on the high seas or in port cities. But to secure their lightly defended enclaves, the Portuguese courted the support of local leaders, whether Indian rajahs or Malay sultans.[79]

In its century-long attempt to control the Indian Ocean, Portugal overcame the extraordinary distance between its capital and the imperial periphery through a supple administrative strategy. At home, the Portuguese crown, unlike larger European states that invested little in exploration, acted as a capitalist entity, an entrepreneur presiding over the imperial enterprise. Abroad, the crown built a resilient network of compact, self-contained *feitorias* to rule a vast oceanic empire that, at its peak, would cover half the globe. From Brazil to eastern Indonesia, Portugal built 50 of these fortified ports, using them as both naval bastions to tax passing ships and counting houses to manage its trade in spices, gold, silver, and slaves. Surrounded by formidable stone ramparts, each of them was a defensible, self-contained community governed by an agent of the crown who regulated private merchants and managed royal trade. To assemble outgoing fleets and market incoming goods, the crown also built a central *feitoria*, the Casa da India on the

Tagus River at Lisbon, where it received rich cargoes from Africa and Asia and consigned them to a merchant syndicate at Antwerp for sale across Europe.[80] In their geopolitical array, Portugal's fortified enclaves arched around that "world island" of Africa and Eurasia, amplifying its global power and allowing it an empire whose resilience went far beyond the country's otherwise-meager resources of men and ships.

Since the Portuguese empire clung to the coasts instead of moving inland to colonize territory, it needed to develop a fluid state for governance of its global archipelago of fortified enclaves. To manage some twenty *feitorias* on the coast of India alone, the crown appointed a viceroy who, after 1530, would rule that country's Estado da India (State of India) from a capital at Goa lined with impressive stone structures that had the look of Iberia in Asia. That enclave would also serve as headquarters for a Portuguese community scattered across Asia that eventually grew to some fourteen thousand, half of them Catholic clerics and the rest officials, soldiers, and merchants. This geopolitical array of forts linked by fleets proved reasonably capable of absorbing attacks by massed Asian levies—repelling assaults from stone ramparts, drawing support from nearby ports, and evacuating safely if necessary.[81] The result: an imperial juggernaut that allowed the Portuguese to dominate the vast Indian Ocean with a few dozen ships and several thousand soldiers, neutralizing more powerful Asian monarchs whose enormous land armies were drawn from a vast Indian subcontinent with 150 million people.[82]

The key figures in Portugal's conquest of this ocean were two military governors the crown dispatched to execute its grand design. Sailing from Lisbon in March 1505 with an armada of 22 ships and 1,500 soldiers, Francisco de Almeida, known as "the Great Dom Francisco," carried the king's appointment as the first viceroy of India and orders for the conquest of an oceanic empire. But he soon found himself on the defensive, fighting a powerful multinational coalition of those displaced by Portugal's capture of the spice trade—both Venetian merchants deprived of their reliable 40 percent profits from the pepper trade, and Egypt's Mamluk Sultanate, which had lost the traditional transit taxes on spice shipments crossing the Suez Isthmus.[83]

As promoters of this alliance, Venice sent timber and shipwrights to assemble a dozen large war galleys at Suez on the Red Sea for Egypt's Mamluk sultan. In February 1507, he dispatched that fleet with 1,500 soldiers to join Indian ships at the port of Diu on the Arabian Sea.[84] Two years later,

Almeida sailed boldly into Diu's narrow harbor with nineteen ships and 1,200 Portuguese soldiers to face a Muslim force of more than one hundred ships and 5,000 fighters. With no room for anyone to maneuver, the Portuguese gunners fired hundreds of rounds point blank into enemy ships, while their soldiers boarded for hand-to-hand combat. With the enemy fleet completely destroyed and the harbor dyed crimson with their blood, Almeida had scored one of the "most decisive" victories in maritime history, in the process giving Portugal control over much of the commerce on India's west coast for the next century.[85]

With that Muslim challenge met, the next viceroy sent out from Lisbon, Albuquerque, spent six years trying to implement his king's grand geopolitical design and did so with such success that he became famed as "the lion of the seas."[86] To secure a capital for Portugal's Asian empire, Albuquerque attacked the Indian port of Goa in 1510, storming the gates at dawn and fighting a bloody street battle to take the city by noon. To capture Southeast Asia's richest prize, Albuquerque commanded an armada of eighteen ships and 1,200 men in an attack on the Malay port of Malacca, routing 20,000 soldiers armed with two thousand cannons in another bloody street battle. Building on that victory, the governor dispatched expeditions to the Moluccas of eastern Indonesia to seize the source of luxury spices—cloves, nutmeg, and mace.[87]

After securing that eastern entrance to the Indian Ocean, Albuquerque tried to capture the fortified port at Aden, gateway to the Red Sea at the southern tip of the Arabian Peninsula. But everything went wrong—cannonballs bounced off the massive fortress walls, troops landed amid submerged rocks, and siege ladders proved to be too short.[88] In his final campaign in 1515, Albuquerque led a formidable fleet to occupy Hormuz Island at the mouth of the Persian Gulf, a windswept outcrop that served as entrepôt for the rich trade between Persia and India. After inviting the local sultan and his influential adviser, an agent of the shah of Persia, for a peaceful parley at his stockade on the shore, Albuquerque ordered the adviser assassinated and forced the sultan to hand over this strategic choke point—a claim that the Persians, reeling from a recent defeat by the Ottoman army, were too weak to resist.[89] By the time Albuquerque died at Goa, his campaigns had fulfilled the king's plans for a *mare clausum* over the entire Indian Ocean—save that one opening at the Red Sea, which would soon become, as historian Michael

Pearson put it, "a vital gap in the Portuguese geostrategic design" allowing Muslim merchants a northern route across the Arabian Sea.[90]

As demonstrated by that naval disaster at Diu, Egypt's Mamluk Sultanate was a regime in decline. It would be quickly eliminated when the Ottoman Empire—which was expanding dynamically in all directions from its capital at Istanbul—marched south in 1517, crushing the Mamluk forces with superior firepower and capturing their entire domain from Syria to Egypt, thus bringing this powerful state to the shores of the Red Sea. Simultaneously, the Ottoman ruler, Selim the Grim, proclaimed himself the universal caliph of Islam and protector of Mecca. With the resources of this now enormously expanded empire, his son and heir Suleiman the Magnificent would pursue that mission by attacking the Portuguese in the Indian Ocean.[91]

In 1538, the Ottoman viceroy of Egypt dispatched an armada of 72 ships, 6,500 men, and excellent artillery across the Arabian Sea to join an even larger Gujarati Indian force for another attack on the Portuguese *feitoria* at Diu, in northern India. Although the timely arrival of a relief fleet from Goa saved the eight hundred defenders from imminent defeat, the Portuguese counterattack at Suez on the Red Sea was easily repulsed. This massive maritime war, with bold strategic gambits on both sides, changed little. In the coming decades, those two rival imperial powers would engage in incessant yet inconclusive combat, sending their troops to support allies among warring kingdoms on the Horn of Africa and fighting naval battles from the Red Sea to the Straits of Malacca.[92]

Ultimately, this mutual failure led to a strategic stalemate. The Ottomans had superior resources, manpower, and local support among fellow Muslims from East Africa to Indonesia. Yet their reliance on the antiquated rowing galley, though effective in defense of the closed, calmer Red Sea, all but assured their defeat against Portuguese sailcraft in the open waters of the Indian Ocean. For over half a century (1507–1565), Portuguese patrols tried to block the access of India's Muslim merchants to the Red Sea, but year after year their ships slipped through, carrying enough spices to break the profitable Portuguese pepper monopoly.[93] During the 1570s, the visionary grand vizier and geopolitical strategist Sokollu Mehmed Pasha developed a lucrative Ottoman spice trade that taxed Muslim merchants and organized convoys of state-owned ships, which sailed up the Red Sea to Suez from Mocha, carrying Yemen's famed coffee crop as well as spices from India.[94]

In the 1580s, however, the intense rivalry for control of the Indian Ocean began to fade as both empires, Ottoman and Portuguese, entered periods of internal crisis. Drained by a protracted sectarian war against the Persian Empire, the Ottoman court at Istanbul became, as historian Giancarlo Casale put it, "locked in a seemingly endless cycle of backstabbing, recriminations, and scandal," epitomized by the assassination of Sokollu Mehmed Pasha in 1579. With him died bold plans to make Istanbul the center of a world empire by the seizure of the Mediterranean from the Christians, the instigation of a pan-Islamic revolt against Portugal across the Indian Ocean, and the construction of canals in both Suez and southern Russia. Through the fatal combination of such palace intrigues, war with the Persian Empire, and escalating military pressures in the Mediterranean, the Ottomans would soon cease to be a "visible political presence" in the Indian Ocean.[95]

Simultaneously, a catastrophic crisis at home finally broke Portugal's century-long attempt to monopolize the Indian Ocean's commerce. In 1578, the young king Sebastian, whose sexual impotence and fiery temperament made him an obsessive "captain of Christ," led the flower of his nation's aristocracy on a latter-day crusade into Morocco. There, at the fateful Battle of Alcácer Quibir, Portugal's army was slaughtered by local Muslim forces. Some eight thousand Portuguese troops were killed and fifteen thousand captured. Only one hundred escaped. The defeat was so devastating that it not only destroyed the king and his court but also precipitated the country's incorporation into the Spanish Empire for the next 60 years.[96] With the constraints from both the Ottoman and Portuguese Empires removed, Muslim merchants and pilgrims could once again move across the Indian Ocean unimpeded.[97]

Through skilled diplomacy and incessant naval warfare, Portugal had spent a century defending its *mare clausum* over two of the world's great oceans, the Indian and South Atlantic. Yet the gains from its naval triumphs and lucrative commerce were surprisingly few. The easy profits from its Asian commerce were wasted by a lavish court in Lisbon and ecclesiastical excess manifest in the construction of large churches and monasteries. Meanwhile, social change was stunted, the formation of a commercial bourgeoisie was blocked, and any capitalist stimulus from imperial conquests was left to the Dutch and British.[98] By 1600, Lisbon's empire was in decline and could no longer compete effectively against Holland, as Amsterdam rapidly emerged as Europe's new commercial center and maritime power. Yet even as Portugal's fragile oceanic venture faded, Spain's more powerful empire would sustain the Iberian world order for another half century.

Spain's Empire of Silver

Although Portugal controlled the Indian Ocean and Spain conquered Latin America in the same four decades after 1500, their empires used contrasting strategies to achieve similar economic outcomes. The Portuguese kept to their coastal enclaves; the Spanish marched inland for conquest. The Portuguese struggled to survive attacks by powerful Asian kingdoms; the Spanish slaughtered Amerindian empires. The Portuguese practiced an oblique geopolitics of encircling Eurasia from the surrounding seas; the Spanish attempted the military occupation of two continents (Europe and Latin America) while exercising global economic influence by making their silver the world's currency. With little more than a million people, Portugal provided few colonists for its vast empire; Spain had at least six times that population to sustain a substantial migration that sent 130,000 Castilians to the New World by 1580.

Transcending these differences, however, was a fundamental similarity in the two empires' aims, abilities, and commercial outcomes. Both countries had an ingrained belief in a divinely ordained human hierarchy headed by a monarch; and both had a surfeit of threadbare aristocrats, descended from the generations of Christian crusaders that had fought Muslim rule on the Iberian Peninsula, who were now eager to seek their fortunes on foreign shores. "We see many men who have sailed from Lisbon to Goa, from Seville to Mexico," wrote a Jesuit priest in 1590, "with as much ease as the farmer goes from his village to the town."[99]

The monarchs of both Spain and Portugal managed their empires as economic hybrids, ruling directly through crown appointees and extracting the "royal fifth" from all incoming cargoes as feudal dues. Once the shipments of gold, silver, and spices were unloaded dockside at the Tagus River in Lisbon or the Guadalquivir River at Seville, those goods were transformed into capitalist commodities that quickly escaped the control of both realms—either marketed by the merchants of Antwerp and Amsterdam or sold to satisfy the bankers of Augsburg and Genoa.[100] For both Iberian powers, this near-effortless flow of vast imperial treasure locked them into a quasi-feudal past and failed to stimulate a capitalist transformation.

Starting a century later than Portugal's, Spain's exploration and exploitation of the Americas proceeded in ways that reflected the character of the realm. The domains of Aragon and Castile were merged by the marriage of the Catholic monarchs Ferdinand and Isabella in 1469 into a single kingdom far greater than the sum of its parts. Ferdinand was prince of Aragon in Spain's northeast, whose chief port, Barcelona, had once been the commercial center of the western Mediterranean. The Black Death and successive epidemics had, however, taken a terrible toll, cutting the population of Barcelona and that of the hinterland around it almost in half. As Barcelona's leading banks collapsed in the 1380s, Genoa's aggressive merchants filled the void, capturing much of its Mediterranean trade and spreading their influence across Spain.[101]

If Aragon was stagnant, Queen Isabella's Castile was dynamic, thriving economically from its prosperous wool trade and expanding militarily through its war with the Muslim emirate in the south of Spain. Not only did Castile cover two-thirds of the peninsula, but its population of five million dwarfed both those of Aragon and Portugal. Through what historian John Elliott has called the "creative exuberance of the Castilians and the organizing capacity of the Aragonese," those two conjugal sovereigns laid the foundations for a powerful Spanish state. During the 30 years between Isabella's coronation in 1474 and her death in 1504, the kingdom's tax revenues soared from just 900,000 reales to 26 million. While Ferdinand ran the realm's foreign policy, Isabella was famed for her patronage of learning, including her expansion of the University of Salamanca to some seven thousand students.[102]

For more than a decade, Ferdinand and Isabella led Europe's last major crusade. In the afterglow of victory that finally came with their capture of the Muslim city of Granada in the south of Spain in 1492, celebrated throughout Christendom as just retribution for the Muslim seizure of Constantinople, the monarchs began building a Catholic empire—incorporating Granada into Castile, expelling nearly two hundred thousand Jews from the kingdom, and planning overseas expansion. Just three weeks after their triumph, the sovereigns met Christopher Columbus and agreed to finance his exploration of a possible westward route to Asia, granting him a tenth of the trade of any new territories he found. Instead of China, of course, he reached the Caribbean, where he tried to create colonies for Spanish settlers.[103]

Over the next 30 years, Spanish governors, including Columbus and his son Diego, presided over a miserable effort to colonize the Caribbean, marked by bitter infighting, the enslavement of local peoples, and limited rewards. In their first two decades, the Spanish collected some fourteen tons of gold from those islands, following which they began to stabilize their ramshackle imperial venture by introducing sugar to the island of Hispaniola. Columbus's successor as its governor, Nicolás de Ovando, established the *encomienda* system, which gave the new colonists not land but control over Amerindians as laborers, creating conditions that Elliott would describe as "barely distinguishable from outright slavery."[104] At this nadir of the Spanish imperial venture, Ferdinand was succeeded by his Habsburg grandson Charles V, whose relentless quest for land and power soon expressed itself in the empire's renewed expansion.

After nearly three decades confined to their Caribbean island colonies, Spain's military would conquer Latin America with a speed and ruthlessness akin to Portugal's sudden sweep across the Indian Ocean. While Lisbon's small fleets used their superior gunnery to best larger Asian armadas, Spanish steel and military skills allowed their tiny militias to slaughter the massed armies of the two great Amerindian empires, the Aztecs and Incas. In one of the most extraordinary campaigns in military history, Spanish soldiers numbering no more than one thousand conquered societies with a combined population of over 30 million. Most of these conquistadors were young, unmarried men with some military training, usually drawn from the lower ranks of the Castilian nobility—those impoverished, desperately ambitious, utterly ruthless, deeply Catholic aristocrats known as *hidalgos*.[105]

In February 1519, the conquistador Hernán Cortés, a poor *hidalgo* grown wealthy as a planter in Cuba, sailed out of Havana's harbor with eleven ships carrying six hundred men, sixteen horses, and some light artillery. "I came here to get rich," he said, "not to till the soil like a peasant." After scuttling the ships near present-day Veracruz to show his men there was no retreat, Cortés led them inland on what became a two-year campaign to conquer Mexico. Although the Aztecs' capital at Tenochtitlan was an awe-inspiring monumental city of a quarter million, their empire was a loose coalition of three cities in the Valley of Mexico that, through a century of fierce warfare, had incorporated outlying states still resentful of their subjugation. Allying with one of these restless satellites, the Tlaxcalans, Cortés attacked an Aztec ally and slaughtered some three thousand of their troops. Exuding an aura of power from that merciless victory, Cortés and his troops marched into the Aztec capital at Tenochtitlan, where Emperor Montezuma welcomed them. After those guests lorded their victory over the city for six months, resentful Aztec chiefs elected a new emperor, stoned Montezuma to death, and drove the Spaniards out of the city, killing hundreds of them.[106]

Retreating to the Tlaxcalan kingdom near the Gulf of Mexico, Cortés drew reinforcements from Cuba and forged an alliance of local city-states that allowed him to march on the capital with nine hundred Spaniards leading an army of ten thousand local forces. To break the Aztec resistance, the Spaniards systematically destroyed the city and slaughtered thousands before finally capturing the new emperor, Cuauhtémoc. The ruins of the great Aztec city of Tenochtitlan would become the foundations for a new Spanish capital they called Mexico City.[107]

Further south, the soldier Francisco Pizarro used his position as mayor of the frontier town of Panama to organize a small exploratory expedition that sailed down the Pacific coast of South America, crossing the equator and reaching northern Peru in 1528. There he heard stories of an inland kingdom encrusted in gold, which was, in fact, one of the world's largest empires. Stretching nearly three thousand miles along the spine of the Andes, the Inca domains covered 350,000 square miles and encompassed ten million people. Though lacking steel, wheels, writing, and draft animals, the Incas had built a strong central state with a powerful military, monumental cities, elaborate irrigation, and 24,000 miles of roads, one of the world's largest networks. Since the Incas worshipped the sun as well as their emperor—the Sapa Inca, "son of the sun"—religion and rule converged in the personage of the venerated monarch. This hyper-centralization of authority also created a vulnerability that would allow a handful of Spanish soldiers to conquer a vast empire. The Inca state was much stronger and more unified than the Aztec one, but it would prove, paradoxically, far easier to subdue.[108]

Following a trip to Spain, where King Charles V appointed him governor of Peru, Pizarro and his four brothers sailed from Panama in January 1532 with a surprisingly small force of 168 men, 62 horses, and some light artillery. By April, Pizarro had made contact with the new Inca emperor, Atahualpa, who was campaigning with his army to suppress a revolt against his authority, leaving his kingdom divided. Surprisingly, the emperor agreed to meet these strangers in the highland city of Cajamarca. Arriving first, Pizarro arranged his soldiers for an ambush in the city's ceremonial plaza. On November 16, the emperor arrived, carried aloft on a gold palanquin by 80 nobles, surrounded by 4,000 unarmed escorts, and defended by 80,000 soldiers at his rear. "The governor then gave the signal," reads a Spanish chronicle, "both cavalry and infantry sallied forth out of their hiding places straight into the mass of unarmed Indians crowding the square. . . . The booming of the guns, the blowing of the trumpets, and the rattles on the horses threw the Indians into panicked confusion. The Spaniards fell upon them and began to cut them to pieces." In the midst of the melee, Pizarro himself fought his way through the crowd, cut down the palanquin bearers, and captured the Sapa Inca.[109]

To pay the ransom Pizarro demanded, Emperor Atahualpa's envoys spent months combing the kingdom for precious metals, delivering the treasures of Inca art to the Spaniard. Running their forges continuously for 34 days, the invaders reduced that hoard to seven tons of gold ingots and thirteen tons of silver. After the ransom was paid, Pizarro ordered Sapa Inca strangled and took his wife, who later bore him two children, as a concubine. As news of their ruler's death spread, countless thousands committed suicide to join their god, and resistance almost ceased. Five months later, the Spaniards occupied the Inca capital of Cuzco without opposition, appointed a new emperor (the teenaged Manco Yupanqui), and spent the next four years crushing resistance in a series of lopsided battles. After an unsuccessful attack on the Spanish garrison at Cuzco, the new Inca emperor led his followers in retreat into the rugged highland fastness around Vilcabamba, where they would remain independent for another half century.[110]

As soon as the Inca armies were routed, the cutthroat conquistadors turned on each other in bouts of bloodstained vengeance. To block a challenge to Pizarro's authority, his brother executed their deputy commander, Diego de Almagro. In reprisal, Almagro's friends assassinated Pizarro himself at Lima. Four years later when Emperor Charles V banned the enslavement of Amerindians, Pizarro's younger brother Gonzalo donned an Inca crown to rule the Andes and led a separatist revolt of slaveholders until a Spanish viceroy executed him in 1548.[111] By the time of his demise, Spain had gained a vast empire, stretching 4,500 miles from northern Mexico to central Chile, with a population of 35 million.

Once the Aztec and Inca war booty was spent, the Iberians sustained their imperial ventures through two industries that required legions of coerced labor—mining and plantations. In 1545, an Amerindian prospector discovered the world's richest silver deposit at Potosí, in the high Andes of Bolivia. By the end of the century, Potosí would grow into a city of 160,000, equal in size to London or Paris and employing 59,000 Indian miners, who produced unimaginable wealth for Spain. A year after that discovery, Spanish colonials found the first of a half dozen major mines along Mexico's silver-rich Sierra Madre mountains. Together, those two places produced the bullion that flowed into the treasure fleets, which sailed every year from Cuba carrying cargoes so rich they eventually tripled Europe's silver supply. For the next three centuries, Spanish America would produce 80 percent of the world's silver.[112]

While the Spanish were mining the mountains of Latin America, the Portuguese were developing sugar plantations along the coast of Brazil. Using seed stocks and milling technology refined years earlier on the islands of Madeira and São Tomé, the Portuguese introduced plantation sugar to the Brazilian coast, from Rio to Recife. By 1630, Portugal had shipped 261,000 African slaves across the South Atlantic to sustain 350 Brazilian plantations that produced more than sixteen thousand tons of sugar annually. With its Indian Ocean spice trade weakening through competition with the Dutch, Brazil's sugar became the economic mainstay of Lisbon's global empire.[113]

Both industries, silver and sugar, were voracious in their labor demands, which became increasingly impossible to sustain from local sources. At first, the Spanish tried to solve their labor deficit by enslaving nearby indigenous peoples. As abuse and disease decimated the local Arawak population of about four hundred thousand on the island of Hispaniola, the Spanish enslaved some 40,000 people in the Bahamas and another two hundred thousand from Nicaragua to supply labor for their growing Caribbean sugar plantations.[114]

As noted earlier, the inhumanity of Spanish enslavement and the ongoing extinction of the Caribbean's entire indigenous population also produced the first sustained political debate over human rights. From the start, the colonists' abuse sparked opposition among the Spanish missionary clergy, most famously by the Dominican friar Bartolomé de Las Casas. In 1502, at the age of eighteen, he came to Hispaniola as an ordinary colonist with one of the first large shiploads of Spanish settlers, primed to subjugate the native population. Within a year, he had won one of Governor Ovando's *encomiendas*, and was assigned a quota of Amerindian slaves. When the Dominican priest Antonio de Montesinos gave his famous sermon in Santo Domingo attacking Spanish abuses, Las Casas was apparently present, and he recorded those angry words verbatim in one of his later histories of the New World. Untroubled by this searing critique, Las Casas joined the brutal Spanish conquest of Cuba, where he witnessed more atrocities and was again rewarded with Indian slaves. Two years later, however, his chance reading of a biblical passage from Ecclesiastes condemning the exploitation of workers prompted an epiphany, compelling him to give up his Cuban slaves and dedicate his life to the Amerindians' cause.[115]

Over the following 40 years of petitions, missions, and manifestos, Las Casas joined the Dominican friars in their impassioned campaign to assert the humanity of Amerindians. While Spanish colonists saw them as subhuman, the Dominicans felt they embodied Aristotle's ideal of the clean slate (*tabula rasa*), upon which they could inscribe the purest forms of Christianity. The Dominicans also believed that liberty was a natural right received on account of God's grace and could not be forfeited through slavery. In his extraordinary lifelong mission, Las Casas attempted to create a utopian community of "free Indians" in Venezuela, developed a doctrine of humane evangelization during travels through Central America, and served as bishop of Chiapas in Guatemala, where he opposed enslavement of the Indians. After 30 years as a missionary, he returned home to become an influential adviser to the Spanish court and its Council of the Indies, pressing tirelessly for reform.[116]

Through the intercession of Spanish clerics like Las Casas, Pope Paul III issued a bull (*Sublimis Deus*, 1537) declaring that "Indians are truly men and that they are not only capable of understanding the catholic faith but . . . they desire exceedingly to receive it." He added that "Indians and all other people who may later be discovered by Christians are by no means to be deprived of their liberty or the possession of their property . . . nor should they be in any way enslaved."[117]

The growing controversy over treatment of the Amerindians began to raise doubts in Madrid about the legal basis for Spain's claim to the New World. At the University of Salamanca, Francisco de Vitoria—a theology professor, Dominican priest, and adviser to Charles V—addressed these questions in his lecture "On the American Indians." Vitoria began by rejecting the commonly held notion that the pope's donation of the Americas to the Spanish crown could override indigenous sovereignty and become a sufficient legal basis for his country's rule. He argued that the Indians "have judgment like other men," manifest in their "laws, industries, and commerce, all of which require the use of reason." As a result, they possess "true dominion, both in public and private affairs." However, the Spanish, he claimed, could serve as their "liberators" by waging just wars with the aim of "putting an end to these sacrilegious rites" of cannibalism and human sacrifice. To govern the Indians "for their own benefit," Spanish princes "might take over their administration, and set up . . . governors on their behalf . . . as if they were simply children," even allowing them to be "governed partly as slaves." In effect, Vitoria argued that Spain's superior civilization justified its suspension of Amerindians' sovereignty, thereby crafting a new legal basis for imperial rule that would be used by succeeding empires.[118]

Meanwhile, Las Casas was at court in Madrid petitioning for an end to enslavement of the Amerindians and drafting his *Short Account of the Destruction of the Indies* in support of that position. In response, Emperor Charles V issued the New Laws in 1542, which limited Indian servitude to a single generation. The royal viceroy who attempted to enforce the reforms in Peru was murdered by Spanish colonists, and his successor only managed to reestablish Spanish authority after the military campaign that culminated in the execution of Pizarro's younger brother Gonzalo. To calm the conflicts among the Spaniards, Charles would simply rescind his reforms, perpetuating slavery and leaving the matter unresolved.[119]

Following further reports of excesses, Charles V ordered a suspension of all further conquests in the New World until a panel of distinguished theologians could decide on ways to assure just treatment of the Amerindians. An ad hoc Council of Fourteen then met at Valladolid to hear a debate between Las Casas and his chief rival, the scholar Juan Ginés de Sepúlveda. On the first day of debate in August 1550, Sepúlveda spoke for three hours, arguing that "the Spaniards rule with perfect right over the barbarians who, in prudence, talent, virtue and humanity are as inferior to the Spaniards as children to adults, women to men, and . . . I might almost say as monkeys to men." For the next five days, Las Casas responded by reading verbatim from a manuscript defending the humanity of the Amerindians and condemning the inhumanity of the Spanish conquest. Although the council reconvened the following April for another month of testimony by the two antagonists, the judges failed to render a verdict.[120]

Despairing of any official remedy, Las Casas moved to Seville, where, in a phenomenal outburst of intellectual energy, he presided over the publication of nine important treatises in two years. Drawing on firsthand experience in the Caribbean, his most accessible work, *A Short Account of the Destruction of the Indies*, detailed "despotic and diabolical" Spanish beatings, burnings, massacres, and "brutal slavery" that had ravaged the Indian population. Citing a litany of atrocities he had witnessed personally in Hispaniola, Las Casas accused his fellow colonists of murderous bloodlust. In Cuba, when Indians there greeted the Spaniards with food and gifts, those Christians, said Las Casas, "were suddenly inspired by the Devil and, without the slightest provocation, butchered, before my eyes, some three thousand souls—men, women and children—as they sat there in front of us." One royal official worked his 300 Indian slaves so hard that only 30 were alive three months later.[121]

Five years after Las Casas died in 1566, the Council of the Indies moved his voluminous manuscripts to Madrid, where they were used in deliberations that led to an ordinance, promulgated by King Philip II, that freed the Indians from further systemic abuse. Thanks to decades of struggle by Las Casas and his fellow clerics, those royal reforms finally ended the outright enslavement of Amerindians—although not of Africans.[122]

Indeed, in his early years as a reformer, Las Casas himself had petitioned Emperor Charles V with the suggestion that African slaves might prove an effective substitute for Amerindians, saying, "Your Highness should maintain in each community twenty Negroes or other slaves in the mines." Whether or not he was influenced by that letter, the emperor did in fact authorize the first direct shipment of African captives to Spanish America just two years later, markedly expanding the slave trade. In his monumental *History of the Indies*, completed five years before his death, Las Casas repented, saying of himself, "As he later saw and ascertained that the slavery of the blacks was as unjust as that of the Indians, he perceived how unwise was the remedy he proposed of bringing in blacks in order to make possible the freedom of the Indians."[123] In another of his last manuscripts, Las Casas arrived at an affirmation akin to an endorsement of universal human rights: "All the peoples of the world are humans and there is only one definition of all humans . . . that is that they are rational. . . . Thus, all the races of humankind are one."[124]

That realization was shared by other Dominicans, notably the archbishop of Mexico, Alonso de Montúfar, who wrote Philip II a scathing letter in 1560 as the first African slaves were arriving. Dismissing the legal and religious justifications for African slavery, the bishop argued that Portuguese traffickers were engaged in a profitable business that conferred few if any "spiritual and corporal benefits" on the captives. Once the traffic was ended, the Holy Gospel could be preached to Africans in their own lands, where "they may be free in their bodies, but more so in their souls." But with thousands of African slaves arriving to replace massive Mexican population losses from disease and overwork, the imperatives of empire eclipsed the bishop's protest.[125]

By the time King Philip II nominally ended the enslavement of Amerindians, major epidemics were already sweeping his empire, producing the "great dying" that would transform the New World. Within a half century of the Spanish arrival, smallpox, combined with the colonists' excesses, had slashed the Indian population of Hispaniola from hundreds of thousands to almost zero. At a slower, but still relentless rate, Spanish rule reduced Mexico's population from 25 million in 1520 to only 1.4 million by 1600. Losses in the highlands of Peru were similarly heavy. Overall, an estimated 60 to 89 million Amerindians died between 1500 and 1600, equivalent to about 15 percent of the world's population.[126]

To fill that deep demographic void, the slave trade would carry some 11 million captive Africans across the Atlantic over the span of four centuries, repopulating much of the New World and producing steady profits for both slave traders and sugar planters. From 1500 to 1630, Iberian traders shipped an estimated 727,000 African slaves to Portuguese Brazil and Spanish America. When Dutch merchants also entered the trade, Africa's slave exports rose rapidly to reach a total of 1.2 million for the seventeenth century. Once Britain's dynamic merchant marine became involved as the next century began, the transatlantic traffic surged to 5.6 million slaves during the eighteenth century. Even after Britain banned the slave trade in 1807, another 3.4 million slaves still crossed the Atlantic, bound for the booming sugar and coffee plantations of Brazil and the Caribbean.[127]

During three centuries of unchecked dominion over Latin America, it would be slave labor that sustained the steady flow of precious metals and profitable commodities to Iberia. In imitation of Portugal's Casa da India, the Spanish crown established a similar office, the Casa de Contratación, to manage the royal monopoly on overseas trade. Between 1500 and 1650, Latin America's colonies shipped 180 tons of gold and sixteen thousand tons of silver to Spain. To deter piracy and assure its monopoly over this wealth, the crown decreed that all ships carrying silver would join an official fleet at Havana every March for the Atlantic crossing to Seville, creating a system that transported this vast treasure with surprisingly few mishaps for nearly 250 years. While that official route carried most of the silver from Potosí's mines in modern Bolivia, an informal "back door" allowed private traders to send about one-third of their output down the Río de la Plata to Buenos Aires for shipment to Portugal, where it funded the slave trade or settled debts in Amsterdam. During the half century after its founding in 1602, the Dutch East India Company would export a stunning five hundred tons of silver to pay for profitable imports from China.[128]

While most literature focuses on the transatlantic silver fleets, the transpacific flow was surprisingly significant too. After Spanish explorers established a colony in the Philippines in the late sixteenth century, a royal galleon began an annual Pacific crossing from Acapulco, Mexico, to Manila that would continue for more than two centuries, carrying outbound cargoes of silver coins and bringing back Chinese silk. Official silver export shipments carried a total of 750 tons of bullion directly to Asia by 1815, and private traders smuggled an average of about 128 tons of illicit silver across the Pacific every year. When a British commodore seized the Spanish galleon *Covadonga* off Manila in 1743, his crew found it stuffed with over 34 tons of silver, much of it hidden from prying official eyes in hollowed beams and even rinds of cheese. During the eighteenth century, British, Dutch, and French companies shipped another 160 metric tons of silver from Europe every year to fund their imports of Asian goods. Through all this trade, minted Spanish dollars became the prime currency for Asian commerce, precipitating Ming China's shift from paper bills and copper cash to silver bullion, so opening its self-contained economy to global trade and making it "the world's silver sink."[129]

More broadly, this phenomenal proliferation of silver created another important legacy of the Iberian age: the world's first common currency. Once permanent mints were established at Mexico City, Lima, and Potosí, Spanish authorities would, for nearly three centuries, produce uniform, unadulterated silver coins worth eight reales, known as "pieces of eight." As world trade carried millions of those minted silver dollars across the globe in the seventeenth and eighteenth centuries, they became the medium of exchange for a growing share of humanity, used by everyone from African chiefs to Virginia planters. Even in European states with their own mints, the flood of silver bullion from the New World allowed mass coinage that put cash in the pocket of every worker and farm laborer. When national revolutions finally closed the Spanish colonial mints in the 1820s, their pieces of eight would become the model for new national currencies in the Americas, including the US silver dollar.[130]

Charles V, Holy Roman emperor, circa 1519 (Credit: Alamy)

The Hand at History's Throat

As the silver shipments flowed regularly and reliably across the Atlantic, Spain soon became the world's wealthiest nation, investing its monarchs with extraordinary resources that they used largely for hopelessly quixotic crusades. Through dynastic descent, the kingdom of Ferdinand and Isabella passed, at their deaths, to the Habsburgs of Austria. And for most of the sixteenth century, just two kings from that venerable Austrian dynasty—Charles V and his son Philip II—reigned over the Spanish Empire's rapid rise and its equally precipitous decline. Rarely has one family placed its withering hand on history's throat with such lasting and fatal effect.

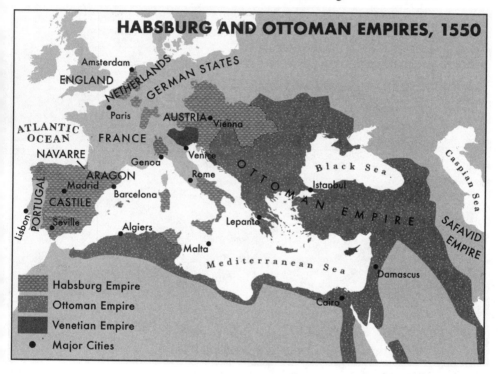

To limit royal pretenders from rival dynasties and so preserve their disparate domains, the Habsburgs repeatedly intermarried with cousins in what became, in the end, something close to sibling incest. Over a period of two hundred years, nine of the eleven marriages among the Spanish Habsburgs involved just such unions. Not only did inbreeding lead to the Spanish dynasty's ultimate extinction in 1700 when its "physically disabled, mentally retarded" heir died childless, but it may have introduced an erratic quality to the reigns of Habsburg kings—manifest in their extreme grandiosity, obsessive religiosity, and monomaniacal willfulness.[131]

By the time Charles V ascended the Spanish throne as a teenager in

1516, generations of strategic Habsburg marriages had accorded him a realm covering much of western Europe and would soon make him history's most powerful monarch. In addition to growing portions of North and South America, his inheritance gave him 72 different domains scattered across Europe—including all of Austria, the Duchy of Burgundy (containing modern Belgium and Holland), four territories that made up half of Italy, and the kingdoms of Castile and Aragon. After his election as Holy Roman emperor, Charles V also became the titular sovereign of Germany's dozens of dominions, whose rule had been complicated by the recent spread of Protestantism among its princes. To knit these disparate territories into a manageable realm, Charles would rely on four key components: his authority as chief defender of the Catholic faith against Protestant heretics and Muslim infidels; massive loans from German and Italian bankers; the cultural flowering of Italy and Flanders; and, above all, the crown of Castile, with its many warriors and vast wealth of silver from the Americas.[132]

To realize his dream of becoming ruler of a united Christendom, Charles V traveled incessantly during his four decades as emperor, mobilizing money and manpower for two endless wars—a dynastic struggle against the king of France, and the defense of Christian Europe from relentless attacks by the Ottoman Empire's army and navy. That formidable Muslim empire was expanding relentlessly under Suleiman the Magnificent, whose long rule coincided almost precisely with Charles's own reign as Holy Roman emperor. Theirs was a bitter struggle over the legitimating mantle of ancient Rome, with Charles aspiring to establish a "universal Christian empire" and Suleiman styling himself, after his conquest of Hungary, as "Caesar of the Romans." Their rival coalitions were ever changing, with Charles V attempting an alliance with the Persian shah and Suleiman aiding both the French navy and German Protestant princes. During these decades of warfare, most of the fighting was a back-and-forth battle along a thousand-mile frontier running from Budapest, down the Adriatic coast, through the Greek islands, and across the eastern Mediterranean. As the trickle of treasure from the Americas turned into a torrent during his reign, Charles V filled his war chest with a phenomenal windfall of some two hundred thousand ducats of silver every year. To wage those endless wars, Charles needed all that and much more, expending a million ducats annually and thereby accumulating a massive debt by the time of his abdication in 1556.[133]

After four decades of unrelenting struggle, an aging, exhausted Charles V stood before his devoted courtiers at the Brussels Town Hall and began the transfer of his many titles. Weeping profusely, he apologized for "many mistakes, big mistakes . . . because of my passions" that had dashed his "hopes of bringing peace among the Christian peoples and uniting their fighting forces for the defense of the Catholic faith against the Ottomans." In a judicious east–west division of his vast domains, he assigned the historic Habsburg lands in central Europe to his brother, Ferdinand. Then he laid hands on his son and heir Philip II, making him ruler of all the rest. Instead of reigning over Europe as Christian Emperor like his father, Philip II would become a true king of Spain, making Madrid the epicenter of an empire with four main domains— the Netherlands, with its thriving commerce; Italy, with money and manpower to sustain his army and navy; Castile, the militarized Spanish kingdom that would provide 70 percent of his European revenues; and the vast lands of the Americas, the source of silver that would sustain this sprawling realm.[134]

Unlike his father, Philip II would try to rule his vast global empire directly, replacing the papal donation of the Americas with his own regal sovereignty and administering these dominions through royal viceroys. This vast empire delivered two million ducats in silver every year, ten times his father's income, thereby funding Philip's obsessive Catholic crusades—one against Islamic Ottomans in the Mediterranean and another against the Protestant Dutch in the Netherlands. Unlike the Venetians and Ottomans, who fielded summer soldiers, Spain's silver sustained Europe's only full-time, professional military, including a regular navy and the famed *tercio* infantry regiments, armed with long pikes and lethal muskets. His campaigns cost him 21 million ducats a year, making the bankers of Genoa and Florence an invisible fifth kingdom within his empire. In the 1590s, the royal treasury calculated that ten million ducats in silver arrived every year from the Americas, but that six million of them left Spain almost immediately to satisfy Italian bankers.[135]

The flow of New World silver financed the defense of the expanding Habsburg empire and made Spain a fulcrum for world trade. But that influx of specie also stifled the country's domestic economic development, slowly crippling its king's imperial ambitions. At the start of Spain's imperial expansion, its domestic economy was already on the cusp of decline, with much of Castile's land devoted to sheep pastures that produced wool for export to the looms of Flanders. As the profits from silver and sugar flowed from

Peru and Brazil into the royal coffers of Spain and Portugal, both crowns wasted their profits on lavish castles, including Philip II's grandiose El Escorial near Madrid and King John V's sumptuous Mafra Palace near Lisbon. El Escorial was a veritable royal city, constructed at incalculable cost over 21 years. Its chapel was the size of a cathedral. Its crypt was cavernous, with tiers of gilded marble coffins holding not only the remains of every Spanish monarch since Charles V, but also the corpse of Spain's economy. By the end of Philip II's reign, silver shipments from the Americas would be funding imports that were slowly suffocating local industry. As cities withered and local manufacturers collapsed, the silver would flow ever more steadily out of Spain to Italy, England, and the Netherlands to pay for mounting debts and a myriad of imported goods.[136]

Ultimately, it would be Philip II's costly campaigns to defend Catholic Europe from the Ottoman Muslims in the Mediterranean and from Dutch Protestants in his Netherlands domain that precipitated the eclipse of his European empire. The long reign of Philip's father had been devoted above all to the defense of Christian Europe from a relentless Ottoman advance that threatened to engulf southeastern Europe. The Ottomans had conquered much of Hungary, but the Habsburgs successfully defended Vienna from Muslim sieges, effectively ending their landward attacks. Nonetheless, the Ottomans continued to advance across the Mediterranean, crushing a Christian armada at Preveza, in the Ionian Sea, in 1538.[137]

As this war between Christian and Muslim empires shifted to the Mediterranean Sea, Philip II suffered a decade of shattering defeats before his Holy Alliance finally began to turn the tide. In 1559, he sent an armada of 150 ships and 12,000 men under Genoan admiral Gian Andrea Doria to capture Tripoli. But an Ottoman fleet sank half the Christian ships and captured 10,000 soldiers, who were paraded in chains through the streets of Istanbul. Six years later, a massive Turkish fleet with 40,000 troops besieged Malta for four months, which was only saved by fanatic resistance from the 2,000 Knights of Malta and the timely arrival of Spanish reinforcements. At the news of this military miracle, church bells pealed across Europe to express a fervent hope that the Ottoman juggernaut had finally been stopped.[138]

That respite, however, would prove illusory. By 1570, the Ottoman navy was again scoring major victories, capturing Cyprus and threatening Greek islands critical to Venice's maritime empire. Under an alliance blessed by the pope and led by Philip II's bastard half brother Don Juan, the so-called Holy League comprising Spain, Venice, and several Italian city-states assembled a massive fleet of 203 galleys that sailed down the Adriatic Sea to engage a similar number of Ottoman ships at Lepanto, in Greece. In one of history's greatest naval battles, 480 ships with 150,000 men and 2,500 cannons faced each other across the narrow entrance to the Gulf of Corinth. After the ships closed on one another with bow guns thundering, infantry in full armor fought from deck to deck, causing horrific carnage on both sides. At the center of the line, Christian troops fought a furious back-and-forth battle on the deck of the Ottoman flagship that only ended when the Muslim admiral, Ali Pasha, fell to a musket ball. In a harbinger of future wars, the Holy League's 1,800 guns, double the Ottoman Empire's 750, decided the outcome. The League annihilated the Turkish fleet, sinking 15 enemy ships and capturing 190 more, while losing only a few of its own galleys. In addition to the 30,000 Turks killed in battle, the Christians captured 8,000 more, many of them skilled mariners who were selectively executed, crippling any future Turkish armada.[139]

Despite the decisiveness of their triumph, the Spanish found Lepanto to be what historian John Elliott has called a "strange anti-climax." After a half century of mortal combat on land and sea, the two empires simply disengaged from their epic struggle. While the Ottomans turned east to fight a rival Persian empire, Spanish forces marched north to suppress a religious revolt by Dutch Protestants.[140]

Philip II's self-proclaimed role as the defender of Christian Europe also had a darker underside. Upon taking the throne at twenty-eight, he was, in the words of historian Henry Kamen, "a cultured, serious and deeply religious" monarch whose "ample experience of the problems of government" would lead Spain into a veritable golden age. Such an assessment, however, ignores an imperious intolerance that made his campaign against Dutch Protestants so relentless and self-destructive that it would eventually consume his empire. "You can assure his Holiness," Philip II wrote the Vatican in 1566, "that rather than suffer the least injury to religion and the service of God, I would lose all my states and a hundred lives if I had them, for I do not intend to rule over heretics."[141]

By virtue of his father's abdication in 1556, Philip II had acquired a Burgundian realm, quite separate from Spain, encompassing modern-day Netherlands, Belgium, and Luxembourg. Instead of ruling it directly from far-off

Madrid, the king appointed his half sister, Margaret of Parma, to administer the so-called Low Countries as governor-general from her court at Brussels. By then, this realm had become the richest in Europe, with a major mercantile center at Antwerp, a flourishing weaving industry, thousands of ships trading across northern seas, and a vital intellectual life that represented a northern Renaissance. This lively culture, however, opened the region to the spiritual ferment of the Protestant Reformation, which had already begun in neighboring Germany. As waves of Lutheran and Calvinist piety swept the Netherlands, Charles V had sent the Inquisition, a Church court charged with enforcing Catholic orthodoxy, into the country, where it publicly executed over a thousand accused heretics and tortured many thousands more. Continuing his father's repression, Philip II ordered his sister to enforce the death penalty for heresy, prompting the Flemish aristocracy to resign their offices and Protestant mobs to smash imagery inside Catholic churches. Margaret responded with moderation, which momentarily restored calm.[142]

Philip II, king of Spain and world's most powerful monarch, 1586 (Credit: Library of Congress)

Determined to extirpate heresy, Philip II ordered his austere Castilian counselor, the Duke of Alba, to march north from Italy with ten thousand troops. "What can an army do," one Dutch aristocrat asked Margaret, "kill two hundred thousand Netherlanders?" Under Alba, known as the "Iron Duke," they would certainly try. He convened a "Council of Blood" that used its extraordinary judicial powers of arrest and execution to begin beheading prominent Flemish nobles. Within a year, the Dutch had risen in revolt under the leadership of William the Silent, who had quit Margaret's court in opposition to the massacre. To spread his fledgling rebellion, William would issue "letters of marque" to eighteen privateer vessels known as the "Sea Beggars"—their captains being Dutch exiles, many of them victims of the Inquisition, who raided Spanish shipping from English ports. When Elizabeth I expelled them from England in 1572, their fleet, which had grown to 84 ships, launched a raid on the city of Brielle in the Netherlands for supplies. In a surprising response, its citizens opened their city gates to welcome the Sea Beggars as liberators. Nearby towns did the same, sparking a popular revolt that soon put most of Holland's cities under rebel control.[143]

Undeterred, the Spanish attacked Protestant cities, setting soldiers loose to slaughter entire populations. At Haarlem, they systematically executed a garrison of more than two thousand Dutch defenders. Repression only increased resistance, so, after six years of failing to break the revolt, Philip relieved Alba from duty and sent a second trusted commander north, who initially opted for more of the same. By the time that governor reevaluated these counterproductive tactics and began making concessions in 1574, the Netherlands campaign had bankrupted Spain. Its unpaid troops mutinied, sacking Antwerp and killing six thousand people.[144]

As the flow of silver from the mines of Peru and Mexico nearly tripled between 1570 and 1600, however, Philip II gained unimagined wealth, enabling another two decades of military ambition. He redoubled his efforts to pacify the Netherlands, while annexing Portugal, attacking England, and fighting France. After twelve years of incessant slaughter and rising Dutch resistance, Philip II turned to his nephew, Alessandro Farnese, to stabilize the desperate situation there. Combining considerable military skill with the usual Habsburg hostility toward heretics, Farnese parlayed military successes into a diplomatic triumph in January 1579 when the Catholic nobles in the southern part of the country signed the Union of Arras, affirming their loyalty to the Habsburg crown. A few months later, Farnese's Spanish and German troops breached the defenses of the Dutch city of Maastricht and rampaged through its streets, slaughtering some ten thousand residents— roughly one-third of the population. Writing to his king with grim satisfaction, Farnese reported that the region "is so ravaged and laid waste that not only is there no food but the whole countryside will be a wasteland for many years."[145]

The success of Spanish arms in the southern Netherlands played very differently in the north, where both Protestant and republican ideals had spread widely. Two weeks after the south declared its royalist allegiance, the seven northern provinces signed the Union of Utrecht, which provided for mutual defense against the Spanish army. That declaration was also Europe's first statement of religious freedom, promising that "each person shall remain free in his religion and that no one shall be investigated or persecuted because of his religion."[146] Two years later, those seven united provinces met at The Hague to declare their independence from Spain in the Act of Abjuration, launching what the Dutch would call the Eighty Years' War against the Habsburgs. In the four years following that declaration of independence, Farnese used a mix of diplomacy and military force to subdue the remaining Protestant resistance in the main southern cities—Bruges, Ghent, Brussels, and the greatest prize of all, the port of Antwerp. With the Netherlands now effectively divided between a Protestant north and a Catholic south, a protracted war would be waged in three distinct phases: first, there would be 30 years of localized Spanish pacification efforts; then, a "Twelve Year Truce"; and, finally, a global Thirty Years' War, fought on five continents.[147]

Meanwhile, Philip II, whose mother was a Portuguese princess, led 47,000 troops in an invasion of Portugal, sweeping across a country still prostrate from the recent slaughter of much of its aristocracy in an ill-fated crusade against Muslim Morocco. With Lisbon's merchants eager for access to Spanish silver and the Portuguese aristocracy either dead or held for ransom, opposition was weak. The conquest proceeded with such speed that, within months, Philip II was king of Portugal. Through this union of the two realms, the Spanish-Portuguese merchant fleet became the world's largest at 300,000 tons, well ahead of the Netherlands (232,000 tons) and England (42,000). Yet, in adding that kingdom to his empire, Philip II unwittingly made Portugal's far-flung colonial outposts legitimate

Dutch targets in this sectarian warfare—a move that would prove, according to historian Jean-Frédéric Schaub, to be "a catastrophe for Portugal's economic interests."[148]

With his domain consolidated, Philip spent four years planning a bold strategic strike to fulfill the Habsburg drive for a "universal monarchy" over all Europe. Not only would a successful invasion of England smother the Protestant heresy in its cradle, but it would consummate Philip II's dynastic claim to England's throne and make him master of yet another ocean, the North Atlantic. Summoning men, money, and materials from every corner of his sprawling empire, Philip II assembled an awe-inspiring Invincible Armada of 130 ships carrying 30,000 troops and 2,500 guns. In July 1588, the fleet sailed from La Coruña, in northern Spain, bound for the port of Dunkirk, on the English Channel. There Farnese had 17,000 battle-hardened Spanish troops waiting to cross to England where, he imagined, the country's restive Catholics would rise in revolt against their apostate queen, Elizabeth I. The campaign would, in fact, become an epic disaster—Dutch ships blocked Farnese's troops from boarding, English broadsides sank five Spanish galleons, and North Atlantic storms took many of the rest. By the time the armada limped back to Spain, half its ships and 15,000 men had been lost.[149]

The fleet's defeat would prove a turning point in the history of the Spanish Empire. At a time when King Philip II's annual budget was around twelve million ducats, the armada alone cost an estimated ten million—a crippling expense. Four years after the fleet's failure, the Spanish crown declared bankruptcy, transforming its deficits into long-term debt that would constrict further imperial adventures. When Farnese died in 1592, leaving the Dutch unsubdued, it was clear that the great crusade against Protestantism was failing.[150]

By the time of Philip II's death in 1598, his long reign had transformed Spain into what anthropologist Eric Wolf would term that "spectral world of decay and disenchantment" so evocatively described in the great novel *Don Quixote*. Its author, Miguel de Cervantes, was himself a veteran of the king's endless naval wars against the Ottomans, wounded at Lepanto and held captive for five years in Algiers. His fable of a delusional knight-errant, wandering an empty Spanish landscape populated largely with sheep, was borne out by the observations of contemporary travelers, who described Castile as a land of moribund agriculture and empty villages. Adding to the aura of decay, the Spanish Inquisition grew during Philip's reign into a repressive apparatus with 20,000 spies who publicly burned two thousand suspected heretics, banned books, and stifled scientific inquiry.[151] Over the next half century, Castile's decline would only continue with its manufacturing towns in ruins, its agriculture fading, and its population dropping. Paradoxically, Spain would remain Europe's chief source of silver and its most important market for manufactures, making Iberia second only to the Baltic region as a source of profits for Dutch shipping.[152]

While Cervantes's novel became a timeless classic, other Spanish writings had a more immediate political impact. During the endless decades of the Dutch revolt, 25 editions of Bartolomé de Las Casas's *Short Account of the Destruction of the Indies* were published in the Netherlands in translation. Drawing on that account, countless Dutch pamphleteers would compare Spanish atrocities in their land with earlier events in the Americas, as did the republic's leader, William the Silent, who wrote a rebel manifesto charging that Spanish conquistadors had first shown "their cruel, covetous, and proud natural disposition" in the Americas.[153]

As the Dutch revolt entered its fourth decade in 1598, a Protestant publisher in Frankfurt released Latin and German translations of the Las Casas history, illustrating his chilling eyewitness account with seventeen lurid copperplate graphics of Spanish atrocities—showing soldiers unleashing attack dogs to feed on Amerindians, chopping off their arms, and hanging dozens on racks over roaring flames. When the Dutch war with Spain resumed in 1621, an Amsterdam press published a new edition of Las Casas's history, bound with a parallel account of Spanish abuses in the Netherlands, juxtaposing those etchings of New World atrocities with images of Dutch citizens being butchered, beheaded, and hung by their genitalia. For the first time in Europe's history, a rising power was using the human rights record of an established empire to challenge its legitimacy and so justify the expropriation of its colonies.[154]

Toward a New World Order

The devastating defeat of the Spanish Armada marked the start of Spain's decline as Europe's dominant power. In one of history's stunning reversals, this global empire encompassing three continents and two oceans would henceforth be on the defensive against an infant Dutch Republic of little more than a million people. In the final round of this epochal conflict, which coincided with the Thirty Years' War (1618–1648), Spain and Portugal would suffer a devastating defeat.

However, in a paradoxical twist with implications for our own era, the influence of the Iberian world order would persist far beyond the eclipse of the Spanish and Portuguese empires. Iberia's global system would, in fact, prove extraordinarily resilient, surviving decades of destructive warfare, the Protestant Reformation, and the rise of powerful new empires. The incessant dynastic and religious conflicts that had culminated in Europe's ruinous Thirty Years' War would cripple Spain and Portugal but leave their world order with sufficient ideological and commercial resilience to continue for another 170 years. Instead of extending their incipient ideas of rights and liberty to include non-Europeans, the rising Protestant powers, England and Holland, would expand the Iberian slave trade to an unprecedented level, while making coerced labor central to the building of their burgeoning empires. Rather than challenge the Iberian concept of imperial sovereignty and its prerogative of territorial conquest, Amsterdam and London embraced it to acquire vast territories in Africa, Asia, and the Americas.

Yet beneath the stable surface of such continuity, a new world order was indeed germinating. The question is: How does an entrenched global system spawn change of sufficient strength to overturn a world order? In the nineteenth century, the German philosopher Georg Wilhelm Friedrich Hegel argued in his *Phenomenology of Mind* that history is driven by a "negative dialectic" that infuses each epoch and its consciousness with "the seeds of its own destruction," creating change that carries humanity through a succession of stages toward the heights of a rationally ordered society. In this process, "World-historical men" like Caesar or Napoleon, although unconscious of "the general idea they were unfolding," still served as history's instruments in reaching the next "sequent step in progress."[155]

If this view of history seems overly mechanistic, it is still useful as a metaphor. While the Iberian world order remained dominant and even hegemonic, its antithesis, in the form of the Protestant Reformation, spread throughout the seventeenth century, seeding change that would flower in the coming centuries. The core Protestant belief in every individual's direct relation with the divine introduced ideas of religious liberty that inspired both the Dutch revolt against Spain in the 1570s and England's Glorious Revolution against a Catholic monarch a century later. Those Protestant religious principles, in turn, grew slowly into broader ideals of human rights that would animate a growing anti-slavery movement in late-eighteenth-century England.

More immediately, Protestant sectarianism allowed the English and the Dutch to defy the Vatican's division of the world between the Iberian powers and to challenge their vast global empires, creating capitalist trading companies that would establish new colonies on three continents. Through their extraordinary profits and relentless expansion, those chartered companies would, as the first modern corporations, play a seminal role in spreading the influence of merchant capital across much of the planet. By 1700, the hallmarks of the Iberian age, slavery and imperial conquest, had clearly survived; yet the market logic of merchant capitalism and the ideals of human liberty were also fusing into a potent force for change. In effect, this long century of Dutch and British imperial hegemony represented a florescence of the Iberian age, carrying its enslavement and expansion to new heights while simultaneously sowing the seeds of change.

By the end of the eighteenth century, Europe's old order had exhausted itself, with absolutist monarchs plunging into one deadly, destructive dynastic war after another, while their royal chartered companies bankrupted themselves by reaching their limits as global instruments. In response, Britain would become progenitor of a new world order, combining a global anti-slavery campaign with a coal-fired industrial revolution to finally end the Iberian age.

Emperor Napoleon I of France, 1806 (Credit: Musée de l'Armée)

Chapter 3
Empires of Commerce and Capital

I n February 1603, a small Portuguese merchant fleet sailing south from Macao on the China coast reached the island of Singapore. Rather than risk passage through the treacherous straits to their destination at Malacca further up the Malay Peninsula in the dark, the fleet's commander decided to drop anchor for the night at the mouth of the Johor River. The convoy's main ship, the massive, 1,400-ton *Santa Catarina*, was a veritable floating city, carrying seven hundred soldiers, a hundred passengers, and a hold packed with Chinese luxury goods. Given its rich cargo, the fleet was lightly armed, reflecting the confidence of an imperial power that had dominated the Indian Ocean and its commerce for nearly a century.

Just after dawn, two Dutch East India Company ships, part of the first fleet the company had sent to Asia, spotted the Portuguese vessels and prepared to attack. In command was Admiral Jacob van Heemskerck, young for the rank at the age of thirty-five, but already renowned for his exploration of a northern route to Asia. On that journey, pack ice had crushed his ship, but he had survived the Arctic winter in a driftwood hut, then rowed five hundred miles across the open sea to safety. Now, however, the admiral's mission was revenge.

Everywhere these early Dutch expeditions had landed in Asia, the Portuguese, determined to defend their commercial monopoly, had responded with gunfire or murder. After capturing a Portuguese vessel off the north coast of Java, Admiral van Heemskerck was enraged to discover letters indicating that Portuguese officials at Macao had recently executed seventeen Dutch sailors, hanging six and throwing eleven into the sea tied to rocks. The admiral's attempt to purchase spices had also been blocked by a Portuguese scorched-earth campaign in the Spice Islands of eastern Indonesia, where groves had been destroyed to deny the Dutch access.

On the morning of the attack, the local sultan of Johor, Alauddin Riayat Shah III, was aboard the Dutch admiral's flagship, the *White Lion*.

He had his own reasons for revenge. To discourage him from trading with the Dutch, the Portuguese had been raiding towns along the Johor River and massacring his subjects.

Before the Portuguese ship could raise anchor and flee, the Dutch warships and several of the Sultan's smaller galleys opened fire, sparking a fierce gun battle that continued through the day and into the evening. Firing with great accuracy, the Dutch gunners followed their admiral's orders to avoid the hull and aim for the mainsails of the *Santa Catarina*, "lest we should destroy our booty by means of our own guns." The other Portuguese ships fled for the safety of Malacca, leaving the *Santa Catarina* on its own and its gun crews hampered by the many passengers on deck.

By the time darkness fell, the Portuguese ship had suffered 70 casualties, lost its sails, and was leaking badly. After its captain raised the white flag of surrender, both sides quickly came to terms: the Portuguese would forfeit the ship and its cargo in exchange for safe passage to Malacca. After the admiral kept his word and delivered the hundreds of Portuguese passengers and crew, Malacca's grateful city council attributed his good fortune in capturing such a rich cargo to a "secret and unknown judgment of God." The Portuguese governor of Malacca, Fernão de Albuquerque, expressed deep regret over the murder of the Dutch sailors at Macao, assuring the admiral that "the culprit has already been arrested and shall . . . pay for his misdeed with his life." Admiral van Heemskerck also attributed his victory to God's grace. "Since the Almighty has blessed our East Indies trade immeasurably," he later told his company's directors, "let us become friends with so many different nations and kings . . . and establish both a spiritual and political Commonwealth."

When the admiral reached home with the *Santa Catarina*'s cargo more than a year later, the extraordinary size of the prize stunned the Netherlands and attracted attention from merchants across Europe. Apart from 60 tons of Chinese porcelains, there were 1,200 bales of raw Chinese silk, numerous spices, woven gold cloth, linen and cotton fabrics, 70 tons of gold, and even a wondrous royal throne inlaid with precious stones. An auction of those goods raised 3.5 million guilders (about $130 million today), equivalent to half the capital of the Dutch East India Company. "When the prize was recently put up for sale," wrote the Dutch lawyer Hugo Grotius, "who did not marvel at the wealth revealed? Who was not struck with amazement?

Who did not feel that the auction in progress was practically the sale of a royal property, rather than a fortune privately owned?"

The richness of the prize sparked all sorts of litigation. After many petitions and much maneuvering, the admiral's crew was awarded 123,380 guilders, and he himself received 31,000 guilders, equivalent to nearly $1.2 million today. But the admiral did not have a chance to enjoy his fortune. Just a year later, as he was leading the Dutch navy in a daring raid that destroyed the Spanish fleet at Gibraltar and helped secure Holland's de facto independence from Spain, he was killed by a cannonball. His body was brought home for a state funeral worthy of national hero. Today his sword and steel armor are displayed at the renowned Rijksmuseum in Amsterdam.[1]

Although it was just one incident among countless battles in the age of exploration, that fight off the shores of Singapore was an early round in what would soon become an epic, 60-year struggle for control of Asia's maritime commerce between two very different kinds of European empires. The Dutch raiders were not part of a royal navy, nor were they even privateers carrying a "letter of marque" from their prince. They were employees of the world's first major corporation, the Dutch East India Company. The windfall profits from its first voyage to Asia showed the pragmatism, and ultimately the superior strength, of this new capitalist approach to exploration and empire.

But most importantly, the labyrinthine litigation spawned by this fabulous prize led the Dutch company to retain the young lawyer Hugo Grotius, providing him with his first international legal case. Infused with the principles of the Protestant Reformation, his brief in defense of the company's seizure of the *Santa Catarina* articulated legal precepts that would prove fundamentally subversive of the Iberian world order. When fully realized two centuries later, his ideas would help overturn both its expansive vision of imperial sovereignty and its narrow view of human rights.

Empire of Commerce and Capital

Admiral van Heemskerck, Hugo Grotius, and the East India Company that employed them embodied the intellectual ferment, maritime prowess, and merchant capital that would make Amsterdam the epicenter of a new kind of empire and the cradle of creativity for the Dutch Golden Age. In the years following the East India Company's founding in 1602, the city's dynamism led to a host of financial innovations that soon made it, as economic historian Jan de Vries put it, "the clearinghouse of world trade." The new Bank of Amsterdam took deposits, transferred funds transnationally, and later stored vast quantities of precious metals in its vaults, helping make the city "Europe's reservoir of gold and silver coin." The Chamber of Maritime Insurance offered coverage for dozens of dangerous destinations, while the newspaper *Amsterdamsche Courant* gave the city's merchants critical information about the prices of goods arriving from those distant shores. Amsterdam also built the world's first stock exchange, where up to five thousand merchants met to trade more than four hundred commodities around a central courtyard that became "the nerve center of the entire international economy."[2]

Dutch cities were also becoming vital intellectual centers, with leading specialists in law, medicine, science, theology, and fine arts. At a practical level, art and science were fused in the field of cartography, making Amsterdam a major center for the production of accurate maps to guide sea captains and inform speculators eager to venture capital for their explorations.[3] In spite of its relatively small population of only one hundred thousand residents, few cities in any era would equal Amsterdam's extraordinary achievements.

The country's drive for innovation also led the Dutch to harness the winds as never before, building sailing ships ten times the size of the Portuguese caravel and powerful windmills that drained their wetlands, enhanced their industry, and most importantly, sawed logs for shipbuilding. With giant sails spanning over 90 feet, a driveshaft weighing five tons, and several sawing frames with six steel blades each, a mill's four-man crew could turn 60 tree trunks daily into uniform planks to maintain the massive Dutch merchant fleet of four thousand oceangoing ships. By 1650, the Zaan region near Amsterdam, arguably Europe's first major industrial district, had over 50 wind-driven sawmills and the world's largest shipyard, launching 150 hulls annually at half the cost of English-built vessels. Many of these were Dutch-designed *fluitschips*, agile three-masted cargo vessels that cut crew size, doubled sailing speed, and carried up to five hundred tons of cargo.[4]

Indeed, Holland was a nation afloat, with an enormous fishing fleet in the North Sea, merchant ships that dominated commerce from the Baltic Sea to Spain, and captains with the skill to explore new routes to Asia and the Americas. Together, Holland and England led Europe in a tenfold expansion of shipping tonnage between 1500 and 1780, raising total capacity to 3.4 million tons and nearly quadrupling overall efficiency in terms of tons carried per sailor.[5]

Holland was also a nation on its knees in prayer. As Protestant ideas spread from nearby Germany, the cities of the Netherlands became centers of religious ferment, embracing reformist beliefs while facing a harsh Roman Catholic Counter-Reformation. Under Habsburg rule, the Catholic courts of Inquisition in the Netherlands commenced in 1523 with the burning of two reputedly heretical Augustinian friars at Brussels. By the time its trials ended in 1576, some 1,300 Protestants had been publicly executed and many thousands more tortured for their religious beliefs.[6]

Holland thus became a nation at arms. During the Eighty Years' War against Spanish rule and its Inquisition, Dutch citizen militias manned the ramparts of every city, ready to repel relentless attacks from Spain's *tercio* infantry, Europe's most formidable armed force. Following the capture of the *Santa Catarina*, however, that war was shifting from land to sea, as a Dutch naval campaign started up that would, in the end, ravage Iberia's overseas empires. Following the war's hard-fought first phase, which had been a battle for the cities of the Netherlands, the Dutch Republic won the so-called Twelve Years' Truce and de facto Spanish recognition of its independence. When the fighting resumed as part of Europe's wider Thirty Years' War, Dutch warships campaigned for decades to break Portuguese control over the Indian Ocean, to capture its prime sugar plantations on the coast of Brazil, and to seize Spanish islands in the Caribbean—all part of a strategy of fighting "the global 'tyranny' of the Habsburg empire" by attacking "its weak colonial underbelly."[7] In its geopolitical design, the Dutch strategy would try to shatter Portugal's encirclement of the tri-continental "world island" by seizing key points from West Africa across the Indian Ocean to Indonesia.

Not only did the infant Dutch Republic, in the end, defeat those vast Iberian empires through decades of struggle, but it also created a purely capitalist form of imperial power that seeded the slow germination of an alternative world order. In just a few decades, the Dutch developed many of the essentials of modern capitalism—including private corporations, low-cost credit, merchant banks, and clever financial instruments like futures trading. While the Iberian empires were economic hybrids, demanding feudal dues from world trade in the form of that "royal fifth," Dutch colonies in both the East and West Indies would be owned and operated solely by joint-stock companies.[8]

The Dutch Republic also became Europe's first avowedly secular state, assuring freedom of worship to all its citizens, advancing science without religious restraint, and grounding its governance in universal principles of law. The fusion of these forces established Dutch corporations and their navy as the world's most powerful imperial enterprise, controlling a far-flung maritime domain spanning four continents. Although this small state could not sustain such an expansive global reach for more than a fleeting half century, the Dutch union with England after 1688 would help steer that latter nation more resolutely in the direction of maritime commerce and naval power—catalyzing trends that would culminate in the British imperial age.

The Dutch Republic aspired to religious tolerance, social equality, and economic vitality, making it a precursor for Europe's modern democracies. Its empire in Asia and the Americas was, however, another matter, refusing to grant its colonial subjects the same rights. Britain developed a similar duality, practicing a form of democracy at home grounded in civil liberties and property rights, while acquiring an overseas empire on the basis of slavery and imperial conquest. Thus, the Dutch and British may have supplanted the Portuguese and Spanish empires in the seventeenth century, but they perpetuated and perfected several essential attributes of the Iberian age.

In an assembly convened in 1618 to resolve theological conflicts within Protestantism, known as the Synod of Dordrecht, the Dutch Reformed Church adopted the Calvinist doctrine of "divine election," which held that certain individuals and groups were favored by God's protection. According to that logic, the Dutch, as God's elect, could struggle confidently against enormous adversity to win their independence from Spain, while denying that same freedom to subjects overseas who lacked such divine grace. Specifically, the Synod ruled that a slave's conversion to Christianity did not confer freedom, implicitly affirming the morality of slavery. As a result, for much of the seventeenth century, the Dutch would, in good conscience, dominate both the transatlantic slave trade and the production of sugar on slave plantations, while using slave labor throughout their Indian Ocean empire, whether in the cultivation of spices in eastern Indonesia or on farms in South Africa. Even in the late eighteenth century, when Enlightenment ideals inspired an abolition movement in England, the Dutch attitude was largely unaffected, and they continued to trade slaves without restraint until the British finally forced them to stop.[9]

Rise of a Republic

The Dutch Republic that emerged in 1581 was a unique mix of economic dynamism and rigid social stratification, with an elite of ten thousand merchants that filled municipal posts and the boards of major corporations—a presence captured in those dour, unsmiling faces of the many Golden Age group portraits. Amsterdam was already a major regional port, providing the labor force and infrastructure for later explorations. There were 1,200 Dutch ships engaged in the Baltic grain trade in 1600, and the North Sea fishing fleet had another thousand ships that employed 450,000 people, over twice the number working in Dutch agriculture. As the bloody Spanish pacification of the southern Netherlands forced Protestant merchants to flee Antwerp for the safety of Amsterdam, they brought along their capital, connections, and experience as brokers in Portugal's Asian trade, helping to make that Dutch city the new center for global finance.[10]

In little more than a decade, all that commercial ferment culminated in a bold Dutch bid to dominate Europe's trade with Asia. When eight ships returned from a fifteen-month voyage to the Indonesian archipelago loaded with lucrative spices, the bells of Amsterdam tolled in triumph and investors rejoiced at the windfall profit of 400 percent. Such an astronomical return set off a frenzy of speculation that soon sent another 65 ships to Indonesia's famed Spice Islands. In 1602, Holland's leading statesmen then consolidated such competing ventures into a unified Dutch East India Company, called the *Vereenigde Oostindische Compagnie* or VOC, which would survive for nearly two hundred years, paying regular annual dividends and fitting out a total of 4,700 ships that would transport almost a million Dutchmen to Asia. Under its state charter, the VOC would, for a time, enjoy a trade monopoly covering half the globe from the Cape of Good Hope to the Straits of Magellan. With delegated state powers to wage war, build forts, administer justice, and negotiate treaties with foreign rulers, the company became what historian Markus Vink has described as a "Janus-faced hybrid institution straddling the divide between merchant and sovereign."[11]

At its peak, this Dutch commercial empire combined a global reach with an austere corporate culture. The VOC controlled the Indian Ocean with ports from Cape Town, South Africa, along the coast of India, all the way to eastern Indonesia. A similar entity, the West India Company, occupied enclaves in West Africa, the northeast coast of Brazil, half a dozen islands in the Caribbean, and the area around Manhattan Island on the coast of North America. To administer this growing empire, the VOC constructed an office building in Amsterdam with a simple meeting room for the company's directors, the famed "Seventeen Gentlemen," or *Heeren XVII*. That modest space is now used occasionally as a midsize lecture hall at the University of Amsterdam—an instructive contrast with the seat of King Philip II's empire at El Escorial near Madrid, a palace so vast that entire cavalry companies could parade in its courtyard.

Only nine years after the VOC's founding, the Dutch navigator Hendrik Brouwer achieved a geopolitical coup by discovering the prevailing winds of the "roaring forties" (40 to 50 degrees south latitude). By running before those strong winds from the Cape of Good Hope straight across the Indian Ocean for six thousand miles, then turning north through the Sunda Straits into the Java Sea, VOC ships gained a direct route to Indonesia's Spice Islands. That southerly route also allowed them to avoid the fortified Portuguese *feitorias* arrayed north of the equator, from South India to the Straits of Malacca. By 1619, the VOC had established thirteen major trading posts in Asia and sent out 246 ships, three times the Portuguese number during that same period.[12]

Although the Dutch company's early ships sailed in search of trade, the VOC soon scored far-greater profits by plundering Portugal's empire. Only a few years after Admiral van Heemskerck's fleet seized the *Santa Catarina*, the VOC had captured at least 30 Portuguese merchant vessels. More importantly, the Dutch quickly occupied most of the Indonesian Spice Islands that Portugal had controlled for nearly a century.[13]

When Portugal challenged the capture of the *Santa Catarina* in Amsterdam's admiralty court, the VOC won a favorable decision. Concerned, however, about the public reaction to an act akin to piracy, the company's directors tasked their lawyer, Hugo Grotius, then just twenty-one years old, with writing a quick defense of their actions. To this end, they supplied him with ample documentation from their archives to establish the "perfidy, tyranny, and hostility" of the Portuguese, and also provided him a copy of lectures by Spanish theologian Francisco de Vitoria that had criticized Spain's denial of sovereignty to the Amerindians. Instead of scribbling a short polemic to justify the ship's seizure, Grotius worked for two years to produce a monumental treatise, replete with pathbreaking theories of sovereignty and human rights. Three years after that work was finished, the VOC, in an attempt to influence ongoing peace talks with Spain, had Grotius rush a chapter from his still-unpublished study into print anonymously, in 1609, under the title *Mare Liberum* (Freedom of the Seas).[14]

Hugo Grotius, Dutch lawyer and diplomat, circa 1640 (Credit: Library of Congress)

In that lengthy extract, Grotius observed that God "had not separated human beings . . . into different species and various divisions, but had willed them to be of one race." God had also "drawn up certain laws not graven on tablets of bronze or stone but written in the minds and on the hearts of every individual" that are "binding on great and small alike," both mighty monarchs and ordinary men. These laws ordain that some things "created for the use of mankind remain common to all." Do not the oceans, he asked, "with which God has encompassed all the earth" and the winds that blow mightily from one quarter to another "offer sufficient proof that Nature has given all peoples a right of access to all other peoples?" As a result, "the subjects of the United Netherlands have the right to sail to the East Indies" under the "unimpeachable axiom of the Law of Nations" that "every nation is free to travel to every other nation and to trade with it." The various papal bulls that the Portuguese had used "to justify their exclusive appropriation of the sea" were deficient because "the Pope is not the temporal lord of the earth, and certainly not of the sea." Echoing Vitoria's earlier argument about indigenous sovereignty, Grotius added that the act of discovery could not make the Portuguese sovereign over Java, Sri Lanka, and the Moluccas because those islands "now have and always have had their own kings, their own government, their own laws." Under "natural or human law from which sovereignty is derived," even pagans are "masters of their own property," and to take it "is no less theft and robbery than it would be in the case of Christians."[15]

As the citizen of a republic in the midst of an ongoing revolt against the Spanish Empire, Grotius thus went far beyond Vitoria's specific criticisms of Spanish imperialism to make sweeping, universal claims about the inviolable, natural sovereignty of all nations, Christian or otherwise. At this apex of the Iberian age, when Grotius was still young, idealistic, and uncompromised by his later diplomatic service, he envisioned an alternative, incipiently modern world order with all humanity gathered as free citizens in their own sovereign states, trading as equals across open seas, and resolving conflicts as a community of nations under international law.[16]

The same sense of moral righteousness and divine destiny that inspired Grotius also sustained the Dutch through their arduous revolt against Spanish rule, allowing them to absorb major reverses on land long enough to win some strategic victories at sea. In 1607, Admiral van Heemskerck organized the regular Dutch navy and sailed into Gibraltar harbor with 26 warships. Although outgunned, his fleet killed some four thousand Spanish sailors and destroyed all of their ships, while losing only one hundred men.[17]

With both sides exhausted from 30 years of a murderous conflict that had pushed Spain to the brink of bankruptcy, diplomats entered into fourteen months of negotiations that culminated in the Twelve Years' Truce in April 1609. Dutch negotiators also extracted an important concession: ships flying their flag could call at all ports in Asia and Africa not under direct Iberian control. In sum, the truce gave the Dutch a narrow maritime opening, which they would soon widen into a global empire.[18]

The Thirty Years' War

Within a decade of Spain's truce with Holland, the powerful Habsburg dynasty's mix of political intrigue and religious fervor culminated in the Thirty Years' War, which became the world's first truly global conflict, ravaging Europe and roiling five continents. After decades of intensive proselytizing by the Catholic League and the Protestant Evangelical Union, the sectarian climate in Europe was tinder dry. In 1618, the Dutch Reformed Church's Synod of Dordrecht condemned the Roman Catholic Church as "the Great Whore of Babylon." A Portuguese chronicler expressed a parallel view common among his countrymen that Hollanders were "fit for nothing save to be burned as desperate heretics."[19]

That same year, the Habsburg heir apparent as Holy Roman emperor tried once again to impose Catholic orthodoxy on his domain in central Europe, sending two imperial representatives to announce the change at an assembly known as the Diet of Prague. Outraged at the potential loss of religious freedom, the Protestant delegates threw the imperial emissaries from a castle window, inflicting serious injuries on them. The incident would be the spark for a religious war that split Europe between a Catholic coalition (Austria, Italy, Portugal, and Spain) and a Protestant alliance (Denmark, Sweden, Holland, and the Germanic principalities). By war's end, eight million people would be dead and the Iberian empires exhausted. But their world order, marked by limited human rights and expansive sovereignty, would persist for another 170 years even as the Dutch and British dominions expanded globally.

When the fighting started, Spain's young Habsburg king, Philip IV, was inclined to join the great sectarian struggle, in part to support his Habsburg relative as Holy Roman emperor but mainly to end the Dutch commercial ascent that had robbed Portugal of its spice trade and Spain of its silver profits. But the royal counselor Baltasar de Zúñiga warned the king that the Dutch state "is at the height of its greatness, whereas ours is plunged in confusion. To promise ourselves that we can conquer Holland is to aim for the impossible." Nonetheless, a Spanish army of 24,000 troops marched north toward the Netherlands with a mission to accomplish just that.[20]

For most of its three decades, the global Thirty Years' War was divided into two quite separate theaters: central Europe and the world's oceans. On land, this bitter sectarian struggle became a firestorm, drawing in ever-larger armies for ever more lethal combat. When King Gustavus Adolphus of Sweden, the greatest general of the age, joined the Protestant side in 1630, his 40,000 troops revolutionized land warfare. Armed with lighter muskets and prepared cartridges for faster loading, his battalions advanced six files deep, with rotating firing lines that threw out a continuous volley of lead, reinforced by lethal fire from their lighter, more maneuverable field artillery.[21]

This murderous form of land warfare inflicted untold suffering on central Europe. Bands of armed men prowled the countryside raping and pillaging, slaughtering villagers like animals. Of the war's 8 million dead, only 1.8 million were military deaths; the rest were civilians. The population of the Holy Roman Empire would take a full century to recover, and Europe would not experience such devastation again for nearly three hundred years.[22]

In striking contrast to these ravages in Germany and Bohemia, the renewed fighting in the Low Countries was comparatively civil. Instead of long marches and murderous infantry charges, both the Dutch forces and Spain's Army of Flanders advanced across the southern Netherlands in river barges, which carried construction equipment and heavy artillery to lay siege to walled cities ringed with Europe's most sophisticated fortifications. Beneath the cover of artillery barrages, the attacking army would usually tunnel toward the city walls. Once powder kegs were in place to blow a breach, the defenders would sensibly surrender before detonation to avoid further fighting. Now that the fanatical Philip II and the Duke of Alba were no longer leading a war of extermination against Protestant heretics, captured cities were treated humanely, armies avoided damaging the densely farmed countryside, and corsairs rescued the crews of any ships they sank. To capture the fortified Dutch town of Breda, Spanish commander Ambrogio Spinola surrounded the city walls with masterful siege fortifications manned by 23,000 troops for nine months before starving the defenders into submission.[23]

The tenor of Breda's surrender, and indeed much of that war, was captured in Diego Velázquez's monumental painting (now at the Museo del Prado in Madrid) showing the triumphant Spinola, with rows of *tercio* pikemen behind him and a smoking battlefield below, bowing magnanimously as he accepts the key to the city of Breda from the defeated Dutch commander.

Yet that costly victory strained the Spanish treasury for a decade, prompting the crown to shift to an attack on Dutch maritime trade.[24]

While such bloody battles and protracted sieges produced an exhausted stalemate on land, combat on the high seas swept across vast distances, changing the face of global empires with comparatively little bloodshed. If the war in Europe was a battle for cities and souls, the naval campaign was a struggle over the spices of Asia, the slaves of Africa, and the sugar plantations of Brazil. To wage such a war of the oceans, the Dutch chartered, in 1621, a new West India Company and built a navy with nine capital ships of five hundred tons.[25]

The war's outbreak coincided with the Dutch East India Company's appointment of a new governor-general for the Indies, Jan Pieterszoon Coen, a ruthless empire builder who would spend the next decade expanding the company's intra-Asian trade, enforcing a monopoly over the Spice Islands and maximizing their production with slave labor. Simultaneously, the company's director for India established half a dozen factories along the subcontinent's west coast while allying with the British to fight the Portuguese.[26]

By attacking individual ports with superior naval forces, the Dutch East India Company slowly severed the once-formidable chain of Portuguese *feitoria* enclaves. The first blow came in 1622 when a Dutch-British fleet, assisted by their Persian allies, captured the Portuguese gateway to the Persian Gulf at Hormuz. With an armada of 85 warships, the Dutch also defeated a Portuguese fleet off Goa on India's west coast in 1638 and then attacked their fort at Batticaloa, Sri Lanka, in alliance with the local monarch, launching a three-year campaign that ultimately captured the island. After a sustained blockade that seized Malacca in 1641, the VOC finally won control of those strategic straits. Although they failed to take the Portuguese port on Mozambique Island, the Dutch found an alternative by settling a small colony at Cape Town. By 1660, the VOC had captured the three strategic choke points that the Portuguese had long used to dominate Indian Ocean commerce, breaking their once-grand geopolitical design into a scattering of isolated enclaves.[27] In a reprise of Portugal's earlier strategy, the VOC's fortified ports now encircled the "world island"—from Elmina and Cape Town in Africa across the Indian Ocean to Sri Lanka, the Straits of Malacca, and the Spice Islands of Indonesia.

Over the next two decades, the Dutch company would reach the peak of its power, controlling much of Asia's spice trade. By inserting itself into intra-Asian commerce from Persia to Japan, the VOC profited at every turn—first swapping Chinese silk for Japanese silver, which it used to buy Indian textiles; next, exchanging those fabrics for Indonesian spices; and, finally, shipping the spices to Europe for sale at a hefty markup. Unlike the Portuguese, who used coercion to exploit existing trade, the Dutch innovated by deepening the connections between countries and continents, profiting enormously in the process. By 1670, the VOC would be the world's richest corporation, with 40 warships, 150 merchant vessels, 50,000 employees, and a chain of 20 Asian forts defended by 10,000 soldiers.[28] As late as 1750, such Asian commerce still constituted a quarter of the Netherlands' foreign trade.[29]

The results the Dutch achieved in the South Atlantic were much more mixed. In a bold bid to capture the profitable Brazilian sugar industry, the Dutch West India Company seized the capital of Portuguese Brazil at Bahia in 1624. Almost immediately, Madrid dispatched the largest fleet ever to cross the Atlantic, 56 ships carrying 12,500 men, which recaptured the city. Five years later, however, the West India Company invaded Pernambuco farther north, and occupied the country's northeast sugar coast for a full quarter century until a sustained local revolt finally drove them out. Across the South Atlantic in Africa, their short-lived bid to occupy Angola ended when a Portuguese relief fleet arrived from Brazil. Indeed, as one Portuguese Jesuit put it, "without Angola, no slaves; without slaves, no Brazil." But Dutch maneuvers around the Gulf of Guinea in West Africa were more successful, as they gained a pivotal position in the transatlantic slave trade by seizing and holding the Portuguese *feitoria* at Elmina, in what is today Ghana.[30]

For two decades, the Dutch company would use that fort to carry as many as five thousand captives annually to sugar plantations on the two dozen Caribbean islands that the British, Dutch, and French had seized from Spain. After that, however, the Dutch role in the slave trade faded to a weak fourth place, and Portugal would again dominate the traffic during the first half of the eighteenth century, shipping six hundred thousand Africans to Brazil's booming coffee and sugar plantations. As the Dutch presence in the Atlantic declined, they formed the chartered Society of Surinam in 1682 and, over the next century, built that "wild coast" and its nearby Caribbean islands into a complex of seven hundred plantations with 85,000 slaves producing ten thousand tons of sugar annually.[31]

In terms of the economic substance of empire, much of this spectacular combat was secondary to long-term trends in global trade. Throughout the Thirty Years' War, Dutch merchants, in an ironic twist, used their central role in the Spanish Empire's finance, commerce, and shipping to win an ever-growing share of the silver arriving from the Americas. Between 1616 and 1661, when Spain needed every bit of bullion to sustain its protracted war effort, the amount reaching Madrid dropped from 50 million pesos a year to just 10 million. In the same period, however, the amount of Spanish silver arriving in Europe actually rose from 50 million to nearly 80 million pesos—with most of that increase going to Dutch merchants and financiers. Such losses beggared the Spanish crown, eventually making it impossible for Madrid to continue its war against the Protestant powers. Dutch mints, by contrast, used the supplies of silver from Spain to produce ample coins for lively foreign trade and domestic commerce, with a per capita money supply double that of England.[32]

As the Thirty Years' War entered its final decade, Spain suffered a series of debilitating reversals that forced it to sue for peace. A German Protestant army captured the Rhineland city of Breisach, cutting the "Spanish road" the *tercios* had long used to march through a stretch of Habsburg lands from Italy to the Netherlands. With their troops now forced to move by sea, a Spanish fleet of some 70 warships and 30 transports carrying 24,000 soldiers was sent to reinforce their forces in Flanders. But a Dutch armada of 96 warships and 9,900 sailors, commanded by Admiral Maarten Tromp, attacked their anchorage in neutral English waters. With the loss of just one ship and 100 men, the Dutch force sank some 30 Spanish galleons and killed 7,000 of their troops—a blow that broke the Spanish navy.[33]

While the war dragged on, Spain itself began to fracture under the strain of the ongoing mobilization of men and money. In 1640, both Portugal and Catalonia rose in revolt against the king's authority. A year later, a Spanish royal army engaged a joint French-Catalan force on the steep slopes of Montjuïc Castle, just outside Barcelona's city walls, and was forced to retreat in defeat after suffering heavy losses. Meanwhile, Portuguese forces in Lisbon rebelled against Spanish rule, seized the royal palace, and proclaimed the Duke of Braganza as King João IV. The Spanish prime minister, the Count-Duke of Olivares, advised the king: "God wants us to make peace, for He is depriving us visibly and absolutely of all the means of war."[34]

Just as the Thirty Years' War was protracted and convoluted, so were the negotiations that ended it. For three years, more than a hundred delegations argued over the three treaties that made up the Peace of Westphalia, which, when finally signed in 1648, resolved some knotty territorial issues and advanced broad principles of international relations. Apart from ending hostilities, the peace settlement recognized the independence of the United Netherlands Provinces and accepted religious tolerance as the new norm for Europe. Although the agreement did not create nation-states with secular sovereignty in the modern sense, it made significant advances in that direction by undercutting the universal authority of both the pope and Holy Roman emperor. Angered at this acceptance of Protestantism, Pope Innocent X raged ineffectually against the Peace of Westphalia, calling it "null, void, invalid, iniquitous, unjust, damnable, reprobate, inane, empty of meaning and effect for all time." With the end of the Vatican's role as the continent's de facto judicial arbiter, European states would henceforth resolve their differences through diplomatic agreements grounded in an evolving body of international law.[35]

While the Peace of Westphalia settled Europe's internal conflicts, its treaties did not tamper with the core Iberian principles of expansive imperial sovereignty and limited human rights. Not only did these agreements treat colonies and their slaves as booty, but they also largely failed to resolve the global war that had swept the world's oceans. Under the Treaty of Münster, also signed in 1648, the Spanish crown had formally recognized Dutch independence and conceded all the territories that Holland's East and West India Companies had seized from Portugal. By then, however, Lisbon's new Braganza dynasty had recovered the country's independence after 60 years of Spanish rule and refused to accept the loss of its overseas colonies. Once those peace talks had removed the immediate threat of a Spanish attack, Portugal resumed offensive operations against the Dutch that quickly recovered Angola as well as two islands off the west coast of Africa, São Tomé and Príncipe. A similarly strong local resistance in Brazil expelled the Dutch from Pernambuco and recovered the sugar plantations that would soon prove Portugal's economic salvation.[36]

By the 1660s, Portugal, exhausted by decades of turmoil, was forced to reach diplomatic settlements with its many enemies—paying the Dutch an indemnity to waive their residual claims to Brazil, conceding the Ceuta enclave in North Africa to Spain for accepting the separation of their two kingdoms, and cementing an alliance with England's King Charles II through his marriage to a Portuguese princess of the Braganza dynasty, along with a generous dowry comprising the ports of Bombay and Tangier, as well as three hundred thousand pounds sterling.[37] Three paintings now displayed at the National Portrait Gallery in London reveal the extent of this sacrifice made by Portugal and its princess. Flanking a likeness of King Charles II, cheeks creased by years of libertine living, are a pair of portraits showing the pious demeanor of his wife, Catherine of Braganza, and the fully exposed breasts of his mistress, the actress Nell Gwyn.[38]

The Aftermath of the Thirty Years' War

By the end of the Thirty Years' War in 1648, the center of European imperial power had moved decisively from south to north, from Iberia to the shores of the North Sea. The Dutch maritime empire, moreover, had attained its final form, which it would maintain for most of the next century. By confining the Portuguese to their enclaves on the coast of India and the Spanish to Manila, the Dutch had become masters of the Indian Ocean from South Africa to Indonesia. In the Atlantic, by contrast, they faced strong competition from Spain in the Caribbean, the Portuguese in the South Atlantic, and Britain in the North Sea and North Atlantic. Though these pressures were formidable, the Dutch still clung to their colonies in the southern Caribbean at Aruba, Curaçao, and several other islands, while maintaining their recent settlements around Manhattan. Though ephemeral, the Dutch victories in the Thirty Years' War affirmed their arrival as the world's largest trading nation, providing ample profits to fund a golden age of governance, commerce, and the arts that made them progenitors of a new kind of society (secular and republican) and a new form of empire (capitalist and commercial).[39]

The speed of the Dutch ascent was matched by Iberia's precipitous decline. By the time these decades of warfare were done, Portugal's empire had been largely reduced to a single source of profit: Brazilian sugar plantations worked with African captives from Angola. It was also clear that Spain's military dominance over Europe was at an end. Despite painful reverses, however, Madrid still maintained the territorial integrity of its empire in the Americas and the Philippines, while preserving the *mare clausum* status of the Pacific Ocean. But the Münster peace accord of 1648 removed the embargo on Dutch merchants, allowing them access to Spain's commerce and accelerating its ongoing economic decline to the rank of a secondary power. Efficient Dutch shipping soon dominated Spain's foreign trade, flooding the country with imports of basic commodities and facilitating the export of its silver to Amsterdam.[40] Both Lisbon and Madrid had lost influence as metropolitan centers of empire, but their respective Latin American colonies were thriving and would remain profitable for centuries to come. In sum, this protracted war, with all its death and destruction, broke the preeminent power of the Iberian empires but was not sufficient to catalyze the transition to a new world order.

Indeed, the Iberian vision of expansive sovereignty—acquisition of terrain by conquest and oceans by exploration—would continue under Dutch and British hegemony, illustrating the capacity of these global systems to survive the empires that created them.[41] As the Dutch extended their colonial rule across Java and the British across India in the eighteenth century, the violence of their transgressions against the sovereignty of indigenous states would approach anything the Iberians had done in Africa or the Americas. Thanks to the British and Dutch decisions to strip their colonial subjects of civil liberties and carry the transatlantic slave trade to new heights, the Iberian hierarchy of human inequality would, in all its cruelty and tragedy, continue.

Dutch Decline, English Expansion

The Dutch Golden Age during the seventeenth century was extraordinary for both its brevity and breadth, as the United Netherlands and its commercial capital, Amsterdam, enjoyed a burst of creativity in almost every field of human endeavor—finance, trade, industry, shipping, warfare, medicine, science, governance, law, and the arts. Its painters, including Rembrandt van Rijn, Frans Hals, and Johannes Vermeer, were among Europe's finest, while Amsterdam was also the thriving hub of the European art market. As Dutch shipping dominated global trade and rich cargoes poured into Amsterdam and Rotterdam, the country became the world's financial capital. With all that wealth, Holland established five new universities, including Leiden, which enrolled eleven thousand students between 1626 and 1650, more than Cambridge in England or Leipzig in Germany.[42]

Yet the downward slide of Dutch imperial power was almost as rapid as its ascent. Only a half century after the country reached its peak circa 1650, the Netherlands would lose its global leadership through a combination of domestic changes and international reverses. Of particular importance, during the late seventeenth century, the Dutch elite shifted from high-risk maritime ventures to more cautious financial investments. Not only had wealth become concentrated in a financial oligarchy, but well over half their capital was now invested in safe government bonds. Holland had accumulated so much capital that interest rates were driven down almost to zero, forcing financiers to move funds overseas. By the 1730s, wealthy Dutch investors owned nearly a quarter of England's public debt, and by the end of the century they held a full quarter of the US national debt as well. Meanwhile, the Dutch share of European shipping fell from a high of 40 percent in 1650 to just 12 percent in 1780.[43]

Cornelis Tromp, Dutch admiral during the Anglo-Dutch Wars, 1675 (Credit: Alamy)

Accompanying these changes, the "old severe and frugal way of living" that had once marked Holland's merchant captains gave way to a luxurious new lifestyle. Admiral Maarten Tromp, son of a ship captain and a washerwoman, ate pickled herring like his sailors and died at sea fighting the English. His son Cornelis also reached the rank of admiral, but his portrait reveals the ruddy, cherubic cheeks of a well-fed aristocrat rather than the weathered lines of an old sea dog. Cornelis married a wealthy heiress and spent the years before his death in 1691 shuttling between an elegant town house in Amsterdam and a lavish country estate at "Trompenberg," which he decorated with large paintings of his naval exploits. By then, Dutch navigation, ship construction, and naval prowess were all in marked decline. Economists, of course, have more abstract explanations for the causes of this crisis (an end to the "classic harmony among its trading, industrial, agricultural, and fishing sectors") but agree about its "profound consequences" (i.e., an "absolute decline to the total output of the Dutch economy.")[44]

Worse yet was the sudden eruption of sustained naval warfare with England. Almost as soon as the Thirty Years' War with the Habsburgs had ended in 1648, Europe's two ascendant maritime powers plunged into their own cycle of conflict as the English challenged Dutch commercial dominance in the North Sea. For decades, the rapid rise of Dutch sea power, particularly its thriving fishing industry, had been a source of tensions with England—manifest in British scholar John Selden's book *Mare Clausum*. Published under royal patronage, his study sought to refute the argument for freedom of the seas that Dutch jurist Hugo Grotius had made 30 years earlier in *Mare Liberum*. Selden asserted that "the sea, by the Law of Nature or Nations, is not common to all men, but capable of private dominion." That principle of the closed sea applied, above all, to the waters surrounding Britain which were, Selden said, "an inseparable and perpetual appendant of the British Empire."[45] Beyond both authors' service to self-interested clients, such book-length treatises represented an early attempt to use secularized international law, based on reason rather than papal authority, as the means to resolve or justify disputes among nations.

In the late 1600s, these two North Sea powers fought three Anglo-Dutch Wars, each marked by several years of naval battles, devastating raids, and lucrative privateering. Determined to establish a *mare clausum* over the North Sea, the British Parliament passed the Navigation Act of 1651, excluding all foreign merchantmen from their ports and imposing a tax on any Dutch ships that fished in "English" waters. A year later, the British closed the English Channel to Dutch shipping, sparking a surge of privateering raids that soon spiraled into open warfare. The first of these wars was a draw. A series of destructive naval battles fought from the Mediterranean to the North Sea eventually forced the two powers to conclude a truce that ended the First Anglo-Dutch War, since neither side had been prepared for full-blown naval combat.[46]

As their naval arms race escalated over the next two decades, however, ever-larger fleets would engage in ever more destructive battles. In 1621, the Dutch navy had only nine ships of five hundred tons. During this first war, British ships such as the *HMS Sovereign of the Seas*, weighing 1,500 tons with 104 guns, had a marked advantage over smaller Dutch ships of some 500 tons. To match the British vessels, the Dutch built a battle fleet of their own, led by *De Zeven Provinciën* (the seven provinces), which also weighed 1,500 tons and carried 80 guns.[47] During these decades, warships would grow to ten times the size of the Portuguese *caravela de armada* that had swept the seas circa 1500, thereby maximizing the potential of wind power for warfare and maritime commerce.

When hostilities resumed in the Second Anglo-Dutch War, these trends were dramatically evident during the St. James Day Fight. In July 1666, fleets of 89 English and 88 Dutch warships, sailing in an enormous "line of battle" that stretched for nine miles along the English Channel, exchanged thundering broadsides for a full day. A month later, an English fleet raided the Zuiderzee waterway north of Amsterdam, burning 140 Dutch merchant ships and razing a coastal city. Outraged, the Dutch navy retaliated the next year in the famed Medway raid, which burned much of the British fleet at Chatham Harbour, inflicting a devastating blow on English morale and effectively ending this round of naval warfare.[48] In sum, this second war was a mutual debacle.

The third of these wars was devastating. England's Charles II brought Louis XIV of France into the conflict through a formal anti-Dutch alliance. Fielding Europe's most powerful army, France joined England in a land-sea pincer attack that should have crushed the small Dutch Republic. As some 150,000 French troops advanced relentlessly across Holland, many wealthy Dutch burghers favored capitulation, but a mass protest movement elevated young Prince William of Orange to the post of empowered lord lieutenant and stiffened his determination "to die . . . defending the last ditch." To dig that ditch, the Dutch opened their dikes to flood miles of fields, thereby forming a "water line" to block a French attack on Amsterdam. When the water froze that winter, some eleven thousand French troops advanced across twelve miles of ice, until an unexpected thaw drowned many of them. Meanwhile, the English fought three massive naval battles against the Dutch navy in the North Sea the following summer. With fleets of 130 to 150 capital ships on each side, the combined firepower of those rival armadas would be an unprecedented ten thousand guns. Skilled seamanship by Holland's legendary admiral Michiel de Ruyter won those North Sea naval battles, breaking a British blockade (aimed at starving Amsterdam into submission) and ending any attempt to land an invading army.[49]

A panoramic painting of the last battle in these wars at Texel Island reveals the confusion, even chaos, of this combat at sea level. Amid the billowing smoke of broadsides and burning ships, Admiral Cornelis Tromp's *Gouden Leeuw* (golden lion) flagship, Dutch flag flying, is firing its 80 guns at the British HMS *Charles*, which answers with 96 guns. Although the Dutch officially won the battle, this was, as historian Timothy Brook argues, "a Pyrrhic victory from which the Dutch Republic was not able to fully recover," ultimately forcing it into an unequal alliance with Great Britain. With the Dutch at the apex of their imperial glory and the English on the ascent, both could do damage, but neither could defeat or destroy the other.[50]

There was, however, an ironic coda that lent lasting significance to these otherwise-forgotten Anglo-Dutch Wars, culminating in what historian Jonathan Israel has called "one of the great events of world history." As the fighting with France continued to threaten Holland's survival, its sovereign, William of Orange (whose wife, Mary, was the eldest daughter of England's king), sought a lasting alliance through a risky, yet successful, attempt to place his wife on the English throne. Simultaneously, England's Protestant nobles, fearing that King James II was plotting a Catholic restoration, invited William, who was a Dutch Protestant, to invade their country. With half the country's investment capital lost since that disastrous French invasion and few prospects for a recovery, Amsterdam's merchants decided to invest their vast financial resources in William's reach for the English crown. This extraordinary convergence of interests culminated in England's Glorious Revolution of 1688. After a mobilization whose speed stunned diplomatic observers, William crossed the Channel with an armada of over 400 transport vessels and 53 warships carrying 40,000 men, including 21,000 Dutch troops with horses and artillery. While regiments stood on deck in parade formation and trumpets sounded, the Dutch army landed unopposed on England's southwest coast. King James II mobilized an army to defend his realm, but many of his troops defected to the Dutch, forcing him to retreat without a fight. A month later, James II fled to France, and William marched into London unopposed. With the throne now vacant, William and Mary were crowned joint sovereigns the following April at Westminster Abby, guarded by Dutch troops.[51]

As a condition for crowning them, Parliament enacted the Bill of Rights 1689, which became the country's "basic constitutional document," lending lasting historical significance to these events. For the first time, all British subjects and their parliament enjoyed the formal protection of their "ancient rights and liberties"—including the right of petition, due process for fines or imprisonment, trial by jury, protection from "cruel and unusual" punishment, free elections, religious toleration, and freedom of speech in parliamentary debate. Subsequent legislation made the calling of Parliament a matter of statute rather than royal prerogative and imposed legislative limits on the monarchy, ending its dynastic character. Though many clauses were particular to this political crisis, the declaration later became the model for the Bill of Rights in the US Constitution, the United Nations Universal Declaration of Human Rights, and the European Convention on Human Rights.[52]

The marriage of crowns was matched by a merger of capital and capital ships. Under an agreement reached at the coronation of William and Mary, a naval alliance would provide warships for future wars on a British–Dutch ratio of five to three. Through what historian Jonathan Scott calls "the Anglo-Dutch financial revolution," William's reign also witnessed a modernization of the British economy along Dutch lines, exemplified by the founding of the Bank of England, the London Stock Exchange, and a profusion of private banks, insurance companies, and joint-stock firms. Not only did the British follow the Dutch by making the national debt a state rather than a royal responsibility, but they went well beyond the fragmented Dutch system by centralizing financial management in the Bank of England. In the following century, British government revenues rose from 3 percent of national income to 20 percent, making the English the most heavily taxed people in Europe after the Dutch and allowing the state to borrow for war without fear of default. By 1760, moreover, Dutch investors would hold a third of the shares in the Bank of England and the British East India Company. Twenty years after that, more than 80 percent of Dutch foreign investment, which had reached an impressive 335 million guilders, was in England. The sum of these changes helped make Britain a trading nation for the first time in its history, raising its total overseas commerce at least fourfold during the eighteenth century.[53]

In addition, during the Anglo-Dutch Wars, a British fleet captured Manhattan, turning New Amsterdam into New York and so consolidating England's control over most of the North American coast from Newfoundland all the way to the Carolinas. Moreover, a regular navy, with purpose-built warships and trained seamen, would henceforth become integral to every strong European state. Indeed, by the 1680s, the Dutch navy had 69 ships of the line, the French 93, and the English 100—each with two or three gun decks and 50 to 100 heavy cannons. The expense was enormous, forcing states to seek expanded revenues. By the 1690s, England's naval dockyards had become the country's largest industry, employing four thousand workers. When warfare again embroiled Europe during that same decade, the Royal Navy would double to 323 ships with 9,900 guns, funded by an unprecedented budget of £19 million (equivalent to £3.6 billion today).[54] The formation of a large navy with a professional officer corps transformed the nature of warfare and the states that engaged in it.

Whatever the financial strain, the growth of the Royal Navy would give Britain an insuperable strategic advantage in the three major conflicts that would roil the continent during the eighteenth century, leaving its homeland unscathed and its empire well positioned to become the world's paramount power. The rise of the Royal Navy as the British state's main military force also created a new elite of officers that, over the span of two centuries, leavened the influence of the country's inward-looking, inherently parochial political leadership: the landed aristocracy. In 1810, the Navy had 145,000 men in service, nearly 3 percent of Britain's male population—a sufficient size to effect social change. According to naval historian Michael Lewis, throughout the eighteenth century "the generality of captains . . . were of middle-class extraction." While a quarter of midshipmen during the Napoleonic Wars were from the landed gentry, 50 percent were sons of professionals and about 10 percent from merchant or working-class backgrounds. Although social connections certainly eased promotion, the relentless rationality of naval warfare allowed commoners to rise, by merit, from ship's boy to lieutenant, captain, or even admiral, sometimes winning peerages that would place them at the right hand of power.[55]

These trends inside the Royal Navy reflected what historian C.A. Bayly has called "a significant growth of the power and aims of the British imperial state." After autocratic rule and a rebellion that cost it the American colonies, Britain moved toward the formation of a permanent civil service and the reform of its government, even starting a postal service. At Cambridge University and two colleges for civil servants in India, meritocratic reforms began creating a cadre of skilled administrators for its expanding state apparatus, at home and abroad.[56]

Colonialism and Mercantilism

The expansion of the Royal Navy throughout the eighteenth century was a manifestation of an extraordinary synergy of overseas commerce and industrial innovation that drove Britain's steady rise toward global power. With its peerless navy securing the unimpeded passage of merchant ships from Asia and the Americas, its overseas trade grew steadily, with exports rising sevenfold, from £6.5 million in 1700 to £43.2 million in 1800.[57]

After their formation circa 1600, the Dutch East India Company (VOC) and its British rival enjoyed such spectacular commercial success that they soon sparked a host of similar ventures. For much of the seventeenth century and well into the eighteenth, the driving force in European colonization would be a myriad of joint-stock companies—notably, the Virginia, Massachusetts Bay, Dutch West India, French East India, Hudson's Bay, Royal African, and many more.

In the process, Europe's empires were evolving away from the quasi-feudal Iberian system toward a more capitalist, market-based commerce. In the metropoles of Amsterdam, London, and Paris, monarchs and legislatures devolved a portion of their state power to those chartered companies, which were the world's first real corporations, with balance sheets, shareholders, elected directors, and legal personae. During the seventeenth century as well, the British East India Company (EIC), like its Dutch counterpart, became a de facto "company state" with delegated royal authority to build forts, make laws, sign treaties, coin money, and make arrests. Out on the imperial periphery, such chartered companies served as the fulcrum for contact between Europe's monarchies and indigenous states, whether Indian maharajahs, Arab emirs, or African chiefs. Thus, they slowly knit European commercial enclaves into territorial empires that would, in the course of the eighteenth century, extend to cover the whole of India and Indonesia.[58]

Right from the start, however, there were significant differences in the character of these trading companies. Reflecting the dynamism of Dutch society in its Golden Age, the VOC was launched with a broad charter, ample initial capital of £550,000, and a surfeit of skilled seamen.[59] Although the British company was awarded a similarly expansive charter in 1600 to conduct itself as a surrogate state, it had inadequate capital of just £68,000, contributed by only 36 shareholders. For the first fifteen years after its founding, the British EIC sent out small trading expeditions to Asia that returned with modest profits and the sobering realization that it could not compete with the Dutch for Indonesia's spices. Nonetheless, those gains were sufficient to attract investors, raising its capital to £418,000 in 1613 and £1.6 million four years later. Now adequately funded, the company established four profitable fortified ports along the coasts of India—Surat in the northwest; Bombay nearby, which soon became a naval bastion of 60,000 people; Madras in the southeast, which grew into a commercial city of 300,000 by century's end; and, most important of all, Calcutta, a busy port with access to Bengal's opium fields and skilled weavers. By the 1750s, some three hundred clerks inside company headquarters at East India House on Leadenhall Street, London, were posting dividends of 8 percent and handling imports of tea, silk, and cotton cloth worth £1 million annually, a hefty slice of Britain's £8 million in total imports.[60]

The last of the major Asian trading ventures, the French East India Company, was founded as a state venture in 1664 and first established a fortified trading post at Pondicherry, on India's southeastern coast. After years of recurring losses, a refugee Scots financier reorganized the company as a quasi-governmental concern, with royal investments and aristocratic officials. While its commercial ventures were only marginally successful, its director-general, Joseph-François Dupleix, formed a company army of Indian troops in 1746 to exploit any opportunities that might arise from the political chaos then engulfing India. The British soon followed his example, using European officers to train Indian troops (sepoys) in modern tactics and so forming a colonial army that would prove central to their future conquest of the subcontinent.[61]

These chartered companies employed a hybrid form of commerce called mercantilism that fused state coercion and commercial monopoly to secure hyper-profits.[62] While the Dutch advocated free trade and open seas in principle, their VOC was ruthless in crushing any competition for the spices of Southeast Asia. To control the export of nutmeg and mace, it curtailed unregulated production in the Banda Islands of eastern Indonesia by slaughtering their populations or deporting them to serve as slaves elsewhere. Even though it had agreed to share port facilities with the British EIC, the head of the Dutch entrepôt at Ambon tortured and beheaded the chief English agent and nine of his colleagues before evicting the company from Indonesia's Spice Islands. By the time the VOC perfected its spice monopoly in the 1680s, native shipping and commerce in eastern Indonesia had been virtually annihilated.[63]

In pursuit of mercantilist profits, European empires active in Asia during the eighteenth century found the trade in addictive substances—coffee, tea, tobacco, and opium—enticingly susceptible to lucrative monopolies. Given the light weight and high value of these drugs, and the certainty that customers habituated to caffeine, nicotine, and morphine would always return, companies were assured of both recurring sales and soaring profits. After discovering the exceptional gains to be made from the India–China opium trade, the VOC headquartered at Jakarta, Indonesia, increased its imports of Indian opium from just 617 kilograms in 1660 to 87 metric tons by 1699, retaining some for local sales and sending the rest to China, where addiction would grow rapidly. Starting in 1720 as well, the VOC used its territorial control over western Java to monopolize exports of coffee to Europe and America, so dominating the global coffee trade that the island's name became a synonym for the beverage. Adopting a similar strategy, the Spanish financed their rule over the Philippines largely through a monopoly on the cultivation and sale of tobacco, first to local markets and later for export to Europe.[64]

But all of these enterprises were dwarfed by the British company's rapid conquest of India and the subsequent growth of its trade in tea and opium. Throughout the eighteenth century, India's once-mighty Mughal Empire was losing power to regional overlords, allowing the British and French to expand their influence at the margins. The French forged an alliance with the ruler, or nawab, of Bengal province in India's northeast to challenge the British. Resentful of their infringement on his sovereignty, the nawab captured the East India Company's enclave at Fort William, near Calcutta in 1756, but the British counterattacked at the Battle of Plassey. Led by its young commander, Robert Clive, a lowly clerk turned talented tactician, the company's fledgling army of some 3,000 troops, largely Indian sepoys, defeated a massive Bengali force of 50,000.[65]

Unresolved tensions between the company and the rulers of India's northeast led to another major battle, upriver from Calcutta at Buxar, where the company's 19,000 sepoys inflicted a shattering defeat on a combined force of 150,000 troops led by Bengal's nawab and the charismatic Mughal emperor, Shah Alam II. Humiliated by this unexpected loss, the Mughal emperor signed a peace agreement in 1765, appointing the company as his tax collector for the provinces of Bengal, Bihar, and Orissa. Through this transformative treaty, the EIC became the virtual ruler of India's most prosperous region, with a population of 20 million. By expropriating two to three million pounds sterling in annual regional tax revenues, the company was freed from any further need to import gold bullion as payment for the Indian cloth, spices, and opium that it exported to Europe and Asia. It then imposed a monopoly over opium production and extracted cotton cloth from local weavers at below-market prices.[66]

In effect, these victories transformed the British company from a tenuous presence clinging to a handful of coastal enclaves into what historian K.N. Chaudhuri called "a powerful territorial force," giving it both the money and military manpower for the subsequent conquest of that vast subcontinent. In the 40 years that followed its victory at Buxar in 1765, the company's armies grew, through half a dozen wars against Indian states, into a formidable force of 120,000 well-trained troops backed by massive arsenals. During a series of hard-fought campaigns at the start of the nineteenth century, the British deployed this superior force to eradicate the residual French presence and subdue the last of India's powerful regional rulers, culminating in the British occupation of the Mughal capital at Delhi and the imposition of a protectorate over the aging Shah Alam II, whose charisma would henceforth lend legitimacy to their rule. Although Britain was a small island nation of just ten million people, it was now well on its way to controlling the subcontinent's population of two hundred million—providing the manpower, military strength, and fiscal resources for future dominance over much of

Asia. "We are now complete masters of India," wrote senior British officer Thomas Munro, "and nothing can shake our power if we take proper measure to confirm it."[67]

The British company's conquest of northeast India also facilitated an explosive expansion of its Asian trade through a synergy of two stimulants— exports of Indian opium to China and imports of Chinese tea to England. Instead of the simple bilateral barter practiced by their competitors, however, British trading companies mastered multilateral exchanges that maximized their profits. Much of England's overseas expansion during the eighteenth century was concentrated on two expanding trade triangles that covered half the globe: one in the Atlantic for slaves, sugar, and manufactured goods; the other in Asia with opium, tea, and machine-spun cotton.

The first leg in the lucrative Asian trade triangle was born of colonial conquest. After winning control over northeast India, the British EIC imposed a monopoly on opium production in the provinces of Bengal and Bihar, forcing peasants in designated districts to cultivate specific amounts and sell to the company's buyers at fixed prices for shipment to southern China where addiction would continue to spread. With its profits on opium exports, which it capped at 280 tons annually, the company and affiliated private traders financed the purchase of Chinese tea for shipment to North America, Europe, and England.[68]

As ever-larger shipments from China fed the English taste for tea, Britain balanced its trade account by exporting iron hardware and machine-spun cotton yarn made by its first textile factories. Through these early industries, Britain was launching an energy transition from the wind and muscle power of the Iberian age to the coal-fired steam energy that would later become a defining attribute of its imperial era. Coal had surpassed wood as England's main source of domestic heat as early as 1620, but it did not become a significant source of industrial energy until the late eighteenth century. As part of its ongoing industrial revolution, Britain began making marked strides in metallurgy, including the smelting and machining of iron used in the production of tools and low-cost muskets. As dozens of new coal-fired furnaces opened in the late eighteenth century, Britain's production of iron increased twelvefold to 250,000 tons circa 1800. By then, England was mining nine million tons of coal annually, representing more than 80 percent of total world production while supplying 90 percent of its thermal energy needs.[69]

In the closing years of the Iberian age, England's energy transition to the era of fossil fuels was well underway, one that would soon free humanity from the massed muscle power of slavery.

Meanwhile, however, just as Indian opium was the prime catalyst driving the Asian trade triangle, so African slaves still played a parallel role in its transatlantic analogue. In the first leg of a three-stage voyage that typically took three hundred days, British merchants sailed from Bristol or Liverpool to fortified ports in West Africa carrying cargoes of manufactured goods—hardware, rum, cotton textiles, gunpowder, and, above all, firearms. Throughout the eighteenth century, there was a striking increase in British shipments of flintlock muskets, which rose from 20,000 guns a year in the 1680s to 200,000 annually by the 1780s, sparking a "gunpowder revolution" along the coast of West Africa. Such weaponry, comprising about 25 percent of British shipments, entered trade networks controlled by militarized African kingdoms—the Asante, Benin, Dahomey, Oyo, Kongo, and others. In exchange for such trade goods, those local states sold slaves who had been captured in war, seized in raids, or punished for derelictions like debt to European forts and trading posts on the coast. "The great quantity of guns and gunpowder which the Europeans have brought," wrote the Dutch director of Elmina Castle at Ghana in 1730, "have caused terrible wars between the Kings and Princes . . . of these lands, who made their prisoners-of-war slaves; these slaves were immediately bought up by Europeans at steadily increasing prices." As a result, the tenfold increase in the import of firearms to West Africa would be matched by a fivefold rise in its export of slaves, reaching a historic peak in the 1780s at 77,000 captives a year.[70]

On the triangle's next leg across the Atlantic, known as the "Middle Passage," each ship carried a cargo of several hundred African captives to the sugar districts of Brazil or the Caribbean, where local plantations had an insatiable appetite for coerced labor. The eighteenth century was, in the words of scholar Eric Wolf, "the golden age of slaving," with about six million Africans forcibly transported to the Americas, nearly five times the number in the previous century. Despite its domestic tradition of liberty enshrined in the Bill of Rights 1689, Britain's burgeoning maritime commerce was responsible for much of the increase, carrying 2.4 million enslaved people, or 40 percent of the total transatlantic traffic. Granted a crown charter in 1672 with a thousand-year monopoly on all British trade with the continent, the Royal African Company established a half dozen trading forts in West Africa. By 1700, it was sending 80 ships across the Atlantic each year with slaves for British plantations in the Caribbean and the Carolinas.[71]

Meanwhile, in a public debate that persisted for two decades, unlicensed British slavers, whose ships were subject to confiscation by the Royal Navy, barraged Parliament with pamphlets and petitions insisting on their freedom, as Englishmen, to trade in enslaved Africans without the encumbrance of a monopoly. Just as unrestricted trade was supposed to be a natural English right on par with trial by jury, so, they argued, the Atlantic should be a *mare liberum* for a free trade in slaves. By the time Parliament finally ended the monopoly in 1712, the Royal African Company had carried close to 150,000 slaves and made enormous profits for its investors. Its longtime principal, Edward Colston, amassed a fortune that secured him a seat in Parliament representing Bristol. His substantial estate of £171,000 (equivalent to £26 million today) was sufficient to endow schools, hospitals, and charities—a munificence that Bristol later commemorated with a statue and plaque to honor "one of the most virtuous and wise sons of the city." (In 2020, that statue would be toppled and tossed into the sea by the Black Lives Matter movement.) With the restraints of monopoly removed, British ships sailing out of Bristol and Liverpool would carry more than two million Africans across the Atlantic by the end of the eighteenth century. By comparison, France and Portugal played a smaller role, transporting about six hundred thousand captives each.[72]

The main markets for English ships sailing the Middle Passage were British, French, and Dutch plantations in the islands of the Caribbean. Dutch traders had introduced sugar technology and a regular supply of slave labor to the British colony on Barbados, prompting a shift among English settlers from small tobacco farms staffed by indentured Irish workers to large sugar plantations worked by African slave labor. By 1667, when the Royal African Company took control of the traffic, Dutch shipments had raised the slave population on Barbados nearly sevenfold, to 40,000. As in Brazil, British planters could extract about seven working years from their enslaved labor, creating a constant need for replacements that sustained the human traffic.[73]

But it was Jamaica that became the center of the British sugar industry. For a time following the seizure of that large mountainous island from Spain in 1655, the British let its capital at Port Royal serve as a pirate's lair for

Captain Henry Morgan, from which he launched his famous raids, with up to 36 ships and two thousand buccaneers, on rich Spanish ports throughout the Caribbean. British settlers, however, had expanded the island's sugar industry so rapidly that Jamaica soon had 775 plantations, worked by 205,000 slaves, who produced 54,000 tons of sugar annually—almost half the total of the Caribbean's exports to England. During the eighteenth century, the West Indies sugar industry accounted for 10 percent of Britain's entire national income, creating wealth for the planters that elevated them into the British elite and causing misery for their slaves, who periodically rose in desperate revolts.[74]

On the final leg of the Atlantic trade triangle, Britain's merchant fleet carried cargoes of cotton, tobacco, sugar, and molasses to England. Only at the very end of the eighteenth century did the American South begin to surpass the British West Indies in the production of raw cotton for British textile mills, inaugurating a slow shift northward of the trade triangle.

The End of the Iberian Age

For well over a century, these chartered-company colonies would remain quintessentially Iberian in their approach to fundamental questions of sovereignty and human rights. Starting in the late eighteenth century, however, a cataclysm of protracted warfare on both sides of the Atlantic—national revolutions in the Americas and the Napoleonic campaigns in Europe—would sweep away those atavisms and release the rationalizing force of industry, science, and Enlightenment ideals to create a new kind of imperial age.

The Iberian world order started to unravel as the British, Dutch, and French chartered companies that ran these early empires became increasingly weak hybrids, incapable of effective colonial rule and increasingly inept at producing profits. Most of these companies—the Royal African, the Dutch West India, the French East India, and even the Dutch East India—were defunct by 1799.[75]

More broadly, a series of incessant, increasingly destructive wars exposed the failure of Europe's royal families—Bourbon, Habsburg, and Hohenzollern—to create a stable state system on the continent, straining their popular legitimacy at home and abroad. That, in turn, unleashed an age of revolution in Europe and the Americas that would, by century's close, shake the foundations of those autocratic regimes. The War of the Spanish Succession (1701–1714) would mark the exhaustion of the Habsburgs as

Europe's dominant dynastic power, while the succeeding Seven Years' War (1756–1763) would block the French monarchy's ambition to assume that position. At the turn of the next century, the devastating Napoleonic Wars (1796–1815) would roil Europe sufficiently to catalyze the emergence of British power and its new world order.

The first of these conflicts was a dynastic dispute with serious implications for the balance of power in Europe. Through two centuries of inbreeding themselves into extinction, the Habsburgs finally placed an heir on the Spanish throne, Charles II, who was chronically ill, with a deformed jaw so large his speech was slurred, and incapable of producing an heir before he died at the age of thirty-eight. To block the Austrian Habsburgs from capturing the Spanish crown and its vast empire, Louis XIV of France, whose wife was a Spanish princess, maneuvered to make their grandson, Philip V, head of a new Bourbon dynasty that would rule Spain and its silver-rich Latin American empire.[76]

Fearful of what this expansion of French power might mean for Britain and Holland, England sided with Austria, sending the largest British army to fight on the continent in more than a century. In 1704, after leading his 21,000 troops, including 16,000 Englishmen, on forced marches for 250 miles into Bavaria, the Duke of Marlborough joined with German allies to destroy a superior French force at the historic Battle of Blenheim. After another major victory over the French at the Battle of Ramillies near Brussels, Marlborough effectively ended Louis XIV's aspirations to dominate Europe. Meanwhile, the Royal Navy used its strategic advantage to strike at will around the continent, inflicting a succession of defeats on Spain. Following fourteen years of fighting marked by three major naval engagements, sixteen protracted sieges, and nineteen bloody battles that left some seven hundred thousand dead, Philip V took the Spanish throne, albeit with a proviso barring any union with the French crown.[77]

Dynastic issues aside, the war's settlement by the Treaty of Utrecht in 1713 confirmed a subtle yet significant realignment of power. Spain emerged unified under a new Bourbon dynasty and preserved most of its empire. Portugal, by contrast, became a British client state, while the Netherlands, another British ally, was reduced to a secondary naval power. Britain had assured its maritime, commercial, and financial supremacy by taking strategic Spanish ports in the Mediterranean, including Gibraltar, and securing the lucrative monopoly contract for the export of enslaved Africans to Spain's Latin American territories.[78] Yet, Britain's duel with France for global dominion remained something of a draw, awaiting a second, definitive round.

Forty years later, unresolved tensions among Europe's ruling families again erupted into devastating war on the continent and another duel between London and Paris for control of the wider world. Starting in 1756 as a dynastic dispute between Prussia and a five-nation alliance led by Austria, the Seven Years' War quickly expanded into history's second global war. In northern Europe, Frederick the Great's disciplined Prussian forces, sustained by British finance, stalemated Austria's superior numbers through 24 bloodstained battles. In southern Europe, an agile Anglo-Portuguese army repulsed three invasion attempts by superior Franco-Spanish forces, slaughtering over half of their 42,000 men. Significantly, some 210,000 soldiers on all sides deserted, indicating that Europe's masses were no longer quite so willing to die for their querulous monarchs. Otherwise, little changed, leaving the war's significant outcomes to battles beyond Europe.[79]

Such fighting overseas would lead to the eclipse of the French Empire and the corresponding rise of British power. Having blocked French ambitions in India, London sent some nine thousand troops to capture Quebec City, in Canada, in the summer of 1758, who then survived a French siege when a relief fleet arrived.[80] By the time the Seven Years' War was done, Britain had become the dominant power in much of North America and India—two key components of its emerging global empire. Through a worldwide naval struggle that culminated in seven major battles, the Royal Navy had also established itself as the most powerful force on the high seas.[81]

Seen from a global perspective, this succession of costly, bloody wars, which left Europe's kingdoms strained to the breaking point financially, catalyzed an age of revolution—a tempestuous half century (1775–1824) that swept both sides of the Atlantic. As British military expenditures in North America soared nearly tenfold, London, for instance, tried to balance its books by imposing, in 1765, the Stamp Act on the American colonies; it also sought to prevent any future Native American uprisings (which it knew would be expensive to suppress) by barring any settlement beyond the Appalachian Mountains. Together, these actions would spark conflicts that culminated in the American Revolution. While the old order trembled, Enlightenment ideals of liberty proved to be tinder for a tempest of riots, rebellions, and revolution that, over the span of half a century, challenged most of Europe's monarchies and wiped out significant parts of their overseas empires. By the end of this revolutionary era, France would lose all of Canada, Britain the thirteen American colonies, Portugal the vast expanse of Brazil, and Spain most of Latin America.[82]

Age of Revolution

As a new age dawned, radical leaders in America, France, and Spain proclaimed principles of human equality that challenged the legitimacy of the Iberian era's slave regime. Yet all of Europe's overseas empires were still economically dependent on slavery to varying degrees, making the issue both critical and complex. On July 4, 1776, the US Declaration of Independence stated: "We hold these Truths to be self-evident, that all Men are created equal, that they are endowed by their Creator with certain unalienable Rights, that among these are Life, Liberty, and the Pursuit of Happiness." Similarly, just six weeks after the start of the French Revolution in 1789, its National Assembly adopted a Declaration of the Rights of Man and the Citizen, which stated in Article I: "Men are born and remain free and equal in rights." During the revolution's most radical phase, the first French government to be organized as a republic, the National Convention, included a specific prohibition on slavery in its 1793 constitution and soon freed all the slaves in its overseas empire. Within a few years, however, both the US Constitution and successive French charters would compromise such declarations of universal rights by creating exceptions that preserved slavery in their plantation economies.[83]

While the French Revolution of 1789 had toppled the Bourbon monarchy and established an egalitarian republic, the ensuing turmoil of social conflict, partisan violence, and economic privation soon created a desire for order and an opening for autocratic leadership. In the midst of this crisis, Napoleon Bonaparte, a young officer from a local gentry family on the Mediterranean island of Corsica, emerged as the progenitor of a new political order for France, along with much of Europe. Indeed, at least one biographer has celebrated him as a "giant of the modern era" who introduced important innovations that "radically transformed the physical, legal, political and cultural landscape of Europe."[84]

Whatever validity that assessment might have from an exclusively

European viewpoint, a historical perspective cognizant of world orders is, on the contrary, apt to consider Napoleon a reactionary figure whose rule was the "inevitable dictatorial epilogue to the Revolution."[85] His brief moment as master of Europe would embody versions of imperial sovereignty and human rights that were the essence of the Iberian age—the seizure of foreign lands by right of conquest, defense of slavery, division of his domains among relatives like a sixteenth-century Habsburg emperor, and creation of a closed continental economy in the manner of seventeenth-century mercantilism. Confronted by an eruption of radical French Jacobin principles of liberty on the Caribbean island of Haiti, where slaves had rebelled to win their freedom, Napoleon dispatched an army that deployed the sort of spectacular cruelty that has been reserved for the suppression of slave revolts since ancient Rome. At home, he formed a pervasive "police state" that suppressed all free expression, a tax office that extracted revenues to sustain his million-man army, and mass conscription that dragooned almost all eligible young male bodies as fodder to feed his insatiable war machine.[86]

By contrast, Napoleon's nemesis, the more conservative British, continued to advocate policies of free trade, open oceans, and abolition of slavery that would make them progenitors of progress and a new global system. Indeed, the millions of deaths and untold devastation from the conflicts of these years, combined with the catalyzing British financial and industrial innovations, would finally bring about a new world order, lending some lasting significance to the decades of incessant warfare.

Promoted to major general at the age of twenty-six amid the political tempest of revolutionary France, Napoleon turned his first command of 40,000 ragtag troops into an all-conquering army. His first show of tactical brilliance was in a campaign that routed opposing forces across northern Italy in just twelve months, and then advanced on Vienna so relentlessly that he could dictate a peace settlement to the powerful Austrian Empire in 1797. Within a year, Napoleon had devised a geopolitical strategy that he summed up in a pithy imperial axiom: "Truly to overthrow England, we must occupy Egypt." Convinced that the Suez Isthmus was the fulcrum to destabilize British India, Napoleon sailed with 36,000 troops to Egypt, where he routed one Ottoman army at the Pyramids; destroyed another at Aboukir, near Alexandria; defeated a third in Palestine, capriciously slaughtering three thousand surrendering soldiers while sacking the city of Jaffa in an "orgy of rape and murder"; and dispatching a fourth in Alexandria, driving it into the sea. To protect India, the British sent one fleet around Africa to blockade the Red Sea and another across the Mediterranean, where it sank the French transports. With the French army being depleted by one bloody battle after another, his deputy remarked presciently that Napoleon "was the kind of general who required an income of 10,000 men a month." As his would-be geopolitical masterstroke veered toward disaster, Napoleon abandoned his ravaged army to suffer its fate and sailed from Alexandria under cover of darkness. Landing in southern France, he proceeded to Paris amid cheering crowds, seizing power as first consul in a military coup; four years later, he would crown himself emperor in Notre Dame Cathedral.[87]

The outcome of the subsequent decade of warfare that spread to five continents was decided by an elusive interplay of geopolitics at multiple levels—global, continental, and regional. Although a tactician of unequaled brilliance who regularly routed superior forces on the battlefield, Napoleon proved a poor geopolitical strategist, failing to translate his many military victories into a stable empire.

The French navy, in alliance with the Spanish, began the Napoleonic Wars as a formidable force. But the British vice admiral Horatio Nelson scored great victories at the mouth of the Nile, Copenhagen Harbor, and Cape Trafalgar that soon severed Napoleon's contact with France's overseas empire and confined his ambitions to Europe.[88] Nelson was an officer whose conventional career led him to an unconventional strategy: not simply to defeat, but to totally destroy the French navy. Born into genteel poverty as the child of a village pastor with eleven children, Nelson joined the Royal Navy at thirteen and was promoted to captain at the age of twenty, with command of a frigate in the Caribbean. Dissatisfied with the standard naval doctrine, which instructed ships of the line to dutifully follow their admiral's flagship in indecisive exchanges of gunfire, he developed new tactics, allowing each ship's captain autonomy to engage and destroy enemy vessels using superior seamanship.[89]

While Napoleon's army was occupying Egypt, Nelson's fleet attacked thirteen French warships at anchor near Alexandria, capturing or destroying eleven of them, and winning control over the Mediterranean. Two years later, the British victory over a Danish fleet at Copenhagen gave the Royal Navy free access to the Baltic Sea. Then, off the Spanish coast at Cape

Trafalgar in 1805, Lord Nelson's legendary "band of brothers" commanded 27 British ships of the line that attacked a larger French-Spanish fleet, capturing or destroying 19 ships while killing fifteen thousand sailors. Not only did that victory give the Royal Navy a strategic advantage in the remaining decade of war, but it also made Britain the world's paramount naval power, with unchecked access to global markets.[90]

Compounding France's difficulties overseas, Haiti, its richest colony, seemed ready to break free after a protracted slave revolt. In the ten years prior to the revolution, France's West Indies plantations had flourished and Haiti had become the world's most profitable colony. As the island's slave population swelled to 470,000, its eight thousand plantations produced a third of the world's sugar and half of its coffee, requiring a thousand ships to carry the rich cargoes to Europe each year. More than any other comparable colony, Haiti had perfected the Iberian era's plantation system—as reflected by a rigid color line, a brutal slave regime, protected markets, and exorbitant profits.[91]

The oppression sparked a massive slave revolt in 1791 that, through a decade of struggle, forged a battle-hardened army and found a brilliant leader, the self-educated slave Toussaint L'Ouverture. As France's hold on the colony weakened, the first to reach for this rich imperial prize was Britain's prime minister, William Pitt the Younger. Eager to capture what he called "the Eden of the Western World," Pitt sent 30,000 British soldiers for an abortive five-year occupation of the island, which ended after 60 percent of those troops had died from disease or in battle against the determined resistance. To recapture that lucrative imperial prize and restore slavery, Napoleon then dispatched 60,000 troops under his brother-in-law, General Charles Leclerc, who quickly contained the revolt and captured L'Ouverture. But once word reached Haiti that France had also reimposed slavery elsewhere in the Caribbean, the revolt revived with such intensity that Leclerc fell back on a campaign of systematic slaughter that only ended when he died from yellow fever. His successor also resorted to mass murder and macabre brutality, but it was not long before disease and combat deaths had winnowed French forces to just ten thousand survivors. Following their withdrawal, Haiti declared independence in January 1804, prompting Paris to sell its remaining North American territories to the United States in the famed Louisiana Purchase. Combined with similar reverses in India, this disaster largely stripped France of its colonial empire.[92] Though overshadowed by the drama of the Napoleonic Wars in Europe, the Haitian Revolution became the world's first successful slave revolt and so played a catalytic role, along with subsequent British abolition efforts, in the eradication of the slave plantation that had been such a defining attribute of the Iberian age.

Denied access to the high seas, Napoleon tried instead to strengthen economic controls over his vast continental empire. Following victorious campaigns across central Europe in 1805 and 1806, he soon forged a dominion of 44 million people, stretching from Spain to Poland, and Norway to Italy. While he introduced modernizing reforms on paper, their effect was undercut by his "elaborate spoils system," which initially allowed his soldiers to plunder conquered lands like a plague of locusts and then divided much of Italy, Germany, and Poland into large feudal estates for the 3,600 members of his imperial aristocracy. To counter a British blockade of his ports, Napoleon formed his famed Continental System, barring any trade with Britain and creating an integrated European economic zone. When British goods continued to enter through Spain and Russia, Napoleon invaded each in turn, miring his army in a fruitless pacification campaign in Spain that cost him three hundred thousand troops and a disastrous winter retreat from Moscow that lost five hundred thousand more.[93] By 1810, his experiment in European economic autarky had produced what French historian François Crouzet termed a "sharp crisis" that "broke the momentum of Napoleonic industrialization."[94]

Compounding these failures, Napoleon's geopolitical maneuvers at the regional level also proved unstable. Like Julius Caesar nearly two millennia earlier, he seemed to view the Rhine River as the fulcrum for control over the continent. After he defeated an alliance of Austria, Prussia, and Russia at the great Battle of Austerlitz in 1805, the French emperor dissolved the Holy Roman Empire that had long ruled central Europe and tried to replace it with a new geopolitical design. Through military operations over the next two years, he cut Prussia's territory by half, seized its great forts on the Oder River, and occupied its capital at Berlin. Simultaneously, he combined some 35 German principalities into a French client state that he called the Confederation of the Rhine, anchored by four large centralized kingdoms—Bavaria, Saxony, Westphalia, and Württemberg. Stretching from Switzerland to the North Sea, this new Germanic state was supposed to serve as a geopolitical buffer to protect France from the military power of Austria and Prussia.[95]

Despite incessant French intervention, the confederation held together for just seven years, at which point Prussia rebelled by joining Austria and Russia in a renewed challenge to Napoleon's empire. To fund its continental allies, Britain provided a massive £22 million in grants and loans, including a million pounds in military supplies shipped directly to Baltic ports. Determined to crush the formidable coalition arrayed against him, Napoleon marched into Germany in the spring of 1813 at the head of his Grande Armée, recently replenished by fresh recruits following devastating losses during that disastrous winter withdrawal from Moscow. After several failed attempts to retake Berlin, he met the enemy at Leipzig, in Saxony, where his troops suffered 73,000 casualties, his Rhine Confederation allies deserted him, and he began a pell-mell retreat back to France. Demonstrating the depth of his geopolitical failure, Napoleon's fleeing forces were attacked by his erstwhile ally, the Bavarian army, which attempted, albeit unsuccessfully, to block the French retreat so the pursuing allies could catch and crush them.[96]

Born of his greatest victory, Napoleon's geopolitical gambit died as the rickety Rhine Confederation crumbled, taking the rest of his European empire with it. After his enemies marched into Paris, sending Napoleon into exile on the small Mediterranean island of Elba, two dozen diplomats gathered for what would be called the Congress of Vienna to reorder their world following a quarter century of warfare. In June 1815, after nine months of grand balls and closed-door negotiations, the major powers reached an agreement that simultaneously granted the victors their spoils and stabilized Europe for a century to come. Just as the 1494 Treaty of Tordesillas had fostered the Iberian world order, so this Vienna summit created the conditions for a new global system, the British imperial era.

Playing a traditional diplomatic game, the victorious powers—Austria, Russia, and Prussia—settled for the usual bits of territory, some symbolic, others substantial. France would emerge from the summit cut down to second-tier size. A third of its territory would be taken, its borders redrawn to increase vulnerability, its empire reduced to a few tropical islands, an indemnity owed that would stifle its economic recovery, and a population reduced by two million war-related deaths. Even though Spanish guerrilla resistance had been critical to Napoleon's defeat, allied diplomats would do little to aid Madrid's recovery from the ravages of French occupation, leaving it so weakened that its Latin American empire would soon break free and fall into London's orbit. British envoys promoted a merger of Belgium and Holland into the United Netherlands to compensate Amsterdam for taking its colonies at Sri Lanka, Cape Town, and Malta.[97] Although the "congress system" of maintaining peace through regular conferences lasted less than a decade, that summit did stabilize Europe by shifting conflict resolution from war to diplomacy.[98]

At Vienna, there was also a significant debate over political principles. Invoking his personalized vision of Christian ideals, Russia's Czar Alexander I advocated an ill-fated Holy Alliance to protect monarchy and quash democracy. Taking a more liberal position, Britain's envoy, Viscount Castlereagh, sought diplomatic support for his country's new campaign against the slave trade, which had started a few years before when Parliament banned the traffic. Through his efforts, the General Treaty signed at Vienna included an article stating that "the commerce, known by the name of 'the Slave Trade,' has been considered, by just and enlightened men of all ages, as repugnant to the principles of humanity and universal morality." All the powers present resolved to end this "scourge, which has so long desolated Africa, degraded Europe, and afflicted humanity." Calling this commitment a "great moral triumph," Lord Castlereagh told Parliament that the Congress of Vienna deserved "the gratitude of mankind . . . for there all the great powers of Europe made a declaration which stamped the slave trade as disgraceful, and made every state anxious to get out of it." To advance such principles, Britain then signed treaties with Spain and Portugal that abolished human traffic north of the equator, but, in an unfortunate diplomatic compromise, left Portugal's South Atlantic slave trade untouched. Despite the ringing condemnation of slavery, Britain would fail to win allied support for its interdiction efforts at two later diplomatic conferences, forcing it to conduct the abolition campaign on its own.[99]

The Legacy of War

In retrospect, the Napoleonic Wars and their diplomatic settlement, by stabilizing Europe and eliminating any further French challenge to Britain's dominion over the world's oceans, facilitated the rise of London's global empire. More broadly, the devastation brought about by decades of warfare, combined with the dynamism of Britain's coal-fired industrial revolution, created conditions ideal for both the rise of the British Empire and the formation of its new world order.

More than any of the earlier eighteenth-century conflicts, the Napoleonic Wars were a maelstrom that roiled the continent through 228 bloody battles and 91 destructive sieges that left six million dead. In contrast to France, which had sacrificed a generation, and Spain, which would soon lose an empire, Britain suffered little loss to its labor force and no material damage. Instead, London gained considerable economic advantage as the banker and workshop for its continental allies. During the century of warfare that ended with the Congress of Vienna, Britain had eliminated every one of its old rivals for overseas empire—Portugal, Spain, France, and the Netherlands. Through the empire's capture of new colonies during those decades of war, the population of British dominions expanded fivefold, from 12.5 million in 1750 to 61 million in 1815.[100]

Not only did the Congress of Vienna draw relatively secure boundaries for Europe that would last another century; it also stabilized relations among its major states. After two centuries of continent-wide warfare, with millions of combat casualties and massive civilian costs, Europe would enjoy nearly a century of relative peace, ruptured only by regional conflicts, particularly at its southeastern periphery in the Balkans.[101]

With the continent stabilized and its maritime competitors eclipsed, Britain was freed to build a global empire and preside over the flowering of an alternative world order whose key principles had been germinating for several centuries. During the seventeenth century, the Dutch Golden Age had articulated new concepts of free trade, freedom of the seas, and human rights. Those broad principles had combined with similar British ideas when their monarchies merged during the Glorious Revolution. In the long eclipse of the Iberian age that followed, however, Britain had proved an imperfect practitioner of those lofty ideals, using its several victories over Spain to supplant the Iberian powers as the key country in the African slave trade.[102] Even so, by the end of the Napoleonic Wars, the principles of free trade and human freedom had gained sufficient moral force for their adoption, however imperfectly, as the foundation for international relations in the succeeding British imperial age.

As Britain set out to shape a new era, its diplomats might wave the banner of free trade to open markets for their country's commerce, but they would also use the principle as a pretext for military interventions that violated the sovereignty of nations worldwide. Even as the Royal Navy seized slave ships in the name of human freedom, Britain was building a vast colonial empire that would subjugate a quarter of humanity on racial rather than religious grounds. During the era of British global dominion, its anti-slavery campaign no doubt advanced the cause of human rights, but the oppressive conditions of its colonial rule would leave much room for further progress.

Louis and Edwina Mountbatten, last British viceroy and
vicereine of India, 1947 (Credit: Alamy)

Chapter 4
Britannia Rules the Waves

On April 22, 1848, the HMS *Grecian*, a sixteen-gun sloop flying the flag of the Royal Navy, was cruising off the coast of Brazil as part of Great Britain's anti-slavery patrols. Late that afternoon, Commander L.S. Tindal saw a "suspicious-looking brig running under all sail before the wind apparently steering for Bahia," where local sugar plantations relied on slave labor.

The commander had good reason to be suspicious. Despite the British navy's seizure of hundreds of Brazil-bound slave ships since 1808, the traffic in human beings was still thriving. In 1848 alone, slavers would smuggle a near-record total of 61,757 captive Africans into that country. The ship's likely destination, the city of Bahia (now called Salvador), was the second largest slave port in the Atlantic, home to a cruel commerce that enriched local elites.

After the HMS *Grecian* fired a warning shot and pursued the suspicious ship for several hours, British sailors finally succeeded in boarding the brig, the *Bella Miquelina*, just before midnight. Below decks they found 517 African men, women, and children chained and suffering from severe hunger. On the ship's other voyages over the previous six months, the death rate on board had reached 10 percent, with 95 of 895 captives lost on one crossing. On this trip, the *Bella Miquelina* had stopped at Lagos Island, on the West African coast, purchased its human cargo from a local leader, King Kosoko, and then spent 30 days crossing the Atlantic.

With the *Bella Miquelina* captured, Commander Tindal now faced a difficult choice. The Africans were clearly weakened from a full month of privation. Since the slave ship suffered "a want of provisions [and had] no more than the sweepings of the provision room to supply the slaves," the commander decided to put a prize crew aboard so that both vessels could sail to nearby Bahia to take on sufficient supplies for a voyage back across the Atlantic to the British colony of Sierra Leone, where an admiralty court would decide the ship's fate. Although Brazil had recently suspended a treaty allowing British inspection of its ships, the Royal Navy continued to seize slavers, and the Brazilians had done little to stop them. Calling at a Brazilian port should not have presented difficulties, so the commander's decision seemed sound.

En route, however, the ships were separated in a terrible storm that swept the South Atlantic. The next afternoon, the *Bella Miquelina*, now manned by the British prize crew, entered the vast Bay of All Saints on its own and dropped anchor just a hundred yards from shore at the port of Bahia. Within hours, Brazilian slave traffickers and local officials had called a meeting of men from the city's poorer parishes and promised them rich bounties in exchange for the slave ship's seizure. Whether in Rio, Pernambuco, or Bahia, slave traffickers, whom one British consul called the "pariahs of the human race," were powerful capitalists who bribed officials and bent local laws to protect their profitable trade.

A little more than five hours later, two market boats loaded with 80 armed men rowed toward the *Bella Miquelina*. The British prize crew "opened fire on the boats immediately on discerning their piratical intentions and continued until they retreated." After gunfire and swordplay lasting no more than fifteen minutes, three British sailors had suffered saber cuts, and three of the traffickers were dead.

British officials were outraged. Just 90 minutes after the attack, consul Edmund Porter called at the home of the local Brazilian governor, Manoel Messias de Leão, informing him of these events and requesting assistance. Several days later, the British ambassador Lord Howden, who happened to be in Bahia, wrote the foreign secretary in London, Lord Palmerston, saying: "Had the expedition from shore succeeded in re-capturing the slaver, there is no doubt that all the prize crew would have been murdered, and the vessel carried out of the harbor, with very little chance of ever identifying the perpetrators of the crime."

Just after dawn two days later, the HMS *Grecian* finally dropped anchor at Bahia. Commander Tindal quickly learned that he was caught in a dangerous situation. Determined to assert his nation's sovereignty, the Brazilian governor had launched an investigation into the attack and demanded that British sailors from the prize crew of the *Bella Miquelina* come to court for depositions. Fearing that mobs might assault the sailors, the commander told Consul Porter that his men would not participate. In reply, the governor grew more assertive, informing Porter that Brazilian authorities alone had the right to decide the fate of the slave ship. Amid these maneuvers, the consul arranged for a local Scottish import-export house, Wilson Sons, to deliver food and fresh water to the slave ship.

"Seeing that the *Bella Miquelina* is ready to sail," Tindal wrote the consul, "I am not able to consent that it might be forced to remain for an unspecified time anchored in this port, and I will depart immediately with her." Defying both the authority of Bahia courts and the governor's assertion of national sovereignty, the two ships soon sailed for Rio de Janeiro, where they took on provisions for the Atlantic crossing back to Africa. Six weeks later, the British vice-admiralty court at Freetown, Sierra Leone, ordered the confiscation of the *Bella Miquelina* for the crime of carrying slaves. As it had done for nearly 30 years, the court then released the Africans into Freetown, where British support groups provided some assistance for their transition to a new life.[1]

In all its high-seas drama and human tragedy, the history of the *Bella Miquelina* reveals both the extraordinary persistence of the African slave trade and the values of the British world order that tried to suppress it. From their own national history, most Americans think of the slave trade as an eighteenth-century phenomenon. But well into the nineteenth century, the human traffic proved remarkably resistant to abolition and remained critical for the plantation economies of Brazil and the Caribbean. Indeed, between 1831 and the early 1850s, slave ships smuggled 738,000 African captives into Brazil alone. The Royal Navy might have ruled the world's oceans in 1848, but when Commander Tindal and his men dropped anchor at that Brazilian port they confronted a resilient slave economy with tentacles that "reached deep into Bahian society." For well over a century, its trafficking syndicates had been a powerful presence in West Africa, even maintaining a major trading fort at Whydah, in Benin. Every facet of this incident reveals the exceptional power of the slave system that the Royal Navy was trying to crush.[2]

Inspired by Enlightenment ideals of liberty and Protestant principles of humanity's equality before God, the British Empire had committed its gathering strength to the extirpation of the slave trade—banning human trafficking by act of Parliament in 1807, abolishing slavery in its own Caribbean colonies in 1833, and deploying the Royal Navy for nearly 80 years to suppress the slave trade. Using its diplomatic clout, Britain signed anti-trafficking treaties with European states, Latin American republics, and African kingdoms. Once the transatlantic trade was suppressed in the 1860s, Britain continued its anti-slavery campaign in the Indian Ocean until the 1880s, leaving human trafficking there reduced but still not entirely eradicated. By its protracted duration alone, this ambitious human rights campaign became a defining aspect of the British world order.

A closer look at the interplay between British and Brazilian officials during those five days in Bahia reveals another key facet of this imperial age: informal empire. Beneath the penumbra of naval power it had cast over the South Atlantic, Britain could control events in this Brazilian port of one hundred thousand people through just five men—the ambassador, the ship's commander, Consul Porter, and a pair of Scottish brothers at Wilson Sons, one of many dynamic British firms ringing the coast of Latin America. Through such barely visible tendrils of trade, capital flows, and naval patrols radiating from London, Britain was, in effect, able to compromise the sovereignty of countries like Argentina, Brazil, China, Egypt, and Persia, thereby sustaining a vast informal empire that controlled much of the globe through a remarkably small cast of characters.

A Global Empire

By the time Commander Tindal seized that slave ship, Britain was building a new world order that repudiated key attributes of the earlier Iberian age, starting with the eradication of human trafficking and the virtual termination of that era's discrimination between Christian and pagan that had long legitimated the enslavement of Africans.

But even as its anti-slavery campaign was ending in the 1880s, Britain continued to embrace one key concept of the Iberian era: the right to strip conquered peoples of civil liberties and subject them to forced labor as unpaid workers in a colonial economy. In a striking instance of imperial duality, the British replaced the religious discrimination that had justified slavery with a racial hierarchy that legitimated European colonial rule over a third of humanity—peoples whom imperialist poet Rudyard Kipling infamously called "lesser breeds without the Law."[3] Even if one accepts that colonialism's denial of civil liberties was less degrading than outright slavery, the loss of national sovereignty and civil rights still made this new imperial era, at best, a halfway house on a continuing path toward human liberation.

Britain's global empire and its new world order had emerged from the long decades of its war against Napoleon. In those years, London had mobilized a million soldiers and sailors to conquer foreign lands, so increasing the population of its empire from just 12.5 million in 1750 to 200 million by 1820. While the whole world felt the growth of British power, its expansion was greatest in the Mediterranean, southern Africa, and the Indian Ocean.[4]

During the era of the Napoleonic Wars, the Royal Navy made the Mediterranean into a latter-day *mare nostrum* (our sea), capturing permanent bases on the islands of Malta and Corfu, while turning the weakened Ottoman Empire into a buffer state to stop possible Austro-Hungarian and Russian expansion into that sea. Britain had also taken full control of the Indian Ocean—capturing Cape Town, South Africa, and Sri Lanka from the Dutch; seizing the island of Mauritius from the French; subduing pirate sheikhdoms in the Persian Gulf; opening ports on the Malay Peninsula at Penang and Singapore; and sending its first settlers to Australia. Finally, the British largely completed their conquest of the vast Indian subcontinent. Even so, they did not yet have an empire in the normal sense of possessing extensive colonies. Given London's "preference for 'trade' over 'dominion,'" its imperium was still what historian Vincent Harlow described as "a chain of trading ports, protected at strategic points by naval bases."[5]

The duration and devastation of the Napoleonic Wars created what another historian, C.A. Bayly, called "the first true world crisis since the Mongol invasions of the thirteenth century," from which Great Britain would emerge with "the ideological and political will for a more vigorous world empire." While Portugal had dotted the coasts of Africa and Asia with its fortified enclaves and Spain's Latin American colonies had produced much of the world's silver currency, Britain would expand upon both those attributes to forge history's first genuinely global empire. Portugal had achieved partial dominion over the Indian Ocean by seizing three of its four strategic choke points, but Britain would soon have all four (Cape Town, Suez, Hormuz, and the Straits of Malacca). Moreover, the Royal Navy would come to control all the waters around the "world island" of Eurasia and Africa as far as Singapore, while British dominion slowly covered much of those continents through direct and indirect imperial rule. Not only would the British pound serve as global reserve currency, but London would also preside over an expanding international system of industry, trade, and capital exports. Meanwhile, railroads, steamships, telegraph lines, and ultimately radio waves would weave the world together. By 1900, the social and economic impact of the British empire would be so profound that scholars have called its century of dominion the "first age of globalization."[6] In the fullest sense, the British imperial era would become a Promethean fire that forged a new world order far more pervasive than any that had come before.

Simultaneously, Britain's industrial revolution brought an energy transition that would move the world definitively beyond the wind and muscle power of the Iberian age. With ample supplies of low-cost coal and pioneering energy research by scientists like Michael Faraday and Lord Kelvin, Britain produced "important inventions . . . that generated and converted energy"—first, coal-fired steam engines starting in 1780, and then coal-driven electrical generators after 1880.[7]

Steam engines began powering factories in 1786, riverboats in 1810, railways in 1825, transatlantic steamships in the 1830s, and the Royal Navy's warships by the 1840s, while the country's coal production climbed steadily from 9 million tons in 1800 to a peak of 292 million tons in 1913.[8] Britain also abolished duties on coal exports and restrictions on the sale of its steam technology, making "the age of coal" a shared global experience. As steam energy spread around the world, global coal production would soar from 80 million tons annually in 1850 to 1.3 billion tons in 1914.[9]

By the 1850s, an armada of steam engines was transforming the nature of work worldwide—driving sawmills, threshing grains, husking rice, pulling gang plows, and crushing sugarcane. Coal-fired construction equipment sculpted the earth's surface, as steam shovels (patented 1839) moved mountains, steam dredges (1844) cut canals, and steamrollers (1867) flattened roadways. Between 1880 and 1900, the number of steam engines in the United States tripled from 56,000 to 156,000, accounting for 77 percent of all US industrial power.[10]

Coal was the catalyst for an industrial revolution that fused steam technology with steel production to make Britain master of the world's oceans. The discovery of the "hot blast" technique for removing impurities raised British iron production thirtyfold, just as the Bessemer and Thomas-Gilchrist processes expanded Europe's steel production from just 125,000 tons in 1861 to a phenomenal 32 million tons by 1913. Innovations in the design of boilers, propellers, and iron-plated hulls allowed British shipyards to launch efficient merchantmen like the 2,200-ton SS *Agamemnon*, which could steam 8,500 miles on a single load of coal, thereby cutting the China run from 90 to 65 days. Not surprisingly then, during the half century after 1860, British ships would make up more than a third of the world's merchant fleet.[11] Instead of extracting sugar profits from the sweat of slave labor on a few tropical islands, the British economy now exported capital and industrial goods to global markets.

Artists like the painter J.M.W. Turner celebrated the advent of steam power in canvases of a monumental scale once reserved for royal portraits or military triumphs. One painting of his depicts the sun setting metaphorically in the background as a squat black tug, spewing steam, tows a three-masted warship: the *Fighting Temeraire*, once triumphant at the Battle of Trafalgar, but now spectral white and stripped of its billowing sails as it heads to the breaking yards. Just as the *Temeraire* and its age of wind power are shown retreating into oblivion, another canvas of his portrays the "Great Western Railway" erupting out of the fog of the past, its steam locomotive almost bursting beyond the frame of the painting as it speeds Britain into the future.[12]

As the wind and muscle power of the Iberian age gave way first to steam and later to electrical and gasoline engines, humankind was slowly liberated from brute bondage in its many older forms—serfdom, peonage, indenture, and, above all, slavery. Indeed, the relationship between Britain's coal-fired industrial revolution and the abolition of slavery was not merely coincidental, but causal. Each step in slavery's eradication was foreshadowed by a new stage in Britain's use of coal-fired energy—including the introduction of steam power in mills and mines by the time Parliament banned the slave trade in 1807; the development of mobile steam engines for land and sea transport prior to the abolition of West Indies slavery in 1833; and the adoption of coal-fired steam power in almost all British industries by the 1850s, when the Royal Navy's anti-slavery patrols reached their coercive climax. Later, new forms of fossil energy—electricity and internal combustion engines—would render even the coerced labor of the imperial age redundant.

But liberation, like all social change of any consequence, came with unexpected costs. Progress won in the unearthing of fossil fuels from the planet's geologic store of carbon took a toll that increased invisibly every year, as carbon dioxide from coal smoke and internal combustion emissions began accumulating in the atmosphere. As Nobel laureate Paul Crutzen has noted, "growing global concentrations of carbon dioxide and methane" in the atmosphere "coincide with James Watt's design of the steam engine in 1784." Indeed, Britain and its industries accounted for 80 percent of global fossil fuel emissions in 1825 and 62 percent in 1850. By the end of the nineteenth century, the Swedish physicist Svante Arrhenius would publish the world's first report on the capacity of industrial emissions to cause global warming. By countless hours of painstaking manual calculations, he predicted with uncanny prescience and considerable precision that "the temperature in the Arctic regions would rise about 8 degrees to 9 degrees C., if the [carbon dioxide] increased 2.5 or 3 times its present value."[13]

Something as vast and complex as the British world order could not and did not appear suddenly like the goddess Athena, leaping fully armed from the head of father Zeus. Britain was the world's preeminent power for more than a century, but its dominance nevertheless evolved through two distinct phases. From 1815 to 1880, it largely oversaw an "informal empire" with a loose hegemony over client states worldwide. In the period of "high imperialism" from 1880 to 1940, however, the empire combined informal controls in countries like China, Egypt, and Iran with direct rule over colonies in Africa and Asia to encompass a full half of all humanity.

In its first half century as a global hegemon, Britain followed the vision of Lord Palmerston, whose policy of informal empire aspired to commercial access without territorial control. During his fifteen years as foreign secretary, he played the major powers against each other, thereby allowing Britain freedom of action to acquire a colony at Hong Kong and cultivate client states in Egypt, Spain, Ottoman Turkey, and Latin America. As prime minister for nearly ten years, he continued to promote the country's overseas interests without expanding its colonies. "Let us try to improve all these countries by the general influence of our commerce," he explained, "but let us all abstain from a crusade of conquest which would call upon us . . . the condemnation of all the other civilized nations." Should such "weaker and less civilized" countries fail to honor their trade treaties, however, then what he called a "display of superior strength," usually by the Royal Navy, could be necessary.[14]

Lord Palmerston, foreign secretary and architect of the
British Empire, circa 1850 (Credit: Alamy)

In parallel with this policy of informal empire, England's economy went through an extended transition as mercantilism, that older form of regulated, restrictive commerce, continued to deliver profits that capitalized a new age of industry, finance, and free trade. In a temporal overlap between eras, the older forms of controlled commerce persisted even while Britain was abolishing slavery in its Caribbean colonies and ending the East India Company's lucrative monopolies over Asian trade. As the industrial revolution gained momentum, Britain's share of world manufacturing grew from 47 percent in 1830 to 59 percent in 1860, overshadowing the United States at 13 percent and Germany at just 9 percent.[15]

When informal empire gave way to formal colonial rule in the period of "high imperialism" after 1880, Britain became one of a dozen different powers competing for colonies, a contest that plunged the planet into an orgy of conquest. By 1900, the world's fifteen empires had acquired 146 colonies covering 40 percent of the globe's land area and governing about 550 million people, a third of humanity—making this era, in the fullest sense imaginable, an imperial age.[16]

Despite growing competition, Britain's foreign trade also continued to expand as its banks sent the bulk of their liquid capital overseas, with investments worth nearly £4 billion earning profits of £200 million annually, about 10 percent of the national income.[17] British engineering firms followed that capital abroad, exporting rails, engines, and rolling stock to build transport grids across the globe, while its telegraph companies laid transoceanic lines for rapid communications.

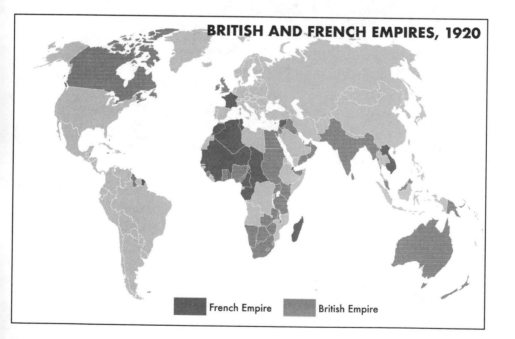

BRITISH AND FRENCH EMPIRES, 1920

French Empire   British Empire

The transition to high imperialism coincided with two important innovations in the use of fossil fuels. After drilling the world's first "gusher" at Oil Creek, Pennsylvania, the United States emerged in the 1860s as the world's premier oil producer, a position it would retain for much of the next century. Following rapid development in the 1870s of the vast Bibi-Heybat oil field near Baku, on the Caspian Sea, European prospectors made similarly rich strikes in Indonesia, Burma, and Iran. By century's end, such discoveries had created a sufficient supply of oil to enable a shift from steam to internal combustion engines in ships, trains, automobiles, and, ultimately, aircraft. Since oil had twice the thermal power of coal, the Royal Navy, under Winston Churchill's leadership as first lord of the admiralty in 1912, decided that all its warships would henceforth be oil-fired. The US Navy soon followed suit. While America had ample supplies of domestic oil, the Royal Navy had none and so invested in the Anglo-Persian Oil Company, providing it capital to develop a remote field in southern Iran and build a massive refinery at Abadan on the Persian Gulf. Oil soon became critical for transport, but it would not supplant coal as the primary energy source in Europe and the US until after World War II, making petroleum's later prevalence synonymous with Washington's world order.[18]

By contrast, electricity moved from introduction to omnipresence in a matter of decades. In 1882, Thomas Edison opened the world's first viable electrical generation station in lower Manhattan, bringing a new form of fossil energy into the home for illumination and onto the factory floor for more efficient production. Three years later, George Westinghouse installed an alternating-current system in Pittsburgh that overcame the distance limitations of Edison's network, thereby creating the technology for a later national electricity grid. In parallel developments, British engineers built the world's first major central power plant at Deptford, London, in 1888, capable of lighting two million electric bulbs. As electrical plants spread quickly, their generators were powered by the first coal-fired steam turbines, producing an unprecedented one hundred kilowatts of power and tying a knot between coal and electricity that persists to this day.[19]

Even as its territorial empire expanded, Britain's economic power ebbed. Its share of the world's industrial output dropped to just 14 percent in 1913, far behind the United States (at 47 percent) and Germany (21 percent). Britain also lagged in the production of chemicals, electrical goods, and steel products that lay at the heart of the "second industrial revolution."[20] From the rise of its global power after the Napoleonic Wars through its sudden demise in the 1956 Suez Crisis, energy, both coal- and oil-generated, shaped the destiny of the British Empire.

Britain's "Informal Empire"

In the decades after Napoleon's defeat, the expanding British Empire culti-vated indirect control through client states that remained nominally inde-pendent while still opening themselves to its trade and diplomatic leadership. Latin America was a prime example, as captured in a casual remark made right after national revolutions had swept away centuries of Spanish colonial rule. "Spanish America is free," said Foreign Secretary George Canning in 1824, "and if we do not mismanage our matters sadly, she is English."[21] With surprising speed, British companies spun a web of shipping routes along both coasts of the continent, tying it firmly to England. By 1860, Britain held 76 percent of Latin America's government bonds and controlled many of its mines, railways, and public utilities. By 1913, such holdings would make up nearly a quarter of all British overseas investments. The British navy was a constant presence, providing a sense of security for these ventures and in-tervening whenever it saw fit.[22] Instead of direct rule by colonial governors, British merchants and bankers handled shipping, insurance, and financial matters in major ports, thus making Latin America an integral part of Lon-don's informal empire of commerce and capital.

This minimalist imperial stance had its intellectual roots in the Enlight-enment critique of absolutist governments, particularly their restraints on individual liberty and free market commerce. In his book *The Wealth of Na-tions*, Scottish philosopher Adam Smith attacked mercantilism, which mo-nopolized trade on the supposition that wealth was finite. He argued instead that both partners would benefit by a free exchange of goods based on their comparative advantage. "To narrow the competition is always the interest of the dealers," said Smith, referring to mercantilism. "It comes from an order of men, whose interest is never exactly the same with that of the public, who have generally an interest to deceive and even oppress the public."[23]

Through Smith's influence and that of fellow Scottish Enlightenment thinkers who developed laissez-faire economics, Parliament rescinded mer-cantilist laws that had protected British commerce for centuries, starting with the abolition of the East India Company's monopolies on Asian trade. Pas-sage of the Great Reform Act of 1832, which expanded the electorate and abolished "rotten boroughs" controlled by rural gentry, was followed by free market reforms that would mark the end of mercantilism. In 1846, Parliament repealed the Corn Laws, which had privileged aristocratic estates by taxing imported grains used to make bread for the poor. Three years later, legislators also rescinded the highly restrictive Navigation Acts that had protected British shipping from foreign competition since the seventeenth century.[24]

In the long transition from mercantilism to free trade, the two trade triangles that had dominated British overseas commerce during the eighteenth century experienced contrasting fates. As noted earlier, under its anti-slavery policy, Britain systematically eliminated the key legs of the old transatlantic triangle, starting with the abolition of the slave trade in 1807. Simultaneously, however, a boom in British textile production created an insatiable demand for cotton that shifted the Atlantic trade circuit north from the Caribbean toward the United States, where it would sustain Southern plantation slavery for another half century. By contrast, Britain's Asian trade triangle continued with remarkably little change, reflecting as it did the key features of the policy of informal empire: the deployment of naval power to force open closed economies like China's, the development of overseas commerce to complement domestic industry, and the diplomatic manipulation of weaker states.

That Asian trade triangle took form through an extraordinary synergy between the mechanization of cotton spinning in Britain and the monopolization of opium cultivation in India. From the 1770s onward, the East India Company alone directed the opium commerce, from cultivation through processing, right up to export. From their refining factories at Patna and Benares in the heart of northeast India's opium growing district, senior British officers supervised two thousand Indian agents who circulated through poppy fields covering some five hundred thousand acres of prime land, extending credit and collecting raw opium from more than a million Indian farmers. Processed under strict supervision at these factories, the drug was dried into balls, packed into wooden chests weighing 140 pounds, and sent down the Ganges River to Calcutta for sale at auction to British and Indian merchants.[25]

China had banned opium as a "destructive and ensnaring vice," but British sea captains bribed mandarins in that country's southern city of Canton and smuggled the chests into China, where the company's brands commanded twice the price of inferior competing products.[26] In managing this trade, the East India Company prized stability above profit. For more than 20 years, the British held India's opium exports at four thousand chests, or 280 tons—just enough to finance its purchase of China's tea crop.[27]

That controlled commerce ended in 1833 when Parliament abolished all the East India Company's monopolies, freeing American and British merchant captains to expand their opium shipments to China. Determined to defend its market share against rival sources of opium from Turkey and the west coast of India, the company tried to "make competition unprofitable" by doubling its poppy cultivation in northeast India. As booming Indian production flooded into Canton, opium imports, still illegal under China's laws, increased nearly tenfold to 2,814 tons by 1840. Instead of the discreet smuggling of decades past, opium clippers crowded anchorages with their illicit cargoes, fending off Chinese customs officers with bribes and artillery barrages. Opium smoking was becoming a major social problem and would, by the end of the century, afflict 27 percent of the country's adult males—an unequaled level of addiction.[28]

Following some five years of this tawdry spectacle, China's emperor appointed the mandarin Lin Zexu as his special commissioner to Canton with broad powers to "go, examine, and act." After Lin dumped 95 tons of British opium in a trench filled with salt and lime, London dispatched a fleet of six warships and seven thousand troops for the First Opium War, capturing Canton and sacking a number of China's coastal cities. Once Britain finished giving China what Lord Palmerston called "a most exemplary drubbing," Beijing ceded Hong Kong in 1842, opened five new treaty ports to foreign trade, and agreed to pay an indemnity of $6 million—concessions that would soon make China part of Britain's informal empire.[29]

During the half century that the East India Company had monopolized northeast India's production, opium exports were both highly profitable and carefully balanced—with £21 million in opium and cotton goods shipped from India to China; £20 million in Chinese tea sent to Britain; and £24 million worth of British textiles and machinery imported back into India.[30] It was that last leg, the export of textiles to India, that tied this Asian trade to Britain's ongoing industrial revolution as the third critical area of technological transformation, after iron production and steam energy.

The industrialization of textile production had surprisingly humble origins. In 1771, Richard Arkwright, an uneducated barber and wigmaker, developed a machine for spinning cotton fibers into thread and built the world's first textile mill on a riverbank in the British Midlands. Eight years later, a textile worker named Samuel Crompton invented the spinning mule, which cut the cost of yarn manufacture and gave Britain an enormous advantage over its main competitor, Bengal in northeast India, then a major producer of both hand-spun thread and handicraft textiles.[31] Although a seemingly small innovation, the mechanized spinning of thread, by far the most labor-intensive part of textile production, gave Britain an edge in making this essential good that it would parlay, over the next half century, into a global commercial reach.

In another critical innovation, the Scots inventor James Watt perfected the steam engine to drive rotary motion, which would then be applied to spinning and weaving.[32] Of the 325 engines Watt manufactured by 1800, nearly a third were installed in textile mills.[33] By 1812, there were five million mule-driven spindles operating in Britain, cutting the time needed to produce one hundred pounds of cotton yarn from 50,000 hours for an Indian hand-spinner to just three hundred hours for a British factory worker. Britain's textile exports to India surged, virtually eliminating Bengal's textile exports by 1860 and displacing 560,000 Indian workers. By then, the main British mill district, in Lancashire, was almost completely steam powered and was burning six million tons of coal annually.[34]

This textile boom also transformed Britain's other trade triangle, in the North Atlantic. In 1793, as the industrialization of British cloth production accelerated, a clever Yankee engineer named Eli Whitney invented a simple machine, the cotton gin, that eliminated the labor-intensive process of separating the plant's seeds from its fibers, making the short-fiber American varieties internationally competitive. As cotton quickly became king, US production surged from just 3,000 bales (weighing five hundred pounds each) to 732,000 by 1830. When plantation owners began the process of moving 835,000 slaves from settled areas on the Atlantic coast to the rich soils of a cotton frontier in the Mississippi Delta, Washington decided to fully open up those lands through the forced expulsion of Native Americans. After 1830, nearly 60,000 members of five tribes—the Cherokee, Creek, Choctaw, Chickashaw, and Seminole—were forcibly marched to Oklahoma on a "Trail of Tears" marked by mass mortality from cold and starvation. On the eve of the American Civil War in 1860, three million African American slaves were producing 4.5 million bales of cotton annually to supply 350,000 British power looms that employed 440,000 workers. Shipments of raw cotton to Britain represented over half of all US exports, while finished cotton textiles made up a similar share of British exports.[35]

The surge in US exports of raw cotton helped change the character of transatlantic commerce. As Britain abolished its own slave system in the Caribbean by degrees, it came to rely on American plantation slavery. In the process, Atlantic commerce shifted north to form an entirely new triangular exchange that carried cotton from the Southern states of the US across the Atlantic to the port of Liverpool. British manufactured goods would then be transported back to Manhattan, and from there down the East Coast to the South.[36] Slavery, of course, remained the driving force in this commercial circuit, adding intensity to the debate over its abolition on both sides of the Atlantic.

Even as steam power transformed factory work in the early nineteenth century, the Southern slave plantation remained a surprisingly productive form of agriculture. Thanks to a mix of the grimmest sorts of coercion, violence, and material incentives, the typical slave field hand was, according to economic historians, "harder working and more efficient than his white counterpart." Right to the eve of the Civil War, the Southern plantation economy remained profitable, earning a 6 percent return from cotton sales; enjoying an annual 7.6 percent capital gain on the rising value of slaves between 1850 and 1860; and even experiencing, in that decade, a rapid expansion of cotton cultivation in the "New South" of Arkansas, Louisiana, and Texas.[37]

With the South firmly wedded to its lucrative slave system and the North determined that this moral abomination should end, a civil war over the issue of slavery was the logical outcome. Reflecting the enormity of the issues at stake, that war was hard-fought for four years and left 750,000 soldiers on both sides dead—more than in all other US wars combined.[38] As the British Royal Navy was discovering in its simultaneous effort to abolish the Brazilian slave trade, armed force would prove essential in the eradication of a plantation system whose exceptional profitability had persisted for four centuries.

The Abolition of Slavery

After dominating the transatlantic slave trade and profiting from Caribbean plantation labor, Britain was on the threshold of an extraordinary reversal. In the last years of the Iberian age, the morality and legality of slavery had faced sharp challenges in both Europe and the Americas. As Enlightenment ideals swept through England, both secular and religious thinkers concluded that slavery was legally and morally wrong. Philosopher Adam Smith branded slave owners "sordid." His colleague in the Scottish Enlightenment, law professor John Millar, remarked on the hypocrisy of America's founding fathers, who spoke of "the inalienable rights of mankind" but had no scruples about denying their slaves "almost of every right whatsoever." English Quakers formed the Society for the Abolition of the Slave Trade, and an Anglican evangelical, William Wilberforce, worked vigorously inside Parliament for the cause. As the abolition campaign spread, some 1.5 million petitioners among Britain's population of 10 million urged Parliament to end the slave trade. When a coalition government formed during the political turmoil of the Napoleonic Wars that included leading abolitionists, both houses of Parliament voted to end the trade. Yet even dedicated abolitionists like Wilberforce felt that the emancipation of those already enslaved in the British Caribbean should be left for some distant debate.[39]

Following the Napoleonic Wars, the Royal Navy had formed the West Africa Squadron, dispatching six ships under explicit orders: "You are to use every means in your power to prevent a continuance of the traffic in slaves." The task would prove far more difficult, costly, and protracted than anyone could have imagined. Seen from the sea, the West African coast was two thousand miles of seamless green, punctured only by an occasional river delta whose mangrove maze could easily hide a slave ship. In light tropical winds, plodding Royal Navy warships were no match for the slavers' speedy Baltimore clippers and had to hug the coast to have any chance of intercepting them, exposing British sailors to malaria and dysentery. When intercepted, the larger slavers were willing to fight, as near the Niger delta when the British sloop *Primrose* boarded the *Veloz Pasagera*, which was carrying 555 slaves, for hand-to-hand combat that left 46 Spanish sailors and three British dead. On the other side of the Atlantic, officials in the three main slave markets of Brazil, Cuba, and the US South colluded outrageously with the traffickers.[40]

Over the 60 years needed to suppress the transatlantic traffic, the West Africa Squadron grew to 32 vessels, capturing 1,800 slave ships and freeing some 160,000 Africans. Just as it did with the *Bella Miquelina*, the Royal Navy escorted most of the seized ships to the British colony of Sierra Leone in West Africa. There the vice-admiralty court awarded substantial prize money from sale of the seized vessels, and the Liberated Africans Department took charge of the freed slaves, registering them as British citizens.

Over the years, 82,000 freed captives passed through Sierra Leone—many remaining, some being recruited as soldiers, and others returning to their homelands. From 1816 to 1867, Britain spent, on average, 2 percent of its national income on this abolition campaign, making it what several scholars have called "the most expensive international moral effort in modern history." About seventeen thousand British sailors died during this effort, some in combat but most from endemic tropical diseases.[41]

By contrast, the US Navy's much-smaller Africa Squadron was generally ineffective. Following a period of many years that had yielded few seizures, the squadron intensified its operations on the eve of the Civil War by capturing 22 slave ships. Notable among them was the merchantman *Erie*, seized near the Congo River, which was bound for Cuba with a cargo of 893 slaves, most of them children, crammed inhumanely below decks. After setting the captives free in Liberia, the Navy vessel escorted the *Erie* back to New York City along with its skipper, Nathaniel Gordon—a resident of Portland, Maine, known among fellow slavers as "Lucky Nat" for his many daring escapes from anti-slavery patrols. After Gordon was convicted of piracy, a capital offense, his lawyers appealed to President Abraham Lincoln, who said: "Any man, who . . . stimulated only by avarice, can rob Africa of her children to sell into interminable bondage, I never will pardon." Although Gordon attempted suicide by taking strychnine, the prison doctor revived him. With his last words, he denounced Lincoln as "contemptible" before walking to the gallows inside the city's Tombs prison. He was the only slaver ever executed in the United States.[42]

After Parliament banned the slave trade, British abolitionists agonized for decades about whether to end slavery on plantations in the British West Indies, expressing concerns that Africans needed "preparation" for freedom. Rejecting that position, more committed abolitionists formed the Anti-Slavery Society in 1823, sending out rousing speakers and printing millions of pamphlets. Backed by wealthy West Indies sugar interests, however, Britain's ruling Tory Party regarded abolition as a "great folly" and blocked any progress during their long years in government. But the general elections of 1830 finally brought the reformist Whigs into government and their emancipation legislation before the House. At that delicate juncture, the African slaves themselves became the agents of their own liberation.[43]

In Jamaica's desperate Christmas Uprising of 1831, some 20,000 slaves fought for over a month against a planter militia and regular British red-coats, burning countless cane fields and plantation buildings before the revolt was crushed. The sordid spectacle of the mass hangings of 340 rebels inspired a renewed burst of anti-slavery agitation in Britain, until Parliament passed a bill emancipating all 775,000 slaves in the British West Indies and Bermuda while providing £20 million in compensation for the planters (and none for the ex-slaves).[44]

Throughout these decades of debate, the British government negotiated treaties with Brazil and Portugal that allowed the Royal Navy's anti-slavery patrols to intercept ships bound for the main slave markets in Brazil and Cuba, where sugar production was still soaring. When Brazil rescinded the treaty allowing searches of its ships, Britain's foreign secretary, Lord Palmerston, ordered the Royal Navy to seize slavers like the *Bella Miquelina* in their home waters anyway, producing pitched battles between British marines and Brazilian troops that cut the country's slave imports from 61,000 in 1848 to just 800 four years later. As Brazil's slave trade faded, however, the traffic to Cuba only expanded. After London and Washington finally began cooperating, the two powers applied sufficient pressure on Cuba to ban the traffic by 1867, effectively ending the transatlantic slave trade after 350 years. Reflecting on these events, Lord Palmerston declared, at the end of his long political career, that "the achievement which I look back to with the greatest and purest pleasure was forcing the Brazilians to give up their Slave Trade."[45]

As the transatlantic traffic came to an end, the Royal Navy shifted its anti-slavery patrols to the Indian Ocean, where, in the late nineteenth century, Arab traders were shipping some 1.6 million captives from the Swahili coast of East Africa to the Persian Gulf. With an abolitionist serving as British consul in Zanzibar and famed missionary David Livingstone exposing the traffic's horrors in East Africa, the campaign to end the "Arab slave trade" became one of the great causes of the Victorian age.[46] But the Royal Navy's East Indies Station had only eleven ships to cover three thousand miles of coast from Mozambique to the Straits of Hormuz, meaning it could not match the earlier effort in the Atlantic. Nonetheless, the British admiralty proclaimed the Indian Ocean slave trade "paralyzed" in 1884, and the campaign's flagship, the HMS *London*, was sold for scrap, finally and formally ending the anti-slavery campaign after nearly 80 years.[47]

High Imperialism

Almost at the moment its abolition effort ended, Britain began moving beyond informal empire to embrace direct colonial rule that created new forms of human bondage. As European colonial regimes expanded across Africa and much of Asia, they usually imposed a labor tax requiring their subjects to work for weeks or even months without pay on roads and canals, while stripping them of their civil liberties—including property rights, due process under law, freedom of expression, and the fundamental right to choose their own government.

More than any other event, the Indian Mutiny of 1857 precipitated this shift to direct colonial rule, on both the subcontinent and in the wider British Empire. During its piecemeal occupation of India in the early nineteenth century, the East India Company had preserved some 560 princely states, producing a crazy quilt of indirect rule that reflected London's preference for informal empire. Under the imperious Governor-General Dalhousie, however, the British Raj began centralizing authority—annexing princely states, dismissing influential Indian tax collectors, and imposing strict discipline upon its two hundred thousand Indian sepoy soldiers.[48]

All the tensions of this transition erupted when three regiments of Indian sepoys mutinied in 1857, killing their English officers. As violence swept spontaneously along the Grand Trunk Road across northern India, the rebels attacked several cities and massacred British civilians. After the rebel soldiers occupied the Mughal capital at Delhi and made its aging emperor their symbolic leader, British forces laid siege to the city until they finally breached its walls. They then proceeded to slaughter civilians indiscriminately and execute rebels in a spectacle of horrific cruelty.[49]

In the aftermath of that atrocious denouement, the British crown abolished the East India Company and formed the Indian Civil Service, which used 1,000 carefully selected Britons, backed by 70,000 British soldiers, to rule 300 million Indians. By 1876, the British had consolidated sufficient control over this vast colony to proclaim Queen Victoria the empress of India in a grand spectacle, complete with maharajahs parading on elephants before a British viceroy, who was seated atop an 80-foot-high dais.[50]

That sweeping change in India also marked the start of an age of empire worldwide that would subject a third of humanity to colonial rule, which was invariably marked by economic exploitation and institutional racism, plus numerous pacification campaigns with high casualties. If high imperialism meant servitude for millions in Asia and Africa, it also brought opportunity for Europe's many poor. As the twentieth century began, Britain's steamship lines, along with their French and German competitors, crisscrossed the oceans on safe, scheduled routes, carrying a hundred million migrants to better lives in Australia and the Americas.[51] Telegraph companies laid 234,000 miles of submarine cables linked to a million miles of landlines, circulating news worldwide at the rate of 40 words per minute.[52] Railroads crossed the continents—North America in 1869, Eurasia in 1904, South America in 1910, and Australia in 1917.[53]

At the epicenter of it all lay London, which became history's first great global city, with seven million residents. As home to the Bank of England and two dozen merchant banks, the City of London at the heart of the metropolis served as the epicenter of the global economy through overseas investments of £3.8 billon and the pound sterling's role as the world's reserve currency.[54] Just to its west were the Inns of Court, a cluster of Elizabethan-era courtyards that housed the city's legal chambers, the embodiment of England's rule of law. Farther on lay the West End theater district, bohemian Soho's cradle of creativity, and Fleet Street, headquarters for the Reuters news service and the world's largest newspapers.[55] Nearby was the official quarter, with Buckingham Palace and the Houses of Parliament, rebuilt after a fire as a gothic fantasy structure crowned by an iconic clock tower. In the opposite direction lay the gritty East End docklands that covered a bend in the River Thames to receive the world's commerce, surrounded by the fetid slums that inspired Charles Dickens's novel *Oliver Twist*. While tunnels for transport, water, and sewage burrowed beneath the streets, countless chimneys burning coal for heat and light cast a permanent canopy of gray soot over the city that blotted out the sun and periodically came to ground as lethal "black fogs," killing thousands.[56]

Adding steel to this global array, the Royal Navy's three hundred warships ruled the seas from a worldwide network of 30 bastions, dominating maritime choke points from Gibraltar to the Straits of Malacca and hinged at the Suez Canal, whose completion in 1869 had halved the sailing distance from London to Bombay. British sea power thus secured the North Atlantic, Mediterranean, and Indian Ocean.[57] With a standing army of only 99,000 men, the entire defense budget consumed just 2.5 percent of the country's gross domestic product—an extraordinary economy of force that allowed a small island nation to sustain a formal and informal empire that covered nearly half the globe.[58] "England without empire," proclaimed the colonial secretary, Joseph Chamberlain, in defense of those global commitments, "would be a fifth-rate nation, existing on the sufferance of its more powerful neighbours."[59]

Joseph Chamberlain, British secretary for the colonies, 1900 (Credit: Alamy)

By 1910, the British Empire encompassed more than 412 million people—about 23 percent of humanity—and covered 12.3 million square miles, or 22 percent of the world's land area. That formal empire was divided into crown colonies and the autonomous dominions (Australia, Canada, New Zealand, and South Africa), while its hegemony extended to half of humanity through informal control over vast areas (Egypt, Persia, China's coast, and much of South America). Eager to share in Britain's success, rival European powers claimed slices of Africa and Asia, while Japan and the United States joined the race for Asian territories in the 1890s, with Tokyo taking Korea and Taiwan as Washington occupied the Philippines and annexed Hawaii. Most imperial powers held just one or two colonies, such as the Belgian Congo or the Netherlands East Indies, although the French Empire was more expansive, covering 4.3 million square miles in Africa and Southeast Asia and boasting a population of 62 million.[60]

Just as the persistence of slavery did not diminish its inhumanity, so the extraordinary reach of colonialism cannot conceal its transgressions. Apart from forced labor, colonized peoples were subjected to the daily degradation of arbitrary arrest, heavy taxes, land confiscation, and political controls that were all justified by their supposed racial inferiority, their inherent unfitness for self-rule.

The Ideology of Racial Difference

Only a year after Britain concluded its anti-slavery campaign, the scramble for colonies in Africa started in earnest, driven by a new form of human hierarchy dressed in the guise of scientific racialism. Although the 1814–1815 Congress of Vienna had launched the British era, it was the 1885 Berlin Conference on Africa that articulated the principles of human rights and imperial sovereignty that became synonymous with Britain's world order.

As tensions among European powers arose over the division of Africa, Germany's iron chancellor, Otto von Bismarck, convened a conference to set rules for rival colonial claims. Much as Portugal and Spain had divided the world at Tordesillas, so the fourteen imperial powers that met in Berlin four centuries later issued a self-serving justification for carving up an entire continent. Reflecting theories of racial difference derived from the pseudoscience of Social Darwinism, representatives of the countries meeting there agreed "to watch over the preservation of the native tribes, and to care for the improvement of the conditions of their moral and material well-being, and to help in suppressing slavery, and especially the slave trade." Through the malign magic of imperial rhetoric, this declaration referred to African "tribes" rather than "nations" or "peoples," thereby justifying suspension of their sovereignty to allow their uplift by supposedly truly civilized powers.[61]

Masked by this racialist doctrine, the colonization of Africa after the Berlin Conference was extraordinarily brutal. From the scramble's start in the 1880s through its end in the 1930s, imperial powers old and new seized territory with capricious abandon, crushed resistance with unrestrained violence, and produced one of the most sordid, sustained records of plunder in human history.

Just as Christianity legitimated slavery during the Iberian age, so a distortion of evolutionary science formed the ideological framework for the British imperial era, creating a racial hierarchy to excuse both the cruelty of European conquest and the harshness of its colonial rule in Africa and Asia. The scientific classification of flora and fauna had begun when famed Swedish naturalist Carl Linnaeus published his 1735 *Systema Naturae*, categorizing all living things by a taxonomy of genus and species. As an afterthought in a later edition of his work, he divided humanity into four "varieties" based on continent and skin color—specifically, *Europaeus albus* (white European), *Americanus rubescens* (red American), *Asiaticus fuscus* (brown Asian), and *Africanus niger* (black African). In 1795, the German professor Johann Friedrich Blumenbach, considered the father of physical anthropology, separated humanity into a hierarchy of five higher and lower races, judging a European cranium from the Caucuses as "the most beautiful form of the skull, from which . . . the others diverge by most easy gradations," thereby creating the racial term "Caucasian."[62]

Following the publication of Charles Darwin's *On the Origin of Species* in 1859, numerous European popularizers espoused a spurious analogy between the evolution of natural species and the advance of human societies, fostering the hierarchy of racial difference that came to be known as Social Darwinism. As colonial conquests accelerated in the Victorian age, Darwin's discovery of evolution merged with erroneous racial theories to effectively erase the Enlightenment belief in human equality that had inspired the British anti-slavery campaign. To create a racial hierarchy of cognitive ability, European museums collected indigenous skulls and scientists measured differences in shape, weight, and cranial capacity. The Royal College of Surgeons in London had a large display of 350 skulls from Australian aboriginals, prized as the lowest rung on this supposed evolutionary scale. In Philadelphia during pre-Civil War decades, a local doctor, Samuel Morton, collected 867 skulls from around the world and used them to argue for inherent racial differences between "Caucasoid" and "Negroid" dating back to the slaves of ancient Egypt—findings a medical journal in the slave-holding South hailed for "giving to the negro his true position as an inferior race." Although the biologist Stephen Jay Gould would later find that "most of the major data sets presented in the name of racial ranking contained evident errors," prejudice shaped science in ways that favored a belief in inherent racial difference. Indeed, the naturalist Alfred Russel Wallace, co-creator of the concept of evolution, said human struggle would produce "the inevitable extinction of all those low and mentally undeveloped populations with which Europeans come into contact."[63] After observing the European extermination of aboriginal peoples in Australia and South America, Darwin himself wrote: "The varieties of man may seem to act upon each other in the same way as different species of animals—the strong always extirpating the weaker."[64]

In its widest application, Social Darwinism developed the theory of "recapitulation," arguing, as that polymath Victorian popularizer Herbert Spencer put it, that "the intellectual traits of the uncivilized . . . are traits recurring in the children of the civilized." In other words, imperialists came to argue that "childlike" Africans and Asians required colonial tutelage to climb the evolutionary ladder toward national maturity—a sentiment Rudyard Kipling captured in a poem that urged America to "take up the White Man's Burden" in the Philippines by sending forth "the best ye breed" to uplift "your new-caught sullen peoples / half devil and half child." In the same spirit, the viceroy of India, Lord Curzon, who proclaimed the British Empire "so great an instrument for the good of humanity," told a friend that the people he ruled were "crooked-minded and corrupt . . . I dare say I am talking rather like a schoolmaster; but after all the millions I have to manage are less than school children."[65]

By the start of the twentieth century, a growing mass media in Europe and America was popularizing these Social Darwinist ideas of racial hierarchy in newspapers and magazines, and even through world fairs—particularly the St. Louis Exposition of 1904, which was visited by half of all American adults. A former chief of the US Bureau of Ethnology, William J. McGee, used the simultaneous presence of the Olympic Games in St. Louis to stage a racial "Special Olympics" at the fair that produced a spurious hierarchy of physical ability, with Nordics at the apex and Native Americans at the bottom.[66] At the center of the sprawling fairgrounds was the Philippine exhibit inhabited by 1,200 Filipinos, largely tribal minorities, who performed sensational shows of archery, ritualized spear combat, and dog eating. Driving home the Social

Darwinist message, the official *World's Fair Bulletin* published a photomontage titled "The Evolution of the Filipino" that described the short black hunter-gatherers in loincloths as the "lowest type humans in the Islands" and the fair, mixed-race Spanish mestizos as "highly educated, refined."[67]

In spite of its swift repudiation by rigorous anthropological research, this doctrine of racial difference allowed Americans to justify their conquest of the Philippines and Europeans to view the colonization of Africa as part of a natural order that would allow the higher races to uplift those supposedly "lesser breeds."[68]

The Scramble for Africa

With dispersed populations and localized kingdoms, Africa's sprawling savannahs, dense forests, and thick jungles became, in the Victorian age, a vast canvas for empowered Europeans to plot epic explorations and draw sweeping lines of colonial division. From every quadrant of the coast, European adventurers plunged inland to explore, enticed by rivers that seemed to them like silvery, sinuous pathways to discovery; they were infatuated first with the hunt for the elusive source of the Nile, and then with the reconnaissance of the greatest and most difficult of them all, the Congo River. Although the press of the day celebrated the heroism of such exploits, exploration was serious imperial business, done to survey terrain and stake claims. In an age when names like Barth, Burton, Brazza, Livingstone, and Rhodes enraptured European imaginations, none could equal the outsized reputation of Henry Morton Stanley.

Born a bastard and raised in a miserable British workhouse, Stanley sought his fortune in America, serving in both the Confederate and Union Armies during the Civil War. Soon after, he began working as a journalist, and in 1871 the *New York Herald* dispatched him to Ethiopia to cover the British invasion of that ancient kingdom. After he scooped the competition by bribing a telegraphist to send his coverage in first, Stanley set off on another mission, hiking eight hundred miles across impassible terrain to find a missing Scots missionary—none other than Dr. David Livingstone. As he finally approached his quarry on the shores of Lake Tanganyika, Stanley uttered those famous words: "Dr. Livingstone, I presume?"[69]

In 1874, Stanley set out again with 353 Africans and three Europeans to follow a river from Lake Tanganyika that he thought might be the source of the Nile but that turned out to be the Congo, the world's second-largest river. After three years paddling 1,500 miles downstream, portaging around rapids, and shooting his way through African settlements, Stanley and just 115 survivors finally staggered into a colonial outpost near the Atlantic coast—accidentally accomplishing the heroic feat of crossing the continent. En route back to London to publish a memoir, *Through the Dark Continent*, Stanley was accosted at a French train station by emissaries from King Leopold II of Belgium. They proposed, unsuccessfully, that he return to Africa posthaste as the monarch's personal plenipotentiary.[70]

Henry Morton Stanley, British explorer, with African servant Kalulu, 1872 (Credit: National Portrait Gallery)

Little more than a year later, however, Stanley was indeed back in the Congo as the official representative of the International African Association, whose humanitarian-sounding title masked King Leopold's avaricious intent. Over the next five years, Stanley founded a private colony for the king there by supervising construction of trading stations along the Congo River, hauling two small steamboats around its lower cataracts, and forming a private army to extract treaties from 450 regional chiefs, which would grant Leopold a commercial monopoly over their territories. Meanwhile, back in Belgium, the king used the former US ambassador to Brussels, financier Henry Shelton Sanford, in a successful bid to lobby Washington for formal recognition of his fabricated claim to the Congo. Leopold quickly parlayed that diplomatic coup into similar concessions by France and Germany. Believing that its long-standing occupation of Angola was under threat, Portugal appealed to Germany's Chancellor Bismarck to resolve these rival claims.[71]

Hence the gathering at the 1884–1885 Berlin Conference. Seated at a horseshoe conference table beneath a giant map of Africa in Bismarck's official residence, diplomats from fourteen nations negotiated for three months to set the ground rules for Europe's continental land grab. The American delegation included the intrepid Stanley, back from the Congo, who commanded rapt attention as he described the landscape with lush adjectives. The senior US delegate, John Kasson, interjected a discordant note, arguing that international law recognized "the right of native tribes to . . . their hereditary territory," but German diplomats deftly sidelined any discussion of indigenous sovereignty, which could have sunk their colonial ambitions. Ignoring any African claims to their own lands, the conference agreed on a principle of "effective occupation" for establishing imperial sovereignty over territory, allowing European powers to spend the next 30 years slicing up Africa without sparking war among themselves.[72]

While France and Britain could expand from their respective footholds in Algeria and the Cape Colony, the Berlin Conference leveled the playing field for the weaker, arriviste powers—Belgium, Germany, and Italy. In the decade following the conference, Germany claimed large colonies, from Tanzania in the east to Namibia in the southwest. To check French expansion beyond their established enclave at Djibouti, the British encouraged Italian ambitions in the Horn of Africa, allowing them to occupy Eritrea and invade Ethiopia. After the ancient Ethiopian kingdom killed over half of their invading army at the Battle of Adowa in 1896, the Italians consoled themselves with substantial coastal strips of Eritrea and Somalia before seizing Libya from the Ottomans. In perhaps the greatest coup of the conference, King Leopold secured diplomatic recognition for his International African

Society's claim to the entire Congo and then quickly dropped the human-itarian facade, making the continent's largest colony his private property, which he called the Congo Free State.[73]

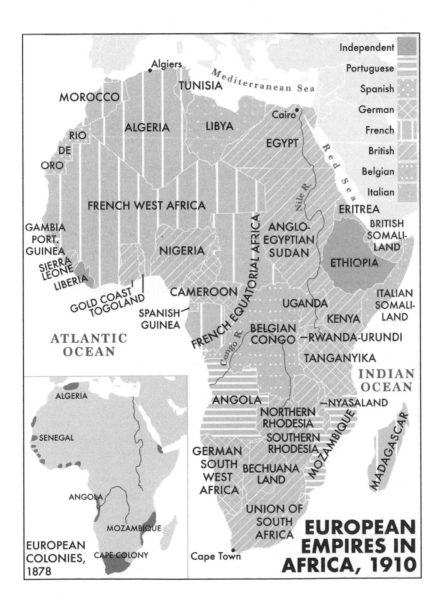

EUROPEAN EMPIRES IN AFRICA, 1910

EUROPEAN COLONIES, 1878

Even in an era indulgent of colonial excess, Leopold's rule over the Congo proved so inhumane that it became the greatest scandal of the imperial age. Despite the so-called Berlin Doctrine, which held that African tribes should be protected, the king's militia of nineteen thousand men, the Force Publique, press-ganged villagers for forced labor and punished any recalcitrance with maiming or death. European officers quickly descended into brutality, notably the Belgian commander at Stanley Falls, Léon Rom, who decorated his post with skulls and a gallows. "The black man's principal occupation," wrote Rom in an 1899 memoir justifying such harsh acts, "consists of stretching out on a mat in the warm rays of the sun, like a crocodile on the sand."[74]

Once the Irish Dunlop Company started manufacturing inflatable rubber tires for the bicycle craze of the 1890s, soaring demand for raw rubber made this capricious cruelty systematic. By taking hostages or severing hands to enforce rubber collection quotas from villagers, the Force Publique was soon extracting an imperial bonanza of eleven million pounds of rubber a year. The impact was devastating, causing some ten million deaths and reducing the Congo's population by 50 percent during the three decades of the king's rule—a mass mortality rate approaching Spain's impact on Mexico in the sixteenth century.[75]

For many years, Leopold posed as a reformer, cultivating allies among an anti-slavery movement that had revived during the 1880s in response to reports of Arab trafficking in Central Africa. Unlike the earlier, exclusively Protestant abolition movement, the current campaign had strong Catholic participation and was led by Cardinal Charles Lavigerie, founder of the Société des Missionnaires d'Afrique. Through Lavigerie's influence, Pope Leo XIII issued an encyclical (*In Plurimus*, 1888) regretting that "each year 400,000 Africans are usually thus sold like cattle, about half of whom, wearied out by the roughness of the tracks, fall down and perish there." Seeking to control the cardinal's movement, Leopold hosted a major international slavery conference at Brussels that culminated in an agreement among seventeen nations "to put an end to the Negro slave trade by land as well as by sea." The king also won the cardinal's help in persuading Belgian Catholics to support a massive government loan for his private colony.[76]

Despite King Leopold's sedulous efforts to control press coverage about his personal colony, missionaries began leaking horrific anecdotes about life in that colonial charnel house. With confidential information from officials of the Congo Free State and photos of gruesome atrocities taken by a missionary, English human rights reformer Edmund Morel published exposés that prompted official inquires by Britain and Belgium. Both documented a forced-labor regime driven by beatings, burning of villages, hostage taking, and maiming. Upon reading such damning conclusions, the Congo's acting governor-general, Paul Costermans, fell into a depression and committed suicide. As abolitionists had done a century before, Morel and his fellow reformers used this careful documentation to stoke public outrage with the aid of renowned writers who crafted a devastating portrait of King Leopold's Congo—Mark Twain by mockery, Arthur Conan Doyle by denunciation, and Joseph Conrad by fiction, in the form of the novella *Heart of Darkness*, born of his own bitter experience as a Congo riverboat captain.[77]

King Leopold II of Belgium, ruler of the Congo Free State, 1903 (Credit: Alamy)

While international, primarily Protestant critics exposed the problems with the Congo Free State, it was left to Belgium and its Catholics to fight for a solution, notably a Jesuit professor of moral theology at the University of Louvain. In his sharply critical 1906 book, *La question congolaise*, Arthur Vermeersch argued persuasively that the monstrosity of Leopold's private colony had to be replaced by responsible Belgian administration. In 1908, as such pressure mounted, the Belgian government finally wrested the Congo from the king's grasp, paying him a premium to transfer his private colony to state control.[78]

This small but significant change revealed an important attribute of the British world system at its peak. Despite a seeming free-for-all in the scramble for Africa, there were still international standards for the recognition of a legitimate state. Just as the Vatican could sanction crowned sovereigns for moral failings during the Iberian age, so the British imperial system required that all states, whether colonial or national, had to meet certain informal standards for human rights that would later be codified by international conventions under Washington's world order.

The savage excesses of Leopold's regime had ended, but the systematic mobilization of coerced labor continued in colonial Africa. Even after all the furor over Leopold's cruelties, the Belgian Congo still required a full 60 days a year of unpaid "communal labor" from its African subjects for the next 30 years—the same servitude that had been the source of all that abuse by the Congo Free State. Under Belgium's colonial labor code, African workers were penalized by forced labor and could be whipped by their employers. For the next half century, the people of the Belgian Congo faced what historian Julia Seibert called a daily "reality of violence, coercion and exploitation."[79]

In its singular focus on King Leopold, the human rights movement also overlooked similar systems of forced labor in other African colonies. Like the Belgian Congo, Portuguese Angola required that villagers provide 60 days a year of unpaid labor; similarly, British colonies demanded up to 30 days, and French West Africa imposed an annual labor tax ranging from five to twelve days.[80] In Asia, the Netherlands East Indies exacted 66 days of forced labor until 1870 and 26 days into the 1920s, while French Indochina stipulated 16 days.[81]

Apart from this forced labor, European empires also recruited legions of indentured workers through long-distance migration. Between 1834 and

1916, more than a million Indians migrated to British colonial plantations worldwide, while about three million Chinese contract workers traveled to Southeast Asia, the Pacific, and the Caribbean. On French rubber plantations near Saigon, some 50,000 Vietnamese contract workers endured floggings with leather whips and experienced extremely high death rates. Similarly, Assam's tea plantations in northeast India relied on "armed musclemen" to recruit 710,000 workers, who were paid about half of free market wages and suffered a mortality rate of 25 percent. Given the coercion common to plantations worldwide, scholars have branded the indentured labor of the imperial age as a "new system of slavery."[82]

Colonialism's expropriation of up to 20 percent of the working lives of poor farmers in Africa and Asia may have been less extreme than outright slavery, but it was nevertheless a severe exploitation and gross transgression of human rights. All the reformers' careful documentation and moving prose had successfully framed the Congo Free State as a unique case, an aberration, rather than the cautionary tale about colonialism that it should have been. It would be another 40 years before the world recognized that empire's excesses were beyond repair and required more fundamental change. Once again, inanimate energy would play an invisible role in facilitating social reform. With the emergence after 1900 of new forms of fossil fuel energy from electricity and internal combustion engines, the need for masses of raw muscle power would decline, rendering coerced colonial labor economically redundant well before its formal abolition after World War II.

Africa's Colonial Wars

Apart from the onerous burden of forced labor, the chief hallmark of high imperialism in Africa was a succession of colonial wars fought with such a marked imbalance of military power that they were often little short of slaughter. In the half century of colonial conquest that followed the Berlin Conference, almost every imperial power seized territory with unrestrained violence, tracking a trail of blood across the continent—the Belgians rapaciously in Congo, the British relentlessly in Sudan and South Africa, the Italians disastrously in Ethiopia, the Germans mercilessly in Namibia and Tanzania, and the French endlessly in North Africa.[83]

Among these atrocities, the German pacification of Namibia was exceptional for its extreme violence that produced what historian Jürgen

Zimmerer has called "important precedents" for later Nazi "genocidal think-ing." When Africans resisted an influx of colonists in 1904, the commanding general launched "the first German genocide" by proclaiming: "I will anni-hilate the rebelling tribes with rivers of blood." Over the next four years, his troops massacred nearly 80,000 people—well over half of the Herero and Nama tribes—using murderous "concentration camps," discriminatory race laws, and tactics of total "annihilation" later manifest in the Holocaust.[84]

As the world's premier power, Great Britain possessed greater force and used it more frequently than any other empire, fighting 72 of these small wars during Queen Victoria's long reign (1837–1901). In their African cam-paigns, British troops would carry two weapons that gave them overwhelm-ing firepower—the new Martini–Henry rifle that fired six shots per minute and the Maxim machine gun that sprayed five hundred rounds a minute.[85] For Social Darwinists, Britain's ability to slaughter Africans in such spectac-ular numbers was clear evidence for the survival of the fittest and Europe's right to rule the tribes of that "dark continent."

At every step in their advance across Africa, British troops used supe-rior firepower to slaughter more numerous native forces. When Egyptian nationalists seized power, 25,000 British troops landed on the shores of the Suez Canal in 1882, routed the Egyptian forces in a hard-fought battle on the road to Cairo, and then captured the city at a cost of only 57 soldiers killed. In the aftermath, the British imposed an informal protectorate that, along with the purchase of a controlling interest in the Suez Canal from Egypt's bankrupt ruler, gave them informal dominion over this nominally indepen-dent nation for the next 70 years. To control such a critical nexus of empire, Evelyn Baring, grandson of the founder of Barings Bank, served for a quarter century as British consul, playing puppet master to Egypt's ruling khedives while his corps of 662 British "advisers" did the same for its bureaucracy.[86]

At the continent's antipode in South Africa, diamond king Cecil Rhodes, acting as the British Empire's advance man, found the Maxim gun essential in capturing much of southern Africa for his private companies that soon became crown colonies. Arriving in South Africa to make his fortune in 1870, Rhodes, a poor parson's son, formed the De Beers Mining Company to monopolize the diamond mines at Kimberley and constructed "closed compounds" with circumscribed civil liberties for his Black workers, thereby creating a model for South Africa's later apartheid system.[87] After the Berlin

Conference, London gave Rhodes a charter for his South Africa Company that covered all land between the Limpopo and Zambezi Rivers. To break the powerful Matabele kingdom, Rhodes dispatched seven hundred mercenaries armed with five Maxims, which cut down 1,500 African fighters in two bloody battles, subduing a territory that would later become the core of Southern Rhodesia (now Zimbabwe).[88]

Cecil Rhodes, South African diamond magnate, 1890 (Credit: Alamy)

The ultimate display of the weapon's power came in 1898 when General Herbert Kitchener, the dour commander of the Anglo-Egyptian army, marched south from Egypt into Sudan with 26,000 troops, armed with 80 artillery pieces and 44 Maxim machine guns, to destroy a Wahhabist Islamic revolt by desert tribes.[89] At Omdurman on the Nile, Kitchener's line of Maxims and artillery fired relentlessly for five hours against 52,000 attacking jihadists armed with muskets and swords, killing 10,800 of them while losing only 49 of their own. A young Winston Churchill, present as a war correspondent, surveyed a battlefield littered with body parts and called it, with unintended irony, "the most signal triumph ever gained by the arms of science over barbarians." The slaughter broke Wahhabist Islamic control over the country, making Sudan a British colonial protectorate for the next 50 years.[90]

At the other end of the continent, Britain's triumphal march across southern Africa ended in a brutal war against two republics, Transvaal and the Orange Free State, filled with Dutch settlers, known as the Boers, whose numbers were so small they could field only 42,000 troops for what would be a white-on-white struggle, rare in the annals of African conquests. A tense truce between the British Cape Colony and these inland Boer republics ended in 1886 when Transvaal struck a gold seam so rich that the city of Johannesburg was soon producing a quarter of the world's bullion. With the secret support of the British colonial secretary Joseph Chamberlain, Rhodes sent six hundred of his company police on a botched raid that failed to spark a British takeover of Transvaal. The Boers saw the raid as a harbinger of British conquest and prepared for war by importing German-made Mauser rifles and field artillery. [91]

Herbert Kitchener, commander, Anglo-Egyptian army,
1895 (Credit: National Portrait Gallery)

In October 1899, the Boers attacked, laying siege to several British set-tlements and keeping the empire's slender force of 22,000 soldiers on the defensive. After raising their troop strength to 87,000, the British launched a counteroffensive that ground down Boer resistance and captured their capitals at Pretoria and Bloemfontein. Instead of surrendering, the Boer commandos, agile horsemen and dead shots, harried the British forces with guerrilla tactics for another eighteen months. In response, London flooded the country with 450,000 troops, and General Kitchener adopted scorched-earth tactics to break Boer resistance—burning 30,000 farmhouses and forc-ing 160,000 settler civilians into concentration camps, where 28,000, mostly children, died of malnutrition.[92]

By war's end, Britain had exhausted its moral and material resources, expending much of its imperial prestige and spending £270 million, or 14 percent of its annual national income. Defeated but not broken, the Boers agreed to become a British dominion in exchange for self-government. Louis Botha, a former Boer commander, became premier of the Union of South Africa with several of his old commandos as cabinet members. In England, the Boer War condemned the long-serving Conservatives to a searing defeat in the 1906 elections and gave the reformist Liberal Party, in alliance with the new Labour Party, an opening to win power under leaders like David Lloyd George, who had denounced the conflict as a "war of extermination" that would "stain the name of this country."[93]

For the next 40 years, however, Africa would remain the prime hunting ground for late arrivals to the imperial scramble. While the Maxim guns of the Victorian age had been murderous, the Spanish and Italian use in Africa of mustard gas, which was banned in 1925 by the Geneva Protocol, proved merciless—causing severe burns, blinding, and internal bleeding on contact, as well as cancer long afterward.[94]

In the first such campaign, Spain tried to subdue 240 miles of the African coast between its two established enclaves at Ceuta and Melilla, which it grandly dubbed Spanish Morocco. When the local Berber tribes rebelled by forming the Republic of the Rif in 1921, the Spanish military launched a six-year pacification effort marked by aerial bombardments with mustard gas, tank operations in villages, and the amphibious deployment of 123,000 troops, who pressed the 12,000 Berber guerrillas mercilessly until they capitulated.[95]

While the world largely ignored the Rif War, public opinion was shocked by the ruthless Italian invasion of Ethiopia. Starting in 1935, Fascist dictator Benito Mussolini unleashed 230,000 troops—backed by seven hundred artillery pieces, 150 tanks, and 150 aircraft—against Emperor Haile Selassie's ill-equipped army, which had only four tanks and a dozen aircraft. Encountering unexpected resistance, Mussolini redoubled his deployments and rained over 80 tons of poison gas on the retreating Ethiopians. At the cost of just 4,300 dead, Italy's mechanized military killed 275,000 Ethiopians—casualties so disproportionate and cruel that they constituted a war crime.[96]

The Geopolitics of World Wars

These late colonial wars in Africa were signs of gathering strains on the British world order. During its century of hegemony, London's global strategy had required both the maintenance of a balance of power in Europe and the assertion of global dominance by a navy that not only protected the empire but secured world commerce. Through its control over the Suez Canal, which served as the strategic link between the Indian Ocean and the Mediterranean, the Royal Navy could assure the passage of the commodity imports and industrial exports that sustained the British Isles. Beneath this calm surface of global dominion, though, were strong riptides of imperial rivalry: Russia was reaching across Central Asia toward India, there were recurring clashes in the Balkans, the French were pressing competing claims to East Africa, and, above all, Germany was building a powerful navy of its own.[97]

As it turned out, the geopolitical strategy that had proved so effective for a peacetime empire would face difficulties when tested by rival powers during two world wars. Starting around 1900, Kaiser Wilhelm II assigned Admiral Alfred von Tirpitz, a self-styled strategic visionary, the task of building a navy large enough to discourage any British attack.[98] In less than a decade, however, that grand strategy collapsed when a genuine naval visionary, British first sea lord John "Jacky" Fisher, decided to build the world's first true battleship, the 17,900-ton HMS *Dreadnought*, driven by steam turbine engines and armed with ten powerful twelve-inch guns. Stunned by the news of the British breakthrough, Admiral Tirpitz countered with a billion-mark program to build his own 18,000-ton battleships, launching an arms race that would force Britain to raise its naval budget by 50 percent and ravage Germany's finances. As the Royal Navy drew ships homeward for defense, Britain had little choice but to jettison its stand-alone foreign policy and begin concluding mutual defense treaties with Japan, France, and Russia that would isolate Germany diplomatically. In 1905, Imperial Navy staff in Berlin war-gamed the outcome of a future Anglo-German conflict and concluded that a Germany cut off from the rest of the world would suffer "a financial and social crisis whose consequences were incalculable."[99]

Alfred von Tirpitz, admiral and architect of the German navy, 1905 (Credit: Library of Congress)

When World War I started, that predicted crisis was not long in coming. The Royal Navy was still sufficiently dominant to bottle up Germany's High Seas Fleet within its home waters and impose a maritime blockade that would cause mass starvation, leading to 763,000 German civilian deaths by war's end. Berlin tried to visit comparable privation upon Britain with unrestricted submarine warfare that sank 5,700 ships, but the Royal Navy's convoys and the sheer size of its merchant fleet made even such heavy losses sustainable. Determined to break the British blockade, Germany's entire High Seas Fleet of 83 ships, led by 6 dreadnoughts, steamed into the North Sea in May 1916 seeking a "decisive battle" of the sort once described by the American strategist Alfred Thayer Mahan. But a devastating shower of shells from a superior British Grand Fleet forced them to turn back, barely escaping annihilation in what became known as the Battle of Jutland.[100]

John "Jacky" Fisher, Britain's first sea lord and father of the
battleship, 1915 (Credit: Library of Congress)

In another strategic move, Britain attacked the Ottoman Empire, a German ally, at its southern frontier in the Persian Gulf, capturing the port city of Basra and securing the Anglo-Persian Oil Company's refinery at Abadan, thereby assuring the Royal Navy's fuel supply. After two more years of blood-soaked stalemate in the trenches on the Western Front, the German war effort collapsed amid crippling hunger—with its navy in open revolt, its army unwilling to fight, famished factory workers on strike, and the kaiser forced to abdicate.[101]

At the cost of a million dead, the British Empire emerged from World War I as the sole "global superpower." Despite all the self-serving rhetoric of freedom, the Versailles Peace Conference at war's end proved to be an imperial banquet, with the victor nations carving up the territories of the defeated Central Powers. In Africa, Britain acquired the former German territories of Tanganyika, Namibia, and portions of Cameroon and Togo, thus gaining an unbroken chain of colonies along the entire length of that vast continent, from Cairo to Cape Town. In the Middle East, it picked up Iraq, Jordan, and Palestine. In the Pacific, the British dominion of Australia was awarded German New Guinea, while New Zealand received German Samoa. By the time those peace talks were done, the British Empire was at the peak of its power with 450 million people under its rule.[102]

Twenty years later, World War II would replay the same geopolitical dynamic, although with a very different outcome for the British Empire. After testing the limits of the international system in Ethiopia and in the Spanish Civil War of the 1930s, the Axis powers—Nazi Germany, Fascist Italy, and Imperial Japan—plunged the world into a war that would strain London's financial strength and geopolitical resilience to the ultimate degree. Leaving aside the Pacific, where Britain played a marginal role after the humiliating surrender of Singapore to the Japanese in 1942, the European theater would prove to be another war of attrition between Germany's continental power and British maritime supremacy. Through its *blitzkrieg* advances across France and Poland, Adolf Hitler's Third Reich came to control nearly all of Europe by mid-1940. However, Germany's geopolitical position was vulnerable at its land and maritime margins. In their rapid expansion, Hitler and the Nazi leadership were guided by the strategic ideas of Dr. Karl Haushofer, a geography professor at the University of Munich who was Germany's leading proponent of geopolitics.

After the initial German conquests of 1940, the Nazi Party published an *Atlas of Victory* outlining its strategy for defeating Great Britain. The study's authors, including Haushofer's son Albrecht, a geography professor at the University of Berlin, used the "new science of geopolitics" to explain how Hitler's Reich would escape the fate of Imperial Germany in the last war. During World War I, the British blockade had defeated Germany by reducing it "to domestic starvation and economic impotence." Now, however, the Third Reich's defeat of France was making it "immune to blockade" while delivering a "shock" to the British supply system by bringing Nazi submarines much closer to England. Moreover, the Third Reich's conquest of Norway in April 1940 had turned the North Sea into "a German Sea," opening a way to the Atlantic and giving its "forces a new position of attack against England's east coast." Instead of enforcing a North Sea blockade just 250 miles across, as it had done in the last war, Britain now faced the impossible task of defending a 2,200-mile maritime cordon from Iceland to Gibraltar, giving Germany and Italy "excellent chances of gaining mastery of the Eastern Atlantic."[103]

Guided by this geopolitical strategy, Hitler's Third Reich made three unsuccessful attempts to bring Great Britain to its knees. Between July and October 1940, the Royal Air Force lost 1,700 aircraft in its resistance of Hitler's attempt to bomb the country into submission. But the Battle of Britain left the island bastion unsubdued, well positioned to threaten the Third Reich's western frontier. Next, Germany turned to submarine warfare in an attempt to cut off the million tons of imports that Britain needed every week to survive. German U-boats would indeed inflict heavy losses on British and American supply ships crossing the North Atlantic, until the Allies' mix of convoys and air patrols slowly turned the tide, allowing a massive buildup of US forces in Britain. By the time the Battle of the Atlantic was over, the Allies had broken the Nazi navy, losing 3,500 merchant ships but sinking 780 submarines.[104]

Simultaneously, Axis forces made repeated attempts to advance across Libya and capture the Suez Canal—a reprise of Napoleon's grand strategy of severing the British empire at its geopolitical fulcrum in Egypt. Although the Royal Navy still dominated the Mediterranean, Italy's colony in neighboring Libya provided bases for the Axis attack. In two massive desert battles at El Alamein, just 160 miles west of Cairo, the British army stopped the German-Italian offensives and began pushing them back across North Africa. At the same time, the Japanese army advanced relentlessly across Southeast Asia and had already captured the British bastion at Singapore, forcing the British army to retreat nine hundred miles through the jungles of Burma to India. To save the empire's crown jewel, the British mobilized an Indian army two million strong to block a Japanese invasion, courting Indian support by promising that country its independence after the war.

With both the Suez lifeline secured and India's frontier defended, Britain's oil concession in Iran doubled production, and its Abadan refinery became the world's largest, supplying Allied forces in Europe, the Soviet Union, and Asia.[105]

Meanwhile, on the eastern front in mid-1942, Hitler sent a million men to invade the southern Soviet Union, aiming, in part, to cut off that country's main pipeline leading from the oil fields on the Caspian Sea and to block critical Allied aid shipments reaching Russia from Iran. For five months, fighting raged at the city of Stalingrad, where the Germans suffered such heavy casualties that their army could no longer stop a Soviet counterattack. Turning to the defense of his empire, Hitler mobilized 32,000 slave laborers to build his famed Fortress Europe (Festung Europa), lining the Atlantic coast with six million mines and tank traps to prevent an Allied invasion across the English Channel. After an amphibious force of nearly three million American, British, and Canadian troops breached that Atlantic wall by landing at Normandy in June 1944, Allied offensives ground their way across France—and, in the case of the Red Army, Poland—before capturing the Nazi capital of Berlin in April 1945.[106]

Despite strong similarities in their geopolitics, there were profound differences in the political outcomes of these two world wars. If the Great War ultimately affirmed imperial rule over the colonized peoples of Africa and Asia, World War II carried the racism of the imperial age to a fatal florescence.

At the end of World War I, the Japanese delegation had come to the Versailles Peace Conference of 1919 to secure a racial equality clause in the charter for the new League of Nations. Despite his promises of freedom and plans for a postwar league to promote world peace, American president Woodrow Wilson was a Southern segregationist who had purged the US civil service of Blacks and hosted a White House screening of *Birth of a Nation*, thereby endorsing the film's celebration of the Ku Klux Klan and its virulently racist depictions of African Americans. British officials had similar concerns that any declaration of human equality would create "extremely serious problems" for their colonial empire. When the Japanese motion nonetheless won majority support at the conference, Wilson used his position as chair of the deliberations to arbitrarily dismiss it, thereby preserving the racial hierarchy of the imperial age. While the conference liberated white Europeans from Austrian and Russian imperial rule, the

League sanctioned continued colonial dominion over the peoples of Asia, Africa, and the Middle East. To preserve imperial rule, the League created a mandate system which instituted a form of suspended sovereignty first advanced in the sixteenth century by the Spanish jurist Francisco de Vitoria. In effect, President Wilson's arbitrary rejection of racial equality crippled the moral leadership of the League of Nations at birth, just as his inept failure to win congressional approval for US participation fatally weakened its international influence.[107]

Little more than a decade after Versailles, Hitler's Third Reich heightened the racial hierarchies of the imperial age and embraced its Social Darwinist logic that the strong should conquer the weak. At this apex of Nazi power, political theorist Carl Schmitt argued that the universal legal jurisdiction of the League of Nations was a fiction now being replaced, thanks to Germany's dominion over Europe, by a division of the world among stronger states. In that spirit, Germany, Italy, and Japan signed the Tripartite Pact aspiring to a new world order grounded in what historian Mark Mazower has called principles "of power, region and hierarchy, not of equality, universality and sovereignty." In a cruel irony, the Axis alliance resolved the contradiction between national sovereignty and imperial rule underlying the British era by making the right of conquest the foundation for its new global system.[108]

After his lightning conquest of Poland at the war's start in 1939, Hitler divided the country, incorporating its western half into Germany and ruling the rest through a Nazi governor who announced that "Poland shall be treated as a colony. The Poles shall be the slaves of the Greater German Reich." As his armies advanced across Eastern Europe, Hitler's Reich moved from enslavement to extermination of peoples that his regime deemed racially inferior—particularly Slavs, Jews, and Romanies. Among Eastern Europe's population of 210 million people, which included 200 million Slavs and 9 million Jews, the Nazis tried to clear *Lebensraum*, or living space, for German colonization by killing some 4 million Ukrainians, 3 million non-Jewish Poles, and more than 90 percent of Poland's Jewish population, estimated at 3 million.[109]

While the slaughter of the Slavs was a haphazard mix of massacres, forced deportation, mass starvation, and, later in the war, brutal slave labor, the Nazi extermination of the Jews was ruthlessly and relentlessly systematic. As a first step, special paramilitary squads massacred about 1.4 million of them until the Nazis began sending sealed trains loaded with Jews from across Europe to six major death camps in Poland. Although there was strong resistance both within the Polish ghettos, where Jews had been concentrated for shipment to the camps, and inside the camps themselves, by war's end the Nazi's "final solution" had resulted in the killing of six million Jews—about two-thirds of Europe's prewar Jewish population. From an imperial view-point, the attempt to make Eastern Europe a breadbasket for the Third Reich only yielded mass starvation, while the systematic plunder of both Jewish assets and the financial resources of various occupied territories, worth about $2 trillion today, proved unsustainable. Ultimately, the regime's economic and racial policies were, in Mazower's view, "completely counterproductive as a philosophy of rule."[110]

While Germany tried to exterminate European peoples it deemed lesser, Japan adopted an assimilationist racial policy for its wartime Asian empire through the enforced dissemination of the Japanese language, culture, and Shinto religion. Just as the Nazis promoted German migration to farm occupied Poland, so Imperial Japan, starting in 1936, dispatched 322,000 of its villagers to settle conquered territory in Manchuria. Infused with a sense of racial-cum-spiritual superiority, its military commanders reacted harshly to any opposition, sparking guerrilla resistance in China and later Southeast Asia.[111]

As the brutality, massacres, and genocide brought by Axis racial policy became ever more evident during the war, the Allies were forced to examine their own failings. Reviewing their empire's racial hierarchy in the Far East, the British Foreign Office concluded, in 1941, that "it is impossible for discrimination to be allowed to exist in the world as it stands today." But progress would be difficult given that the "Americans also are far from any real belief in racial equality." By 1944, however, the influential US Commission to Study the Organization of Peace concluded that "Hitler's gospel of Aryan superiority . . . planted the seeds of war." Chastened by the memory of President Wilson's "rejection at Paris of the principle of racial equality," the commission urged postwar measures to advance human rights, saying: "Through revulsion against Nazi doctrines, we may . . . speed up the process of bringing our own practices in each nation more in conformity with our professed ideals."[112] In 1945, the Allies drew up a charter for the United Nations with principles of racial equality that would become foundational for the postwar world order.

Although the Nazis had, in Mazower's words, "brought home the realities of colonialism" to the peoples of occupied Europe, it would still take a decade or more for officials in The Hague, London, and Paris to fully absorb that lesson. More immediately, however, the postwar Nuremburg trials of Nazi war criminals documented the Holocaust of European Jewry in great detail, creating a template for later truth commissions to assay the crimes of authoritarian regimes. That documentation also contributed to the ratification of the UN Convention on Genocide in 1948, a landmark for the world's emerging body of human rights law.[113]

The extraordinary extent of the war's devastation still exceeds the limits of the human imagination. Through new technologies of mass destruction, World War II was responsible for an estimated 77 million deaths. To reap this lethal harvest, the world's armies had procured 600 million mines, 2 million artillery pieces, 450,000 fighter-bombers, 300,000 tanks, 170,000 heavy bombers, and 4,000 naval vessels. It was as if all the world's industrial might had been given over to forging an enormous engine for death and desolation. Two-thirds of the war's fatalities were civilians, compared to 20 percent in World War I. Bombing had destroyed about 30 to 40 percent of all housing in the major cities of Germany and Japan, while European nations had lost 20 to 30 percent of their dwellings.[114] All this destruction amounted to a cataclysm of sufficient scale and scope to end an imperial age that had covered the globe with colonies for more than a century.

Britain's triumph in World War II had come at an extraordinary cost: its cities were damaged, its finances strained, and its people were exhausted. Among the 4.7 million military personnel mobilized, equivalent to 20 percent of all British males, 403,000 soldiers had died. Moreover, German bombing had killed 60,000 civilians, wrecked industrial machinery worth £900 million, and destroyed or damaged more than a million homes. To fight a global war for six long years, Britain had held an imperial "fire sale" by pledging its assets to borrow £2.7 billion from the empire and £5.3 billion in lend-lease aid from the United States—a lifeline that Washington immediately cut at war's end. Poor harvests meant postwar food rationing was stricter than the wartime version and would persist for another decade. After suffering so much, the British people favored domestic reconstruction and better social services at home over the expense of empire, while the colonies themselves were no longer willing to accept foreign rule.

Britain was faced with a choice: it could either give up its empire—still an almost-unimaginable idea—or find a way to make it a source of profits to rebuild its shattered domestic economy.[115] In the aftermath of history's most destructive war, its quixotic attempt to preserve that empire would plunge it into two decades of extraordinary political turmoil.

Postwar Decolonization

As European cities sifted through the rubble, Africa and Asia were at the threshold of one of modern history's greatest transformations. During the 20 years that followed the war, the ten empires that had ruled a third of humanity would give way to 100 newly independent nations. Just six months after Japan's surrender, Philip Bagby, a minor US diplomat who had been posted to Calcutta and Casablanca during the war, reported with what would prove striking accuracy: "The world is going through a colonial crisis unparalleled in history. The great empires built up by the Western European powers during four centuries . . . are crumbling before our eyes."[116]

As an epochal event that buried one world order and birthed another, decolonization would at times be extraordinarily violent. Hard-fought revolutionary wars in Indonesia, Vietnam, Algeria, Kenya, and other African colonies would achieve independence at a staggering cost in human lives. Even the negotiated transitions in Burma, India, and Malaya would spark bitter internal disputes that left lasting social scars.

Although the age of empire had clearly ended, a number of emerging nations would find themselves forced to fight recalcitrant colonial regimes clinging ferociously to the last vestiges of imperial power. At war's end, Washington tried to promote peaceful decolonization by including a Trusteeship Council in the UN, but its European allies insisted on exempting their empires. "I will have no suggestion that the British Empire is to be put in the dock," said Prime Minister Churchill at the 1945 Yalta Conference, "and examined by everybody to see whether it is up to their standard." During the drafting of the UN Charter later that year, Britain succeeded in limiting discussion of decolonization to a vague requirement that rulers be mindful of "the interests of the inhabitants" of their colonies and plan for "self-government or independence" at some undefined future point. Caught between principle and power, Washington softened its anti-colonial position to accommodate the British and French, but took a hard line against the Dutch.[117]

In the Netherlands East Indies, the Dutch refused to accept the reality of Indonesian nationalism and maneuvered desperately to curtail its influence. When Indonesia's leaders declared independence in August 1945, the Dutch mounted a determined military effort to restore colonial rule, eventually dispatching 140,000 troops. After four years of a brutal yet unsuccessful pacification campaign replete with atrocities, the Dutch only withdrew when Washington applied heavy diplomatic pressure. Even then, the Netherlands insisted on retaining the western half of New Guinea as a rump colony, until more international pressure forced a final retreat in 1962.[118]

The decolonization of France's global empire was even more tempestuous, marked by bitter anti-colonial wars that dragged on for fifteen years after World War II. In Indochina, full-blown combat from 1946 to 1954 killed 45,000 French forces and 175,000 Vietnamese troops.[119] Simultaneously, a nationalist party in Madagascar launched a desperate uprising along the island's eastern coast, but French pacification killed 89,000 people, leaving the country traumatized and ill-prepared when independence finally came in 1960.[120]

If Indochina and Madagascar were far-off fires, Algeria was a nearby inferno that embroiled France in political turmoil and civil war. For more than a century, French colonial rule had created an apartheid regime in that North African land, which was now tinder-dry for revolution. While nine million Muslims were denied employment or adequate schooling, a million French colonists, called *pieds-noirs*, expropriated the best agricultural land and monopolized government jobs. Every attempt at reform crashed into a wall of *pied-noirs* privilege, defended vigorously with arguments that Muslims were racially inferior.[121]

After eight years of revolutionary struggle killed 17,500 French troops and left 141,000 liberation fighters dead, President Charles de Gaulle used his enormous prestige to extricate France from empire, not only negotiating an end to the Algerian War but also granting fourteen other African nations full independence in 1960.[122] Taking the bitter French experience as a cautionary lesson, Belgium quit the Congo precipitously that same year, leaving behind an ill-prepared nation that would plunge into a decade of chaotic conflict. In the end, Portugal was the first and last of global empires, fighting a fifteen-year war against liberation movements in Angola, Guinea, and Mozambique, until the collapse of its authoritarian regime at home in 1974 finally paved the way for a close to colonial rule in Africa and Southeast Asia.

Like the other European powers, Britain struggled after World War II to adapt its vast formal and informal empire to this changed world that would ultimately make decolonization an inescapable reality. Even in the darkest days of World War II, Conservative Party imperialists of the "Victorian generation" like foreign secretary Anthony Eden still exuded what historian Chris Bayly called an "indomitable self-confidence" in their empire's future. Despite its socialist principles, the postwar Labour government proclaimed its support for the "jolly old Empire." Both political parties shared the conviction that the colonies would need many years of preparation before independence. Once India broke free in 1947, British governments spent the next decade trying to co-opt nationalist aspirations and concoct schemes to retain their remaining colonies; for the Labour Party, the principal motive was to fund its social welfare programs, while the Conservatives sought to revive the economy and preserve Britain's aura of global power. Starting with the bloodletting that accompanied India's independence, a succession of colonial crises in Malaya, Palestine, Egypt, Kenya, and elsewhere gradually led British leaders to the belated realization that the imperial age was over, spurring their rapid retreat. Through the sum of these pressures, in the 20 years after World War II the population within the British Empire fell from 700 million to only 5 million.[123]

With minimal negotiations to guide the transition, Britain's retreat from its informal empire would often prove more tempestuous than the process of formal decolonization. Along the China coast from Canton to Shanghai, British banks and trading houses were swept away by a communist revolution in 1949, except in Hong Kong, where they hung on for another half-century. In Iran, the national government's bid for equitable revenues from the Anglo-Iranian Oil Company and its enormous Abadan refinery culminated in a tumultuous coup by the US Central Intelligence Agency that replaced a once-pervasive British influence with its American counterpart. In Egypt, a begrudging British retreat would become a death knell for empire.

In their formal empire of colonies and protectorates, the British spent the fifteen years after World War II in an ad hoc decolonization, much of which was led by ambitious but bigoted aristocrats whose foibles compounded these imperial debacles. To cite the prime example, Britain's woefully inadequate preparations for the partition of India and Pakistan, involving the sudden movement of eleven million people, contributed to mob violence and sectarian massacres that left at least a million dead.[124]

There is ample blame to go around, but it was the last viceroy of India, Lord Louis Mountbatten, a cousin of the British king, who mismanaged the move to independence in ways that maximized the potential for violence. Arriving in March 1947, Mountbatten, knowing little about the Hindu–Muslim divisions that roiled this land with one-seventh of the world's population, quickly decided that partition into two nations was the solution and that speed was imperative. After slicing ten months off London's already tight deadline, Mountbatten presided over the independence celebrations in August, posing for photos in his immaculate white naval uniform. Only when press coverage celebrating this "peaceful" transfer of power was complete would he allow the release of detailed maps that showed what one historian called "hastily and ineptly drawn lines of partition," thereby preventing any preparation to mitigate the suffering for millions of refugees. Those horrors cut a wound across the subcontinent clearly evident even 75 years after these tragic events. Years later, Mountbatten, reflecting on his role, told a BBC journalist with disarming frankness, "I fucked it up."[125]

With the nettlesome problem of India resolved, London did try to cobble together a three-part strategy for a sustainable, if vastly reduced, postwar empire: first, consolidate smaller colonies into cost-effective confederations; next, control their exports to capture hard-currency profits; and finally, cling to military bases critical for imperial defense. For instance, it merged nine sultanates and two crown colonies into the Federation of Malaya to control the US dollars earned from its rubber exports, which provided, by 1952, 35 percent of Britain's net balance of payments with the dollar area. So critical was this cash flow that London dispatched 50,000 troops, who would fight for a decade to crush a communist revolt and keep Malaya in the British Commonwealth. Similarly, the Central African Federation combined three colonies to secure the dollars from Zambia's copper exports while supporting a small number of white settlers in Zimbabwe (then Southern Rhodesia), who had been allocated 50 million acres of farmland, compared to only 29 million for Africans. In the Persian Gulf, British Petroleum explored for oil while British advisers led seven sheiks into a federation that later became the petro-rich United Arab Emirates. Over the longer term, the Federation of Malaya and the United Arab Emirates proved relatively stable independent states, while their Central African counterpart broke apart, after mass protests and inept colonial repression, into the nations of Malawi, Zambia, and Zimbabwe.[126]

The economic and military aspects of this British imperial strategy had more mixed results. To protect the flow of oil from British-operated fields in Arabia, Iraq, and Iran, London retained its naval base at Bahrain in the Persian Gulf and turned the Suez Canal Zone into a military bastion with ten airfields and bases for two hundred thousand troops. Farther south in East Africa, Britain planned to keep Kenya as a site for an air base and, as one colonial governor put it, "a white man's colony" for 60,000 English settlers whose large farms denied many of the country's six million Africans access to land. Elsewhere in East Africa, the colonial government in Tanganyika set aside another five million acres for English settlers, while the imperial marketing board in Uganda sold the country's coffee for one hundred times the amount it gave the poor African growers. In West Africa, the Colonial Office manipulated the Cocoa Control Board, paying Ghanaian farmers below-market prices and banking over half their dollar earnings—worth a substantial $50 million in 1948. Through such intensified exploitation, Britain's postwar economy did, in fact, recover rapidly from extensive war damage, with colonial exports of coffee, copper, cocoa, oil, and rubber strengthening the country's currency. Simultaneously, its own industrial exports grew sixfold by 1951 to £2.5 billion, with over half of them going to the empire. While this imperial strategy solved Britain's short-term economic problems, it aroused deep antipathy in the emerging African nations, ultimately leading to some violent ruptures.[127]

The geopolitical core of Britain's compact postwar empire was the Middle East. From bases in the Suez Canal Zone, Britain's huge force of heavy bombers served as its "prime means of deterrence," ready to strike the industrial heartland of southern Russia should the Soviet Union attack British occupation forces in West Germany. From a security corridor composed of bases in Bahrain, Suez, and Kenya, the Royal Navy could still protect shipping lanes to Southeast Asia and the movement of oil from the Persian Gulf to Europe. More broadly, British leaders, both Conservative and Labour, saw the Middle East as their "greatest geostrategic asset," which allowed them to claim "co-leadership" of the Western alliance with Washington.[128]

The limits of Britain's postwar imperial strategy were first evident in Kenya, where a doomed attempt to make an African homeland into a white dominion brought a decade of ruthless repression. For the previous half century, British rule had squeezed Kenya's population into just 20 percent of the country's land and reserved seven hundred thousand prime acres in the "white highlands" for European settlement. In 1952, when miserably poor Africans formed the Mau Mau resistance movement, Kenya's colonial governor, Evelyn Baring, son of the British proconsul who had once ruled Egypt, imposed a state of emergency. Believing that the Mau Mau "was evil and had to be suppressed," Baring transformed the once-prosperous colony into a police state with the aim of quashing all talk of independence. With twelve army battalions backed by a 25,000-strong Home Guard, British troops killed eleven thousand guerrillas, swept a million Africans into 850 enclosed villages, and confined 70,000 suspected rebels in 50 prison camps where they were systematically tortured. Although these measures suppressed the revolt, press reports of the terror and torture damaged Britain's international reputation. In 1960, as Washington pressed for some resolution to counter Soviet propaganda, London began talks with jailed nationalist leader Jomo Kenyatta. Three years later, he would become the new East African state's prime minister after Britain capitulated, conceding full independence.[129] By then, London would scarcely be able to resist US demands, having sacrificed its international prestige in a crisis over the Suez Canal.

Evelyn Baring, governor of Kenya, inspects the King's African
Rifles, 1957 (Credit: Imperial War Museum)

The Suez Crisis

After a decade of relentless pressure to withdraw from one colony after another, the accumulated emotional stress pushed Britain's ruling Conservative Party into a disastrous attempt to reclaim the Suez Canal from Egypt. This failed military intervention, in turn, caused a "deep moral crisis in London" over what a former foreign minister would term the "dying convulsion of British imperialism."[130] In retrospect, the unfolding crisis would reveal not only the decline of British power but also the degeneration of the country's ruling Conservative establishment. Through their fantasies of endless empire, illusions of racial superiority, and backstabbing political intrigues, the country's ruling elite showed they were no longer capable of global leadership.[131]

Just as Americans once regarded the Panama Canal as a triumph of their nation's engineering prowess, so British Conservatives had long seen the Suez Canal as a vital lifeline that tied their small island to its global empire. Although it had been nationalized by Iran in 1951, British Petroleum's Abadan refinery on the Persian Gulf still shipped its oil production through the canal—fueling the Royal Navy, domestic transportation, and much of the country's industry. As late as 1953, Britain maintained 80,000 soldiers and a string of military bases to secure the Suez Canal Zone.[132]

Once bilateral negotiations with Egypt led Britain to withdraw its forces from Suez in late 1954, the country's charismatic president, Gamal Abdel Nasser, who had only recently ousted the pliably corrupt British client ruler King Farouk, asserted Egypt's neutrality in the Cold War by purchasing Soviet bloc arms, thereby raising tensions with London and Washington.[133] Other hammer blows to Britain's position in the Middle East had come in steady succession—its withdrawal from Palestine "amid humiliation and confusion" in May 1948; anti-British riots in Cairo that had burned hundreds of buildings, including the iconic Barclays Bank, in January 1952; and the expulsion of the British diplomatic mission from Tehran that October.[134]

Britain's man of the hour in dealing with this growing Middle East crisis was its foreign secretary, Anthony Eden, whose name would soon become synonymous with the empire's decline, much as Lord Palmerston's had been with its steady ascent. Born the son of a baronet and a society beauty on an eight-thousand-acre estate in 1897, he inherited elegance from his mother and a "violent temper" from his sire. As a fourth son, however, Eden would have to work for a living and so paid attention to his studies at Oxford University, where he majored in Oriental languages, becoming fluent in Persian and Arabic.[135]

British Foreign Secretary Anthony Eden and Egyptian President Gamal Nasser, Cairo, 1955 (Credit: Getty Images)

After inheriting a small fortune from his father and marrying a banker's daughter, Eden had entered politics as a Conservative, serving as Winston Churchill's foreign affairs secretary during World War II and again when he returned to power in 1951.[136] To shore up fading British influence in the Middle East, Eden formed a mutual security agreement, known as the Baghdad Pact, with Turkey, Iraq, Iran, and Pakistan—but not Egypt, since Nasser condemned it as divisive. During a visit to Cairo in February 1955, Eden tried to charm the Egyptian leader at an embassy reception with his fluent Arabic. When Nasser said it was interesting to be inside the place that had governed his country, Eden replied smugly, "Not governed perhaps, advised, rather," a transparent falsehood that further alienated the Egyptian president.[137] Shortly after his return from Cairo, Eden, chafing under Churchill's seemingly endless tenure, pushed his mentor aside to become prime minister himself.[138]

To sway Nasser from his Soviet dalliance, Britain and the United States offered to match a $200 million World Bank loan for the construction of the Aswan High Dam on the Nile River, which promised to lift millions of Egyptian farmers from abject poverty.[139] But Egypt angered the administration of President Dwight Eisenhower by recognizing the People's Republic of China. After Washington withdrew its aid for the dam's construction that July, Nasser sought alternative financing by nationalizing the Suez Canal, in a move that electrified the Arab world and elevated him to the first rank of world leaders.[140]

Although British ships still passed freely through the canal and Washington was insisting on a diplomatic resolution to the crisis, Eden and his chancellor of the exchequer, Harold Macmillan, found Nasser's assertive nationalism deeply unsettling. "What's all this nonsense about isolating Nasser or 'neutralising' him as you call it?" Eden berated his foreign minister, Anthony Nutting. "I want him destroyed, can't you understand? I want him murdered."[141]

Once the canal was nationalized, Eden gave orders to make good on that threat, operating as if the empire were still at the peak of its powers. In late July, the government formed a special Egypt Committee, led by Eden and Macmillan, that agreed its "immediate purpose" was "to bring about the downfall of the present Egyptian government." In recruiting Egyptian exiles and officers for an assassination plot, MI6, Britain's counterpart to the CIA, selected the deputy chief of Egypt's air force intelligence as its prime asset. He turned out be a double agent loyal to Nasser, facilitating the arrest of "virtually the entire network" of four Britons and eleven Egyptians.[142]

With that option off the table, Eden and his Egypt Committee began formulating a secret military operation to seize the canal. Behind a smoke screen of sham diplomacy designed to deceive their American allies, the British foreign secretary met secretly with the prime ministers of France and Israel at a safe house near Paris, where they agreed on a duplicitous two-stage seizure of the Suez Canal.[143]

On October 29, 1956, the Israeli army, led by the dashing General Moshe Dayan, swept across the Sinai Peninsula, destroying Egyptian tanks and positioning troops within ten miles of the canal. Using this fighting as a pretext for an intervention to restore peace, Anglo-French amphibious and airborne forces quickly joined the attack. Starting on October 31, a devastating bombardment from six allied aircraft carriers and planes from British airfields on Cyprus smashed the Egyptian air force in just three days, destroying 104 of its new Soviet MiG jet fighters and 130 other aircraft.[144] After Egypt's military virtually collapsed from the destruction of its air arm and troop losses in Sinai, Nasser deployed a strategy brilliant in its simplicity. By filling dozens of rusting cargo ships with rocks and scuttling them at the canal's northern entrance, he quickly closed Europe's oil lifeline to the Persian Gulf. By the time 22,000 British and French forces began storming ashore at the canal's north end on November 6, their objective, to secure the free movement of ships, had already been snatched from their grasp.[145]

From the moment the British bombing started, Eden's government faced a formidable diplomatic backlash. At an emergency meeting of the UN General Assembly, the United States and the Soviet Union both backed a motion calling for an immediate cease-fire. In Washington, President Eisenhower felt any American support for the British "might well be to array the world from Dakar to the Philippine Islands against us." Breaking with his prime minister to back the proposed cease-fire, Macmillan told the cabinet that "there had been a serious run on the pound, viciously orchestrated in Washington," and heightened the sense of economic crisis by falsely reporting that the country's gold reserves had hemorrhaged a breathtaking £100 million (it was actually £32 million). In a transatlantic phone call that same day, Eisenhower reportedly asked, "Anthony, are you mad?" Chastened, Eden agreed to a temporary cease-fire just 48 hours after his troops had landed in Egypt.[146]

When Washington next demanded a complete withdrawal from the canal zone as the price of a bailout for a collapsing British economy, Eden's imperial bluster began to crumble. Britain finally capitulated by announcing an immediate departure of all troops, and the White House, in response, arranged an emergency $1.8 billion support package for the British pound.[147] Humiliated by the forced withdrawal and looking like a broken man, Eden apparently compensated psychologically by ordering another vengeful assassination attempt on Nasser. Scrambling for assets, MI6 turned to some "renegade Egyptian officers," but the plot fizzled when weapons cached outside Cairo proved duds.[148]

As criticism of Eden's handling of the Suez Crisis mounted, his partner in planning the invasion, Harold Macmillan, maneuvered with skillful skulduggery to replace his former ally as prime minister. Just weeks after the last British soldier left Egypt on December 22, Eden, discredited and disgraced, was forced to resign after only 21 months in office.[149]

The Suez Crisis, in other words, revealed the rot deep inside Britain's apparatus of power, even as the party that had built the British Empire refused to admit the disastrous nature of the Suez invasion. Of the 20 ministers in Eden's cabinet, which had backed the intervention fully, over half were titled lords, making his irrational attachment to the canal more a mark of his class than an individual aberration. The Royal Navy that had once ruled the waves was forced to retrieve aging warships from mothballs and landing craft from ferry companies to form its invasion fleet.[150] Instead of leading world diplomacy as it had at Vienna in 1815 and Versailles in 1919, Britain found itself rebuked by the international community at the UN. Once the world's banker, London now lacked the finances for even such a relatively modest military intervention, forcing it to accept the International Monetary Fund's very first bailout to avoid the collapse of its currency. Even its legendary secret service proved inept. In the aftermath of this debacle, the United States would henceforth replace Britain in the Middle East because, as Eisenhower put it, "the British and French have forfeited their position there and have no influence."[151] The once-mighty British lion emerged from the Suez Crisis looking like a tamed circus animal that would henceforth jump through hoops whenever Washington cracked the whip.

Within four years of the Suez debacle, multiple pressures, political and economic, led Prime Minister Macmillan to the painful realization that Britain could no longer afford its empire. Although he won a strong majority in the 1959 elections for Parliament, British voters showed little interest in the remnants of the empire, and many of the newly elected Conservative members shared that view. The next year, the UN General Assembly adopted, without any dissent, Resolution 1514 calling for an end to colonial rule, stating that "alien subjugation, domination and exploitation constitutes a denial of fundamental human rights." Speaking in white apartheid South Africa, Macmillan, abandoning his advocacy of empire, said: "The wind of change is blowing through this continent and . . . this growth of national consciousness is a political fact." During the decade following his historic declaration, Britain would grant independence to 30 former colonies in Africa, Asia, the Caribbean, and the Pacific, liquidating its global empire. The coup de grace would come in January 1968 when Labour Prime Minister Harold Wilson announced that Britain would withdraw all its forces east of Suez within three years, ending both its role as an Asian power and any pretentions to global leadership. Finally, in 1973, Britain would complete its descent from global power to regional player by becoming one of nine member states in the European Union.[152]

Eclipse of Empire

The end of the British imperial era resulted from a mix of rising nationalism, domestic economic decline, and strategic shifts that made the US nuclear armada more significant than traditional British sea power. The result: a new world order under Washington's leadership—with a dominant superpower presiding over a new international community of some 190 sovereign nations.

After nearly a century as global hegemon, Britain's geopolitical strategy of encircling the Eurasian landmass with a string of naval bastions had culminated in searing defeat. In 1904, as construction of the Trans-Siberian Railway crawled across the continent toward Vladivostok, the geographer Halford Mackinder warned that the age of sea power, which had allowed Europe's maritime empires to dominate Eurasia, was coming to an end.[153]

While Mackinder's prediction was premature, his geopolitical insight was acute. With its military resources stretched to the limit, the British Empire's encirclement of Eurasia—like Portugal and the Netherlands before it—never extended much beyond Singapore. To fill that serious strategic gap, London negotiated the Anglo-Japanese Alliance in 1902, which allowed the Royal Navy to concentrate its forces in the Atlantic to defeat Germany during World War I. After that treaty lapsed in 1922 and Tokyo joined the Axis powers, Britain could not prevent Japan from sweeping down the Pacific littoral at the start of World War II, seizing its naval bastion at Singapore and so starting the empire's unraveling east of Suez. Such strategic vulnerability on Britain's part highlights the historic import of Washington's postwar geopolitical position as the first power in a millennium to control both axial ends of Eurasia.

The British imperial century also fostered a host of contradictions that subverted its once-stable world order and left Washington an ambiguous legacy. Most immediately, British diplomacy failed to build a stable alliance system, allowing tensions among rival empires to erupt into murderous conflicts in 1914 and again in 1939. In the end, the monumental destruction of World War II became a cataclysm comparable to the Black Death, bringing Britain's imperial era to a close and allowing the ascent of Washington's world order. While most of the 15 million deaths in World War I had been concentrated along the Western Front in France, World War II spread its devastation globally, with over 70 million killed and cities ravaged across Europe and Asia, including two Japanese cities that were targets of the first nuclear bombs—weapons that would soon hold the power to destroy life on the planet.[154]

As world war gave way to the Cold War, the British eventually recognized the reality of their empire's end and managed the imperial retreat in ways that would maintain overall global stability. In addition to supporting Washington's formation of institutions for a new world order, the British also transferred key imperial assets to their American allies, through both formal diplomacy and covert collaboration. In a striking reprise of the smooth shift from Dutch dominion to British maritime power during England's Glorious Revolution of 1688, this transatlantic imperial baton pass from London to Washington ensured a surprisingly seamless global transition. Amid the rapid decolonization of Europe's empires and a military confrontation with the Soviet Union, this stable Anglophone alliance assisted Washington's bid to become both history's most powerful empire and the architect of a new world order.

Not only did London assist Washington's ascent, it also left an important legacy for the exercise of global power. Earlier European empires had acquired enclaves and colonies that covered large portions of the globe. Britain, however, was the first to create a penumbra of power that transcended territory to encompass the entire planet. At a surprisingly low cost in blood and treasure, the Royal Navy proved an agile instrument for projecting such power—securing the sea-lanes for world trade, protecting investments, and enforcing an imperial order. Given its leading role in Britain's human rights campaign against the slave trade, that navy also played a seminal role in infusing its world order with moral authority. As banker to the world, London achieved a stable synergy between sharing its technological innovations and assuring the profitability of its industries. Its secret services provided timely, accurate intelligence, and its diplomats were deft in their maximization of influence with minimal use of military force. Through this multifaceted synergy, Britain built a duality of global power that balanced a liberal world order with a self-aggrandizing empire, creating the template for Washington's world system.

Britain also left another, even more ambiguous, legacy in the form of an energy transition that will likely contribute to the decline of that very US global order. For throughout the nineteenth century, it was Britain that developed the technology for coal-fired steam energy that would then migrate across the Atlantic to make the United States into the world's premier industrial power. By the end of the nineteenth century, Britain was also a leader in a global exploration for oil that provided ample supplies of liquid carbon to fuel the automobiles, aircraft, and maritime transport that would become synonymous with Washington's world system.

Over the longer term, however, the British imperial era's energy transition to fossil fuels also inaugurated a relentless 70-fold increase in the annual rate of global carbon emissions—rising from just 28 million tons in 1800 to 2 billion in 1900, and nearly 5 billion by 1940. From the "preindustrial" baseline of 280 parts per million in 1880, carbon dioxide concentrations in the atmosphere kept climbing to 410 ppm by 2020, thus causing climate change that could ultimately destabilize US hegemony, along with much else.[155] Through both its global empire and its central role in this energy transition, Britain left a mingled legacy that would profoundly influence both the rise and decline of Washington's world order.

President Theodore Roosevelt welcomes Great White Fleet, 1909 (Credit: Naval History)

Chapter 5
Pax Americana

On February 22, 1909, President Theodore Roosevelt stood on a steel gun turret aboard the battleship *Connecticut*, wearing a top hat and stylish overcoat to cut the winter winds blowing off the sea at Hampton Roads, Virginia. Beneath the barrel of a massive twelve-inch gun, hundreds of sailors pressed close to catch his words as Roosevelt hailed the return of the "Great White Fleet" of sixteen brand-new battleships from an epic fourteen-month voyage around the globe.

"Officers and men of the Battle Fleet," he said, "the hearts of all who saw you thrilled with pride as the hulls of the mighty warships lifted above the horizon.... You have steamed through all the great oceans; you have touched the coast of every continent." They were, he told them, "the first battle fleet that has ever circumnavigated the globe."[1]

In response to the forceful rise of Japanese naval power, Roosevelt had sent the ships of the Atlantic fleet around Cape Horn to show Tokyo that the United States was indeed a Pacific power. But the wider world saw in that gesture a different message. As the fleet rounded Cape Horn and crossed the Pacific to Hawaii and Australia, vast cheering crowds were stunned by the sheer size of the American armada. For the countless thousands who witnessed the passage of those warships and the millions more who read about them in daily newspapers, this voyage marked America's arrival as a major military power.[2]

Forty years later, in September 1948, Theodore Roosevelt's niece Eleanor, the widow of recently deceased president Franklin Roosevelt, stood before an audience of diplomats and students at the Sorbonne University in Paris, wearing her usual unpretentious black dress. "I have come this evening to talk with you on one of the greatest issues of our time—that is the preservation of human freedom," the former first lady began in her high, lilting voice. "The future must see the broadening of human rights throughout the world. . . . In a true sense, human rights are a fundamental object of law and government in a just society."[3]

Eleanor Roosevelt, chair, UN Commission on Human
Rights, 1947 (Credit: United Nations)

At a time of rising tensions with the Soviet Union, Eleanor Roosevelt was making a plea for the passage of a human rights declaration by the General Assembly of the United Nations. Through 85 bitterly adversarial sessions with 1,400 separate procedural votes over the next two months, she would, as chair of the UN Human Rights Commission, fight with steely determination for those principles against strenuous Soviet opposition. "All human beings are born free and equal in dignity and rights," read the first article of the draft declaration, ringing with an uncompromising rhetoric of individual liberty. "They are endowed with reason and conscience and should act towards one another in a spirit of brotherhood." The Moscow press, strongly opposed to such bourgeois individualism, derided her as the "garrulous, feeble old Eleanor Roosevelt."[4]

But at four minutes before midnight on December 10, 1948, the UN General Assembly voted 48 to 0—with the Soviet bloc, South Africa, and Saudi Arabia abstaining—to approve her text for a Universal Declaration of Human Rights. When the body's president announced the vote, the General Assembly, for the first and only time in its history, burst into a spontaneous standing ovation for an individual delegate. Eleanor Roosevelt, said its president, had "raised a great name to an even greater honor."[5]

Yet the honor was not hers alone. Much of the language of that declaration was nearly three hundred years in the making, deriving from the English Bill of Rights, the French Revolution's Declaration of the Rights of Man, and the US Declaration of Independence. Throughout World War II, allied leaders, including her husband, Franklin, had proclaimed just such universal principles in an effort to inspire the war effort. Now, at this cusp between a world war and a Cold War, Washington had ample prestige and power to persuade the world's nations of the need for such an uncompromising declaration.

In fulfilling this commitment to human rights, the United States would face some exceptional challenges. Unlike earlier imperial powers, it was, after all, a former colony with a long history of slavery and a succeeding system of racial segregation that would compromise its commitment to those principles at home. As its global power grew during these postwar decades, Washington would cultivate anti-Communist allies among authoritarian leaders in Asia, Africa, and Latin America, tacitly endorsing torture and repression in their lands. Even as the US practiced racial segregation at home and backed ruthless dictators abroad, civil society groups worldwide would continue to fight for human rights, just as African Americans would struggle for their civil rights at home, making this universal principle a defining attribute of Washington's world order, almost in spite of itself.[6]

The Duality of US Global Power

Juxtaposed, those two speeches celebrating power and principle reveal the ambiguity that has long lain at the heart of US global hegemony. Even at its peak of power in the decades after World War II, Washington's pursuit of unilateral military might was balanced, however tenuously, by its promotion of an international community of sovereign states governed as equals under the rule of law. By the time Washington's world order was fully formed in the late 1950s, the unequaled power of its nuclear-armed bombers, its overseas military bases, and its covert interventions in the affairs of countless nations coexisted tensely with a new world order, epitomized by the UN, that was meant to protect the sovereignty of even small states and promote universal human rights. This underlying duality of Washington's version of world power would manifest itself in numerous contradictions during its 70 years of global hegemony.

Elihu Root, secretary of war and architect of US global
power, 1902 (Credit: Library of Congress)

From the time the US stepped onto the world stage circa 1900, such ambiguity in its foreign policy would be embodied in the careers of two men who proved to be progenitors of its global presence. With the publication of his influential treatise on sea power in 1890, Captain Alfred Thayer Mahan, head of the Naval War College, became a forceful advocate for building a blue-water navy that would allow the country to project its power to foreign shores. During his decade as secretary of war and secretary of state, Elihu Root built an elaborate apparatus for the formation of the country's foreign policy, while shaping its signature commitment to the international rule of law. This stark duality of raw military power joined uneasily to internationalist principles would remain a hallmark of American hegemony in the twentieth century, even as the country rose to unprecedented global power.

Root has been largely forgotten today, but he presided over the country's transformation from an insular continental nation into a major player on the world stage.[7] Despite his modest background as the son of a math professor at Hamilton College and his lack of Ivy League credentials, Root rose quickly by dint of his impressive legal acumen and his skilled cultivation of patrons among the Gilded Age power elite, including two future presidents and numerous financiers. After 30 years as a New York corporate lawyer defending monopoly trusts, robber barons, and corrupt city bosses, Root would devote the rest of his long career to public service. Yet even as an official, he practiced the delicate art of courting patrons, bending their wealth and power to serve his own unbending aims.[8]

As cabinet secretary, senator, and then special diplomatic envoy, Root built the apparatus of US global power and simultaneously placed the nation's imprint on the character of an emerging international community.[9] To transform the weak US state of the Gilded Age into an instrument for world power, he spent a quarter of a century pursuing three intertwined objectives: the renovation of the federal government into an effective apparatus for overseas expansion, cultivation of a consensus among the country's elites for such an activist foreign policy, and establishment of new forms of global governance susceptible to Washington's influence. In sum, Root worked to move both his own country and the community of nations beyond the British imperial age, with its colonial conquests and gunboat diplomacy, to a new global system of sovereign states resolving disputes through international law.[10]

As secretary of war from 1899 to 1904, Root transformed the US Army from a small force focused on coastal defense into an agile apparatus for foreign intervention—in China, the Caribbean, the Philippines, and ultimately Europe. To adapt a republic to the task of running an empire, he dealt with the troubled aftermath of the Spanish-American War of 1898 by establishing colonial regimes for Puerto Rico and the Philippines. He also ended the US occupation of Cuba by dictating terms for its independence that conceded his own country a large naval base at Guantánamo Bay and the right to intervene whenever it chose in that island's affairs.[11]

While secretary of state from 1905 to 1909, Root led a sustained effort to increase America's diplomatic influence, simultaneously using that leverage to advance the international rule of law. As the first secretary of state to tour the globe, he made Washington a major player in international relations. After a "triumphal visit" to Rio de Janeiro for an International American Conference in 1906, he circled the South American continent on a Navy cruiser, greeted by cheering crowds at every port. A year later, at the Second Hague Peace Conference in the Netherlands, US delegates had sufficient diplomatic leverage, with the support of the 17 Latin American republics among the 44 nations present, to advance the idea of a permanent international court as an alternative to armed conflict. To house that court, which became the first institution for global governance, Root turned to his good friend, steel baron Andrew Carnegie, for $1.5 million to build an ornate Peace Palace in The Hague, within which he helped establish the Academy of International Law.[12]

As secretary of state and then a US senator from 1909 to 1915, Root cultivated a close alliance with Britain. In particular, he promoted treaties to resolve territorial disputes that had roiled relations with the world's pre-eminent power for the better part of a century—work that won him the Nobel Peace Prize. Even as a retiree in his seventies, he served on a League of Nations committee that established the Permanent Court of International Justice in 1920. Although he failed repeatedly to persuade Congress to join that court, it still embodied his long-held vision of an international community governed by the rule of law and served as the immediate precursor to the UN's International Court of Justice.[13]

Root also cultivated new social networks, merging New York financiers, Washington politicians, and academic experts in a distinctively American process that formed foreign policy through civil society dialogue. For that tour he made of Latin America, Root plucked Dr. Paul Reinsch from the political science department of the University of Wisconsin, launching the young academic on a diplomatic career that would later take him to China as ambassador. Through his close friendship with Andrew Carnegie, Root presided over the investment of a significant part of that tycoon's vast fortune in the erection of an institutional architecture for America's unique way of engaging the world. In the process, Root established, and chaired, both the Carnegie Institution for Science and the Carnegie Endowment for International Peace. This effort culminated in 1921 when Root led a group of financiers, industrialists, and corporate lawyers in the establishment of the Council on Foreign Relations in New York City, which soon became the country's premier forum for the promotion of an expansive foreign policy. In short, he wove key elements of the American elite into a layered nexus of money, influence, and intellect, thereby creating a unique foreign policy establishment that would help define the country's diplomatic priorities for the century to come.[14]

If Root represented the liberal principles of democracy and the rule of law that would later infuse Washington's world order, then Mahan personified the military might that would ultimately propel it to global power. He was a realist who felt that the nation's security lay in the construction of battleships and the seizure of naval bastions. As a delegate to the First Hague Peace Conference of 1899, he was deeply opposed to his own delegation's attempt to create a permanent court of arbitration, writing at the conference's close: "Men forget what they have owed, and still owe, to the sword."[15]

Respected, even revered as the country's leading strategist, Mahan was born at West Point, where his father taught military science to army cadets from his own textbook for nearly 40 years. Although "an aloof and solitary figure" at Annapolis and a Navy misfit whose service at sea was undistinguished, Mahan had rare analytic gifts that would make him the country's only original military strategist. Assigned to instruct mid-career officers at the newly established Naval War College, Captain Mahan spent his first year developing lectures that became the foundation for his renowned 1890 study, *The Influence of Sea Power upon History, 1660–1783*. With the same pithy maxims that had marked his father's writings on land warfare, Mahan posited that sea power was the determinative factor in the rise and fall of empires. To attain the status of a great power required command of the sea, which could only be achieved through both naval superiority and maritime trade with overseas colonies and foreign markets. That work of his was wildly popular in its day, read as gospel by everyone from Kaiser Wilhelm II to

Japanese admirals. His maxim that major wars turn on a "decisive battle" at sea would shape German strategy in World War I and guide Japanese naval operations in World War II.[16]

Alfred Thayer Mahan, US naval strategist, circa 1910 (Credit: Library of Congress)

Written at a time when America was just beginning its ascent to global power and expanding its navy, Mahan's book made the crucial argument that Washington needed both to build a battle fleet and to capture island bases that could control the surrounding sea-lanes—particularly in the Pacific. In marked contrast to the Royal Navy's chain of fortified bastions that made an "extensive empire, like that of England, secure," US warships with "no foreign establishments, either colonial or military" would be "like land birds, unable to fly far from their own shores. To provide resting-places for them . . . would be one of the first duties of a government proposing to itself the development of the power of the nation at sea."[17] In reviewing the book for the *Atlantic Monthly*, a young Theodore Roosevelt wrote: "Captain Mahan shows very clearly the practical importance of naval history. . . . We need a large navy, composed not merely of cruisers, but containing also a full proportion of powerful battleships."[18]

During the 1870s, the US had the world's twelfth-largest navy, behind both Chile and Turkey. Its first steel-hulled cruisers were vastly inferior to British or French ships, and its still-insular mindset was fully replicated in a major modernization program under the Navy Act of 1890 that allowed for only a defensive fleet of "short-range torpedo boats" and "sea-going coastline battleships." Congress even restricted the ships' range by limiting their capacity for carrying coal.[19]

But America was changing. As waves of immigrants tripled the nation's population, the US replaced Britain as the world's leading economic power. In 1860, Britain produced 59 percent of the world's industrial wealth, and America just 13 percent. Five decades later, the US share was at 48 percent and rising, while Britain's was down to a mere 15 percent and falling.[20]

In 1904, President Roosevelt, Mahan's friend and admirer, started construction of the "most powerfully armed and longest-range battleships afloat." Within three years, the nation's shipyards had launched eleven new battleships, making the US Navy second only to Britain's in capital ships. Then, to announce the country's arrival as a Pacific power, Roosevelt sent the Great White Fleet of sixteen battleships on that epic voyage around the globe. After Britain escalated the naval arms race by launching the HMS *Dreadnought*, with its unprecedented speed, size, and firepower, the United States kept pace by building, within six years, an impressive armada of fourteen dreadnought-class battleships, including the USS *Pennsylvania*, which at 31,400 tons was three times the size of older coastal warships.[21]

In his influential essays, Mahan also argued that the construction of a canal across the Isthmus of Panama was essential for the nation's commercial future, adding that protection of such a canal would require Washington's dominion over the Caribbean. Writing in the *Atlantic Monthly*, he argued forcefully that the control of any future canal across the Isthmus of Panama would be critical for the country's "full development and . . . its national security." If another power were to build such a canal, it would be, he said, "a disaster to the United States" and would be "especially dangerous to the Pacific coast."[22]

America's overseas expansion would first be felt in the Caribbean. As early as 1895, Washington pressed London to give up its informal empire over Latin America and recognize US hegemony in the Western Hemisphere. When tensions arose over the boundary between British Guiana and Venezuela, Washington insisted that "the United States is practically sovereign on this continent," effectively forcing the British to back off. Three years later, Spain's ruthless repression of Cuban nationalism prompted US intervention. During the four short months of the Spanish-American War, Washington annexed Puerto Rico and liberated Cuba in exchange for that permanent naval base at Guantánamo Bay. When an Anglo-German-Italian fleet blockaded Venezuela's main port to compel bond payments, President Roosevelt sent the Navy to prevent troop landings, in an action he later justified by proclaiming "an international police power" to prevent "flagrant cases of wrongdoing or impotence" anywhere in Latin America.[23]

In 1903, Roosevelt sent warships to the Caribbean, blockading the coast of Colombia while rebels in the country's province of Panama declared their independence. Within three days, so quickly that the *New York Times* branded the whole affair an "act of sordid conquest," the new republic granted Washington a perpetual lease to a 50-mile-wide canal zone across Panama. For the next ten years, a force of 68 massive steam shovels and 40,000 contract workers battled tropical disease and rugged terrain to cut the channel across the mountainous isthmus that would become the world's largest and most successful civil engineering project. Apart from the sheer power of a 95-ton machine that could scoop up eight tons of earth, those steam shovels, along with hundreds of pneumatic drills and hydraulic rock crushers, were symbolic of a new kind of empire that would use fossil fuels to replace coerced colonial labor. When completed in 1914, the canal could, in just eleven hours, lift a 50,000-ton battleship 85 feet above sea level with three massive, precisely engineered locks, carry it across the world's largest artificial lake, and finally lower the ship through three more locks into the Pacific.[24]

As the canal neared completion, the US already had a chain of overseas military bases with permanent troop deployments across the Caribbean, including army posts in Puerto Rico, the naval base at Guantánamo Bay, and coastal artillery at both ends of the Panama Canal. When it finally opened, President Woodrow Wilson tried to secure the country's southern flank by launching long-term military interventions in Nicaragua, Mexico, Haiti, and the Dominican Republic.[25]

Mahan was also convinced that the US had to become a Pacific power. So important were naval bases in the Pacific for America's defense that, as he argued in a popular article, "it should be an inviolable resolution of our national policy that no European state should henceforth acquire a coaling position within three thousand miles of San Francisco"—a distance that encompassed the Hawaiian Islands and much of the Pacific Ocean, which soon became America's next frontier of overseas expansion.[26]

While US claims to dominion over the Caribbean during the 1890s met no real opposition, the Pacific was another matter altogether. The East Coast was secured by elaborate coastal fortifications and an ad hoc alliance with Great Britain, but the West Coast and its Pacific frontier were largely undefended. As Britain, Germany, and Japan plunged into a naval arms race in the 1890s, Republican Party leaders decided to turn Mahan's axioms into action. "As regards Hawaii, I take your views absolutely," Roosevelt wrote to the strategist. "If I had my way we would annex those islands tomorrow." When the Cuban crisis came to a boil after the mysterious sinking of the USS *Maine* at Havana in early 1898, Roosevelt, as acting secretary of the Navy, telegrammed Admiral George Dewey's Asiatic Squadron, then anchored in Hong Kong, to prepare for "offensive operations in the Philippine Islands." After Washington declared war on Spain in April, Dewey's ships steamed into Manila Bay to score a crushing victory, sinking seven Spanish cruisers while suffering no US losses.[27]

Although 75,000 American troops would be needed for a four-year pacification campaign that would kill 200,000 Filipinos and defeat a nascent Philippine Republic, Dewey's victory at Manila Bay served, from an international perspective, to establish US sovereignty over those islands.[28] A month after its Manila victory, a ship assigned to the Asiatic Squadron seized the island of Guam from Spain, and a month after that, President William McKinley signed a congressional resolution annexing Hawaii. A year later, the US secured the sea-lane between Honolulu and Manila by seizing Wake Island, and then reached across the equator to claim Samoa. By the time this burst of expansion was complete with the acquisition of the Panama Canal Zone, Washington had, with stunning speed and surprisingly little planning, won an empire of islands that reached nearly halfway round the world, skipping along the Tropic of Cancer from Puerto Rico across the Pacific to the Philippines.

Like many advocates of geopolitics, Mahan had used seemingly precise strategic concepts to project his country's current position into a murky, uncertain future. His persuasive pleas for a blue-water, bicoastal navy and an expanded Pacific defense perimeter seemed, in their day, a sensible response to the rise of Japanese naval power. As those strategic principles slowly took shape in an ever-changing international context, however, the result was an indefensible strategic position in the Pacific. Instead of a resilient triangle of naval bastions reaching no further than Honolulu, the US had acquired a vulnerable string of bases stretching all the way across the ocean to Manila Bay.

Pacific Century

By its sheer size, the Asia-Pacific region has represented a persistent geopolitical challenge for US foreign policy. The Pacific, the largest and deepest of the oceans, comprises nearly half of the world's waters and a full third of the earth's surface.[29] After four centuries as a closed Spanish sea, in the era of high imperialism that ocean became a site second only to Africa in its importance in the competition for colonies. In the more populous South Pacific, European claims had come in rapid succession—Germany in New Guinea and the Bismarck Archipelago; Britain in Fiji, Papua, and the Solomons; and France in Tahiti and Bora Bora.

North of the equator, the sailing distances across the Pacific are double those of the Atlantic, with only sparse islands for landfall. Across those seven thousand miles of open ocean, the US occupation of Hawaii, Wake, Guam, and the Philippines made it the dominant imperial power, although Germany acquired the Northern Marianas and most of Micronesia. Along the ocean's western rim is an offshore arc of islands that form a Pacific littoral from Japan through the Philippines to Indonesia. Beyond that, the vast Eurasian landmass was home to half of humanity and the site of intense imperial rivalry between a rising Japan, a strife-torn China, and an expansive Russia.

In the century plus since it first pushed across the Pacific, Washington has tried to balance three geopolitical components—a vast ocean, a volatile island littoral, and a populous continent—in an effort to maintain a viable strategic position in the Asia-Pacific region, which has long been central both to its domestic defense and its global presence. In the continuing struggle to control this strategic frontier, Washington has been at war somewhere in the Asia-Pacific region for 50 of the past 80 years. Just as Portugal's global empire was synonymous with its dominion over the Indian Ocean, so America's has been, and likely will be, shaped by its experience in the Pacific.

From the outset, Washington's headlong plunge across that ocean created a formidable challenge for its national defense. Appointed president of the Navy's General Board in 1900, Admiral George Dewey recommended the dispatch of a major battle fleet to the Pacific, supported by the construction of a fortified base in the Philippines. President Roosevelt obliged, securing a million-dollar appropriation for the construction of a major naval base at Subic Bay, a deep-water harbor just north of Manila.[30]

The outcome of the Russo-Japanese War in 1904–1905 quickly forced Washington to abandon its plans for a major naval presence in the western Pacific. With its victory over Russia's Pacific Fleet at Port Arthur and its spectacular destruction of the Tsar's Baltic Fleet in the Tsushima Straits near Korea, the Japanese navy established itself as the dominant power there. Recognizing that strategic reality, Theodore Roosevelt ordered the last US Navy battleship out of the Pacific in 1906 and, a year later, authorized appropriations for construction of a new Pacific bastion at Pearl Harbor, Hawaii, instead of Subic Bay in the Philippines. In a letter to his secretary of war, Roosevelt clarified the strategic implications of his decision, saying "the Philippines form our heel of Achilles," a realization that would soon lead him to favor immediate independence for the Islands.[31]

In the aftermath of the Russo-Japanese War, US military planners struggled to identify a strategy that could defend its Philippine colony from the seeming inevitability of a Japanese attack. For more than fifteen years, the War Department planned for Army troops to respond to such a scenario by holding the fortifications around Manila Bay for an indefinite period, until the Atlantic Fleet could arrive to relieve the garrison. Such planning carried with it a sober strategic assessment of the possibility of a partial or total naval defeat in Philippine waters.[32]

The outcome of World War I redoubled this strategic conundrum. At war's end, President Woodrow Wilson arrived at the Versailles Peace Conference to popular acclaim for his proposal to establish the League of Nations, which would assure "independence and territorial integrity to great and small states alike." But he failed to win congressional ratification of US membership in the league, effectively isolating the country from European affairs and inadvertently increasing the importance of the Pacific to its national defense.

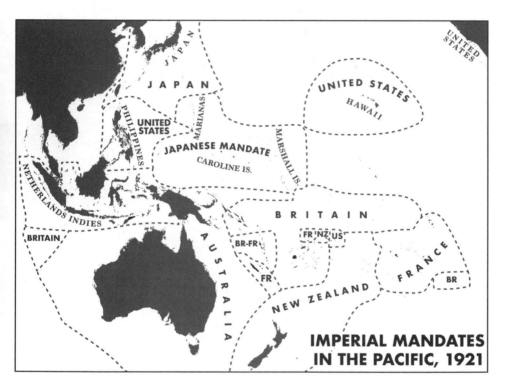

IMPERIAL MANDATES IN THE PACIFIC, 1921

Nonetheless, the Versailles peace settlement also granted Tokyo a colonial mandate over much of Micronesia—the Caroline, Marshall, and Mariana Islands—that suddenly placed the Japanese navy astride the central Pacific sea-lanes between Pearl Harbor and Manila Bay. Compounding the problem, the 1921–22 Washington conference on naval disarmament conceded Japan superiority over its home waters in the western Pacific and barred any further fortification of US bases there. While Japan's bombers had a short 550-mile flight to Manila from its colony at Taiwan, the US Navy had to steam for 5,300 miles from Honolulu. With its strategic posture crippled by such diplomatic blows, Washington's new "War Plan Orange" required that Army forces in the Philippines fight a desperate defensive campaign against Japanese invaders while the main battle fleet at Pearl Harbor traveled through the Japanese-dominated central Pacific to save US forces from surrender.[33] According to military historian Louis Morton, this strategy was "more a statement of hopes than a realistic appraisal."[34]

Advent of World War II

Although Washington had seemingly jettisoned its strategic vulnerability in 1935 by launching the Philippines on a ten-year transition to independence, imperial illusions would bring US forces back to the islands on the eve of World War II. Convinced that the brand-new B-17 bomber had somehow ended Japan's naval dominion over the western Pacific, Secretary of War Henry Stimson sent squadrons of those scarce "Flying Fortresses" to Manila with the mission of destroying any future invasion fleet. This flight of strategic fantasy was uncharacteristic for such a sober statesman. As a former law partner and protégé of Elihu Root, Stimson had followed his mentor's career path from corporate law to public service, taking on the post of governor-general of the Philippine Islands and thereby forming a deep emotional attachment to the colony.[35] Now, as secretary of war facing rising tensions with Japan, Stimson was almost euphoric at the discovery of a wonder weapon that would at long last bring those islands securely inside America's defensive perimeter.

Stimson became aware of the B-17's potential in early 1941 when subordinates began reporting that the Flying Fortress was the world's first effective long-range, daylight bomber. "At irregular intervals in history some new development has altered the art of warfare and changed the fate of peoples and the world," the assistant secretary of war for air, Robert Lovett, told Stimson. "Today that development is the large airplane, particularly the fast bomber. It has annihilated distance."[36]

Over the opposition of British and American commanders, who wanted the scarce bombers placed elsewhere, in August Stimson convinced President Franklin Roosevelt to send a massive fleet of 165 Flying Fortresses to the Philippines—the bulk of the 220 planes scheduled for production in the latter half of that year.[37] By the time the Japanese attacked in December, the Army had 74 heavy and medium bombers in the Philippines, 35 of them B-17s.[38]

While the bombers were crossing the Pacific to Manila, Stimson shared his epiphany with the president in a revealing letter. "A strategic opportunity of the utmost importance has suddenly arisen in the southwestern Pacific," he wrote. "We are rushing planes and other preparations to the Philippines from a base in the United States which . . . bids fair to stop Japan's march to the south and secure the safety of Singapore, with all the revolutionary consequences of such action." Not only could the bombers defend the Philippines; they would, he argued, make America master of the entire Pacific and thus "remove Japan from the Axis powers."[39]

Henry Stimson, US secretary of war, 1940 (Credit: Library of Congress)

As more sober minds might have predicted, such a vision of victory through airpower would evaporate within hours when war came suddenly on December 7, 1941. Japanese fighters, flying from bases on nearby Taiwan, would soon destroy most of those B-17s on the ground near Manila in the first days of the war, prompting Stimson to complain: "Now we have to sit helpless while our thirty years' successful experiment in laying the foundations of free government in the Philippine nation goes down in fragments under the military autocracy of Japan."[40]

War with Imperial Japan

Although most historians treat World War II as a single global war, from an imperial perspective the fighting in the Pacific seems a separate conflict, arising from a half century of regional rivalry between Tokyo and Washington. While the triumph in Europe would be shared with both Britain and the Soviet Union, victory in the Pacific would remain largely an American effort, allowing the US unchecked authority over the postwar occupation of Japan and South Korea.

In the first one hundred days of World War II, Japanese forces swept across Southeast Asia and the western Pacific in a lightning offensive, covering vast distances to crush the armed forces of three allied empires—the British, Dutch, and American—and thereby seize lands with nearly two hundred million people. Not only was the population of Japan's "Co-prosperity Sphere" then larger than that of the British Empire, but it was also history's quickest conquest of so much land and so many people. In retrospect, however, Japan's rapid, ill-planned expansion was riven by strategic flaws that would make it not only the world's most populous empire but also its most ephemeral.

With 36 of its 51 army divisions tied down in its ongoing war in China, Japan had only 11 divisions left with which to conquer Southeast Asia, forcing it to economize its forces by using a two-phase strategy. Instead of driving due south for the oil fields on the Indonesian islands of Borneo and Sumatra that were its main strategic objective, Japanese forces struck first at Allied bases on their flanks that might threaten later lines of communication—the British bastion at Singapore in the west and US bases at Manila Bay and Pearl Harbor in the east. With an Allied oil embargo strangling the fuel supplies that powered its army and navy, Japan desperately needed those oil fields to fuel its modern military. Acutely aware of his country's "oil predicament" and its inability to compete with US industry in a long war, the commander of Japan's navy, Admiral Isoroku Yamamoto, decided to determine "the fate of the war on the very first day" by destroying the US fleet at Hawaii—a fateful decision that would shatter American "isolationism" and finally force its population to mobilize for war.[41]

Isoroku Yamamoto, commander, Japan's Combined Fleet, 1942 (Credit: Alamy)

That first phase of Japan's strategy was remarkably successful. The December 7 surprise attack, involving six Japanese carriers, targeted the main US Navy base at Pearl Harbor, seeking to cripple the Pacific Fleet while pushing its own defensive perimeter deep into the central Pacific. With minimal losses, two waves of 353 Japanese fighters sank ten US ships, including four battleships, and turned America's Pacific bastion into a smoking ruin. Stunned by his own victory, the Japanese admiral in command failed to send a third wave of aircraft to attack the base's infrastructure.[42]

Arriving two weeks later to assess and salvage the situation, the new commander in chief of the Pacific Fleet, Admiral Chester Nimitz, quickly determined that the damage at Pearl Harbor was not as bad as it looked. Focused on the battleships, which the Japanese thought would be key to the war's outcome, they had missed the aircraft carriers, which were at sea. Nor did they attack the submarine piers, the ship repair facilities, or the massive oil reserves at the base. "All of the oil for the Fleet was in surface tanks," Nimitz explained. "We had about 4½ million barrels of oil out there and all of it was vulnerable to .50 caliber bullets. Had the Japanese destroyed the oil it would have prolonged the war another two years." Realizing that battleships were largely superseded, Nimitz quickly began building a new triad of vessels for the Pacific campaign to come—the fast aircraft carrier, the amphibious landing craft, and, for the combat service he knew best from his years at sea, the attack submarine. From such slender beginnings, the Pacific Command would grow into a massive force of 730 ships, one thousand B-29 Superfortress bombers, 20 Army divisions, and more than four hundred thousand marines.[43]

Chester Nimitz, commander, US Pacific Fleet, 1945 (Credit: Library of Congress)

Continuing their devastating southern sweep, the Japanese landed on the main Philippine island of Luzon and quickly occupied its capital, Manila, leaving General Douglas MacArthur's army contained on the nearby

Bataan Peninsula. After Japanese bombers from Saigon sank the two British capital ships sent to defend Singapore, Japanese forces under General To-moyuki Yamashita swept down the Malay Peninsula, defeating the demoralized British defenders in every battle. After just seven days of fighting, the British command at Singapore, with 85,000 troops and ample munitions, surrendered their greatest bastion east of Suez to a force of just 35,000 Japanese—a humiliation that Winston Churchill called "the worst disaster and largest capitulation in British history."[44]

In February 1942, Japan launched its second-phase strike for the main strategic targets in Southeast Asia. In an initial thrust, 20 warships pushed south into the Java Sea where they quickly destroyed the combined American-Australian-British-Dutch fleet, sinking ten ships and killing two thousand Allied sailors. In March, its army units swept across the islands of Java and Sumatra, capturing 98,000 Dutch colonial troops without a fight. After receiving reinforcements, Japan's forces in the Philippines defeated MacArthur's troops who were holding out on the Bataan Peninsula. In May, its forces based in Thailand invaded Burma, driving the British Army westward into India. Simultaneously, the Japanese navy captured Guadalcanal, in the Solomon Islands, placing their forces at the edge of the Coral Sea, within striking distance of the Australian coast for the first time.[45]

With the sudden check of Japan's southern advance at the Battle of the Coral Sea in May 1942 and the defeat of a parallel naval thrust eastward into the Pacific at Midway in June, Tokyo's advance was stopped, and its vast empire reached its peak. At Midway, Admiral Yamamoto gambled most of his surface fleet on a "decisive battle" to break the US Navy. He lost that bet badly and was forced to retreat after losing four carriers, 248 aircraft, and many of his best pilots.[46] Even after these defeats, Japan remained a formidable foe. After all, Tokyo's expanded empire stretched from the central Pacific to central China, from Manchuria to Southeast Asia—a vast domain of 540 million people, almost a quarter of all humanity, rich in oil, minerals, agriculture, and industry.[47]

Yet this hemispheric imperium, conquered at such unprecedented speed, was also rent by serious geopolitical weaknesses. Most fundamentally, the empire's industrial complex in northeastern Asia was fueled by oil shipped from Southeast Asia via a vulnerable maritime corridor through the South China Sea to Japan's home islands. With a porous defensive perimeter arching across the central Pacific from Alaska to Indonesia, the Japanese Navy had no way of stopping US submarine warfare from cutting off that flow of oil.

On account of its faith in Captain Mahan's maxim that major wars are settled by a single "decisive battle," the Japanese Navy's command had not prepared for a modern war of attrition fought with submarines and air attacks. "For a generation," wrote historians David Evans and Mark Peattie, "the guiding principle of [Japan's] tactical doctrine . . . had been the single, annihilating surface victory." Not only did that doctrine create "a fighting force that was both one-dimensional and brittle," but it also left the Japanese navy ill-prepared for a protracted war against a major industrial power.[48] While London and Washington used convoys to defeat "wolf packs" of Nazi submarines in the Battle of the Atlantic, Tokyo failed to devise a strategy to protect its shipping from daring hunter-killer attacks by individual American submarines in the western Pacific.

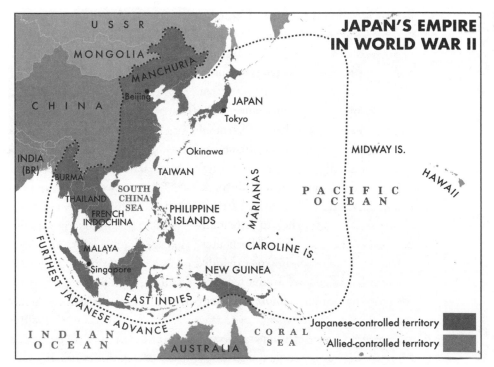

Playing upon these strategic flaws, US Navy submarines penetrated Japan's porous maritime frontier, gradually cutting off the critical supply of oil from Southeast Asia. For the first eighteen months of war, submarine operations were slowed by a torpedo design flaw and by skippers who had been trained to use the subs passively, for reconnaissance. After the Navy removed nearly 30 percent of its Pacific sub commanders in 1942, younger captains created high-risk tactics like firing "down the throat" shots at the bow of an oncoming Japanese warship. The revitalized submarine fleet and its newly daring captains struck with lethal effect, sinking 492 enemy ships and destroying two-thirds of Japan's tankers, cutting its shipping capacity from seven hundred thousand tons to just two hundred thousand. By war's end, a relatively small US fleet of 234 submarines had sunk 1,114 Japanese merchant ships, crippling its industries, constraining its air and naval operations, and collapsing its empire from within well before the emperor's formal surrender in August 1945.[49]

The US Navy's capture of the Northern Mariana islands of Guam, Saipan, and Tinian finally brought Japan's home islands within range of the new US strategic bomber. Developed at a cost of $3 billion, the B-29 Superfortress was the war's most expensive weapon—a behemoth powered by four engines to speeds of 350 miles per hour and equipped with a pressurized cabin that allowed it to fly at 32,000 feet, above the range of Japanese fighters. After months of indifferent results from precision daylight bombing, an aggressive new commander, General Curtis LeMay, switched to a tactic that would have appallingly lethal effects: the mass firebombing of Japanese cities. On the night of March 9, 1945, an air armada of 279 Superfortresses dropped 1,665 tons of incendiary bombs on Tokyo, unleashing a firestorm that incinerated a quarter of the city and killed 83,000 people. Over the next four months, LeMay's fleet of 600 bombers conducted continuous raids that dropped 167,743 tons of bombs and razed almost every major Japanese city.[50]

That devastating campaign culminated in attacks on two Japanese cities by a totally new weapon. On August 6, 1945, a single B-29 Superfortress dropped an atomic bomb on Hiroshima. The mushroom cloud rose to 50,000 feet. The temperature on the ground surged to 3,000°C, melting granite and steel. Of the city's 76,000 structures, 70,000 were destroyed. More than 78,000 people were killed in the blast. Another 150,000 later died from radiation exposure. Three days after that, another B-29 dropped an atomic bomb on Nagasaki. Even though the surrounding hills absorbed much of the shock, 12,700 of the city's 51,000 buildings were leveled. At least 23,800 people died. Six days later, Japan finally surrendered. By then, the bombing campaign had killed 330,000 people, obliterated 67 cities, destroyed 2.5 million homes, and left 30 percent of all Japanese homeless.[51]

The US paid a heavy price for its Pacific victory. In contrast to Europe, where Allied forces outnumbered Americans, its troops did most of the fighting in the Pacific and suffered accordingly. In destroying 686 Japanese warships and killing 298,209 of their personnel, the US Navy lost 79 ships and 31,485 servicemen, while the US Army suffered 50,385 killed in action.[52] By the end of the war, the US had won absolute dominion over the Pacific. But even more importantly, nuclear weapons had become an essential element of geopolitical power.

In addition, by war's end, the increasing range of strategic bombers, combined with the advent of the atomic age, had transformed Stimson's air power fantasy into strategic reality. As effective ranges grew from 2,000 miles for the B-17 Flying Fortress to 3,250 miles for the B-29 Superfortress, the War Department planned to extend America's defensive perimeter by securing military bases along the Pacific littoral from Japan to the Philippines.

As the US had fought its way across the Pacific, both the Navy and War Department had advocated the retention of captured Japanese islands, particularly the Carolines and Marianas, for postwar military bases. Concerned that the US example might prompt the Soviets to do the same in Eastern Europe, the Roosevelt administration honored the international mandate and Washington later put those islands under UN trusteeship.[53]

The Pentagon, however, was still determined to acquire postwar bases in the Philippines. In November 1943, General Thomas Handy of the War Department's Operations Division advised Stimson: "Present studies concerning US post-war military requirements . . . envisage the establishment of a chain of outlying bases as a defense ring around the Western Hemisphere." To "insure against a major surprise attack on our shores," the War Department should press the Philippine Commonwealth for base concessions "so sweeping in nature that as to permit exact locations to be determined by US military and naval authorities upon conclusion of the war."[54] After the president of the Philippine Commonwealth, Manuel Quezon, who headed a government-in-exile in Washington, agreed in principle to these concessions, Congress passed a resolution in mid-1944 authorizing negotiations for postwar US bases in the Philippines.[55]

Briefing the delegation to the UN conference in April 1945, Stimson defended the proposed bases as a corrective to the conundrum that had bedeviled the American position in the Pacific for the past 40 years. "I went on and pointed out the errors which we had made in not keeping a path open across the Pacific to enable us to guard the Philippines and our interests in the Far East," Stimson explained. "I told them Mr. Wilson had been warned against giving the Mandated Islands [in the central Pacific] to Japan but nevertheless allowed it to be done. . . . We thus shackled ourselves and placed our reliance upon treaties which the Japanese promptly broke, and I earnestly begged them never again to repeat that error."[56]

In the immediate postwar period, the US would, in fact, transform the island chain off the coast of Asia into the front line of its Pacific defense, seizing military bases along the length of Japan and transforming the island of Okinawa into a military bastion. Washington then exploited Manila's desperate need for war reconstruction aid to extract a 99-year lease on 23 military bases in the Philippines, for all of which Washington was granted unrestricted use for offensive operations. Clark Field and Subic Bay soon became two of the largest overseas US bases.[57]

Thus, even as it advocated formal protection for the sovereignty of all nations at the UN, Washington was securing Pacific military bastions under terms that would infringe on the sovereignty of close allies, thus revealing the underlying tensions between its internationalist ideals and the gritty reality of its geopolitics.

Washington's World Order

The widespread death and devastation of World War II brought an end to the age of empire and allowed the emergence of a new world order. Not only did the war ravage three continents and leave some 70 million dead across the planet, but it was also an ideological struggle that destroyed the idea of imperialism as a legitimate form of governance—for both colonizers and colonized alike.

To counter Axis propaganda during the war, the Allies had forged a common commitment to a postwar world in which all humanity would live as equals in their own sovereign states. In January 1941, Roosevelt proclaimed his famous four freedoms—of speech and worship as well as from want and fear. Articulating a principle that would later legitimate American global power, the president added, "Freedom means the supremacy of human rights every-where." That August, Roosevelt and British prime minister Winston Churchill issued the Atlantic Charter from the deck of a British battleship, promising to "respect the right of all peoples to choose the form of government under which they will live." Churchill soon made it clear that he was speaking about the nations of Nazi-occupied Europe and not their colonies.[58] But by 1944, as evidence of Axis race-based atrocities mounted, Roosevelt announced: "The United Nations are fighting to make . . . a world in which all persons regardless of race, color, or creed may live in peace, honor, and dignity."[59]

In the aftermath of history's most destructive war, the United States used its unmatched power to form a new global order. Like Britain at the end of the Napoleonic Wars, America had emerged from global war with little damage and much advantage—its economy expanded, its military modern-ized, and its citizens united. While American war dead numbered 416,000, that figure paled before the 19 million killed in Europe, the 20 million more in China, and the 24 million in the Soviet Union.[60] While industries in Europe, Russia, and Japan were damaged or destroyed, the US had doubled the size of its economy during the war. By 1945, it accounted for 60 percent of the world's industrial output. With just 6 percent of the world's popula-tion, the US had 46 percent of the world's electrical power and 59 percent of its proven oil reserves. Much of Europe and Asia were suffering from serious food shortages, but American agriculture was producing swelling surpluses to feed a hungry humanity. At war's end, its military had grown to more than twelve million troops, its Navy ruled the seas with more than a thousand warships, and its Air Force commanded the skies with 39,000 military aircraft. The United States was, as President Harry Truman put it, "the most powerful nation, perhaps, in all history."[61]

Over the next decade, Washington would, through the stark duality of its global power, build both an empire of unprecedented reach and a world system that espoused liberal principles of inviolable sovereignty and human equality. In retrospect, the sharp contrast between Mahan's realism and Root's idealism, evident at Washington's debut on the world stage, was no less manifest a half century later, when the country achieved global hegemony.

Washington's visionary world order took form at two major confer-ences—at Bretton Woods, New Hampshire, in 1944, where 44 Allied nations forged an international financial system exemplified by the World

Bank, and at San Francisco in 1945, where they drafted a charter for the UN that created a community of nations. The old order of competing empires, closed imperial trade blocs, and secret alliances would soon give way to an international community of emancipated colonies, sovereign nations, free trade, and peace through law. In essence, the UN Charter's many clauses rested on just two foundational principles that would soon become synonymous with Washington's world order: inviolable national sovereignty and universal human rights.[62]

Yet within the UN and the world system it represented, there would be a recurring tension between the prerogatives of sovereign states and the principle of human rights. When the so-called Big Four Allied powers— the US, Great Britain, China, and the Soviet Union—met at Dumbarton Oaks near Washington, DC, in late 1944 to draw up plans for a successor to the League of Nations, they all agreed that they would control an empowered Security Council, while the rest of the world's nations would be limited to advisory discussions in a powerless General Assembly. As President Roosevelt put it, this assembly "should meet about once a year" to allow "all the small nations . . . to blow off steam." China's pressure for commitments to human rights and racial equality met strong opposition, particularly from officials in the State Department, which rejected any encroachment on US sovereignty that might allow a challenge to its system of racial segregation.[63]

Once deliberations moved outside the closed doors at Dumbarton Oaks to public debates by 51 sovereign states and dozens of US civic groups in San Francisco, the tenor of the discussions changed markedly. The Latin American delegations arrived with a unified agenda urging that the new United Nations make "every effort to prevent racial or religious discrimination." Colonized peoples insisted that their freedom was required for lasting world peace. US labor and religious groups urged fulfillment of wartime commitments to human rights and racial equality. These pressures forced the Big Four powers to modify their plans, producing a UN Charter that protected human rights, created a General Assembly authorized to make recommendations about all forms of rights, and a Trusteeship Council to supervise the end of colonial rule. Even though those were important changes, the Big Four still emerged from San Francisco with their prerogatives in the Security Council unchecked.[64]

On the credit side of history's ledger, the new UN Charter rejected the right of conquest prevalent in the imperial age and espoused the "principle of the sovereign equality of all its Members," who "shall refrain . . . from the threat or use of force against the territorial integrity or political independence of any state." The Trusteeship Council charged the remaining colonial powers to "accept as a sacred trust to promote to the utmost . . . self government or independence."[65] By the time decolonization was complete in 1980, the number of UN member states would triple to 155.

In the debit column of that historical accounting, the UN Charter compromised its commitments to racial equality and colonial liberation by adding clauses that made state sovereignty paramount. The Charter's Article I stated that one of the UN's prime purposes was "encouraging . . . fundamental freedoms for all without distinction as to race, sex, language, or religion." Yet the major powers at San Francisco also inserted a legal loophole, Article II (7), providing that none of the charter's clauses would allow the organization "to intervene in matters which are essentially within the domestic jurisdiction of any state." With this sweeping limitation on the equality promised under Article I, South Africa protected apartheid, Britain exempted its colonial empire, and the bloc of Southern states in the US Congress saw no threat to racial segregation. Indeed, the American delegate John Foster Dulles, a Republican conservative and future secretary of state, crafted Article II (7) precisely to avoid any international pressure for reform of what he called "the Negro problem in the South"—code words for the harsh system of racial segregation that had succeeded slavery. This loophole was so large and so controversial that it plunged the UN into two years of intense debates over human rights, culminating in the unanimous approval of the Universal Declaration of Human Rights in 1948 that proclaimed "equal and inalienable rights of all members of the human family."[66]

In effect, Washington's new order, as embodied in the UN, rejected the religious and racial divisions of the previous five centuries, articulating principles of equality that would lend moral support to the struggle against colonial rule worldwide, apartheid in South Africa, and even racial segregation in the US. In the first years after the UN's founding, domestic civil rights groups would cite its charter in their legal challenges to the many forms of racial discrimination that were then such an established part of American life, including covenants barring housing sales to minorities, systematic disenfranchisement, and segregation in the South enforced by thousands of lynchings. Although Washington would back away from human rights during much of the Cold War, plaintiffs still cited the UN Charter in the landmark Supreme Court cases of 1954, *Brown v. Board of Education* and *Bolling v. Sharpe*, which argued for an end to the racial segregation of public schools.[67]

Even with all the compromises involved, the UN represented a real advance in international relations. Just as the British imperial system was much more pervasive than its Iberian predecessor, so Washington's world order went far beyond both to become rigorously systematic and deeply embedded. The Congress of Vienna had been an ephemeral gathering of two dozen diplomats whose influence largely faded within a decade. In contrast, the United Nations and its 193 member states have, for nearly 75 years, sustained thousands of permanent staff with broad international responsibilities for health, human rights, education, law, labor, gender, development, food, cultural heritage, peacekeeping, and refugees. Under its broad charter, the UN formed specific affiliated groups such as the World Health Organization (WHO) to fight smallpox, polio, plague, and other pandemics that had scourged humanity for centuries. In addition to such broad governance, the UN would also host treaties that regulated sea, space, and climate change. Not only did the Bretton Woods Conference create the International Monetary Fund (IMF) and the World Bank, but it also led to the formation of the World Trade Organization (WTO), which regulates commerce among 164 member states. Such a comprehensive system for global governance, integrated into almost every aspect of international intercourse, should, in theory, have sufficient resilience to survive even major upheavals.

Moreover, the UN was just one of many international initiatives that followed World War II. After 1945, as political scientist John Ikenberry has pointed out, "the United States pushed onto the world a breathtaking array of new institutions—multilateral, bilateral, regional, global, security, economic, and political."[68] Starting with its $13 billion Marshall Plan for the reconstruction of war-torn Europe, Washington supplemented the work of the World Bank by providing billions of dollars in bilateral aid to fund reconstruction and development in nations old and new.[69] Through such efforts, the portion of the world's population living in extreme poverty fell steadily from 40 percent in the early 1980s to just 10 percent by 2015, with projections as low as 3 percent by 2030. However, in 2015 there were still some 3.4 billion people, nearly half the world's population, living on five dollars a day—conditions that underscore the pressing need for major development efforts in Asia, Africa, and Latin America.[70]

The Realpolitik of US Global Power

Yet all that liberal internationalism coexisted alongside a grittier dimension of US global power. "We have about 50 percent of the world's wealth but only about 6.3 percent of its population," said George Kennan in 1947, when he was chief of policy planning at the State Department. "Our real task in the coming period is to devise a pattern of relationships which will permit us to maintain this position of disparity without positive detriment to our national security. To do so, we will have to dispense with all . . . high-minded international altruism." If the UN, formed in a burst of idealism amid the great allied victory over fascism, embodied that altruism, then the Cold War instruments that Kennan would help to create represented the darker side of a duality that permeated Washington's postwar programs, large and small. Foreign aid would rebuild a war-torn Europe and alleviate poverty worldwide, while covert operations fomented assassinations, conducted coups, and rigged elections in countless nations. Washington's new clandestine services developed cunning techniques of psychological torture and mass propaganda that became tools of political oppression, while its development agencies promoted land redistribution in Asia, Africa, and Latin America that, for millions of tenant farmers living in that structural legacy of colonialism, represented something akin to economic liberation.[71]

Once its World War II alliance with the Soviet Union collapsed into the Cold War, Washington forged a national security apparatus that served, simultaneously, to contain Communism and create the capacity for global hegemony. Under the National Security Act of 1947 and subsequent legislation, Washington formed the basic instruments for its exercise of global power—the Defense Department, the US Air Force, the National Security Council, and the Central Intelligence Agency. That legislation also established the Pacific Command at Pearl Harbor, which, according to historian Bruce Cumings, was "the core of the nation's global power," with 362,000 troops and 220 ships by the close of the Cold War.[72] For more than 30 years, a succession of battle-hardened World War II veterans designated commander in chief of the Pacific Fleet—steely admirals like Harry D. Felt and John S. McCain, Jr.—would serve in this post as veritable viceroys for the Pacific and field marshals for all of Asia.

On this realpolitik side of the duality that marked its foreign policy, the US sought to contain the Communist bloc, led by the Soviet Union and the People's Republic of China, behind an "Iron Curtain" (to use Winston Churchill's famous phrase) that would stretch five thousand miles across the Eurasian landmass. To control the world's nations on its own side of that divide, advance its global dominion, and protect its extraordinary wealth and power, Washington constructed a formidable four-tier apparatus—economic, military, diplomatic, and clandestine.[73]

The foundation and first element for Washington's hegemony was an economy of exceptional strength. Not only did America account for half of global output in the aftermath of a devastating world war, but the global economy it built at Bretton Woods was based on the US dollar, which had long surpassed the British pound as the leading international currency. The experts at that meeting, led by famed British economist John Maynard Keynes, created the IMF to attenuate the rigidity of the prewar gold standard, an aim it achieved by setting exchange rates for all currencies based on that dollar and then making it convertible to gold at $35 per ounce. Apart from effecting an increase in liquidity that would spark economic growth for a quarter of a century, the system established the dollar as the global reserve currency. Whether spending $13 billion to rebuild a ravaged Europe or billions more to construct hundreds of overseas military bases, Washington could simply print paper dollars, and foreign governments had to bank them as if they were gold bars. Although Moscow quickly rejected the IMF, President Harry Truman was undeterred, crowing, "We are the giant of the economic world."[74]

At the core of US power was its second key element—an unmatched military with hundreds of overseas bases that circled the globe, a formidable nuclear arsenal, massive air and naval forces, and many client armies. Within a decade of the end of World War II, Washington already had five hundred overseas military bases ringing Eurasia, and a chain of mutual defense pacts stretching from the North Atlantic Treaty Organization (NATO) in Europe and North America, to the Australia, New Zealand, US Security Treaty (ANZUS) in the South Pacific. Washington also signed the Rio Treaty with Latin American republics, which was based on the principle of collective defense. These treaties and the many military bases that went with them created what Cumings has called "an archipelago of empire."[75]

In marked contrast to the landed aristocrats presiding over the British Empire's decline, the US military also provided a talented generation of upwardly mobile leaders, rigorously selected and tested in combat, who extended Washington's global reach to far-flung countries and continents. When the Cold War's first battle erupted—the Greek Civil War in 1946—Washington selected General James Van Fleet, the son of a failed Florida businessman and a 1915 graduate of West Point, to head a contingent of 450 US military advisers. They would guide the Greek army as it hammered the Communist guerrillas for 20 months, until their resistance collapsed. Sent to the divided peninsula of Korea, where a disastrous war backed by Cold War superpowers was underway, Van Fleet led US and South Korean troops in the maintenance of constant pressure on Chinese forces, finally leading to an armistice.[76] Even in retirement, he founded the Korea Society in 1957 to promote "cooperation between the people of the United States and Korea." (On a memorable day three years later, I met the general when he visited my grandfather's cattle ranch in Dade City, Florida, while purchasing a truckload of prime breeding bulls. The people of South Korea, he said, needed a new source of protein.)[77]

James Van Fleet, commander of UN forces, Columbia Orphanage, Seoul, South Korea, 1952 (Credit: Author's Collection)

The president who presided over the military operations that had accompanied America's ascent to global power was Dwight Eisenhower, the son of a failed general-store owner in Abilene, Kansas, and another member of the West Point class of 1915. During World War II, he had forged the Allied coalition that defeated the Germans in North Africa, mounted a massive amphibious landing in France, and breached Germany's last defenses. As president during the Cold War decade of the 1950s, he oversaw the synthesis of science, industry, and weapons procurement into what he called a "military-industrial complex" to maintain America's technological edge.[78]

By the end of the Eisenhower presidency in 1960, the Pentagon had built a nuclear triad of weaponry that gave it "a virtually invulnerable strategic deterrent." While the US Navy's fleet of five nuclear-powered submarines cruised the ocean depths carrying sixteen nuclear-armed Polaris missiles each, its fourteen attack carriers, including the atomic-powered USS *Enterprise*, were also equipped for nuclear strikes. Moreover, the Strategic Air Command had 1,700 bombers ready to drop nuclear payloads on the Communist bloc, including six hundred behemoth B-52s with a range of eight thousand miles. Meanwhile, the Air Force had developed Atlas and Titan ballistic missiles that could carry nuclear warheads more than six thousand miles.[79]

Drawing on the country's economic strength, the Pentagon lavished funds—growing rapidly from $33 billion annually in 1959 to $87 billion in 2009—on scientific research.[80] Its close alliance with defense contractors produced incessant technological innovation, including the world's first system of global telecommunications satellites, which would evolve during the Cold War into its chief means for military navigation, intelligence, and communication.[81] To exercise its dominion over the skies, Washington would elaborate on the British Empire's doctrine of "freedom of the seas" to include the sky and even space, where its military satellites could orbit without restraint.[82]

Such a massive military apparatus rested on geopolitical foundations of extraordinary strength. As historian John Darwin has explained, Washington achieved its "colossal Imperium . . . on an unprecedented scale" after World War II by becoming the first power in history to control the strategic axial points "at both ends of Eurasia." Indeed, when the Cold War reached Asia at the start of the Korean War in 1950, the National Security Council issued a memorandum (NSC-68) stating that "Soviet efforts are now directed toward the domination of the Eurasian land mass" and requiring that the US expand its military "to deter, if possible, Soviet expansion, and to defeat, if necessary, aggressive Soviet or Soviet-directed actions." To encompass Eurasia, the defense budget increased almost fourfold from $13.5 billion to $48.2 billion, launching an increase of military appropriations that continues to this day.[83] In defense of its dominance over that vast continent, Washington would, over the next 40 years, fight two hot wars in Korea and South Vietnam to check communist expansion, while the CIA waged large covert operations around its southern edge, probing relentlessly for vulnerabilities in the Sino-Soviet bloc.

While Washington defended the western axis of Eurasia through a multilateral defense pact with a dozen NATO allies, its position in the East was secured by bilateral pacts with four nations—Japan, South Korea, the Philippines, and Australia—as well as a five-thousand-mile chain of military bases along the Pacific littoral. In the aftermath of the Korean War, Washington would maintain permanent garrisons in South Korea, adding to the one hundred military installations it had seized during the postwar occupation of Japan. Further south, the US had an anti-Communist redoubt on the island of Taiwan, massive military installations at Clark Field and Subic Bay in the Philippines, and access to ports at Sydney and Brisbane in Australia under the ANZUS alliance. At its peak, the British Empire's reach around the tri-continental "world island" of Africa and Eurasia had not extended much beyond Singapore, but now Washington controlled these continents from military bastions in Europe and the entire Pacific littoral.

By serving as the frontier for the defense of one continent (North America) and a springboard for its dominance of another (Eurasia), the Pacific littoral would become the geopolitical fulcrum for the entire US global defense posture. By 1955, these early enclaves in Japan and the Philippines had been integrated into a global network of hundreds of overseas bases aimed largely at containing the Sino-Soviet bloc behind the Iron Curtain. Anchored by massive military bases at Ramstein, Germany, and Subic Bay in the Philippines, these axial points were tied together by layers of steel, including strategic bombers, ballistic missiles, and massive naval fleets in the Mediterranean, the Persian Gulf, and the Pacific.[84]

At the midpoint of those arcs of steel around Eurasia lay the Middle East, which would become a recurring flash point for American global hegemony. After World War II, the British initially maintained an informal empire there by backing the region's conservative monarchs, but the US slowly gained influence over its oil—first in Saudi Arabia and later, after the 1953 CIA coup that elevated the shah to direct rule, in Iran. As Britain ended its protectorates over Iraq, Kuwait, and finally in 1971 the Persian Gulf emirates, Washington quickly filled the breach by taking over the Royal Navy base at Bahrain in the Persian Gulf and forging a close alliance with Iran. But the shah's downfall in that country's Islamic Revolution of 1979 removed the geopolitical keystone for the US position in the entire Middle East. Through three major wars over the next 40 years, Washington would struggle unsuccessfully to achieve a new strategic balance in a region that served as the main source of oil for the global economy.[85]

Just as Britain's imperial age coincided with its coal-driven industrial revolution, so Washington's world order relied on crude oil to feed the voracious energy needs of its global economy. Although the country first struck oil in 1859, coal would remain its prime energy source for most of the next century. Even on the eve of World War II, when America produced two-thirds of the world's petroleum, oil accounted for only one-third of its energy supply and just 10 percent for other industrial societies like Europe and Japan. As US automobile ownership climbed from 40 million units in 1950 to 213 million in 2000, oil consumption surged from 6.5 million barrels daily to a peak of 20 million barrels. During those same decades, the federal government spent $370 billion to cover the country with 46,000 miles of interstate highways, allowing cars and trucks to replace much of the older fuel-efficient railway system. As a result, the US remained the world's main source of carbon dioxide emissions throughout the twentieth century—accounting for 36 percent of the total in 1900, 48 percent in 1950, and 24 percent in 2000.[86]

To drive the carbon-fueled economy of Washington's world order, there would be a dramatic, fivefold increase in the global consumption of liquid fossil fuels during the last half of the twentieth century. As the number of cars and trucks worldwide kept climbing, crude oil rose from 27 percent of global fossil fuel consumption in 1950 to 53 percent by 1973, surpassing coal to become the world's main source of energy. To meet this relentlessly rising demand, the Middle East's share of global oil production would climb from just 7 percent in 1950 to 40 percent in 1973. By then, America's auto registrations would reach one hundred million, demand for oil would outstrip domestic production, and imports would surge to provide 36 percent of its petroleum supply. Oil accounted for 46 percent of total energy needs in the US, 60 percent in Western Europe, and an overwhelming 73 percent in Japan. Reflecting this rising dependence, Washington made itself guardian of the Persian Gulf and would, under the Carter Doctrine of 1980, struggle to secure the region's vast oil reserves (63 percent of the world's total) through an endless succession of wars in the Middle East—from the Gulf War of 1990 through its ongoing involvement in Iraq.[87] Yet such interventions in search of stability seemed only to fuel the Middle East's continuing volatility.

Whether negotiating mutual security pacts, courting Middle East monarchs, or forging consensus at the UN, diplomacy would supplement raw economic and military strength to become an important third element in Washington's array of global power. As decolonization progressed throughout the Cold War, the Eisenhower administration had to develop a new form of global hegemony, replacing the British Empire's collaboration with local elites (chiefs and maharajahs) with cooperative national leaders (presidents and prime ministers). From its inception, the US system did not create mere surrogates or clients, but allies who worked, even if from a weaker position, to maximize their own national interests. To manage such contentious allies, Washington deployed the salve of foreign aid and the sting of clandestine operations.[88]

These covert operations were a fourth and final element of US global power during the Cold War. Through surveillance by the NSA and secret interventions by the CIA on five continents, Washington manipulated elections and promoted coups to assure that national leaders on its side of the Iron Curtain would remain compliant "subordinate elites," friendly to America.[89] As a result, from its founding in 1947, the CIA became a critical mechanism for the resolution of a contradiction that lay at the heart of Washington's world system: How could the US intervene in the internal affairs of independent nations in the exercise of its global hegemony without being seen to violate their inviolable sovereignty under the UN Charter?

The answer was to do so covertly, using the agency's (at least theoretically) traceless tools to invisibly compromise the sovereignty of countless nations. At the start of the Cold War, George Kennan, then the State Department's architect of Washington's anti-Soviet containment strategy, drafted a revealing directive (NSC-10/2). To counter "the full might of the Kremlin's political warfare," the US, he wrote, should mobilize its "resources for covert political warfare" by placing "responsibility for them within the structure of the Central Intelligence Agency." To expand the agency's operations beyond its original intelligence function, the National Security Council formed the Office of Policy Coordination (OPC) within the CIA to undertake a wide range of covert activities—notably "sabotage, anti-sabotage, demolition and evacuation measures, subversion against hostile states, including assistance to underground resistance movements, guerrillas, and refugee liberation groups." Over the next four years, the OPC grew rapidly from just 302 agents to 5,954 personnel operating from 47 CIA stations worldwide with a budget of $82 million. At the same time that it was codifying the laws of war through the Geneva Conventions and its own Uniform Code of Military Justice, Washington, in a clear illustration of the duality of its hegemony, exempted the CIA from any legal or ethical restraints in carrying out these covert missions.[90]

George Kennan, director, Policy Planning Staff, US State
Department, 1947 (Credit: Library of Congress)

As the Iron Curtain came down across Europe, the OPC's initial mission was twofold: to promote active anti-Communist resistance in Eastern Europe and to curb Communist influence in the West. For about four years starting in 1949, the OPC recruited hundreds of Eastern European exiles, trained them in espionage, and parachuted them behind the Iron Curtain. Whether in Albania, Poland, Romania, Russia, or Ukraine, all were quickly captured, and almost all were killed by ruthlessly efficient Soviet bloc secret police. In marked contrast to that dismal failure, CIA operations in Western Europe seemed, at the time, stunningly successful. Its operatives blocked the Communist Party from a certain victory in the 1948 Italian elections, while simultaneously splitting the Socialists and Communists in France to keep the left out of power. Under its Operation Gladio, the CIA embedded clandestine networks inside countries across Western Europe, ready to mobilize mobs or break out arms from covert caches should Communists threaten to take power.[91]

With Europe secured by the early 1950s, the CIA applied similar techniques to assist the ascent of compliant national leaders in Asia, Africa, and Latin America. Between 1945 and 2000, the US intervened in 81 consequential elections worldwide, including eight times in Italy, five in Japan, and many more in Latin America.[92] Between 1958 and 1975, military coups, many of them American-sponsored, changed governments in three dozen nations—a quarter of the world's sovereign states—fostering a distinct "reverse wave" in the global trend toward democracy.[93]

During the first decades of the Cold War, a national leader critical of America could face a CIA-sponsored coup that left him locked up for life (Iran), forced into exile (Guatemala), tortured to death (Congo), or left murdered on the capital's streets (South Vietnam). Apart from coups, which were often difficult to organize, the agency attempted assassinations, which usually failed (Congo, Cuba) but sometimes hit the mark (Dominican Republic).[94] More than any other aspect of foreign policy, those secret CIA operations clearly violated the national sovereignty assured in the UN Charter, lending an irresolvable ambiguity to the US exercise of global power.

Even the most altruistic of Washington's foreign policy initiatives reflected aspects of that ambiguity. While the Marshall Plan did give Europe $13 billion for postwar reconstruction, recipient nations had to provide the plan's overseas offices with an equivalent amount of local currency—creating what reporter Tim Weiner called a "global money-laundering scheme" that allowed the CIA to expropriate 5 percent of those funds, totalling $685 million, for its covert operations. With all that cash, the agency recruited European assets, created "all-out liberation movements" behind the Iron Curtain, funded conservative discussions among intellectuals to shape public discourse, delivered "small fortunes" to right-wing labor groups, and paid gangsters in Naples and Marseilles to serve as bare-knuckles strikebreakers.[95]

This new clandestine weapon would, however, soon prove a double-edged sword. During its first decade, covert CIA interventions at first seemed like stunning victories—including the manipulation of the 1948 Italian elections to favor of the moderate Christian Democrats over the Communists, the replacement of the prickly Iranian prime minister Mohammad Mosaddegh with the pliable shah, and the ouster of Guatemala's socialist government under Jacobo Árbenz to install a reliable military regime. Over time, however, the Christian Democrats proved both corrupt and inept, the shah became a brutal autocrat determined to crush the democratic yearnings Mosaddegh had so clearly embodied, and Guatemala's military grew genocidally murderous in their effort to extinguish the peasant land-hunger that had inspired Árbenz's moderate reforms. Nonetheless, in Washington those seeming victories encouraged what diplomatic historian David Milne called "illusions of consequence-free omniscience" that soon led the agency to attempt the overthrow of Fidel Castro's entrenched Cuban government with 1,500 ill-trained exiles, producing a monumental foreign policy disaster at the Bay of Pigs. Even when they were seemingly brilliant in their short-term tactical expediency, numerous CIA covert operations had disastrous long-term strategic consequences for both the US and the subject society. Secret intervention to change a society's political direction could and often did fracture a delicate political balance, plunging a weaker state into protracted instability marked by endemic violence. As the heavy costs of the agency's covert capacity accumulated, State Department official Kennan called its creation "the greatest mistake [he] ever made."[96]

Waging the Cold War

Viewed through the lens of actual warfare, the Cold War was modern history's largest, longest, and—paradoxically—least destructive conflict. While the threat of a thermonuclear holocaust prevented direct combat between the rival superpowers, a succession of surrogate wars effectively divided the

40 years of the Cold War into three distinct phases. First, there was a nuclear standoff in Europe between Washington's NATO allies and Moscow's Warsaw Pact (1948–1962). Next, following the nuclear brinkmanship of the Cuban missile crisis, the superpowers waged a surrogate war in South Vietnam (1962–1975). The final phase (1975–1989) was marked by murderously destructive conflicts in southern Africa, Central America, and Central Asia. In each successive phase, as the costs and dangers of massive standing armies became prohibitive, conventional and nuclear forces gave way to covert operations and proxy warfare, culminating in Angola, where Russian and American clients fought for a full quarter of a century without any combatants from either superpower ever being on the ground.

During the Cold War's initial phase, mechanized armies squared off across the heart of Europe—with 150 Warsaw Pact divisions facing 25 active-duty NATO divisions, both backed by armadas of artillery, tanks, strategic bombers, and nuclear-armed missiles.[97] To compensate for its inferiority in conventional forces, the US built a superior nuclear arsenal, with a staggering 6,800 warheads by 1964 compared to the Soviet Union's 500.[98] Such weaponry, however, produced its own paradox. Nuclear weapons were so efficient in their destruction that they could never be used, meaning that actual warfare during the Cold War shifted to live battlefield combat—first in Greece, when the US aided the royalist government in defeating a Communist insurgency, and then in Korea, where UN forces saved the South from a Communist invasion. Since these limited wars carried a risk of dangerous nuclear escalation, both superpowers preferred to probe the other's weaknesses covertly, making espionage and clandestine operations defining features of their global rivalry.

Under President Eisenhower, the National Security Council became his central command post for fighting the Cold War, meeting weekly to plan foreign policy for a fast-changing world, while the CIA served as his secret strike force for securing the support of the hundred new nations emerging from colonial rule. During his eight-year term, the agency conducted 170 major covert operations in 48 nations, largely on the US side of the Iron Curtain.[99]

The first major one came when the CIA (helped by British intelligence) supplanted the prime minister of Iran, after he nationalized the Anglo-Iranian Oil Company in 1951. By orchestrating terror bombings and hiring mobs to riot, the agency replaced Mosaddegh with the so-called shah—the young, inexperienced son of an ousted military dictator. After the coup, the CIA helped consolidate the shah's control by establishing the most important of his brutal secret police units, the SAVAK, and training its officers in torture techniques—one of the earliest signs of the agency's program of secret research into psychological torture that it would, in defiance of international conventions, disseminate among allies worldwide.[100] As opposition to the shah grew in the 1970s, the SAVAK would torture dissidents cruelly, sparking Iranian student protests in Europe against his abuse of 50,000 political prisoners.[101] In an interview with the French newspaper *Le Monde*, the shah said: "Why should we not employ the same methods as you Europeans? We have learned sophisticated methods of torture from you."[102]

After angry demonstrators forced the shah from power in 1979, Iranian poet Reza Baraheni claimed that "at least half a million people have . . . been beaten, whipped, or tortured by SAVAK"—charges he documented with gruesome autopsy photos of mangled bodies. By buttressing the shah's rule with riot police and ruthless interrogation, the CIA destabilized Iranian democracy and unleashed a political process that eventually allowed the ascent of a rigidly theocratic Islamic regime. Although the agency's analysts concluded the success of its 1953 coup that put the shah in power "was mostly a matter of chance," it still became what the *New York Times* called "the blueprint for a succession of CIA plots to foment coups and destabilize governments during the cold war."[103] The agency's recurring complicity in such tortures, all banned under Article 5 of the UN Universal Declaration of Human Rights, highlighted the stark duality between Washington's principles and its exercise of power.

Within a year, the Iran coup was followed by the CIA's ouster of the democratic government of Guatemala, which was trying to redress the country's pervasive rural poverty by expropriating idle land from the US-owned United Fruit Company. By broadcasting propaganda from a pirate radio station to create the illusion that a small coup force was, in fact, a powerful rebel army, the CIA drove President Jacobo Árbenz into exile and established the first of a dozen military dictatorships that would rule the country for the next 30 years. As military repression mounted, frustrated peasant farmers joined guerrilla groups, and the countryside plunged into a 36-year civil war. In its bloodiest year, 1982–1983, General Efraín Ríos Montt led a junta, supported by US military aid, in the slaughter of 70,000 rural residents. The country's truth commission later called these "acts of genocide against groups of Mayan people." By the time a formal peace was signed in 1996, the Guatemalan military had destroyed 460 villages, displaced a million villagers, and killed two hundred thousand civilians—all in a society of only five million people. With violence so ingrained in the country's culture, Guatemala would remain, for the next two decades and beyond, one of the world's most unstable nations, with an astronomical murder rate and a profusion of criminal gangs whose 22,000 members controlled half its territory.[104]

Following those two supposed successes, Washington authorized another 330 such covert operations during the next decade, making the CIA its preferred instrument for the exercise of global power. Success bred hubris, and the agency soon met its nemesis when Fidel Castro crushed its invasion force of Cuban exiles. In a plan inspired by its Guatemala operation, the agency's invasion force of 1,500 exiles landed on the country's south coast with the doomed mission of marching 60 miles through an impassable swamp and across a deep bay without boats to a mountain redoubt where the Cuban masses would supposedly rally to their flag. The exiles never made it off the beach. Those not killed were all captured. Seizing the opportunity to break out of its geopolitical isolation, Moscow soon deployed nuclear missiles in Cuba, bringing the superpowers to the brink of thermonuclear war.[105]

In the aftermath of the Cuban missile crisis, both sides shifted their superpower competition to Southeast Asia, inaugurating the sanguinary second phase in the Cold War. Between 1963 and 1975, the superpowers armed their respective Vietnamese surrogates for a sustained conflict whose intensity far exceeded the strategic significance of that small country. When conventional combat by 540,000 US troops failed to defeat North Vietnamese regulars and Viet Cong guerrillas, Washington, flailing about for a winning strategy, deployed the CIA to terrorize South Vietnamese villages through its Phoenix Program, which would ultimately be responsible for 40,994 extrajudicial executions. Not only was the agency ruthless in its use of torture on a mass scale, but it was also inept. Indeed, a Pentagon study found that in 1970 and 1971, only 3 percent of the suspects "killed, captured, or rallied were full or probationary Party members above the district level," and over half the supposed Viet Cong captured or killed "were not even Party members." One CIA veteran was even more critical, saying "never in the history of our work in Vietnam did we get one clear-cut, high-ranking Viet Cong agent," raising the possibility that the program had been manipulated by the enemy's counterintelligence service into eliminating neutralists and even anti-Communists. Meanwhile, the US Air Force ravaged the South Vietnamese countryside and parts of North Vietnam with 6.1 million tons of bombs—more than three times its total tonnage in World War II.[106] By the time North Vietnamese forces captured the Southern capital of Saigon in 1975, nearly four million people had died, including 2 million civilians, 1.1 million North Vietnamese and Viet Cong troops, 250,000 American-allied South Vietnamese soldiers, and 58,000 members of the US military. (And that does not even count the massive casualties from the parallel secret wars the US was waging in those years in neighboring Cambodia and Laos.)[107]

In a complementary effort elsewhere in Southeast Asia, Washington conducted a bloody covert operation against the Indonesian Communist Party (PKI), then the world's largest outside the Iron Curtain. When rival military factions mounted a coup and countercoup in October 1965 in that country, the CIA collaborated with British intelligence in a broadcast of lurid propaganda charging that a PKI women's group had emasculated captured military commanders and danced wildly waving their severed members. As inflamed Islamic fundamentalists and army units began slaughtering suspected Communists, the US embassy provided the Indonesian military with comprehensive lists of PKI leaders, thereby encouraging massacres that eventually claimed nearly a million victims. The embassy in Jakarta cabled Washington that the list of top Communists it had provided "is apparently being used by Indonesian security authorities who seem to lack even the simplest overt information on PKI leadership." Amid the turmoil, the mercurial President Sukarno—co-founder of the new Non-Aligned Movement of nations that sought a middle way during the Cold War, to Washington's consternation—gave way to the rightist General Suharto, who would remain a reliable US ally for the next 32 years. This operation was so extraordinarily successful, reported journalist Vincent Bevins, that "far-right groups around the world began to draw inspiration from the 'Jakarta' model," sparking copycat programs that "pushed the Latin American death toll into the hundreds of thousands."[108]

At multiple levels, the Vietnam War was a watershed in US foreign policy. With costs climbing to $2 billion a month at its peak and Washington's balance of payments thereby destabilized, the conflict compelled the administration of President Richard Nixon to curtail the costly nuclear arms race through détente with the Soviets. While Washington was wasting its military resources on ground combat in Vietnam, Moscow had expanded its intercontinental missile stockpile from 400 to 1,500, forcing National Security Adviser Henry Kissinger to admit that US global power had "passed its historic high point." In May 1972, President Nixon and Soviet leader Leonid Brezhnev signed an interim Anti-Ballistic Missile Treaty capping Moscow's arsenal at 1,618 missiles and Washington's at 1,054, and so effectively ending the nuclear arms race. By then, US defense spending had fallen from its Cold War peak of 14 percent of gross domestic product to only 6 percent, where it would remain for the rest of the decade.[109]

During the Vietnam War, as economic expansion in Europe and Japan surpassed America's, the value of US dollars held overseas began to exceed the sum of Washington's gold reserves. In August 1971, to staunch the hemorrhaging of its bullion, the Nixon administration announced that the Treasury would no longer exchange dollars for gold. With central banks worldwide holding billions of dollars and Middle East petro-states still demanding dollars for oil, the world had little choice but to continue using the dollar as its global reserve currency. Within two years, however, an ongoing volatility in dollar flows forced Washington to dump the Bretton Woods system of fixed exchange rates and float the dollar with daily, market-driven fluctuations in value, effectively yielding control over its currency rates to global financial markets. The convergence of a growing economic and military weakness in the early 1970s meant one thing: the end of unchallenged American dominion globally and the advent of a more fluid international system in which deft diplomacy would be required to maintain Washington's world leadership.[110]

Once the Vietnam War ended in 1975 and détente curtailed the nuclear arms race, the Cold War's final phase would be marked by a maelstrom of surrogate warfare in Central America, Central Asia, and southern Africa. By fusing the primordial passions of religion and ethnicity with the destructive power of modern weaponry, such regional wars would prove extraordinarily brutal, leaving ravaged lands in their wake. From Washington's perspective, however, those conflicts were remarkably cheap to fund—costing a few million dollars for automatic rifles instead of many billions for nuclear-armed missiles. Throughout the 1980s, the administration of President Ronald Reagan would order the CIA to mobilize the exiled right-wing Nicaraguan rebels known as Contras to launch military forays into that country, seeking to topple its leftist Sandinista regime. Simultaneously, Washington would back tribal revolts against Angola's revolutionary government across two decades of civil war that killed a half a million people, displaced a third of that nation's population, and sowed the countryside with fifteen million land mines. While the US was allied with South Africa's apartheid regime in trying to destroy the region's liberation movements, China was building an ambitious two-thousand-mile railway across the continent—the first of many such foreign aid projects that would earn it exceptional influence throughout Africa. By the time CIA covert intervention in Angola ended circa 1990, Washington had won the Cold War and lost a continent.[111]

Even Angola's devastation, however, paled in comparison with the desolation that would be visited on Afghanistan. As 30,000 Red Army troops were mobilizing to occupy the capital Kabul in December 1979, national security adviser Zbigniew Brzezinski persuaded President Jimmy Carter to authorize $500 million for Operation Cyclone, a bold CIA geopolitical campaign aimed at destabilizing the Soviet Union by arousing militant Islam inside its Central Asian republics. "We didn't push the Russians to intervene," Brzezinski later explained, "but we consciously increased the probability that they would do so. This secret operation was an excellent idea. Its effect was to draw the Russians into the Afghan trap."[112]

Zbigniew Brzezinski, US national security adviser, 1977 (Credit: Library of Congress)

Even so, US military aid to the Islamist guerrillas, who were intent on driving the Russians out of their country, remained limited until April 1985, when President Reagan signed a classified order to do just that "by all means available." That directive soon doubled the CIA's covert arms budget there to $350 million a year. After the president approved the delivery of advanced shoulder-fired Stinger missiles, Afghan fighters used those lethal ground-to-air weapons to shoot down some 270 Soviet aircraft in the last two years of that war. Through an expenditure of just $2 billion over a decade, the CIA's Afghan version of surrogate warfare destroyed 995 Soviet armored vehicles and 745 aircraft, killed 15,000 Red Army troops, and produced unsustainable losses of $96 billion. To staunch what Soviet leader Mikhail Gorbachev came to call the "bleeding wound" of Afghanistan, the Red Army was forced to withdraw in defeat.[113]

As the covert war in Afghanistan wound down in 1989, the Western alliance failed to sponsor a peace settlement or finance reconstruction of any sort—leaving behind a devastated country with 1.5 million dead, 3 million refugees, a ruined economy, and well-armed warlords primed to fight for power in a civil war that would ravage the country for another decade.[114] It also just so happened to leave behind a young Saudi militant who had founded a group called al-Qaeda during the US-backed Islamic crusade against the Soviets and would now have to reconsider where to direct his efforts. His name: Osama bin Laden.

A survey of the wastelands left by this and other CIA secret wars brings to mind what the ancient Scots chieftain Calgacus once said of the Roman Empire: "They make a desolation and they call it peace."[115]

In 1991, exhausted by the nuclear arms race and the Afghan War, its economy in ruins, the Soviet Union simply imploded, allowing its 22 satellite states and captive republics to finally break free. By contrast, the US military had become a global behemoth with more than seven hundred overseas bases, an air force of 1,763 jet fighters, more than a thousand ballistic missiles, and a navy of nearly six hundred ships, including fifteen nuclear carrier battle groups—all linked by the world's only global system of communications satellites.[116] By then, however, global defense was consuming 4.5 percent of the country's gross domestic product, twice the British rate at its peak as an imperial power.[117] For the next 20 years, Washington would enjoy what Defense Secretary James Mattis called "uncontested or dominant superiority in every operating domain. We could generally deploy our forces when we wanted, assemble them where we wanted, operate how we wanted."[118]

As the US became the world's sole superpower after the Cold War, Brzezinski, a specialist in Eurasia's elusive geopolitics, warned that Washington should take care to avoid three conditions that could erode its global power—first, the loss of its strategic "perch on the Western periphery" in Europe; next, the rise of "an assertive single entity" in the "middle space" of Eurasia; and finally, "the expulsion of America from its offshore bases" in Asia.[119]

The weakening of those "offshore bases" had already started in 1991 when the Philippines, unwilling to accept Washington's ambiguous commitment to its defense, refused to extend the lease on the Seventh Fleet's bastion at Subic Bay. As US Navy tugs towed Subic's floating dry docks homeward to Pearl Harbor, the Philippines gained full responsibility for its own defense, which it largely failed to fund. As a result, during a raging typhoon three years later, China occupied some shoals in the Spratly Islands—the first step in what would be a stealthy bid for control over the South China Sea and its later challenge to US power in the Pacific. Instead of air and navy patrols, the Philippine military grounded a rusting US-surplus ship on nearby Ayungin Shoal in 1998 to serve as a base for a squad of barefoot soldiers, who were forced to fish for their rations.[120] Meanwhile, in those years the US Navy underwent a 40 percent reduction in its pool of surface warships and attack submarines, further weakening the US position on the Pacific littoral.[121]

While Washington scaled back its global military presence after the end of the Cold War, its economic influence expanded markedly through the pervasive process of globalization. Following a two-tier strategy to open the world to unchecked capital flows, Washington presided over the formation of the multilateral World Trade Organization in 1995 while pursuing a parallel series of bilateral pacts, starting with the North American Free Trade Agreement (NAFTA) with Canada and Mexico. To create a business climate ideal for multinational corporations, the WTO pushed financial deregulation, protected Big Pharma's medical patents, and removed restrictions on genetically modified food crops. Simultaneously, the IMF and the World Bank pressed open market "structural adjustment programs" on developing economies worldwide, including former socialist states in Eastern Europe, ex-military dictatorships in Latin America, and emerging nations in Africa.

With this powerful one-two punch, neoliberal economists smashed tariff barriers worldwide, helping create a unified capitalist market that covered the globe. Meanwhile, US foreign investment surged nearly tenfold, from $700 billion in 1990 to $6.3 trillion in 2014. Simultaneously, Washington spent $2 billion promoting free market democracy and dispatching "democracy trainers" to foster "color revolutions" in former Soviet satellites, while also weaponizing human rights to justify armed intervention in Kosovo, Iraq, and Afghanistan.[122]

To integrate this fast-expanding world economy, corporations spent many billions weaving a worldwide web of fiber-optic cables. By 2017, there were 420 submarine cables stretching for seven hundred thousand miles around the globe. Simultaneously, the US led the world in orbiting 1,327 satellites for improved aircraft navigation, weather forecasting, and television transmission.[123] At the start of the twenty-first century, Washington thus had the open, globalized world economy it wanted. By fraying social safety nets while eroding many structures that protected unionized workers and local businesses, American neoliberal reforms penetrated societies worldwide—reducing the quality of life for many, creating inequality on a staggering scale, and stoking a working-class reaction that would erupt, a generation later, in an angry right-wing populism. Beyond that economic policy, US elites failed to craft a shared vision to replace the Cold War's anti-Communist containment, producing a fragmented foreign policy that would lead, over the next 30 years, to what one specialist called "overextension and exhaustion."[124]

The War on Terror

That extraordinary decade of economic globalization hit the pause button on September 11, 2001, when aircraft flown by nineteen Islamic fundamentalists sent by Osama bin Laden, most of them Saudi, destroyed the World Trade Center in New York City and damaged the Pentagon in Washington. In the aftermath, the epicenter of US military operations would shift, for the first time in the country's history, away from the Atlantic or the Pacific to the Middle East. During the decade from its invasion of Afghanistan in 2001 to its "withdrawal" from Iraq in 2011, the US military moved its focus away from the heavy weaponry of great-power conflict to small-unit counterterror operations. Then, in the years after 2011, the Pentagon would maintain smaller deployments in Afghanistan, Iraq, and Syria in a desperate attempt to foster a political balance favorable to its interests.

In the months following the 9/11 terrorist attacks, Washington launched what it called a Global War on Terror with a combination of a not-quite-covert intervention in Afghanistan and a conventional invasion of Iraq. In turn, each operation would quickly segue from sudden, heady triumph to grinding, demoralizing defeat. To topple the fundamentalist Taliban regime that had harbored Osama bin Laden and his al-Qaeda terrorists, Washington used the CIA to mobilize Afghan warlords, backing them with massive US airpower. With just a handful of Americans on the ground to hand out cash and call in airstrikes, US bombs smashed Taliban lines while its warlord allies swept across the countryside, capturing the capital, Kabul, in little more than a month. Although the Taliban offered to surrender, Washington, in an act of imperial hubris, refused to deal with what it called "barbaric criminals." But as billions of dollars from a subsequent US nation-building effort sank into the quagmire of Afghani corruption over the next five years, the Taliban would slowly begin to capture significant parts of the countryside. Compounding the problem, Washington ignored the country's burgeoning opium traffic during the early years of its occupation, effectively conceding this lucrative source of local finance to the Taliban for its expanding guerrilla operations. The US would then spend fifteen years and nearly $9 billion in a failed effort to control opium production and thereby curtail the Taliban's hold on the countryside. Instead, the harvest soared dramatically from just 185 tons in 2001 to 9,000 tons by 2017—providing nearly 90 percent of the world's illicit heroin supply.[125]

To contain the spreading insurgency, in 2009 the new administration of President Barack Obama opted to undertake a "surge" that brought US troop strength in that country to one hundred thousand, in a bid for a knock-out blow against the Taliban.[126] But Obama also signaled the limits of US commitment by announcing a deadline of December 2014 for ending major combat operations there. Amid that scheduled drawdown of allied forces and a parallel reduction in air operations, the Taliban launched new offensives, killing record numbers of Afghan army troops and police.[127] Stunned by that group's sudden success in capturing up to half the countryside, Washington seemed forced to slam on the brakes, leaving some 14,000 combat troops that were nevertheless unable to contain the relentless advance by 60,000 full-time rebel guerrillas, backed by many thousands more part-time fighters. Finally abandoning its eighteen-year effort to pacify Afghanistan, Washington, under the administration of Donald Trump, signed a tentative peace agreement in February 2020 that made the Taliban rebels potential partners in a coalition government, while agreeing to further substantial cuts in its own troop strength—a tacit admission of defeat in America's longest war. A year later, as Taliban guerrillas advanced relentlessly, capturing the countryside and threatening cities, President Biden announced that, regardless of consequences, he would mark the twentieth anniversary of the 9/11 terrorist attacks by withdrawing all American troops from Afghanistan.[128]

The costs of this incipient defeat were heavy indeed. During two decades of that failed pacification effort, the 775,000 US troops deployed to Afghanistan suffered 2,442 killed and some 20,000 wounded. An estimated 170,000 Afghans died, including 47,000 civilians. The total US costs for this conflict reached $2.2 trillion, including nearly a trillion in military expenditures alone. "What did we get for this $1 trillion effort? Was it worth a trillion?" Jeffrey Eggers, a White House staffer and Navy SEAL veteran, asked a government investigation of the Afghan war in 2015. "After the killing of Osama bin Laden, I said that Osama was probably laughing in his watery grave considering how much we have spent on Afghanistan." With a similar sense of regret, Douglas Lute, an Army general who directed Afghan war policy for the Bush and Obama administrations, added: "We were devoid of a fundamental understanding of Afghanistan—we didn't know what we were doing."[129]

The US occupation of Iraq would prove even more disastrous. On the basis of bogus intelligence that the country's Baathist regime was about to acquire nuclear weapons, the Bush administration invaded that country in March 2003 with an overwhelming force of 177,000 troops and total air superiority, capturing Baghdad in just nineteen days. On May 1, President George W. Bush proclaimed, "Mission accomplished."

Almost as soon as jubilant US troops had triumphantly pulled down the statue of autocrat Saddam Hussein in a central square in Baghdad, the troubles began. Only weeks after arriving in the Iraqi capital, Paul Bremer, a retired diplomat with absolutely no Middle East experience, exercised his extraordinary authority, akin to that of a colonial viceroy, as head of the new Coalition Provisional Authority and eradicated the previous Iraqi government with two strokes of his pen. With no clear plans for what might follow, he issued Order Number 1 on his fifth day in office, decreeing a sweeping purge of all senior Iraqi officials previously affiliated with the ruling Baath Party. "By nightfall," warned the CIA chief of station, "you'll have driven some 30,000 to 50,000 Baathists underground. And in six months you'll really regret this." Imperiously waving away what he called "a sea of bitching and moaning," Bremer plunged ahead, forcing at least 85,000 Iraqi officials out of office. US commander Ricardo Sanchez would later call this policy decision "a catastrophic failure."[130]

Ignoring both White House instructions and military advice, Bremer soon issued Order Number 2, aimed at "dissolving Saddam's military and intelligence structures to emphasize that we mean business." With that second stroke of his pen summarily dismissing 335,00 police and 385,000 soldiers without salary, severance pay, or pensions, Bremer created a vast cadre of what the US Army's official war history would call "seasoned military men who suddenly had no livelihood."[131]

As Bremer's two orders "sent shockwaves throughout the country," there were angry anti-American demonstrations and "violent confrontations" between Iraqi ex-soldiers and coalition forces. Those demobilized former soldiers also included countless trained experts with access to cached military munitions and knowledge of how to build lethal improvised explosive devices, or IEDs. Three days after Bremer's Order Number 2, a US Army private died when the first of these new weapons exploded under his vehicle. Over the next ten years, IEDs would kill 3,100 US servicemen and wound 33,000 more, including 1,800 amputations—forcing the Pentagon to spend $75 billion to prevent fatalities from a weapon as cheap as a pizza. "Orders 1 and 2 led to a far more sweeping implosion [of the Iraqi state] than US leaders intended," the US Army's official war history later reported, "after which factions of all kinds, including extremist militants, rushed to fill the void."[132]

In the midst of a spreading insurgency, the Abu Ghraib prison torture scandal erupted in April 2004 when CBS broadcast disturbing photos of American troops torturing Iraqi prisoners. Subsequent investigations found that the Bush administration had authorized the CIA to revive its Cold War psychological torture techniques. Desperate for intelligence to stop lethal IED attacks, the US command in Baghdad had tacitly authorized such tortures to extract intelligence. These revelations, in turn, sparked a decade of congressional investigations that uncovered a CIA global network of "black sites" from Thailand to Poland, where suspects from the ongoing War on Terror were subjected to a Dantesque hell of abuse. As these well-publicized investigations documented the cruelty of psychological torture, the US forfeited its claim to moral leadership of the international community.[133]

Meanwhile, Iraq plunged into a four-year maelstrom of urban guerrilla attacks and intra-Islamic sectarian warfare. As IEDs ripped through military convoys, American combat deaths passed one thousand in September 2004. Once US counterinsurgency specialists started training Shi'a death squads that trolled the streets for sectarian enemies, the number of mangled, tortured Iraqi bodies dumped in Baghdad reached 1,100 monthly in July 2005. To save a desperate situation, President Bush dispatched another 21,500 US troops in 2007, bringing the total to 170,000. Along with the 74,000 Iraqi militia mobilized by the US command, this "surge" in troop deployments momentarily stabilized the situation, enough to enable staged drawdowns of US forces until 2011. By December of that year, only a small contingent of seven hundred trainers remained to work with the Iraqi army.[134]

Three years later, however, a revived insurgency—formed, ironically enough, inside an American prison camp in Iraq—raised the black banner of the Islamic State and swept aside a demoralized Iraqi army, which the US had rebuilt in its image at a cost of many billions of dollars, quickly capturing the northern third of the country and a similar swath of neighboring Syria. In a counterattack, massive US airstrikes would pulverize major Iraqi cities like Ramadi, Mosul, and the Syrian provincial capital of Raqqa, while a coalition of Iraqi troops and civilian Shi'a militia, many of them aligned with neighboring Iran, advanced relentlessly, until the Islamic State lost its last foothold in the country by late 2017. Some eighteen months after that, the US-backed Syrian forces captured the last Islamic State territory inside that country, effectively defeating a de facto government that had controlled, at its peak, a territory the size of Britain and an army of some one hundred thousand. However, the defeat of the Islamic State was hardly a victory. The militant Islamicist movement continued to spread across the Middle East and northern Africa. In these years, moreover, neighboring Iran, as the heart of Shi'a Islam, had played upon its political ties to Iraq's Shi'a majority and turned that country into a virtual client state—taking over abandoned CIA intelligence assets, controlling murderous Shi'a militias, cultivating allies in the cabinet, and courting politicians from mayors to prime minister.[135]

As in Afghanistan, the US military concluded that its overall performance in the Iraq War had been nothing short of dismal. Nearly 4,500 American soldiers were killed and 32,000 more wounded. Estimates of Iraqi civilians killed by US military operations ranged from two hundred thousand to more than one million. The direct costs of the war reached nearly $2 trillion. After spending countless billions during a decade of reconstruction, the desperate US bombing campaign to defeat the Islamic State had ruined the country's cities and ravaged its infrastructure. The Army's official war history concluded that "US efforts . . . were inefficient, disjointed, and ultimately unsuccessful" in the critical task of rebuilding a stable society. After the United States expended a "staggering cost" in blood and treasure, the study concluded, "an emboldened and expansionist Iran appears to be the only victor."[136] For the Army, those wars in Afghanistan and Iraq were dismal defeats, but for the wider world they were an undeniable sign that US military power could no longer order the globe as it wished. From a strategic perspective, by the time Washington wound down its Iraq operations in 2018, America had achieved energy independence and oil was joining cordwood and coal as a fuel whose days were numbered, rendering the future Middle East geopolitically irrelevant.

While Washington was struggling to constrict the territory controlled by armed Muslim extremist movements in Afghanistan, Iraq, and Syria, affiliated militant groups were springing up from Nigeria to the Philippines. To counter them, the US military launched regular drone strikes and dispatched special operations forces. By 2015, the unified Special Operations Command had 69,000 elite troops drawn from the Army Rangers, Navy SEALs, and Air Force Commandos deployed to 147 countries, or 75 percent of the world.[137] By then, the Air Force and CIA had ringed the Eurasian landmass with a network of 60 bases for its growing arsenal of Reaper and Predator drones—all the way from the Sigonella Naval Air Station in Sicily to Andersen Air Force Base on the island of Guam.[138] With a flying range of 1,150 miles when armed with its full payload of Hellfire missiles, the Reaper could now strike counterterror targets almost anywhere in Africa or Asia. To fulfill its expanding global mission, the Air Force planned to have 346 Reapers in service by 2021, including 80 for the use of the CIA.[139]

Gradually, it became apparent that such short-term tactical operations from Africa to Southeast Asia reflected a broad strategic shift in US defense policy toward a more diffuse global array of military bases. To cover the whole globe after the Cold War, the Pentagon adopted an agile stance of dispersed "lily pads"—that is, small forward operating sites with pre-positioned weapons for sudden strikes against rogue actors anywhere on five continents. By 2009, Washington had assigned 305,000 service personnel to 909 overseas military bases, most of them far smaller than the massive bastions that it had built during the Cold War.[140]

By the time the War on Terror began to wind down, the heavy-metal strategic forces long central to US defense were at a low ebb. Between 1998 and 2014, the Navy's fleet had declined from 333 ships to just 271. That 20 percent reduction, combined with a shift to long-term deployments in the Middle East, weakened the Navy's position in the Pacific. With a smaller fleet and crews straining under the pressure of ever-extending tours of duty, the once-powerful Pacific Command was ill-prepared to meet an unexpected challenge from China.[141]

The Rise of China

Only a decade after Brzezinski's warning about the centrality of Eurasia to US global power, China began to contest America's control of that strategic landmass. While the US military was mired in the Middle East for a full decade after 2001, Beijing was quietly attempting to control more of that vast "middle space" of Eurasia and maneuvering to neutralize America's offshore bases along the Pacific littoral—thus compromising two of Brzezinski's three conditions for the continuation of US global hegemony.

When China was admitted to the WTO in 2001, Washington's foreign policy elites were confident that Beijing would play by established rules and become a compliant member of the international community. There was almost no awareness of the massive geopolitical shifts that could occur when a full fifth of humanity joined the world system as an economic equal for the first time in three centuries.[142] In just four years, however, China's surging trade surplus and swelling dollar reserves sparked charges that it was gaming the global system through currency manipulations and depressed wages.[143]

In the decade following the devastating 2008 recession, the US competitive position vis-à-vis China weakened markedly in three key

areas—economic, technological, and educational. At the seeming peak of
Washington's global power in 2012, the US National Intelligence Council
warned about the rise of a "potential rival" to America's leadership. "By 2030,"
it reported, "Asia will have surpassed North America and Europe combined
in terms of global power, based on GDP, population size, military spending,
and technological investment. China alone will probably have the largest
economy, surpassing that of the United States a few years before 2030." To
explain America's decline and Asia's rise, the council reduced this protracted
historical process to a single PowerPoint slide. Throughout its rise to world
power from 1820 to 1870, Britain increased its share of gross world product by
just 1 percent per decade, while America's rose by 2 percent during its ascent
from 1900 to 1950. By contrast, China was increasing its slice of the world
pie at an extraordinary pace of 5 percent from 2000 to 2020.[144]

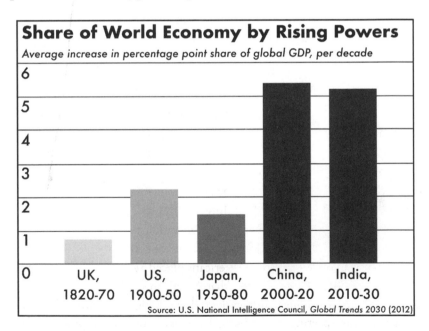

While China was growing at hyper-speed, the US share of the global
economy had fallen from 40 percent in 1960 to 22 percent by 2016. And if
we use the more realistic index of purchasing power parity, which measures
what money can actually buy in each country, America's slice of the global

economy was down to just 15 percent in 2019. If we then project that decline into the future, the US share will fall to 12.2 percent in 2030, 9.1 percent by 2040, and a mere 6 percent by 2050. Using that same index, the accounting firm PricewaterhouseCoopers calculated that China's economic output had already surpassed America's in 2014 and was on a trajectory to become 40 percent larger by 2030.[145]

Beijing also launched a challenge to US technological dominance that it branded "Made in China 2025," planning for a quantum leap to global high-tech leadership in ten key industries—including aerospace, artificial intelligence, information technology, and telecommunications.[146] As shown in the race for worldwide patents, American leadership in technological innovation was clearly on the wane. Two years after passing the US in 2011, China filed 825,000 patent applications, compared to 572,000 by Americans.[147] Of the three million patent applications filed worldwide in 2016, China accounted for 43 percent, the US 20 percent, and Japan just 10 percent.[148]

With supercomputing becoming critical for everything from code breaking to consumer products, China's Ministry of National Defense outdid the Pentagon in 2010 by launching the world's fastest supercomputer.[149] Eight years later, the US was back on top after spending $200 million to build the even-faster Summit machine at Oak Ridge National Laboratory. In an indication of the intensity of this competition, both Beijing and Washington already had plans to create supercomputers at least five times faster than the Summit.[150]

Finally, the American education system, long its critical source of future scientists and innovators, began falling behind its competitors as well. In 2012, the Organisation for Economic Co-operation and Development tested 510,000 fifteen-year-olds worldwide, finding that those in Shanghai came first in math and science; while Americans placed 20th in science and 27th in math. The OECD also reported that American students "have particular weaknesses in performing mathematics tasks with higher cognitive demands, such as . . . interpreting mathematical aspects in real-world problems."[151] Three years later, that gap had only widened when the US fell to a miserable 39th in math. After billions in federal aid was targeted expressly at test performance, American results in math did creep up slightly to 36th in the 2018 test, but scores still lagged 20 percent below Chinese students, who once again placed first.[152] By the landmark year of 2030, those fifteen-year-old test takers will have shed their braces and backpacks to become China's new generation of cutting-edge scientists and engineers.

By 2011, a decade of economic growth, averaging 10 percent annually, had allowed China to accumulate an unprecedented $3 trillion in currency reserves that created the potential for a rapid, radical shift in the global balance of power.[153] Absorbed in its endless wars in the Middle East, Washington initially struggled to grasp these new global realities and was slow to react.

Obama's Geopolitical Strategy

Following Barack Obama's 2009 inauguration, the president and his closest advisers became among the first in Washington's leadership to recognize the signs of a serious geopolitical challenge. Even while spending much of his first term partially extricating the US military from the Bush administration's Middle East wars, Obama had a long-term strategic vision for checking China that was manifest in what he called his "pivot to Asia." After two long wars in Iraq and Afghanistan "that cost us dearly, in blood and treasure," he announced, "the United States is turning our attention to the vast potential of the Asia Pacific region," which is "home to more than half the global economy."[154]

To check China's rise, the Obama administration developed a multifaceted strategy involving a pivot of strategic assets toward Asia, accompanied by a scale-down of military commitments in the Middle East and reduction of the US dependence on imported oil to obviate the need for further intervention in that troubled region. Rejecting established policy that made Washington the perpetual guardian of the Persian Gulf, Obama withdrew most American forces from Iraq and refused to commit more of them for regime change in Syria. As his second term was ending, he explained that Middle Eastern countries were "failing to provide prosperity and opportunity for their people. You've got a violent, extremist ideology, or ideologies, that are turbocharged through social media." Southeast Asia, by contrast, was "filled with striving, ambitious, energetic people who are every single day scratching and clawing to build businesses."[155]

The reduction of US dependence on Middle East crude oil complemented Obama's commitment to slow climate change while encouraging hydraulic fracturing, or fracking, in US oil shale deposits, whose growth, in these years, earned the country the ironic title "Saudi America." In marked contrast to his predecessor, Obama's term was marked by major initiatives on global warming, including an increase in the fuel standard for cars to 55 miles per gallon by 2025, realization of a US–China deal on emissions, adoption of the UN's 2015 climate change accord, and the launch of the Clean Power Plan to cut power plant emissions. By 2016, US emissions fell to their lowest level in 25 years as renewable wind and solar power climbed to 7 percent of US electrical generation. Nonetheless, fossil fuels and nuclear power still supplied 85 percent of the country's electricity, leaving a great deal of room for progress.[156]

To avoid the need for more military involvement in the Middle East, the US reduced its net oil imports from 11.1 million barrels daily to just 2.3 million, with only 16 percent of that latter figure coming from the Persian Gulf. Building on those gains, America became a net oil exporter for the first time in 70 years, thanks in part to the proliferation of fracking across America.[157] By the end of Obama's term, the US economy no longer needed the Middle East.

As Obama withdrew troops from Afghanistan and Iraq, Washington began rebuilding its chain of military bases and strategic alliances along the Asian littoral. In March 2014, a full battalion of US Marines was deployed at the port of Darwin, Australia, on the Timor Sea, well positioned to access the strategic Lombok and Sunda Straits that lead to the South China Sea. Five months later, the two powers signed the US–Australia Force Posture Agreement allowing for the basing of American troops and warships at Darwin.[158]

Further north, in February 2016, the South Koreans completed a naval facility on Jeju Island, between that country and Japan, giving the US Navy access to a strategic port astride the East China Sea. Washington also signed an enhanced defense agreement with the Philippines, allowing use of several military bases astride the South China Sea.[159] In combination with its eight established air and naval bases in Japan, Washington had effectively rebuilt its chain of military enclaves at the edge of Asia.[160] To operate them, the Pentagon planned to "forward base 60 percent of our naval assets in the Pacific by 2020" along with a similar preponderance of Air Force fighters and bombers, which would be bolstered by "space and cyber capabilities."[161] By strengthening long-standing bilateral alliances, the Obama administration had taken the first steps, militarily speaking, toward rebuilding the US axial position on the Pacific littoral, which had long been central to its control over the vast Eurasian landmass.

While Washington was spilling its blood and treasure into desert sands, Beijing had been investing much of its accumulated trade surplus in the integration of the "world island" of Africa, Asia, and Europe into an economic powerhouse. Drawing on its now $4 trillion in currency reserves, by 2015 China had invested $630 billion in foreign infrastructure projects under what it dubbed the "Belt and Road Initiative," largely within that tri-continental expanse.[162] Through another trillion dollars in projected investments, China had also doubled its annual trade with Africa to $222 billion—three times America's total. Hobbled by strict eligibility requirements, Washington's smaller development initiatives for Africa had largely failed, and the continent's non-oil exports to the US were stalled at just $4.1 billion.[163]

Throughout his two terms, Obama nevertheless pursued a countervailing strategy that sought to split Beijing's world island economically at its continental divide in the Ural Mountains, through two trade pacts that would give the US preferential access to 60 percent of the world economy. Along the eastern axis of Eurasia, the Trans-Pacific Partnership (TPP), which pointedly excluded China, was the keystone to his strategy for drawing Eurasia's trade toward America and rendering Beijing's Belt and Road Initiative a hollow shell. Surpassing any other economic alliance except the European Union, this treaty was designed to integrate the economies of eleven Pacific-basin nations that generated 40 percent of gross world product.[164]

Even so, Obama's scheme faced ferocious opposition within his own Democratic Party from leaders sharply critical of the secret negotiations, closed arbitration panels, and potential degradation of labor and environmental laws covered by the TPP.[165] In the face of such strong criticism, the president had to rely on Republican votes to win Senate approval for "fast track" authority to complete the final round of negotiations—signs of opposition that would ultimately prevent the agreement's approval before he left office.[166]

To pull at the western axis of China's would-be world island, Obama also pursued negotiations for a Transatlantic Trade and Investment Partnership with the EU, whose $18 trillion economy was the world's largest, accounting for 20 percent of gross world product.[167] Apart from eliminating the few remaining taxes and tariffs, this treaty sought fuller economic integration between Europe and America through a closer regulatory alignment

that could have added \$240 billion to their annual trade. However, an oppo-
sition coalition of 170 European civil society groups protested that the treaty
would transfer control over regulation of consumer safety, the environment,
and labor from democratic states to closed corporate arbitration tribunals.[168]
That opposition slowed the EU's adoption of the agreement, leaving it un-
ratified when Obama's term ended.[169]

Finally, in a personalized campaign of diplomacy that much of the
US media misconstrued as a sentimental journey, Obama courted African
nations aggressively, convening a White House summit for more than 50
African leaders and making a state visit to East Africa.[170] With its usual
barbed insight, Beijing's *Global Times* identified the real aim of Obama's
Africa diplomacy as "off setting China's growing influence in this continent
and recovering past US leverage."[171]

By the time Obama left office, however, his grand geopolitical strategy
for checking China remained largely unfulfilled. The continuing military operations against Islamic fundamentalists in Iraq and Afghanistan had slowed
his signature military pivot to Asia. Meanwhile, a populist revolt against
economic globalization at home and abroad had blocked ratification of the
trade agreements central to his geopolitical design.[172]

Trump's Foreign Policy

Both the rejection of Obama's trade initiatives and popular support for his
successor's disruptive diplomacy reflected broader global trends that were
shaking the economic foundations of Washington's world order. Following
a quarter century of accelerating globalization that came with the end of
the Cold War, displaced workers and disadvantaged businesspeople around
the world began mobilizing politically to oppose an economic order that
privileged corporations and economic elites above all else. Emerging with
surprising speed and simultaneity from the margins of their respective societies, a generation of right-wing populist leaders gained influence by giving
voice, often with violent or virulent inflections, to public concerns about the
social costs of globalization.

Anti-globalization sentiment grew dramatically from the few thousand
left-wing demonstrators protesting the WTO conference at Seattle in 1999
into a wider working-class anger, largely on the right side of the political
spectrum, a decade later. By mid-2016, only 19 percent of Americans polled

believed that trade creates more jobs, despite numerous economic studies showing otherwise. A survey of public opinion in 44 countries found that only 26 percent of respondents felt trade lowered prices. Adding to this skepticism, Chinese imports eliminated 2.4 million American jobs between 1999 and 2011, closing plants for furniture in North Carolina, glass in Ohio, and auto parts and steel across the Midwest. Most trade deals in decades past had involved a balanced exchange among industrial nations, but China's unprecedented admission to the WTO in 2001 meant that a developing economy with an enormous workforce gained open access to markets in Europe and the US, leading to the rapid erasure of countless factory jobs.[173] As nations worldwide imposed a combined 2,100 restrictions on imports to staunch the loss of employment, world trade started to slow and then to fall during the second quarter of 2016—the first time it did so during a period of economic growth since World War II.[174]

Across Europe, hypernationalist parties like the French National Front, Greece's Golden Dawn, Alternative for Germany, and the British Independence Party won voters by cultivating nativist reactions to just such trends, often attacking the economic globalization that had become a hallmark of Washington's world order. In the most visible rejection of international integration, the British public voted in June 2016 to leave the European Union. Simultaneously, a generation of populist demagogues won power in nominally democratic nations around the world—notably Viktor Orbán in Hungary, Vladimir Putin in Russia, Recep Tayyip Erdoğan in Turkey, Narendra Modi in India, Rodrigo Duterte in the Philippines, and, of course, Donald Trump in the United States.[175]

In the decade before Trump's inauguration, there were already signs that US global influence was in long-term decline and its signature effort at economic globalization was under challenge worldwide. Not only would the Trump administration's diplomacy accelerate that trend, but it also cast a strong light on the dynamics of the downward trajectory of Washington's world order. Yet a certain logic did lurk beneath all the diplomatic tumult of his administration. With each succeeding year, Trump's foreign policy moved from ruptured relations with allies to a fraught courtship of autocratic leaders before lurching into a volatile confrontation with China over trade.

Right after taking office in January 2017, Trump curtailed trade talks with Europe and withdrew from the TPP, saying: "We're going to stop the ridiculous trade deals that have taken . . . companies out of our country, and it's going to be reversed."[176] By jettisoning Obama's geopolitical strategy and failing to craft another, his transactional foreign policy would slowly diminish Washington's international influence over the next four years.

That May, Trump rejected the advice of close foreign allies and announced his withdrawal from the landmark Paris climate accord, saying it was "unthinkable that an international agreement could prevent the United States from conducting its own domestic affairs." Over the next four years, he would systematically reverse almost all of Obama's major climate change initiatives—weakening the fuel standards for automobiles, rolling back restrictions on methane leaks from oil and gas wells, and removing requirements that coal-fired electrical plants reduce emissions.[177]

Trump's fervent climate change denial not only abdicated America's international leadership on this critical issue, but also blocked remedial measures that might have slowed the damage and so preserved Washington's world order. Driven by the profligate consumption of fossil fuels, carbon concentrations in the atmosphere had climbed from 316 parts per million at the start of US hegemony in the 1950s to 400 ppm in 2015, a level that one science writer called "a clear red line into a danger zone of climate change." If carbon levels continue to rise at that rate, the world will reach 500 ppm by 2070, raising average global temperatures to 3°C above the preindustrial benchmark and so bringing on a dangerous rise in sea levels, mass migration of climate change refugees, the destruction of the Amazon rain forest, and ever more extreme weather and wildfires.[178]

During his first overseas trip to Europe, Trump previewed the disruptive foreign policy that would, over the next three years, weaken the US position at the axial ends of Eurasia and open the continent to Beijing's expanding influence. Instead of the usual US support for the NATO security pact, Trump chided the country's European allies for failing to pay their "fair share" of military costs and pointedly refused to endorse its core principle of collective defense.[179]

Trump's first Asia tour that November included an address before the Asia-Pacific Economic Cooperation (APEC) in Vietnam, which provided a stark contrast between two competing visions for a new world order.[180] After denouncing an ever-lengthening litany of foreign trade violations as nothing less than "economic aggression" against America, the president invited everyone to share his "Indo-Pacific dream" of the world as a "beautiful constellation" of "strong, sovereign, and independent nations," each working, like America, to build "wealth and freedom."[181]

In contrast to Trump's narrow economic nationalism, China's President Xi Jinping played the global statesman, calling upon APEC to support a world economic order that would be "more open, inclusive and balanced." Just as China had lifted 60 million of its own people out of poverty in only five years, so he urged a more equitable world system "to bring the benefits of development to countries across the globe." To advance such a transformation, China would "make US $2 trillion of outbound investment"—an apparent reference to the $1.3 trillion Belt and Road Initiative for Eurasia and another $1 trillion in aid and investment for Africa.[182] On a similar note, the remaining eleven TPP partners, led by Japan and Canada, announced major progress toward the finalization of that agreement—significantly, without the United States.[183]

Press headlines from the Trump administration's first twelve months indicated that Washington's international influence was fading with surprising speed. Consider the first seven days of December 2017, when a series of *New York Times* reports showed nation after nation pulling away from Washington. First, Egypt, after receiving $70 billion in US aid over the previous 40 years, opened its bases to Russian jet fighters.[184] Next, Burma, despite the Obama administration's assiduous courtship, was now moving closer to Beijing.[185] Then, Australia, America's stalwart ally for the last century, began adapting its diplomacy to accommodate China's dominant position in Asia.[186] Finally, Germany, long the US bastion in Europe but now China's close trade partner, announced a widening divide with Washington, saying relations would never be the same.[187]

Compounding all this were the diplomatic ruptures caused by Trump's daily tweets, which prompted Mexican president Enrique Peña Nieto's cancelation of his state visit after a tweet that Mexico would have to pay for a border wall, outrage from British leaders when he retweeted a racist anti-Muslim video, and a chilling of relations with Pakistan after a New Year's Day blast that accused it of "nothing but lies and deceit."[188]

Since there are only around 40 or 50 nations with enough wealth to play even a minor role in global politics, the loss of friends and allies at such a pace would soon leave Washington's international influence diminished—something Trump experienced that same December when he defied numerous UN resolutions by announcing US recognition of Jerusalem as Israel's capital. That act of unilateral diplomacy earned the White House a fourteen-to-one reprimand from the UN Security Council. After US ambassador Nikki Haley warned that the administration would be "taking names" to punish those that dared vote against it, and Trump threatened to cut aid to those that did, the General Assembly nonetheless voted overwhelmingly, 128 to 9, to condemn the recognition—a stunning repudiation of Washington's international leadership.[189]

By the end of Trump's first year in office, American global stature had fallen markedly. In a survey of 134 countries, Gallup pollsters found worldwide approval of US leadership had plunged from 48 percent in 2016 under Obama to a record low of 30 percent under Trump—just a notch below China's 31 percent and significantly under Germany's 41 percent.[190] In a year-end assessment, conservative CNN commentator Fareed Zakaria rued the "Trump administration's foolish and self-defeating decision to abdicate the United States' global influence," opening a power vacuum that will be filled by illiberal powers like China, Russia, and Turkey.[191]

During the administration's second year, the president's torrent of tweets and off-the-cuff remarks began to form a more coherent vision of America's place in the world. Instead of reigning confidently over international organizations, multilateral alliances, and a globalized economy, Trump seemed to see America as standing alone in a troubled world—exploited by self-aggrandizing allies, battered by unequal terms of trade, threatened by tides of illegal immigrants, and betrayed by self-serving elites too timid or compromised to defend the nation's interests.

In lieu of multilateral trade pacts like the TPP, NAFTA, or even the WTO, Trump favored bilateral deals rewritten to the advantage of America. Instead of democratic allies like Canada and Germany, Trump had begun weaving a web of personal ties to avowedly nationalist and autocratic leaders like himself—Putin in Russia, Orbán in Hungary, Modi in India, Abdel Fattah al-Sisi in Egypt, Benjamin Netanyahu in Israel, and Mohammad bin Salman of Saudi Arabia. Instead of old alliances like NATO, Trump favored a loose coalition of like-minded powers, notably the "Quad" or Quadrilateral Security Dialogue of Indo-Pacific powers (Australia, India, Japan, US) aimed at checking China's expansion in the Indian Ocean. And in lieu of continuing multilateral efforts to block nuclear proliferation, Trump quit the 2015 nuclear pact with Iran and began to cancel Cold War nuclear arms agreements with Russia while pursuing bilateral negotiations with North Korea.[192]

Each of his overseas tours in 2018 served, almost by design, to disrupt or even damage alliances that had long been the foundation for US global power. During a second, divisive visit to NATO headquarters at Brussels, Trump charged that Germany was "a captive of Russia" and pressed allies to immediately double the share of their GDP for defense to an unrealistic 4 percent—a demand they all ignored.[193] Just days later, he again questioned the wisdom of the alliance's core principle of common defense, remarking that if "tiny" NATO ally Montenegro decided to "get aggressive," then "congratulations, you're in World War III."[194]

Moving on to England for a state visit, Trump kneecapped a close ally, Conservative prime minister Teresa May, telling a British tabloid that she had bungled the Brexit withdrawal from the EU and killed off any chance for a US trade deal.[195] He then went on to Helsinki for a summit with Putin—a meeting the *New York Times* labeled "the humiliating Trump-Putin cuddle-fest"—where he abased himself before NATO's nemesis so completely that there were protests even from leaders of his own Republican Party.[196]

His second year also saw a continuing erosion of America's alliances in the Pacific, long the fulcrum for its defense of North America and dominance over Asia. Even after ten personal meetings and frequent phone calls from Japan's Prime Minister Shinzo Abe, Trump imposed heavy tariffs on Japanese steel imports.[197]

The limitations of Trump's deal-cutting diplomacy were most evident on the Korean Peninsula. After leaving a meeting of the Group of Seven at Quebec City in shambles by refusing to join the usual communiqué and calling for Russia's readmission to the organization, Trump flew to Singapore for an amiable but inconsequential summit with North Korean dictator Kim Jong-un. Trump emerged to claim that country was "no longer a nuclear threat" and rewarded its leader with an indefinite suspension of joint US military maneuvers with South Korea—something Pyongyang had long desired.[198]

Within a month, however, satellite intelligence revealed that North Korea was building new missiles capable of striking anywhere inside the United States.[199] And inside of two months, the conservative *Wall Street Journal* editorialized glumly that "the prospect of complete, verifiable and irreversible denuclearization looks further away now than it was before Singapore."[200] A second summit at Hanoi followed early the next year, where Kim rejected Trump's attempt "to go big" with a denuclearization deal, and the talks collapsed. In the aftermath of that debacle, Pyongyang tested some highly maneuverable solid-fuel rockets, confirming the most pessimistic assessments of Trump's version of personal diplomacy. In November 2019, Trump tried to revive talks with Pyongyang by tweeting Kim playfully, "See you soon!" but North Korea replied that it had "no intention to sit at the table with the tricky US."[201]

Trump was even more solicitous in courting another autocratic leader, Vladimir Putin, remaining silent while Russia launched a succession of withering cyberattacks that compromised a domain increasingly critical for US national security. As the first major power to recognize the potential of the internet for cyberwarfare, Washington had formed the US Cyber Command in 2009 and scored some early successes, infecting computers in Iran's nuclear facilities with devastating effect and conducting cyber-surveillance of national leaders worldwide.[202] During the 2016 presidential elections, however, Russian intelligence, the Senate later reported, "used social media to conduct an information warfare campaign destined to spread disinformation and societal division," which was, in fact, "part of a broader, sophisticated and ongoing information warfare campaign."[203] Worse was yet to come. In March 2017, the hackers' website *Wikileaks* released a kit of the CIA's top secret hacking tools, forcing the agency to notify allies of a serious lapse in its security. In the Trump administration's last weeks, the private cybersecurity firm FireEye notified the US government of a possible breach that turned out to be massive. Through an operation "whose sophistication stunned even experts," Russian security services had inserted a Trojan horse software upgrade into eighteen thousand private and government users—including Commerce, Homeland Security, State, and Treasury Departments, as well as the Pentagon.[204] In the twenty-first century, a global hegemon hacks the communications and computers of subordinate nations; a declining power, by contrast, gets hacked.

Acting as if the United States were still a superpower that could bend China to its will, the president also launched an all-out trade war, starting with tariffs on $60 billion of Chinese imports in March 2018, then raising those duties to record levels that September.[205] Beijing replied in kind, imposing crushing duties on US agricultural exports and disrupting its industrial supply chains. After an eighteen-month standoff with much damage on both sides, Trump finally capitulated, rescinding many of his tariffs in exchange for unenforceable promises from Beijing to import more US goods.[206]

About the time officials from both countries were signing that trade deal at a celebratory White House ceremony in January 2020, a new coronavirus, Covid-19, began to spread rapidly in the central Chinese city of Wuhan. Through its enforcement of a strict quarantine and an effective underlying public health system, China quickly contained the virus at just 83,000 cases, with 4,600 deaths, and succeeded in largely reopening its economy safely by mid-May. In the United States, by contrast, Trump dithered for the better part of two months, dismissing the virus as a seasonal flu that would soon fade and effectively abdicating any federal role in control of the pandemic. Compounding the problem, the Centers for Disease Control and Prevention, once the world's premier public health agency, bungled the development of a virus test, lending the government the aura of a failed state. Instead of leading the international public health campaign as it had done for decades, Washington absented itself from a global vaccine summit and then quit the WHO, seeking to blame it and China for its own woefully inept response. By the end Trump's term, America had more than a quarter of the world's Covid-19 cases with nearly 24 million individual infections, over four hundred thousand deaths, and 40 million job losses—with much worse to come. While the US economic recovery was fitful at best, China quickly bounced back to a 6 percent increase in GDP, producing at least 30 percent of global growth in 2020. China also became the world's top destination for foreign investment, surpassing the US for the first time. This striking disparity in state performance accelerated China's trajectory to pass the US as the world's largest economy (at market exchange rates) by 2028 and, with all that financial clout, become its preeminent power.[207]

As the pandemic continued to spread across America, the country was issued a forceful reminder of its colonial past as a slave society and its subsequent century of racial segregation. Captured in graphic cell phone recordings, the murder of two black men, one by vigilantes in Georgia and the other by police officers in Minneapolis, were the catalyst that plunged the nation into months of protest. Some 140 cities across the country and dozens more around the world saw spontaneous demonstrations under the banner of Black Lives Matter, shutting down highways and holding mass vigils in parks and plazas. Most of the protests took the form of marches, whose demands included police accountability for the murders, along with the redistribution of police department funding to community initiatives. Others took more direct forms of action, toppling statues of historical figures identified with every phase of slavery's tragic history—Columbus in St. Paul; Edward Colston, head of the Royal African Company, in Bristol, England; King Leopold II in Antwerp, Belgium; and Confederate president Jefferson Davis in Richmond, Virginia. Instead of addressing the discrimination and violence that were the subject of the protests, President Trump denounced the demonstrators as "thugs" and, paraphrasing a racist Southern police chief from the Jim Crow era, threatened brutal repression, saying, "When the looting starts, the shooting starts."[208]

And so, at yet another turning point in the country's history, the legacy of slavery impinged upon its exercise of global power. In the five years preceding the protests, police violence had killed a thousand African Americans every year. Black men also suffered a disproportionate rate of incarceration, comprising, in 2009, nearly half of the country's bloated prison population. From a historical perspective, the lynchings and convict chain gangs of the old segregated South were the direct precursor—as coercive means of enforcing systemic inequality—of contemporary police shootings, mass incarceration of African American men, and lasting disenfranchisement of felons. Apart from their expression of anger over police violence, the protests also heightened awareness of racial disparities in access to education, housing, employment, and health care (with the Covid-19 pandemic hitting minority populations harder than majority-white ones nationwide). "Our country has a birth defect," wrote former secretary of state Condoleezza Rice, in an appeal for racial redress after those two incidents. "Africans and Europeans came to this country together—but one group was in chains." Over time, a political consensus might well form to address such unresolved issues through programs of racial reparations and social equity that could make a long-term claim on federal funding, reducing resources for overseas military operations.[209]

Trump's presidency brought a growing realization, at home and abroad, that Washington's world leadership was ending far sooner than anyone had imagined. Like Britain's former prime minister Anthony Eden, Trump did not cause the decline but clearly accelerated it. It is indicative of that loss of influence that when he called the Group of Seven meeting in Washington in June 2020, the country's closest allies—Britain, Canada, and

Germany—refused to cooperate with his plans to invite Russia; as a result, the summit, for the first time after 45 meetings, became engulfed in controversy and was postponed. Reflecting its antagonistic relations with long-term allies, the Trump White House retaliated by announcing the withdrawal of 9,500 troops from Germany, just as it had earlier suspended joint maneuvers with South Korea without consulting Seoul.[210]

After decades of promoting democracy to legitimate its global leadership, a US president, Donald Trump, spent his last months in office denouncing a fair American election as fraudulent. In the culmination of that bizarre spectacle, on January 6, 2021, Trump sent a mob of ten thousand to storm the Capitol, where Congress was ratifying the transition to a new administration. Adding to the failed-state aura, the country's once-formidable national security apparatus crumpled like a tropical constabulary as right-wing militia members breached the frail security cordon around the Capitol and stormed its halls like a lynch mob, hunting congressional leaders. When Congress was finally back in session, the Capitol rang with Republican calls for forgetting in the name of national unity, echoing the impunity that has long protected fallen military juntas in Asia or Latin America from any accounting for their crimes. In the aftermath, the Republican Party rallied to Trump, embracing his fantasy of electoral fraud as an article of faith and making personal fealty its sole platform. Just as the Conservative Party's chimera of endless empire had accelerated Britain's decline, so the Republican Party's retreat from rationality into a delusional obeisance signaled a marked diminution in US capacity for global leadership. Suddenly, the exceptional nation seemed tragically ordinary, no longer capable of inspiring others to follow its principles, or even to acquiesce to its power.[211]

Beyond Trump

Succeeding administrations can readily revise or reverse Trump's domestic policies on trade, the environment, and health care, but his disruptive diplomacy is an altogether different matter. Global leadership lost is not readily recovered, particularly when rival powers are prepared to fill the void. As Washington's strategic position weakens, China has been pressing relentlessly to displace it and dominate Eurasia—a key step on its path to global primacy. After winning the 2020 presidential elections, Joe Biden proclaimed "America is back" and promised to revive its liberal international leadership. But European leaders, mindful of Trump's battering of NATO, continued to make plans for their own common defense without America. "We aren't in the old status quo," said one French diplomat, "where we can pretend that the Donald Trump presidency never existed and the world was the same as four years ago."[212]

Some twenty years after Brzezinski issued his warning, all of his geopolitical conditions for the decline of US global power were in the process of being met. Washington's "perch on the Western periphery" of Eurasia has indeed been eroding, through both internal conflicts within the EU and the Trump administration's attacks on the NATO alliance. That vast "middle space" of Eurasia was threatening to become "an assertive single entity" under Beijing's economic leadership. Through China's diplomacy and Washington's diplomatic failings, conditions were also developing that could eventually expel America from its offshore bases along the Pacific littoral.[213]

Within the stark duality that is Washington's world order, a decline in US power could also ultimately threaten liberal international institutions like the UN, the IMF, the WHO, and the WTO. America's ongoing withdrawal from the global arena had created an opening for illiberal powers like China, Russia, Iran, India, and Turkey, whose advance could well damage the liberal international order by weakening its core principles of universal human rights and inviolable state sovereignty.

There was, however, another far more fundamental force compounding the pressures for a change in world orders. After 70 years of profligate fossil fuel consumption that had become synonymous with Washington's world system, climate change had gained sufficient force to cause profound disruptions of the human community. Through 20 years of bipartisan denials, evasions, and compromises, the US had failed to launch a transition to renewable energy sources. Denmark already derived 47 percent of its energy from wind, and Germany generated 46 percent of its power supply from renewables; but the US, as of 2019, produced only 17 percent of its electricity from renewables and 20 percent from nuclear while still relying on fossil fuels for 63 percent. As European oil majors led by BP and Shell were moving to alternative energy and making plans to leave company oil reserves buried forever, their US counterparts Chevron and ExxonMobil were doubling down on oil drilling and dismissing renewables as "a low-profit business." The situation was even worse in China, which secured only 13 percent of its energy from renewable sources and depended on fossil fuels for a full 85 percent. The underlying problem was an imbedded inertia. After 150 years of dependence, the "production, delivery, and consumption of fossil fuels," explains energy expert Vaclav Smil, "constitute the world's most extensive, and the most expensive, web of energy-intensive infrastructures that now span the globe, with many of its parts expected to serve for decades."[214]

In any transition beyond fossil fuels, the world's two largest economies would have to play a determinative role. After all, if you were to add up all fossil fuel emissions during the century and a half from 1870 to 2014, a full quarter of that total occurred in the fifteen years between 2000 and 2014, when the US and China dominated the global economy. As global carbon dioxide emissions rose by a staggering 50 percent from 22.2 gigatons in 1997 to a peak of 33.3 gigatons in 2018, China and the US together accounted for 43 percent of the world's total. Not only was the gross tonnage going up, but the rate of increase in global emissions was rising as well—from 1 percent per annum in the 1990s to 3 percent during the fifteen years before the 2015 Paris climate accord.[215]

Looking into the future, the impending cataclysm from climate change, combined with China's geopolitical challenge, has the potential to end Washington's world order and allow the ascent of an alternative global system—while simultaneously ushering in an era of catastrophic environmental disruption.

President Xi Jinping of China announces Belt and Road
Initiative, Astana, Kazakhstan, 2013 (Credit: Alamy)

Chapter 6
Beijing's World System

In September 2013, China's new president, Xi Jinping, stood smiling and confident before an audience at Kazakhstan's Nazarbayev University to give an address that went far beyond the usual platitudes of a state visit. After praising the country's long-serving dictator and calling the friendship between the two nations "as close as lips and teeth," Xi offered a personal anecdote about that land's historic role at the heart of the Silk Road between China and Europe. "Shaanxi, my home province," he said, "is right at the starting point of the ancient Silk Road. Today, as I stand here and look back at that episode of history, I could almost hear the camel bells echoing in the mountains and see the wisp of smoke rising from the desert. It has brought me close to the place I am visiting."

Then, in a quick pivot from the personal to the geopolitical, Xi asked the audience to join him in building an "economic belt along the Silk Road" that would "forge closer economic ties, deepen cooperation and expand development space in the Eurasian region." Through trade and infrastructure "connecting the Pacific and the Baltic Sea," this vast region inhabited by close to three billion people could, he said, become "the biggest market in the world with unparalleled potential."[1]

Though seemingly focused on commercial issues, Xi's address also posed a challenge to US global power and its liberal world order. At the most visible level, that speech marked the start of Beijing's bold development scheme, dubbed the Belt and Road Initiative (BRI), to make Eurasia into a single market by investing a trillion dollars in its infrastructure. But it was also the beginning of China's attempt to break the US military's encirclement of that vast continent. After ten years of compliance with Washington's rules for good global citizenship, Beijing's actions following that address would slowly reveal a stealthy strategy for breaking American global power.

By spending a trillion dollars to build a transcontinental grid of railroads, oil pipelines, and industrial infrastructure, China would begin to harness Eurasia's vast resources in a bid to become the world's premier economic power.[2] Next, building upon its new role as the world's top manufacturing nation, Beijing would use trade and investment to assert itself in Europe in ways that would neutralize the North Atlantic Treaty Organization (NATO), while deploying parallel pressure to weaken Washington's bilateral ties to its Asian allies. Finally, China would surround Africa and Asia with naval patrols, commercial ports, and a growing number of military bases, effectively ending Washington's strategic control over both continents. In sum, by realizing Sir Halford Mackinder's geopolitical vision of merging Asia, Africa, and Europe into a single "world island," Beijing was attempting to unite Eurasia as the epicenter of a new global system with the potential to accelerate both the decline of US global hegemony and the ascent of a new world order.[3]

In that speech, Xi's silences were no less important than his bold statements. He avoided any mention of carbon emissions or sustainable energy. Indeed, as it took form, the BRI's pell-mell pursuit of growth would promote increased use of coal-fired electricity, potentially contributing significantly to global warming and ultimately harming the poor it purported to assist. Like the three world orders that preceded it, Beijing's emerging global system thus came to exhibit a marked duality—in this case, between economic development that would promise to lift many millions out of poverty and a hypernationalism that would disregard both carbon emissions and human rights, thereby degrading the long-term quality of life for those same millions.

Beijing's Grand Strategy

As America squandered time and treasure on military misadventures in the aftermath of the Cold War, China spent the same decades building industries that would make it the world's workshop. In a major strategic miscalculation, Washington admitted Beijing to the World Trade Organization (WTO) in 2001, bizarrely confident that a compliant China would somehow join the global economy without changing the balance of power. "Across the ideological spectrum, we in the US foreign policy community," two former members of the Obama administration later wrote, "shared the underlying belief that US power and hegemony could readily mold China to the United States' liking. . . . All sides of the policy debate erred." A bit more bluntly, former national security adviser H.R. McMaster concluded that Washington had empowered "a nation whose leaders were determined not only to displace the United States in Asia, but also to promote a rival economic and governance model globally." Over the span of fifteen years, Beijing's exports to the US grew nearly fivefold to $462 billion, and its foreign currency reserves surged from just $200 billion to an unprecedented $4 trillion by 2014. Meanwhile, Washington was wasting $5.4 trillion on profitless wars in the Middle East in lieu of spending on infrastructure, innovation, or education—a time-tested formula for imperial decline.[4]

While Americans were mired in their endless wars, Beijing was using its growing capital reserves to build a tri-continental infrastructure that would incorporate great swaths of Africa and Asia into its version of the world economy, simultaneously lifting many millions out of poverty. During the Cold War, Washington had presided over the reconstruction of a ravaged Europe and the economic development of a hundred new nations that emerged from a century of colonial exploitation. But when the Cold War ended in 1990, more than a third of humanity was still living in extreme poverty. Even as late as 2015, nearly half the world's population, about 3.4 billion people, were struggling to survive on little more than five dollars a day.[5] Ultimately, it was the BRI's bold geopolitical gambit, combined with its strategy for improving the lives of humanity's forgotten millions, that gave Beijing's scheme sufficient force to shake the established global order.

Social change began at home. Starting in the 1980s, the Communist Party presided over the transformation of China from an impoverished agricultural nation into an urban industrial powerhouse. The first step in the construction of Chinese state capitalism entailed the breakup of Maoist collective farming and the deregulation of agricultural prices, allowing farmers freedom to work where they pleased. With stunning speed, in less than three decades the proportion of China's workforce in agriculture plummeted from 70 percent to just 30 percent, while its gross domestic product soared from an impoverished $156 per capita to a comfortable $7,740. As workers left the villages to the very old and very young, some 87 percent of all those between sixteen and thirty-five years old found full-time off-farm employment. Amid a rapid shift of population to the cities, 229,000 village elementary schools closed in just a decade. Confident that urbanization was, in the words of

Premier Li Keqiang, "the most powerful . . . internal driving force for economic growth," China's government planned to have a billion people, about 70 percent of the country's population, living in cities by 2030.[6]

Propelled by the greatest mass migration in human history, China's economy grew an average of nearly 10 percent annually for 40 years—the fastest sustained rate ever recorded by any country. Meanwhile, its industrial output increased from $1.2 trillion in 2006 to $3.2 trillion in 2016, surpassing both the United States at $2.2 trillion and Japan at just $1 trillion.[7]

Much of that economic dynamism derived from Beijing's decision to encourage private entrepreneurship in two key sectors—industrial production in export zones and the commercial development of cyberspace. Starting in the 1980s, China opened its first special export zone at Shenzhen, just across the river from Hong Kong, which grew, in just 30 years, from a town of 30,000 people into a metropolis of 10 million. At first, those zones attracted multinational corporations that produced the great bulk of the country's industrial exports, until the government began requiring them to share technology—a decision that sparked the dramatic growth of domestic firms.[8] Soon after China joined the WTO, that strategy encouraged a rapid expansion of cyber-commerce, with Huawei becoming the world's largest producer of communications equipment by 2012. Two years later, the e-commerce giant Alibaba raised a record-shattering $25 billion at its initial public offering on the New York Stock Exchange.[9]

By the time the Obama administration awoke to China's challenge and responded with its strategic pivot to Asia, it was too late. Beijing had already become an industrial powerhouse with ample capital to fund massive infrastructure developments across Africa and Eurasia. As its foreign reserves reached $4 trillion in 2014, Beijing established the Asian Infrastructure Investment Bank, with 56 member nations and an impressive $100 billion in capital. Beijing also formed its own $40 billion Silk Road Fund for private equity projects.[10] When a Belt and Road Forum of 29 world leaders convened in Beijing in May 2017, President Xi hailed the initiative as the "project of the century," which was already "bearing rich fruit" of "enhanced infrastructure connectivity" and eradication of "poverty, backwardness and social injustice," raising half of humanity out of unending misery.[11] Indeed, two years later a World Bank study found that BRI transport projects had already increased the gross domestic product in 55 recipient nations by a solid 3.4 percent.[12]

Although the American media has often described the BRI's individual projects as wasteful, sybaritic, exploitative, and even neocolonial, its sheer scale and scope merits closer consideration.[13] Beijing is expected to commit $1.3 trillion to this project by 2027, making it the largest investment in human history. Adjusted for inflation, that monumental sum is over ten times more than the foreign aid Washington allocated to its famed Marshall Plan to rebuild a ravaged Europe after World War II. By 2016, China's low-cost infrastructure loans to 70 countries from the Baltic to the Pacific were building the Mediterranean's biggest port at Piraeus, a major nuclear power plant in England, a $6 billion railroad through Laos, and a $46 billion transport corridor across Pakistan, among other projects.[14] If successful, such investments could knit Asia and Europe—home to 70 percent of the world's population—into a unitary landmass and a unified market without peer on the planet.

Amid this flurry of flying dirt and flowing concrete, Beijing seems to have an underlying design for transcending the vast distances that have historically separated Asia from Europe. The foundation for this ambitious transnational scheme is a monumental construction effort that, in just three decades, has covered the country with a massive transport triad: pipelines, roads, and high-speed rail. Starting in 2008, the China National Petroleum Corporation collaborated with Turkmenistan, Kazakhstan, and Uzbekistan to launch the Central Asia–China gas pipeline, a system that will eventually extend more than four thousand miles.[15] In only a decade, Beijing built a comprehensive network of transcontinental gas and oil pipelines to import fuels from Siberia and Central Asia for its own population centers. When the pipeline system, the first arm in its transport triad, is complete around 2025, there will be an integrated inland energy network, including Russia's extensive grid of pipelines, that extends for six thousand miles, from the North Atlantic to the South China Sea.

The rapid growth of these natural gas pipelines has been part of a multifaceted attempt to reduce the country's dependence on coal and thereby cleanse the air above its cities, which are blackened by lethal particulates from home heating and electrical generation. To power its headlong development, China raised domestic coal production exponentially, from just 32 million metric tons to 3.7 billion tons by 2015, forging an extraordinary dependence. Even those massive gas pipelines, together with a dozen import terminals, had only increased the share of the country's energy supplied by liquefied natural gas to 6 percent. China was the undisputed world leader in wind power, but it nevertheless accounted for only 3.3 percent of its total energy supply. Beijing had also built the world's biggest dam, but hydropower provided a mere 8 percent of its energy needs. Even its massive oil imports, the world's second largest, supplied a modest 18 percent of the country's energy. In spite of all those monumental efforts, China still produced 40 percent of the world's coal, which supplied almost 65 percent of its energy use.[16] Nothing, it seemed, could break its insatiable hunger for the dirtiest of all fossil fuels.

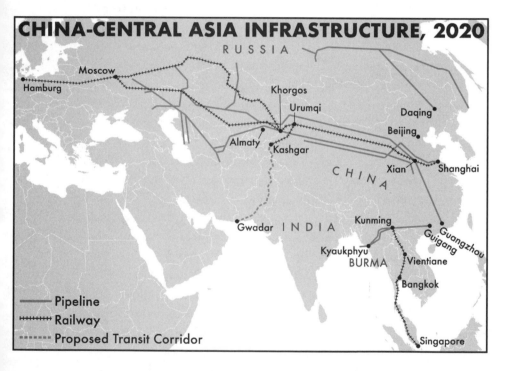

The second arm in that transport triad, roads, represented a problematic continuity with Washington's carbon-fueled world order. Beginning in 1990 without a single expressway, by 2017 China had built 87,000 miles of those concrete roadways, creating a nationwide complex nearly double the size of the US Interstate Highway System. Even that breathtaking number cannot begin to describe the extraordinary engineering feats that tunnel through steep mountains, span wide rivers, dance across deep gorges on towering pillars, and spin concrete webs around massive cities.[17] Meanwhile, China had also become the world's largest auto manufacturer, and the total number of cars and trucks on those roads soared to 340 million in 2019, exceeding America's 276 million vehicles. By clinging to coal while reaching for a bigger slice of the world's oil imports, China's contribution to global greenhouse gas emissions doubled from 14 percent in 2000 to 29 percent in 2017, far surpassing America's. With only 150 cars per thousand people, as compared to 850 cars per thousand in the United States, today China's auto industry still has a vast potential for future growth—good news for its economy, but bad news for the world's climate.[18]

Completing its transport triad, Beijing has built the world's largest high-speed rail system, with more than 15,000 miles in operation and plans for a network of nearly 24,000 miles by 2025. Although the rolling stock was initially imported, China quickly developed a domestic industry that now exports trains to Indonesia, Thailand, Turkey, and Russia. Compared to an average speed of only 66 miles per hour on America's fastest line, China's trains regularly travel at 160 miles per hour, virtually eliminating all short-distance air travel. Not only does China have the world's fastest passenger train (220 miles per hour), but it also has the longest high-speed line (1,400 miles). And keep in mind that such a massive domestic network is just the first step toward a transcontinental rail system for passengers and freight, starting with an expansion of the "Eurasian Land Bridge" track that runs from China through Kazakhstan to Europe.[19]

To supplement such transcontinental trunk lines, Beijing also made bold plans for spur railroads running due south toward Singapore and southwest through Pakistan. Apart from expanding Beijing's own network, each new section stimulates local infrastructure investment. As a $6 billion railroad bored through China's rugged southern mountains toward the Laotian capital at Vientiane in mid-2019, the government of neighboring Thailand announced complementary plans to construct 2,000 miles of high-speed rail, at a cost of $65 billion, to make Bangkok the hub of a network stretching for 1,600 miles from southern China to Singapore.[20]

Illustrating the BRI's strong stimulus effect, Beijing's $6 billion Lao rail project in effect sparked Bangkok's $65 billion match, which will amplify the impact of China's original investment tenfold. Not only did Beijing's new spur line breach the formidable mountain barrier that had long separated

southwest China from its southern neighbors; in tandem with Bangkok's effort, it will also integrate the transport infrastructure of six Southeast Asian
nations and, simultaneously, improve the Thai capital's congested links to
its outlying industrial zone. Even if many of these Belt and Road projects,
including new railroads in Ethiopia and Kenya, remain unprofitable, they
could still have important spillover effects, stimulating the economies of
their respective regions.[21]

Paralleling this transcontinental infrastructure, Beijing also acquired
special access through loans and leases to more than 40 seaports encompassing its own latter-day "world island"—from the Straits of Malacca, across
the Indian Ocean, around Africa, and along Europe's extended coastline
from the Greek city of Piraeus to the town of Zeebrugge, in Belgium.[22] To
crown that network, in 2019 President Xi made a state visit to Italy for the
first signing of a Belt and Road agreement with one of the Group of Seven
nations. Under the terms of this economic entente, China gained access to

the ports of Genoa and Trieste, both strategically sited with direct rail links through the Alps into the heart of Europe.[23] To take advantage of Arctic waters being opened by global warming, Beijing also began planning for a "Polar Silk Road" that is to coincide with ambitious Russian and Scandinavian plans for a shorter shipping route along the continent's Arctic coast to the nations of northern Europe.[24] In geopolitical terms, China's string of seaports mimed the Portuguese Empire's agile array of 50 fortified enclaves (*feitorias*), which once extended along the coasts of Africa and much of Asia. But Beijing also added immeasurable strength with its trans-Eurasian grid of railroads, gas pipelines, and infrastructure projects.

Although Eurasia remained its prime focus, China also pursued economic expansion in Africa and Latin America to create what might be dubbed the Strategy of Four Continents. To tie Africa into its Eurasian network, Beijing planned, circa 2015, a massive infusion of capital expected to reach a trillion dollars within a decade, with much of that invested in commodities extraction that would make the continent China's second-largest source of crude oil.[25] Similarly, Beijing invested heavily in Latin America and the Caribbean in order to access their commodities—gaining control, for instance, of over 90 percent of Ecuador's oil reserves. Nor is it surprising that China's trade with Latin America doubled within a decade, reaching $244 billion in 2017, considerably greater than US commerce with its own southern neighbors.[26]

By the end of the BRI's fifth year, China's export of its economic model for state-controlled enterprises had generated a good deal of criticism from recipient countries. For one thing, Beijing's infrastructure loans were usually tied to contracts with Chinese construction companies, leaving little room for local participation. Sharp criticism of the initiative's projects arose in Zambia, Myanmar, Sri Lanka, Malaysia, Pakistan, and the Maldives, because they regularly lent support to authoritarian leaders, encouraged corruption, and fostered debt-trap dependency. Adding to the chorus of dissent, environmentalists faulted the BRI for committing over $20 billion to coal-fired electrical generation, particularly in Bangladesh, Pakistan, and Indonesia. Chinese officials acknowledged the problem, and regulators clamped down on aggressive overseas lending by the country's banks, momentarily slowing the breakneck pace of the BRI.[27]

At its second Belt and Road Forum, which 150 nations attended in April

2019, Beijing responded to the criticism with its launch of what the director of the International Monetary Fund (IMF), Christine Lagarde, called "BRI 2.0." In the future, she said, China would emphasize "low-carbon and climate-resilient investment," while requiring "increased transparency, open procurement with competitive bidding, and better risk assessment."[28] China's finance minister, Liu Kun, addressed the debt-trap charge by releasing a sustainability framework for future loans based on IMF standards. With that reset, the initiative extended another $128 billion in foreign loans, bringing the scheme halfway to its target of $1.3 trillion.[29]

To investigate Washington's accusations that China was using debt "to hold states in Africa captive to Beijing's wishes," researchers at Johns Hopkins University studied one thousand Chinese loans worth more than $140 billion, concluding that most of the criticism was unfounded.[30] Despite inevitable problems with such a massive scheme, it remained the world's largest development program, dwarfing all competing efforts. Not only did the rival US BUILD Act have just $60 billion in capital, but its conditions for infrastructure projects in Asia and Africa were burdensome for borrowers.[31]

The China–US Trade War

As Beijing's global influence continued to grow, the administration of Donald Trump declared a trade war on China. Amid a major purge of moderate White House personnel in early 2018, the president formed a hard-right foreign policy team, promoting his loyal adviser Peter Navarro from deputy assistant to head of a new Trade Office, co-equal with the older National Economic Council.[32]

As a top White House aide, Navarro applied his prickly persona and idiosyncratic views to reshape the trade war. Despite a doctorate in economics from Harvard and a professorship at the University of California, Irvine, he remained an angry outsider, denouncing special interests for "stealing America" in his first book.[33] During a busy decade in the 1990s, Navarro had launched five losing political campaigns for offices ranging from city council member to congressional representative. He detailed his crushing defeat in the latter race in a tell-all book, *San Diego Confidential*, that dished out disdain for "sellout" Bill Clinton, dumb "blue-collar detritus" voters, and just about everybody in between.[34] Following his final losing campaign for a seat on San Diego's city council, Navarro spent the next decade churning out books attacking China, starting in 2006 with a jeremiad that denounced Beijing's foreign trade, followed by another filled with torrid tales of lethal Chinese consumer products.[35]

President Donald Trump and trade adviser Peter Navarro,
White House, March 2020 (Credit: Reuters/Alamy)

With his third book, 2015's *Crouching Tiger*, however, Navarro put aside polemics for a serious study of geopolitics, complete with detailed maps and admiring references to Alfred Thayer Mahan, arguing that China's "anti-access, area denial" strategy could effectively challenge the US Navy's control over the western Pacific.[36] To check China, the Pentagon had already prepared two aggressive containment strategies that it labeled "Air-Sea Battle" and "Offshore Control." Both, said Navarro, were fundamentally flawed. The first planned to blind China's satellites and knock out its missiles, but the probability of hitting Beijing's mobile missile systems was, he said, "extremely low."[37] The second proposed a blockade of China's entire coastline with mines at six maritime choke points from Japan to Singapore. However, the same blockade would, Navarro observed, also deliver "crushing blows" to the US economy.[38] The only realistic solution was, therefore, "the imposition of countervailing tariffs to offset China's unfair trade practices."[39]

As chief defender of Trump's belief that "trade wars are good and easy to win," Navarro used his new White House position to confront his China nemesis.[40] In March 2018, the president fired the opening shot of his trade war, imposing heavy tariffs on steel imports targeted at China. Just a few weeks later, he promised to impose yet more of them on $60 billion of its imports.[41] When those tariffs began in July, Beijing immediately retaliated against what it called "typical trade bullying" by levying similar duties on US goods.[42] In September, Trump escalated the trade war with tariffs on an additional $200 billion in Chinese goods, while threatening duties on another $267 billion if China dared to retaliate.[43] Tit for tat, Beijing promptly hit back with its own, this time on just $60 billion in goods since its duties already covered 95 percent of all its US imports.[44]

In his third year in office, Trump escalated his trade war to include Beijing's high-tech industrial program, "Made in China 2025." Calling that slogan a "label for a Chinese strategy to achieve dominance," Navarro told the media in December 2018 that "China is basically trying to steal the future of Japan, the US and Europe, by going after our technology."[45] The first US target was China's premier telecommunications firm, Huawei. Concern about it had initially arisen earlier that year after an Australian intelligence agency, the Foreign Signals Directorate, ran a cyberwar exercise that led it to advise US officials that Huawei's role in the emerging 5G internet infrastructure, which is one hundred times faster than its 4G predecessor, represented a serious security risk. Suddenly, Washington decided that Huawei represented a "grave national security danger" and that to let it into their communications networks would be "tantamount to opening Troy's gates to the mythical Trojan Horse," as national security adviser H.R. McMaster later put it. Only three of 61 countries that American officials approached initially agreed to boycott Huawei's 5G technology, but the president still signed an executive order in May 2019 that banned the company's equipment from all US networks on national security grounds, precipitating a short-term plunge in company revenues.[46] However, Huawei already had nearly a third of the global market for communications equipment, was the world's second-largest maker of cell phones, and had 2,570 patents for 5G, so the company's revenues quickly rebounded, increasing 13 percent, to $65 billion, in the first half of 2020.[47]

That attack on Huawei, along with Trump's demand that Beijing codify its trade concessions into Chinese law, stifled negotiations until June 2019, when Trump and Xi met at the Group of Twenty summit in Osaka. During a tête-à-tête chat at the opening dinner, Xi explained why he was building "concentration camps" for the Uyghur Muslim minority in Xinjiang Province. According to presidential adviser John Bolton, Trump replied that China "should go ahead with building the camps, which he thought was exactly the right thing to do." During their bilateral talks the next day, Trump, in Bolton's recounting, "stunningly turned the conversation to the coming US presidential election"—stressing "the importance of farmers . . . in the electoral outcome." He then told the Chinese leader: "Make sure I win. . . . Buy a lot of soybeans and wheat and make sure we win." Emerging from these private meetings, Trump announced triumphantly that China would buy a "tremendous amount" of American agricultural products and that he, in turn, would allow exports of US components critical for Huawei products.[48]

After a few weeks of inconclusive diplomacy and none of the promised food purchases, Trump grew impatient and took steps that soon sent relations with China into free fall. In a midnight tweet on August 1, the president announced a 10 percent tariff, effective in just 30 days, on the remaining $300 billion in Chinese imports.[49] That announcement sparked a stock market plunge from investors' concern that the continuing trade war was slowing the economies of both Germany and China. Rattled by the unexpected market response, Trump retreated momentarily from his attack by suspending about half the tariffs for, he said, "the Christmas season, just in case some of the tariffs would have an impact on US consumers." Meanwhile, Navarro publicly defended the tough tactics, promising "a huge economic rebound later in the year."[50]

As a condition for rescinding the tariffs, Navarro insisted that China end "seven acts of economic aggression" and make structural changes to its economy. The president, Navarro added, could not compromise with the Chinese "because if you meet them halfway, they'll only be stealing half as much as they're stealing and killing half as many of Americans"—remarks indicating an animus so deep and demands so broad that any final resolution of the trade war would prove difficult.[51]

At the end of August, on the eve of the 2019 Group of Seven summit in France, China struck back, announcing new tariffs on $75 billion of US imports.[52] Infuriated at Beijing's refusal to bend, Trump fired off more tweets, in which he threatened to raise tariffs further on all $550 billion in Chinese imports, demanded US companies quit China, and denounced Xi as an "enemy." Although Trump calmed sufficiently during the summit's three days to hail Xi as a "great leader" (albeit not great enough for Trump to reduce his retaliatory tariffs), all the tumult indicated that the White House aspired to changes in the relationship that would be far more fundamental than mere tariffs. By the time those new duties took effect on September 1, Trump had raised the average US tariff on Chinese goods from 3.1 percent to 21.2 percent, the highest on any country in more than 50 years. Meanwhile, Beijing began charging a 33 percent duty on US soybean imports, contributing to a dramatic drop in US agricultural exports to China from $24 billion in 2014 to just $9 billion in 2018.[53]

By December of 2019, those tensions were damaging the US economy, prompting the White House to beat a hasty retreat and agree to an interim trade deal. Beijing's hardliners were, said the *New York Times*, "jubilant and even incredulous" when Trump gave up his demands for structural reforms of their economy and agreed to what he called a "big, beautiful" trade deal. Indicating the scope of his surrender, at the agreement's signing ceremony in January 2020 the administration slashed tariffs on $100 billion of Chinese goods in exchange for Beijing's "wildly ambitious" promise to import $40 billion in US goods.[54]

After months of deploying almost every weapon in its diplomatic arsenal, Washington had proven incapable of changing the character of China's massive state-managed economy. Over the previous fifteen years, China's industries had become fully integrated into the American consumer economy, producing a commercial synergy that accounted for 40 percent of world economic output. Even though Trump's State Department felt Beijing harbored "hegemonic ambitions" aimed at "displacing the United States as the world's foremost power" and "transformation of the international order," Washington still lacked leverage, as a fading superpower, to force change upon China.[55] In sum, the United States had reached the limits of its global power and no longer had sufficient strength to check China's rise as the world's leading economy.

While the Trump White House obsessed over how to game these bilateral ties, Beijing outmaneuvered Washington by pursuing two multilateral trade agreements that stole a page right out of Obama's strategic playbook. In November 2020, Beijing led fifteen Asia-Pacific nations in signing a Regional Comprehensive Economic Partnership that created the world's largest free trade zone, encompassing 2.2 billion people and nearly a third of the global economy. Just a month later, President Xi scored what one expert called "a geopolitical coup for China" by signing a draft agreement with European Union leaders for closer integration of their financial services. In effect, the accord, when finally ratified, would give European banks easier access to the China market, thus drawing the continent more closely into Beijing's orbit. So serious was the shift away from Washington that President Biden's national security adviser Jake Sullivan publicly urged the NATO allies to consult first with the new administration before doing the deal—a plea they simply ignored. In a stunning inversion of Obama's bold yet unrealized geopolitical gambit of using multilateral pacts to direct Eurasia's trade toward America, these two agreements will give Beijing preferential access to nearly half of all world trade. In years to come, these accords could, along with the Belt and Road Initiative, steer a growing share of Eurasia's capital and commerce toward Beijing. China's inclusion could well mean America's exclusion from much of the burgeoning trade that makes that vast continent nothing less than the epicenter of the global economy.[56]

China's Naval Gambit

Complementing its bid for economic dominance over Eurasia, China expanded its blue-water navy of glistening white ships and built a network of overseas bases in the Arabian and South China Seas. As Beijing stated in a 2015 white paper, "[T]he traditional mentality that land outweighs the sea must be abandoned. . . . It is necessary for China to develop a modern maritime military force structure commensurate with its national security."[57] Although it could not yet compete with the US Navy's global presence, China seemed determined to dominate a vast arc of oceans surrounding Asia—from the Horn of Africa, across the Indian Ocean, and along its own coast all the way to Korea. Strategists at the RAND Corporation were among those who recognized the seriousness of this challenge, reporting in 2015 that Beijing had made such "tremendous strides" in missiles, fighters, and submarines that "the net change in capabilities is moving in favor of China."[58]

Beijing's bid for overseas bases had begun quietly back in 2011, when it spent $200 million to transform a sleepy fishing village on the Arabian Sea at Gwadar, Pakistan, into a modern commercial port only 370 miles from the mouth of the Persian Gulf.[59] Four years later, Xi committed $46 billion to build a China–Pakistan Economic Corridor of roads, rails, and pipelines stretching nearly two thousand miles from China's western provinces to a now-modernized port at Gwadar, still avoiding any admission of military aims that might alarm New Delhi or Washington.[60] In 2016, however, Pakistan's navy announced that it was opening a base at Gwadar, soon strengthened by two Chinese-built warships, adding that Beijing was also welcome to base its own ships there.[61]

That same year, Beijing began building a military facility at Djibouti, on the Horn of Africa; in August 2017, it opened its first official overseas base, giving its navy access to the oil-rich Arabian Sea.[62] Simultaneously, Sri Lanka settled its billion-dollar debt to China by ceding its strategic port of Hambantota, at the epicenter of the Indian Ocean, thus creating a potential dual-use port to support future Chinese military and commercial operations.[63]

As controversial as all these enclaves might be, they paled before China's attempts to claim an entire ocean—one that holds 12 percent of global fisheries and 190 trillion cubic feet of natural gas reserves. Back in 1949, Beijing had drawn a looping "nine-dash line" on a map to mark its territorial claim to most of the South China Sea.[64] Starting in April 2014, Beijing escalated its bid for exclusive territorial control over that sea by expanding Longpo Naval Base, on its own Hainan Island, as a homeport for four nuclear-powered ballistic missile submarines.[65]

Without any announcement, Beijing also began to dredge artificial atolls for military airfields at the center of that sea, in the disputed Spratly Islands. In just four years, Beijing's armada of dredges sucked up countless tons of sand to build permanent bases on seven shoals. Just two years after those islands took final form, Beijing landed its first aircraft at a new three-thousand-meter airstrip on Fiery Cross Reef.[66] By 2018, China's army was operating a jet runway protected by anti-aircraft missile batteries on Woody Island, had mobile missile launchers near runways ready for jet fighters at three of the new Spratly "islands," and had installed military radar on the southernmost atoll, Cuarteron Reef, to guide its DF-21D carrier-killer missile batteries on the mainland in any future strike they might make on US ships.[67]

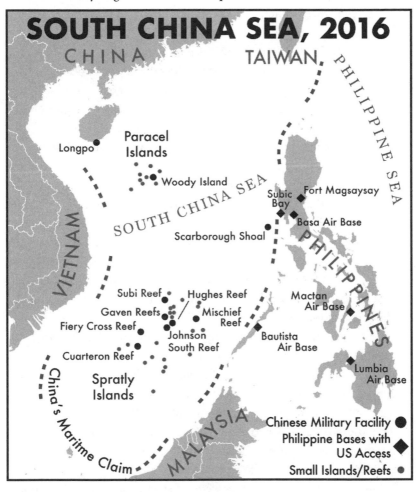

In response, the US Navy began staging "freedom of navigation patrols" that steamed close to these islands, to little effect.[68] With naval patrols alone unable to check China's claim to that strategic waterway, the Philippines again became critical for the US position in the Pacific. In April 2014, its ambassador to Manila signed an Enhanced Defense Cooperation Agreement with the Philippines, allowing the United States permanent facilities inside five Philippine bases, including two on the shores of the South China Sea.[69] Concerned about Chinese expansion into its exclusive economic zone, in July 2015 Manila opened its own military installations at Subic Bay, the former US naval bastion, to house two frigates and a new squadron of Korean-built FA-50 jet fighters.[70]

Paralleling these military moves, the Philippines also filed a complaint about China's incursions into its waters before the Permanent Court of Arbitration at The Hague. In 2012, Beijing had responded to Philippine naval inspections of Chinese fishing boats at Scarborough Shoal by occupying that reef, forcing the Philippines to defend its exclusive economic zone before the court.[71] "China's claims to historic rights, or other sovereign rights or jurisdiction," wrote the unanimous panel of five judges in July 2016, "with respect to the maritime areas . . . encompassed by the relevant part of the 'nine-dash line' are contrary to the [UN Convention on the Law of the Sea] and without lawful effect." In other words, with unambiguous clarity, the court ruled that China's dredging of artificial islands gave it no right whatsoever to the seas surrounding them. In response, China's Ministry of Foreign Affairs rejected the court's decision, stating flatly that it was "invalid and has no binding force."[72] Not only had Beijing claimed a *mare clausum* (closed sea)—a throwback to the Iberian age—but it had also signaled its disdain for the international rule of law, which had long been a hallmark of Washington's world order.

Further north, in 2013 Beijing imposed a unilateral Air Defense Identification Zone over the entire East China Sea. It also maintained relentless pressure on the Japanese-controlled Senkaku Islands, at the edge of that sea, prompting Japanese fighters to scramble 571 times in 2015 alone to counter Chinese incursions into the area's airspace. Should Beijing succeed in dominating those two seas, it would control all its coastal waters as far as the "first island chain" running from Okinawa to Borneo. As one senior Japanese official put it: "China is determined to create a great wall in the sea."[73]

While fighters and submarines were the stealth pawns in China's opening gambit for control of those strategic seas, Beijing also began preparing to checkmate Washington with a future armada of aircraft carriers, the dreadnoughts in this latter-day game of empires. After acquiring an unfinished Soviet *Kuznetsov*-class carrier from Ukraine in 1998, China's naval dockyard at Dalian retrofitted its rusting hulk and launched it in 2012 as the county's first aircraft carrier, the *Liaoning*. That carrier's hull was, of course, already 30 years old at its launch, an age that often sends warships to the scrapyards.

Though not combat-capable, the ship could still train China's first generation of naval aviators in the uncommon skill of landing a speeding jet on a
heaving deck in high seas. In marked contrast to the fifteen years needed to
retrofit this first ship, the Dalian yards took just five years to construct, from
the keel up, the first-ever Chinese-built carrier: the *Shandong*, a much-im-
proved version of the old Soviet design that was capable of full combat operations.[74] A third and larger carrier, built from China's own blueprints at
the Shanghai yards, is planned for launch in 2021, and will boast a superior
cruising range, a complement of 40 "Flying Shark" fighters, and a faster elec-
tromagnetic catapult system.[75] Through this accelerating tempo of training,
technology, and construction, by 2030 China might have enough aircraft
carriers, a Pentagon report warned, to make the South China Sea "virtually
a Chinese lake."[76]

Such carriers served as the vanguard for a sustained naval expansion
that, by 2020, had already produced a modern navy of 360 ships (more
than America with 297), backed by land-based missiles, jet fighters, and
a global system of military satellites.[77] By constructing submarines at the
breakneck pace of two a year, China had assembled a fleet of 57, both die-
sel- and nuclear-powered, that was destined to become an undersea armada
of 76 by 2030—outnumbering the United States, which will have 66 subs.
Each of its four nuclear submarines carried twelve ballistic missiles with the
range to strike anywhere in the western United States.[78] In addition, Beijing
had launched dozens of amphibious ships and coastal corvettes, giving it
naval dominance in its home waters.[79] While China's anti-ship ballistic
missiles already had a range of 2,500 miles, it was also making strides in
its mastery of a volatile new technology: impossible-to-stop hypersonic
missiles with speeds up to 5,600 miles per hour.[80]

So it was that the Pentagon could say, already in 2010, that Beijing had
the world's "most active land-based ballistic and cruise missile program"
and could target "its nuclear forces throughout . . . most of the world, including the continental United States." Moreover, accurate missiles would
provide "the People's Liberation Army (PLA) the capability to attack ships,
including aircraft carriers, in the western Pacific Ocean." China also began to contest American dominion over space and cyberspace, with plans
to dominate "the information spectrum in all dimensions of the modern
battlespace." With the development of the Long March 5 booster rocket

and the launch of five satellites by mid-2010, China began building "a full network" of 35 satellites for global command, control, and communications that was completed on schedule in June 2020—thereby breaking Washington's 50-year near-monopoly on the militarization of space.[81] The implications of China's space program for the US satellite system, critical for all of its military communications, became obvious in 2007 when China used a ground-to-air missile to shoot down one of its own satellites.[82] Reinforcing the Pentagon's concerns, a RAND Corporation study, *War with China*, warned that Beijing's improved capabilities meant a US victory was no longer certain in a conflict that "could involve inconclusive fighting with steep losses on both sides."[83]

Well before China's military prowess was so pronounced, President Obama broke with Washington's consensus about a benign Beijing and developed a deft geopolitical strategy to counter China's rise—a pivot of strategic military forces to Asia and a twelve-nation trade pact, the Trans-Pacific Partnership, that was designed to drain Beijing's Eurasian infrastructure of its commercial lifeblood. In spite of Trump's reversal of much of this trade policy immediately following his 2017 inauguration, the administration still enacted an expanded $700 billion defense budget to fund 46 new ships by 2023, which will eventually raise the Navy's total to 326.[84] After declaring Obama's "pivot to Asia" officially dead, the Trump administration announced its own version: a "free and open Indo-Pacific" founded on the Quadrilateral entente of four supposedly kindred democracies—Australia, America, Japan, and India.[85]

While the Trump administration's foreign policy stumbled through a succession of minor crises, his admirals, mindful of Mahan's strategic dictums, were acutely aware of the geopolitical requisites of US global power and vocal about their determination to preserve it. China's naval expansion, along with advances in Russia's submarine fleet, led to a fundamental shift in the Navy's strategy away from limited operations against regional powers like Iran, and toward full-spectrum readiness for "a return to great power competition."[86] After a sweeping strategic review of his forces in 2016, the chief of naval operations, Admiral John Richardson, reported that China's "growing and modernized fleet" was "shrinking" the traditional US advantage. "The competition is on," the admiral warned, "and pace dominates. In an exponential competition, the winner takes all. We must shake off any vestiges of comfort or complacency."[87]

Meanwhile, the commander of the US Navy's surface force, Admiral Thomas Rowden, proclaimed "a new age of seapower" with challenges from "near-peer competitors" that must be met, in the event of attack, with a "distributed lethality" capable of "inflicting damage of such magnitude that it compels an adversary to cease hostilities." Summoning the ghost of Captain Mahan, the admiral warned: "From Europe to Asia, history is replete with nations that rose to global power only to cede it back through lack of seapower."[88]

After a decade of bipartisan repair, the United States still held an overall superiority of forces over China. Against Beijing's fleet of three hundred ships, with just two carriers and numerous antiquated submarines, the Pacific Command, now renamed the Indo-Pacific Command, had two hundred ships, including five carrier strike groups, nearly a thousand combat aircraft, and 368,000 personnel. Most of these units were highly mobile, including two Marine Expeditionary Forces with 86,000 troops and 640 aircraft, as well as the US Army Pacific with 106,000 personnel, 300 aircraft, and five ships.[89] Under a new Pentagon strategy for "Access and Maneuver in the Global Commons," which replaced the older "Air-Sea Battle" doctrine, these forces were deployed in a state of readiness to counter "determined potential adversaries." The fear was, of course, focused on China, whose "new capabilities constitute an unprecedented array of antiaccess/area denial (A2/AD) capabilities that threaten the US and allied model of power projections and maneuver." This new doctrine plans to counter such "A2/AD" threats by integrating "all five warfighting domains (land, sea, air, space, and cyberspace)" to successfully "confront a near-peer, modern competitor."[90]

By 2022, however, says the Office of Naval Intelligence, China will "complete its transition" from a coastal force to a modern navy capable of "sustained blue water operations" and "multiple missions around the world," including full-spectrum warfare. Indeed, the Pentagon's 2020 Report to Congress warned that China was on track, through ever-expanding defense budgets, to build "a military by mid-century that is equal to—or in some cases superior to—the US military." Beijing was already ahead of Washington in three key areas, including, "the largest navy in the world" (with 350 ships compared to 293 for the US), an armada of 1,250 ground-launched missiles with ranges up to three thousand miles, and "one of the world's largest" air defense systems. Even though China's capabilities were already "the most robust within the first island chain," it aims to strengthen its capacity "to reach farther into the Pacific Ocean." Some "major gaps and shortcomings remain," but China's military was fast becoming an effective instrument for Beijing's "increasingly global interests and its aims to revise aspects of the international order."[91]

While China's ongoing military modernization will slowly erode the US strategic advantage, the likely zone of any future conflict will be its own home waters, inside that first island chain from Okinawa to Borneo, where Beijing's land-based aircraft and missiles will give it outright superiority. In the process, it will become the first power in 70 years to challenge the US Navy's once-absolute dominion over the entire Pacific basin. Observing these developments, political scientist Graham Allison noted that this "tectonic shift in the balance of power" will require Washington to accept "the reality that there are spheres of influence in the world today—and not all of them are American spheres."[92] Whatever the outcome, Washington's determination to dominate the Pacific while Beijing seeks control over a growing share of that ocean has placed the two powers on a possible collision course.

Naysayers who dismiss China's challenge might say that its navy only operates in two of those metaphoric "seven seas"—a pale imitation of the US Navy's robust global posture. Yet its rising presence in the Indian and Pacific Oceans will have far-reaching geostrategic implications for Washington's world order, opening Eurasia to Beijing's dominion and potentially allowing the rise of a new global order in its image.[93]

China's Emerging World System

As US global power has begun to fade, Beijing has been working sedulously to build a successor system that will be, in certain critical areas, strikingly different from its predecessor, some of whose essential principles it has already rejected. Most fundamentally, China has subordinated human rights to overarching national sovereignty, vehemently rejecting foreign criticism of its harsh treatment of Tibetan and Uyghur minorities, just as it ignores egregious rights transgressions by countries like North Korea or the Philippines. Beijing has swept more than a million Uyghur Muslims into reeducation camps scattered across Xinjiang Province in an elaborate effort to extirpate their ethnic and religious identity. Instructing the Communist Party leadership to ignore international criticism, Xi told them, "Don't be afraid if hostile forces whine, or if hostile forces malign the image of Xinjiang."[94]

By January 2020, Beijing's abuses had become so sustained and systemic that the New York–based Human Rights Watch branded China "an existential threat to the rights of people worldwide." At home, the Chinese Communist Party, it reported, had "constructed an Orwellian high-tech surveillance state and a sophisticated internet censorship system" to suppress any domestic dissent that might threaten its "ruthless autocratic rule." Abroad, Beijing "flexes its political muscles with . . . vigor and determination to undermine the international human rights standards." If China's stance is not somehow checked, the Human Rights Watch report warned, the world faces "a dystopian future in which no one is beyond the reach of Chinese censors, and an international human rights system so weakened that it no longer serves as a check on government repression."[95]

In a further extension of its state prerogatives, China has also defied the long-standing doctrine of open seas, which are today sanctioned by a UN convention, to claim adjacent oceans as sovereign territory. Adding volatility to China's claim, the South China Sea is one of the world's most strategic waterways, similar in geopolitical sensitivity to the Persian Gulf. Asia's sustained economic growth during the 1990s drew 40,000 ships and two-thirds of the world's liquefied natural gas supplies through those waters, which have proven oil reserves of 7 billion barrels and estimates, according to optimistic Chinese sources, of 130 billion barrels—second only to Saudi Arabia.[96] More immediately, the South China Sea ranked fourth among the world's nineteen major fisheries, producing one-fifth of the world's catch in 2010.[97]

As its dissatisfactions with the existing global order grew, Beijing began to explore alternatives. To counterpoise the NATO security pact on the continent's western extremity, in 2001 China founded the Shanghai Cooperation Organisation, including Russia, India, and Pakistan as a development and security bloc weighted toward the eastern end of Eurasia.[98] In lieu of the World Bank, with its restrictive stipulations for fiscal probity and human rights, Beijing formed the Asian Infrastructure Investment Bank, which quickly attracted 70 member nations and a capital of $100 billion.[99] Meanwhile, China's Belt and Road Initiative began mobilizing up to $8 trillion in matching funds for 1,700 projects aimed at the economic integration of dozens of nations across Africa and Eurasia.[100]

China's attempt to fashion a new global order has become increasingly focused, extending into the critical realm of news and information.

According to a 2019 report by the Paris-based Reporters without Borders, Beijing has "been going to great lengths . . . to establish a 'new world media order' under its control" that "poses a threat to press freedom throughout the world." Not only are international media groups "forced to submit to censorship if they want access to the Chinese market," but Beijing has exported its media-control model to Southeast Asia, where "authoritarian regimes are adopting Internet control regulations based closely on Chinese legislation." In a 2011 op-ed in the *Wall Street Journal*, the head of China's Xinhua News Agency, Li Congjun, called for a "new world media order" that would respect "the unique cultures, customs, beliefs and values of different nations." During a visit to the newsrooms of China's top three media outlets, President Xi himself reinforced the deeper meaning of that message, saying: "The media run by the party . . . are the propaganda fronts and must . . . love the party." In effect, according to Reporters without Borders, China's leaders are promoting a "theory of cultural relativism" diametrically opposed to the "universality of the UN's Universal Declaration of Human Rights."[101]

With its repudiation of current ideals of human rights and the international rule of law, Beijing's future world order seems likely to be governed by the realpolitik of commercial advantage and mutual self-interest. Just as Beijing has revived the medieval Portuguese doctrine of *mare clausum* to claim entire oceans as sovereign territory, so its human rights policy will likely be a throwback to the imperial age that placed national interest above universal principles.

China as Global Hegemon?

While a weakening of Washington's global reach seems likely, the future of its world order is still unclear. At present, China is the sole state to have most (but not all) of the requisites to become a new global hegemon. Its economic rise, coupled with its expanding military and growing technological prowess under the "Made in China 2025" program, has given it many of the elements fundamental to superpower status. Spared the sudden, wrenching changes that have marked recent British and American foreign policy, China's Communist Party is likely to continue its unwavering pursuit of international influence, giving it certain advantages in its global rivalry with the United States.

Yet as the 2020s began, no state seemed to have both the full panoply of power to supplant Washington's world order and the skill set to establish global hegemony. Indeed, apart from its rising economic and military clout, China has a self-referential culture, recondite non-roman script (requiring four thousand characters instead of 26 letters), nondemocratic political structures, and a subordinate legal system that will deny it some of the chief instruments for global leadership.

In addition to the essentials of military and economic power, "every successful empire," observes historian Joya Chatterji, "had to elaborate a universalist and inclusive discourse" to win support from the world's smaller, subordinate states and their leaders.[102] Successful imperial transitions driven by the hard power of guns and money also require the soft-power salve of cultural suasion if they are to achieve sustained and successful global dominion. During its near century of hegemony from 1850 to 1940, Britain was the exemplar par excellence of soft power, espousing an enticing political culture of fair play and free markets that it propagated through the Anglican church, the English language and its literature, mass media such as the British Broadcasting Corporation, and its virtual creation of modern athletics (including cricket, football/soccer, tennis, rugby, and rowing). Similarly, US military and economic dominance after 1945 was made more palatable by the appeal of Hollywood films, civic organizations like Rotary International, and popular sports like basketball and baseball. On the higher plane of principle, Britain's anti-slavery campaign invested its global hegemony with moral authority, just as Washington's advocacy of human rights lent legitimacy to its world order. While Spain espoused Catholicism, and Britain an Anglophone ethos of rights, so the United States, at the dawn of its global dominion, courted allies worldwide through soft-power programs that promoted democracy and development.[103]

China still has nothing comparable. Both its communist ideology and its popular culture are avowedly particularistic. To overcome such deficiencies and exercise some soft-power influence, China spent $2 billion between 2008 and 2016 to open five hundred Confucian Institutes worldwide that were to teach its language and culture. But, in marked contrast to the Alliance Française, the British Council, or the Goethe-Institut, these have become controversial thanks to ham-fisted state censorship of sensitive issues such as Taiwan, Tibet, or the Tiananmen pro-democracy protests. According to an investigation by the US Senate, funding for each of the hundred Confucian Institutes in the country "comes with strings that can compromise academic freedom." Testifying to the seriousness of such constraints, by June 2019, no less than 24 American universities had canceled their contracts.[104] However, Beijing's Belt and Road Initiative does offer the impoverished millions of Africa and Asia, many of them long forgotten by Western international finance, access to capital and a path to progress.

China has been a command-economy state for much of the past century, and as such has developed neither the legal culture of an independent judiciary nor an autonomous rules-based order complementary with the web of law that undergirds the modern international system. From the foundation of the Permanent Court of Arbitration at The Hague in 1899 through the formation of the International Court of Justice under the UN Charter, the world's nations have aspired to the resolution of conflicts via arbitration or litigation rather than armed conflict. More broadly, the modern globalized economy is held together by a web of conventions, treaties, patents, and contracts grounded in international law that has limited purchase in Beijing.

From its founding in 1949, the People's Republic of China has given primacy to the Communist Party and the state, slowing the growth of an autonomous legal system and the rule of law, as it showed when it rejected the Permanent Court of Arbitration's unanimous 2016 ruling against its claims to the South China Sea.[105] In the exceptional vehemence of its response, Beijing seemed to dismiss both the decision and the entire apparatus of international law that had produced it.[106]

If, however, Beijing's potentially immense infrastructure investments, history's largest by far, succeed in unifying the commerce of three continents, then the currents of financial power and global leadership may indeed flow, as if by natural law, toward Beijing. But if that bold project falters or ultimately fails, then, for the first time in five centuries, the world could face an imperial transition without a clear successor as global hegemon.

Weighing Beijing's global future, it seems safe to assume that it can gain enough strength, at minimum, to weaken Washington's global grip and that it might serve, in concert with the accelerating impact of global warming, as a catalyst to effect such a fundamental change. There is certainly mounting evidence, visible in the daily news, that climate change is accelerating, and will create a cataclysm capable of further shaking Washington's international system.

At the 2019 UN Climate Change Conference in Madrid, Secretary-

General António Guterres summarized the signs of an impending catastrophe, saying that "the point of no return is no longer over the horizon. It is in sight and hurtling toward us." With carbon dioxide in the atmosphere reaching 408 parts per million in 2018, well past the "unthinkable tipping point" of 400 parts, the secretary-general began listing the danger signs. "Ice caps are melting," he said. "In Greenland alone, 179 billion tonnes of ice melted in July. Permafrost in the Arctic is thawing 70 years ahead of projections. Antarctica is melting three times as fast as a decade ago. Ocean levels are rising quicker than expected, putting some of our biggest and most economically important cities at risk." Despite these danger signs, the nations of the world were still failing to meet their carbon-reduction commitments under the Paris climate accord, while the Trump administration had simply withdrawn from it. If current trends for emissions continue, global warming would, he warned, reach as high as 3.9°C by century's end, with "catastrophic" consequences for all life on the planet.[107]

From scientific evidence, it seems clear that, for the first time in seven hundred years, humanity is facing another cumulative, century-long catastrophe akin to the Black Death of 1350 to 1450 that could, once again, rupture a global order and set the world in motion.

The Geopolitical Impact of Climate Change

The problematic response in Europe and the Unitd States to the world's first waves of climate change refugees indicates the potential of their ever-rising numbers to profoundly rupture the current world order. Not surprisingly, the geopolitical consequences of global warming were felt most immediately in the Mediterranean basin, home to 470 million people. While the average global temperature increase in 2016 was still just 0.85°C above preindustrial levels, temperatures in this dry region had already risen by 1.3°C.[108] That accelerated warming brought the threat of drought to a historically arid area bordered by sprawling deserts in North Africa and Saudi Arabia.

From 2007 to 2010, climate change caused the "worst three-year drought" in Syria's recorded history—precipitating unrest marked by "massive agricultural failures" that drove 1.5 million people into city slums. That forced migration, in turn, contributed to a devastating civil war that forced five million refugees to flee the country.[109] As more than a million migrants (led by 350,000 Syrians) poured into Europe in 2015, and 181,000 Africans crossed the Mediterranean from Libya to Italy in 2016, the European Union plunged into political crisis, as anti-immigrant parties gained popularity—and sometimes power—across the continent. For instance, it was largely over the immigration issue that Britain voted to exit the EU. To contain the crisis, the EU paid Turkey $6.6 billion and funded the Libyan Coast Guard to hold back the refugee tide, momentarily stilling the political turmoil. Then, in 2020, during a summer heat wave that set records across the Middle East, the temperature hit 125°F (51.7°C) in the Iraqi capital of Baghdad—a city that not only had a failing electrical grid, but was also still devastated from the aftermath of the American invasion. It was only a taste of what is to come.[110]

In these same years, a strikingly similar political dynamic was evident along the US–Mexico border. In Central America's northern triangle of Guatemala, El Salvador, and Honduras, the devastating impact of climate change upon the region's agriculture played a catalytic role in crises that have sent migrant caravans trekking northward through Mexico. That triangle, which lies at the northern end of Central America's "dry corridor," regularly sees storms, flash floods, and droughts that extend all the way down to Panama and make life tenuous for the zone's ten million inhabitants. An increase in average temperatures of 0.5°C since 1950 has had a "dramatic impact" on its weather, rainfall, and soil quality, reducing agricultural yields and forcing families to migrate. With temperatures projected to rise by at least another 1.0 to 2.0°C by 2050, erratic weather patterns will deliver protracted drought in some areas and increased flooding in others, damaging the viability of smallholder farming in this impoverished region and generating a recurring flow of migrants north toward the United States.[111]

In the highlands of Guatemala, climate change manifested itself in killer frosts at nine thousand feet elevation as well as heat surges, drought, and torrential rains at lower altitudes. After decades of steady, manageable migration, the numbers surged in 2018 when 50,000 Guatemalan families were apprehended at the US border, about half of whom came from this troubled mountain range. "There are always a lot of reasons why people migrate," a Guatemalan forestry expert, Yarsinio Palacios, told *New Yorker* reporter Jonathan Blitzer. "But in every situation, it has something to do with climate change."[112]

Farther south, in the western highlands of neighboring Honduras, rising temperatures were making coffee cultivation difficult as drought, pests, and blight damaged the harvest, greatly reducing the number of coffee growers. Not surprisingly, Honduran agricultural workers made up a substantial part of the migrant caravans that reached Tijuana, Mexico, in the fall of 2018. With climate change projected to reduce the land suitable for coffee by more than 40 percent across Central America by 2050, ample economic pressure will drive more migrant waves north toward the US border.[113]

As increasing numbers of Central Americans reached that border, Donald Trump had become another of those populist leaders worldwide to gain power by stigmatizing refugees as alien invaders. Throughout his 2016 presidential campaign, he had led mass rallies across America in fiery chants of "Build the Wall," his synecdoche for sealing the border. Indeed, during his first year in office, he would issue unprecedented executive orders that made entry into the United States painfully difficult: first he separated families detained on suspicion of undocumented entry, some of whose children were never reunited with their parents; then, he forced asylum seekers, many of whom were fleeing violence, to await their hearings in Mexico instead of the United States. During the midterm elections two years later, he ordered 5,200 troops to the southern border—a publicity stunt whose nominal mission was to block any further crossing. When the UN adopted the Global Compact for Migration, which recognized climate change as a cause for such displacement, his administration refused to join the 164 nations that approved the agreement. Then in March 2019, the president cut all aid to El Salvador, Guatemala, and Honduras, saying, "We're not paying them anymore because they haven't done a thing for us."[114]

According to calculations in a 2018 World Bank report, by 2050 climate change will displace as many as 143 million people in three world regions alone—sub-Saharan Africa, South Asia, and Latin America. The UN estimates the total will reach 200 million worldwide. By then, the number of migrants from Central America and Mexico arriving at the US border will likely reach 1.5 million annually, and the forced migration of so many millions will also undoubtedly produce profound political disruptions.[115] Lest we forget, all the political turmoil that led to the rise of anti-immigrant populism in Europe, as well as Britain's withdrawal from the EU and Trump's call to "Build the Wall," was caused by the movement of less than two million refugees.

The Middle East will likely become a bellwether for the destabilizing political impact of climate change. In 2019, the US National Intelligence

Council warned that "climate hazards" like "heat waves, droughts, and floods" were increasing "social unrest, migration, and interstate tension in countries such as Egypt, Ethiopia, Iraq, and Jordan."[116]

Translate those sparse words into a future scenario, and you can gain a sense of how global warming might weaken the sort of international cooperation that has been a key part of the current world order. Sometime between 2030 and 2040, when *average* global warming reaches a dangerous 1.5°C above preindustrial levels (if not more), the Middle East will likely experience a disastrous temperature rise that will exceed 2.3°C. Such intense heat will produce protracted droughts, sparking water wars among the nations that share the Tigris and Euphrates Rivers. This future heat surge will likely unleash havoc across the Middle East, sending millions of refugees fleeing toward Europe. Under such unprecedented pressure, far-right parties could take power across the continent, and the EU would be strained as every nation asserted sovereignty and sealed its borders. Under similar pressures, NATO, which already suffered a "severe crisis" during the Trump years, would likely weaken further from internal division, leading to a strategic vacuum that might finally allow Russia to seize portions of Ukraine and the Baltic states, further rupturing the world order.[117]

Pressures on US Global Presence

In the United States, the impact of climate change is a key factor—along with economic pressures and demographic change—that will likely force a reduction or even a retreat from its worldwide military commitments. More broadly, the juxtaposition of just a few key trends indicates the potential role of a gathering environmental crisis in catalyzing the shift to a new world order. First and fundamentally, America's share of the gross world product has declined steadily, from 50 percent in 1950 to a projected 15 percent by 2024. But its defense budget has moved in the opposite direction, rising 150 percent from $274 billion in 2000 to $720 billion in 2019, with planned increases to $747 billion by 2024.[118]

Complicating Washington's ability to sustain the high costs of its global military presence, its own 2018 *National Climate Assessment* predicted the country will face multiple consequences of climate change by 2050, if not before—including sustained drought, proliferating wildfires, coastal storm surges, far more intense hurricanes, damaged infrastructure, and declining harvests—all of which it is already experiencing to some degree. The combined impact of "rising temperatures, extreme heat, drought, wildfire on rangelands, and heavy downpours" will cut US agricultural production back to the level of the 1980s. Indicating the lack of preparation for such cascading changes, the report warned: "The potential need for millions of people and billions of dollars of coastal infrastructure to be relocated in the future creates challenging legal, financial, and equity issues that have not yet been addressed." Indeed, another government report, issued in 2020, warned that 40 percent of the US population lives in coastal areas vulnerable to sea level rise, which has accelerated rapidly. By 2100, seas worldwide are very likely to rise at least twelve inches above their level in 2000; however, if carbon emissions continue unchecked, they could surge as much as 8.2 feet.[119]

Confronted by an ever-widening gap between rising military budgets and declining fiscal resources, Washington will likely have to reduce expensive overseas deployments and turn increasingly to a cost-effective covert triad for national defense—cyberwarfare, special operations forces, and satellite surveillance. As its share of the world economy declines, Washington's fiscal and political capacity to maintain its troop commitments to NATO is already fading. At the other end of Eurasia, Beijing's expanding economy will draw longtime US allies into China's orbit, weakening their support for American bases and joint military operations. China's growing dominance will eventually make the costs of US overseas garrisons prohibitive, and Washington will likely retreat to some version of hemispheric hegemony.

Adding to the pressure for such a global retreat, two social forces, working in tandem, will likely decrease US capacity for overseas military missions. Most immediately, the escalating tempo of natural disasters from global warming will demand domestic troop deployments. "Climate change is an urgent and growing threat to our national security," the Pentagon told Congress in 2015, "contributing to increased natural disasters, refugee flows, and conflicts over basic resources such as food and water." Already, there have been major deployments for hurricane relief, and the need will only grow as disasters increase in scale and frequency with each passing decade.[120]

America also faces escalating social costs to sustain an aging society. By 2034, the United States will reach what the Census Bureau calls "a new milestone," when people over age sixty-five (77 million) will outnumber children under eighteen (76.5 million). Those older Americans will generate "greater demands for healthcare, in-home caregiving and assisted living facilities" that will likely divert fiscal resources from defense to social services.[121] The Congressional Budget Office predicts that federal spending on people older than sixty-five (Social Security, Medicare, and Medicaid) will climb steadily from 20 percent of the federal budget in 2019 to 50 percent by 2049, while both the labor force and the economy will grow at much slower rates than in decades past.[122] The ever-increasing costs of supporting senior citizens is likely to leave far less money for overseas bases or military interventions. From this synergy of domestic and foreign pressures, Washington's global presence will probably start to fade within a decade.

Compounding such internal problems, an ever-increasing flow of climate change refugees from Mexico and Central America reaching the southern border may well contribute to an upsurge in populist nationalism within the United States. While the political consequences of anti-immigrant xenophobia are unpredictable, they could lead to sealed borders, a less welcoming society, and Washington's further retreat from international leadership.[123]

As tensions over climate change refugees rise on both sides of the Atlantic after 2030, the United Nations could become paralyzed by a great-power deadlock in the Security Council, as well as by rising recriminations over the role of its High Commissioner for Refugees. Pummeled by these and similar crises from other climate change flashpoints such as Bangladesh, East Africa, and Southeast Asia, the international cooperation that lay at the heart of Washington's world order for the previous 80 years would come under severe pressure amid faultfinding and reprisals.

In a world battered by global warming with millions of migrants streaming across borders worldwide, the hypernationalism of the Chinese global system will probably prove more appealing. As the international cooperation that was once the hallmark of the current world system recedes, Beijing's transnational system marked by transactional diplomacy could slowly achieve something akin to global hegemony.

In the earlier transition to the Iberian age, the cataclysm of the Black Death converged with European conquests in Asia and the Americas to create a new world order. Similarly, the industrial revolution, combined with the cataclysm of the Napoleonic Wars, led to the emergence of the British imperial era. In a possible reprise of such a process, the geopolitical impact of China's growing economic dominance over Eurasia, catalyzed by the mounting disruption of climate change, could gain sufficient force to supersede Washington's world order with something new.

Washington's Eclipse, Beijing's Ascent

When will this convergence of geopolitics and climate cataclysm produce such a change? Beijing plans to complete both the technological transformation of its own economy and much of its massive trans-Eurasian infrastructure by 2025. That projected date complements a prediction by the US National Intelligence Council that "China alone will probably have the largest economy, surpassing that of the United States a few years before 2030." The accounting firm PricewaterhouseCoopers projected that by 2030 China's GDP would grow to $36 trillion—over 40 percent larger than America's of $25 trillion.[124]

Since Beijing's and Washington's defense budgets represent 2 and 3 percent of their respective economic outputs, China's military, already the world's second largest, should be comparable or even more powerful than America's around 2030, leaving Washington militarily dominant only in the Western Hemisphere. In late 2019, the *New York Times* reported that "in 18 of the last 18 Pentagon war games involving China in the Taiwan Strait, the US lost." Rather than ramp up its defense of those straits, where more US aircraft carriers would simply mean bigger targets, in 2020 Washington encouraged Taiwan Semiconductor Manufacturing Co., maker of 84 percent the world's most advanced computer chips, to build a $12 billion factory in Arizona. Those outcomes may explain how Beijing's growing strength in the South China Sea could become the first step in Washington's retreat from the Pacific littoral. As China pushes its maritime frontier farther into the Pacific, engulfing and threatening Taiwan, Washington may well be faced with a difficult choice—to either abandon an old ally, or fight a war it might lose.[125]

In sum, climate change pressures on the current international system will likely converge with China's expanding economic and military power around 2030 to catalyze the transition to a new hegemon and a new world order cast in its image. If so, the impact on the three intertwined issues that have long been the hallmark of global governance—national sovereignty, human rights, and energy—will be profound.

Compared to the way the unrivaled US military dominated the globe for the past 80 years, China's hegemony will likely be more diffuse and less direct. Given its deep commitment to the defense of its frontiers, Beijing will probably concentrate its military forces near home, pushing the US Navy back toward Hawaii. Moreover, the Chinese state is run by Communist mandarins unaccustomed to and dismissive of the legalistic negotiations of international organizations, meaning it is likely limit its global leadership to bilateral economic exchanges with individual nations or regional blocs.

Adding all this up, the Chinese global hegemony that may take shape around 2030 will be a looser world order than its American predecessor. Instead of military intervention or covert manipulation to assure compliance with preordained political standards, Beijing will ignore the corruption, incompetence, or inhumanity of its international partners to focus on the mutual advantage of economic exchange. Instead of aspirations to human rights and adherence to the judgments of international tribunals, its world order will privilege national sovereignty over universal principles. And instead of hundreds of overseas military bases and worldwide troop deployments, China will likely concentrate its forces in the western Pacific and Indian Ocean. In this more diffuse world order, each hegemon would dominate its immediate region—Brasilia over South America; Washington, North America; Beijing, East and Southeast Asia; Moscow, Eastern Europe; New Delhi, South Asia; Tehran, Central Asia; Pretoria, southern Africa; Ankara and Cairo, the Middle East.

Judging from Beijing's past actions, it seems likely that this divergence of its emerging global order from Washington's will be especially marked in the defining areas of national sovereignty and human rights. From its suppression of Tibetan Buddhist identity in the 1960s through its repression of the Uyghur Muslims a half century later, its leaders have been unconcerned about the human rights of its religious minorities, just as it ignores such abuses by its allies.[126]

As the first global hegemon in five centuries to emerge outside the succession of Western powers, China's ruling Communist elite does not share the same ingrained cultural references. The shift in global power from Madrid to Amsterdam, London, and then Washington was smoothed by a continuity in the debates over human rights within the same Western legal tradition. So China's rise represents a real rupture. After centuries of struggle to establish the principles of individual liberty articulated in the UN's Universal

Declaration of Human Rights, that seminal document's moral imperative will probably fade during the coming decades. Similarly, the recognition of the world's oceans as a shared commons for commerce among nations, hard won after centuries of war and diplomacy, will likely diminish as Beijing defends its claim to a *mare clausum* over the East and South China Seas.

In parallel with President's Xi's political ascent since 2013, a generation of statist intellectuals has celebrated China's rise as a new kind of empire and rejected most Western influences. Arguing that "the history of humanity is surely the history of competition for imperial hegemony," prominent statist scholar Jiang Shigong posits that the Anglo-American powers created the UN as nothing more than "a site of struggle in the construction of world empires." Now that the United States and its empire are suffering "state failure, political decline, and ineffective governance caused by . . . decadence and nihilism created by cultural liberalism," China must, he says, take advantage of the current "historical transition . . . to construct world empire 2.0."[127] Judging from its diplomacy to date, Beijing will try to bind its world system together with the rhetoric of economic progress, while leading a global campaign to lift humanity's forgotten millions out of their material misery.

Yet Beijing's embrace of economic growth as the basis for both its domestic legitimacy and international influence may well condemn its global leadership to an early death. In its hell-bent drive for development, Beijing has fouled the air of its cities with coal smoke and auto exhaust, damaged its greatest river by damming it for cheap electricity, and fished its coastal waters to exhaustion.[128] To repair the damage from that environmental degradation, Beijing adopted a generally successful five-year Air Pollution Action Plan in 2013 to cut coal consumption for home heating and reduce fine particulates in the air of major cities below 60 micrograms per cubic meter (still far above the World Health Organization's maximum of 10 micrograms.) To combat global warming, President Xi announced in 2020 that China would reach carbon neutrality by 2060—a date so far in the future that it might well be too late to stop the feedback loops of tropical fires and Arctic permafrost melting that are already creating an environmental crisis.[129]

On the global stage, Beijing has been similarly conflicted. During the UN's 2019 Madrid climate summit, China claimed a leadership role while simultaneously joining the United States and India in blocking the call for stricter emission targets. Abroad, Beijing was unapologetically promoting coal-fired power. In early 2020, the trade group Institute of International Finance reported that 85 percent of all projects under the BRI entailed high emissions of greenhouse gases, particularly the 63 coal-fired electrical plants the project was financing worldwide. At home, moreover, China remained the world's leading emitter of carbon dioxide (CO_2) and even raised its coal-fired electrical capacity in 2018–2019 by 4.5 percent, while use elsewhere in the world declined. Between 2015 and 2020, Beijing built an impressive 440 gigawatts of wind and solar energy, but it also added a hefty 225 gigawatts of coal-fired electricity that increased its share of the world total for coal-generated power to a daunting 53 percent. As global CO_2 emissions only rose, China's combination of increasing oil imports and continuing coal production made it the largest single source of pollution on the planet, accounting for 29 percent of the world's total in 2017.[130] Both at home and abroad, China's global influence has thus become a major barrier to curbing greenhouse gas pollution.

The recent American record has been marked by a parallel lack of progress, particularly under a climate change–denying president whose administration was focused on giving free rein to fossil fuel producers. Despite Donald Trump's impassioned defense of the coal industry, market forces driving the shift to natural gas for electrical generation cut the country's coal consumption by 18 percent. Nevertheless, rising pollution from natural gas and a continuing reliance on gasoline for road transport meant US emissions actually increased. Instead of meeting its commitment under the Paris climate accord for a 28 percent reduction in greenhouse gas emissions within a decade, the Trump administration adopted anti-environmental policies that will add 1.8 billion metric tons of CO_2 to the atmosphere by 2035—equivalent to the annual combined emissions of Britain, Canada, and Germany.[131]

Together, China and the United States accounted for 44 percent of total CO_2 emissions in 2019, but they have failed, unlike the Europeans, to exercise a commensurate role in the ongoing transition to renewable energy.[132] In spite of the visible proliferation of photovoltaic panels and turbine towers worldwide, it will take an enormous effort to move the planet beyond its current dependence on fossil fuels for 80 percent of its total energy needs. The UN's "middle-of-the-road scenario," which aims to keep the global temperature increase to 1.5°C above preindustrial levels, requires that electricity from all renewables (solar, wind, hydro, modern bioenergy) reach 48 percent in 2030 and 63 percent by 2050. That is a steep climb from the current world total, circa 2020, from those four sources of just 11 percent.[133] Since 72 percent of all greenhouse gases come from energy for industry, heating, and transport, their reduction requires a sweeping two-phase transformation—first, a shift of all three activities to appropriate forms of electricity, and then a simultaneous conversion of the electrical grid to renewables.[134]

To transform an energy infrastructure built up over the past 150 years will require several decades of sustained investment and an ironclad political will, still largely absent in both China and the United States. Just as Beijing has promised to become carbon neutral by 2060, so Washington under the Biden administration has made the same commitment for 2050. As a critical first step, the president announced in April 2021 that the US would, within a decade, cut emissions by 50 percent from its peak level in 2005. To advance toward that ambitious goal, the US needs to make some drastic, even daunting, changes by 2030: it must close all of its remaining 200 coal-fired power plants, convert a quarter of the country's homes to electrical heat pumps, raise annual sales of battery-powered cars from the current 1.5 percent to 50 percent of the total, and expand the nation's electrical grid by 60 percent. The country will also need to double, and then redouble, the annual pace of renewable energy construction, until solar and wind installations cover an area bigger than Colorado and Wyoming combined. If all that were done, the US would cut its pollution per person, which is currently the world's highest at 17.6 tons of CO_2 every year, to 8.8 tons, comparable to Europe where emissions are 7.4 tons. Even if America and China meet those ambitious goals, there will still be enough residual CO_2 accumulated in the atmosphere for the inertia of "committed warming" to drive world temperatures well past the UN's target of 1.5°C to a dangerous average of 2.3°C. In sum, the world can still slow the pace of climate change and avoid the most disastrous scenarios, but even a maximum effort cannot prevent the advent of serious environmental and social disruption.[135]

Over the past three hundred thousand years, humanity has made three basic energy transitions: first came the mastery of fire, then the domestication of draft animals and agriculture, and most recently reliance on fossil fuels. Without more effective leadership from the global titans, humanity's fourth transition to renewable, non-emitting energy sources will likely be too slow to contain global warming at manageable levels.[136]

As Washington's dominance fades and its share of the world economy falls steadily, leadership in this critical transition to renewable energy will probably fall to Beijing. Assuming that China indeed ascends to global hegemony sometime after 2030 and that it continues its long-standing policy of prioritizing the economy over the environment, Beijing's global leadership will fail to slow the relentless pace of climate change, quite likely contributing to an untimely end to its own hegemony and leaving humanity without a functioning world order for the first time in five centuries. If that happens, then the latter half of the twenty-first century could be a period that is not only afflicted by incalculable problems, but also holds the potential, even the promise, of inaugurating a very different kind of world order.

Undocumented Central American immigrant riding the "death train" through Mexico toward the US border. (Credit: Alamy)

Chapter 7
Climate Change in the Twenty-First Century

Through its ever-increasing intensity, global warming will have a destructive impact on world orders for the rest of the twenty-first century and beyond. For America's "baby boom" generation born in the decades right after World War II, climate change seemed until quite recently a distant threat, likely to have limited effect during their lifetimes. It is an altogether different matter for the youth of the world. Born early in this century, they may, with luck, live to see its last decades, experiencing all the devastation and disruption to come. For that older generation of "boomers," the dates in the discussion that follows—2050, 2070, 2100—are just numbers without much meaning, but for the world's youth and their children, they will be the signposts of their lives.

If Washington's current world order indeed fades around 2030, Beijing's hypernationalist hegemony will have just a couple of decades of dominance before it too begins to suffer the calamitous consequences of unchecked global warming. From clear scientific evidence, it seems likely that the accelerating pace of climate change will affect China so adversely by 2050 that it will be compelled to retreat from many of its foreign commitments, abandoning whatever sort of global system it might have constructed. And so, as we peer dimly into the decades beyond 2050, the international community will have good reason to forge a new kind of world order unlike any that has come before.

To grasp these possibilities, three critical issues need to be considered: first, the nature and extent of climate change; next, its social and economic impact by midcentury; and finally, the way such changes could affect the world system in the latter half of the twenty-first century and beyond.

To engage the nature of climate change, we should begin with the basics, as explained by the Earth Observatory at the National Aeronautics and

Space Administration (NASA). Under ordinary circumstances, the planet maintains a relatively constant level of carbon dioxide (CO_2) storage in four linked areas—the atmosphere, land, plants, and the oceans. When anything, whether natural or human, changes the carbon level in one of these reservoirs, "the effect ripples through the others." As the earth's orbit, which is constantly changing, moved closer to the sun ten thousand years ago, the amount of CO_2 released into the atmosphere increased, temperatures rose, and an ice age ended in the Northern Hemisphere. In another 30,000 years, the earth's orbit will again change sufficiently to reduce sunlight to "the levels that led to the last Ice Age."[1]

But now, according to the Earth Observatory, "changes in the carbon cycle are happening because of people . . . burning fossil fuels and clearing land." From the start of the industrial revolution to 2021, the atmosphere's concentration of CO_2 rose from 280 parts per million to 415 ppm. Given that the atmosphere's carbon level had remained at or below 275 ppm for the previous eight hundred thousand years, this sharp increase has profound implications for the future of life on the planet.[2]

Before excess carbon started accumulating in the atmosphere, the earth absorbed energy from the sun and then radiated about 30 percent of it, in the form of infrared light, through the atmosphere and back into space. When all that extra CO_2 and methane (another powerful gas released by production of fossil fuels) began accumulating in the atmosphere, those greenhouse gases formed a layer of molecules that began absorbing some of that energy, blocking it from escaping into space and sending it back down toward earth, thereby raising the average temperature of the planet.[3]

The Impact of Global Warming at Midcentury

In assessing the likely impact of climate change on the world order by 2050, one question is paramount: How quickly will we feel its impact?

For decades, scientists thought that climate change would arrive at what science writer Eugene Linden called a "stately pace." In 1975, the US National Academies of Sciences still felt that it would "take centuries for climate to change in a meaningful way." As late as 1990, the Intergovernmental Panel on Climate Change (IPCC), a group of leading scientists working under United Nations auspices, drew upon available evidence to conclude that the Arctic permafrost, which stores both CO_2 and the even more dangerous methane, was not melting and that the Antarctic ice sheets were stable. Concerns about the climate, though still modest, were nevertheless sufficient for the world's nations to meet in June 1992 at Rio de Janeiro, where they drafted the UN Framework Convention on Climate Change. In that agreement, they outlined minimal, nonbinding guidelines to encourage the "stabilization of greenhouse gas concentrations in the atmosphere . . . within a time-frame sufficient to allow ecosystems to adapt naturally to climate change." Note that key word "adapt," meaning the earth was supposed to achieve a new, natural balance even without major measures to stop global warming. In 1993, however, scientists conducted precise studies of ice cores extracted from Greenland's ice cap and discovered that there had been 25 "rapid climate change events" in the last glacial period. There was, in other words, clear, convincing scientific evidence that the "climate could change suddenly and massively in just a decade or two."[4]

With such evidence mounting rapidly, the world's nations reconvened in December 1997 at Kyoto, where they replaced Rio's open-ended adaptation to climate change with a strict program of "quantified emission limitation and reduction commitments within specified time-frames" for 38 developed nations. In 2002, moreover, in a report titled *Abrupt Climate Change: Inevitable Surprises*, the National Academies announced a fundamental paradigm shift: "Large, abrupt climate changes have affected hemispheric to global regions repeatedly," with "changes of up to 16 degrees Celsius and a factor of 2 in precipitation . . . in periods as short as decades to years." Driven by a strong scientific consensus that the globe was facing accelerated change, representatives of 196 states met in 2015 at Paris, where they adopted stringent targets that required a 45 percent reduction in global greenhouse gas emissions by 2030 and net carbon neutrality by 2050 to limit global warming to 1.5°C above preindustrial levels. This, they argued, would be sufficient to avoid the disastrous impacts sure to come if levels reached 2.0°C degrees or higher.[5]

However, the bright hopes brought by the Paris conference that the world could slow the impending environmental damage quickly faded. Within three years, the scientific community was in near-unanimous agreement that the cascading effects of global warming to 1.5°C above preindustrial levels would be evident, not in the distant future of 2100 as once thought, but by 2040, impacting the lives of most adults alive today. In the IPCC's 2018 "doomsday report," scientists warned that the impact of warming at 1.5°C would be much worse than first estimated, with significant coastal flooding, ever more intense storms, fierce droughts, wildfires, and heat waves causing damage worth $54 trillion—an amount equivalent to 40 percent of the global economy in 2018. At the more dangerous level of 2.0°C, damages would reach $69 trillion. Even at 1.5°C, the temperature increase would be unevenly distributed, reaching 3.0°C in the warm season in the tropics and 4.5°C in the Arctic, with disastrous consequences for both regions. According to the *New York Times*, global warming would, absent heroic carbon-reduction measures, reach 2.0°C a few decades after 2040 and "perhaps four degrees Celsius by 2100."[6]

In September 2019, the United Nations reported that worldwide mitigation efforts, though increasing, still fell "far short of an unprecedented transformation needed to limit impacts of climate change." That sobering assessment was soon corroborated by a report from the International Energy Agency on projected global energy consumption to 2040, which warned that greenhouse gas emissions would continue to rise for the next 20 years, meaning "the world will miss its climate goals by a very large margin." By then, reported the *New York Times*, more than 90 percent of the world's population will experience direct, deleterious effects of climate change—including a high risk of water scarcity, increased flooding, extreme heat stress in Africa and parts of Latin America, a near doubling of California wildfires, and more intense cyclones along the Pacific littoral.[7]

Lending credence to those concerns, the summer of 2019 saw massive forest fires that ravaged disparate ecosystems around the globe—including 830,000 acres of European woodlands, 2.3 million acres of the Amazon rain forest, 2.5 million acres of Alaskan tundra and snow forest, 6 million acres of Siberian forests, and a vast, unknown area of Central Africa's savannah. When summer reached the Southern Hemisphere at the end of the year, Australia erupted in its worst fire season in more than a century.[8] The continent experienced its highest temperatures yet recorded amid hundreds of bushfires that burned 46 million acres—an area larger than Syria. "This is not a bush fire," said one official. "It's an atomic bomb."[9]

But in many parts of the world, the fire season in 2020 was even worse. In Brazil, exceptionally dry conditions burned 8.5 million acres of the Amazon rain forest and 3 million acres of the biodiverse southern wetlands known as the Pantanal, which a NASA official called "really unprecedented."

On the US West Coast, massive fires, driven by strong winds, burned nearly 6 million acres. In California, the state's worst fire season ever—sparked by thousands of freak lightning strikes and temperatures reaching a world record of 130°F (54.4°C) in Death Valley—ravaged over 4 million acres, forcing utility companies to impose rolling power blackouts. "What we're experiencing right here is coming to communities all across the United States of America," said California governor Gavin Newsom, "unless we can act on climate change." In neighboring Oregon, "unprecedented" fires covering a million acres destroyed five towns, forcing 40,000 residents to flee and turning thousands of buildings into ash and twisted metal. In Washington State, where 600,000 acres burned, Governor Jay Inslee, whose presidential campaign on the climate issue had failed to gain traction, said these were "climate fires" not wildfires. Adding to the toll, Colorado lost over 400,000 acres to dozens of fires, including one that was the largest recorded in state history. "This climate change connection is straightforward: Warmer temperatures dry out fuels," said a bioclimatologist at Columbia University. "In areas with abundant and very dry fuels, all you need is a spark."[10] Showing the feedback loops that can accelerate climate change, these disparate blazes worldwide were, at least in part, sparked by rising temperatures that, in turn, accelerated carbon accumulation in the atmosphere through both the flames and the forests' reduced capacity to retain CO_2.

Extreme weather events like cyclones, floods, and landslides displaced seven million people worldwide in the first half of 2019—the highest figure in nearly two decades of record keeping. In early 2020, US government researchers reported that the past decade had been the hottest on record and that every decade since 1960 had been hotter than the one before it. Illustrating the immediacy of this change, Australia's average temperature was already 1.5°C higher than in the mid-twentieth century, southern Africa faced a serious drought that had brought worsening food shortages, and the Bering Sea off Alaska's northwestern coast had been ice-free for much of the previous winter.[11] In January 2019, using new data from sophisticated floating sensors, scientists reported that the world's oceans were heating 40 percent faster than estimated only five years earlier, in a shift that would unleash more powerful storms with more frequent coastal flooding.[12]

The immediate and medium-term effects of climate change are amplified by the unevenness of the earth's warming, producing marked differences in regional impacts. According to a *Washington Post* data analysis, by the 2014–2018 period the world already had significant "hot spots" that recorded an average rise of 2.0°C above the preindustrial norm. As the sun strikes tropical latitudes, huge columns of warm air rise and then are pushed toward the poles by greenhouse gases trapped in the atmosphere, until they drop down to earth at higher latitudes, thereby creating spots with faster-rising temperatures in the Middle East, Western Europe, and the Arctic. By averaging the findings of five studies, the *Post* found that, as of September 2019, about 10 percent of the earth had already experienced a temperature increase of 2.0°C, while 20 percent of the planet had seen rises of at least 1.5°C.[13]

The melting of ice sheets in Greenland and Antarctica, further advanced than previously thought, will intensify the impact of climate change. Satellite measurements by the National Oceanic and Atmospheric Administration (NOAA) in September 2019 indicated a 33 percent decline in summer sea ice across the Arctic region. If average global temperatures rise by 2.0°C over preindustrial levels by 2050, then Arctic oceans will likely be entirely ice-free in the summer, allowing those open waters to absorb six times more solar energy than ice-covered surfaces. The loss of the white shield of sea ice during the long summer days of midnight sun would, says a report in *Geophysical Research Letters*, "drastically shorten the time available to adapt to climate changes and . . . for achieving carbon neutrality."[14]

A parallel report in the journal *Nature* warned that meltwater from Greenland will disrupt the North Atlantic's "overturning circulation," producing extreme weather events in both Europe and North America. Meanwhile, Antarctic meltwater will trap warm water under the sea's surface, accelerating the breakup of the West Antarctic Ice Sheet. As early as May 2014, NASA called a press conference to announce that this massive ice sheet had "gone into irreversible retreat," and the news has only gotten worse since. Six years later, NASA participated in a study that found the breakup of two massive glaciers was accelerating, with the potential to trigger a "feedback process" that would cause a collapse, in the distant future, of the ice sheet, which holds enough ice to raise sea levels worldwide by ten feet. And even while it remains intact, the increased meltwater from both poles will double the frequency of flooding events in low-lying areas worldwide by 2050 and, on their own, raise the sea level by at least twelve inches by the end of the century.[15]

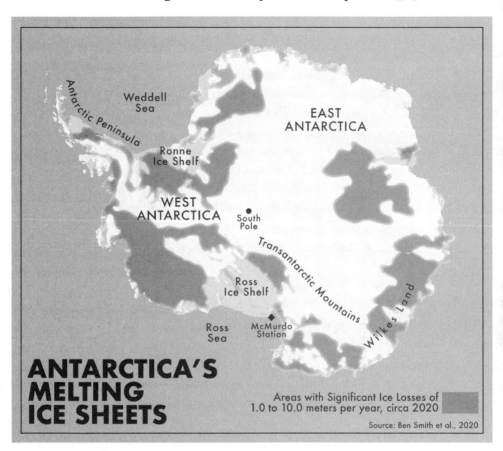

Weddell
Sea

EAST
ANTARCTICA

Antarctic Peninsula

Ronne
Ice Shelf

WEST
ANTARCTICA

South
Pole

Transantarctic Mountains

Ross
Ice Shelf

Wilkes Land

Ross
Sea

McMurdo
Station

ANTARCTICA'S MELTING ICE SHEETS

Areas with Significant Ice Losses of
1.0 to 10.0 meters per year, circa 2020

Source: Ben Smith et al., 2020

Adding to concerns about rising seas, the larger East Antarctic Ice Sheet is also shedding massive amounts of ice. According to a study published by the National Academy of Sciences, annual loss averaged 252 gigatons of ice from 2009 to 2017—a sixfold increase over the 1979–1990 period. "The Wilkes Land sector of East Antarctica," said lead researcher Eric Rignot, "has always been . . . more sensitive to climate [change] than has traditionally been assumed, and that's important to know, because it holds even more ice than West Antarctica and the Antarctic Peninsula together." By 2020, scientists using images of Antarctica from NASA's new ICESat-2 satellite found substantial losses of mass in the ice shelves at the edge of the sea, weakening the large sheets that cover the continent. "It's like an architectural buttress that holds up a cathedral," said glaciologist Helen Amanda Fricker, a co-author of the study. "The ice shelves hold the ice sheet up. If you take away the ice shelves, or even if you thin them, you're reducing that buttressing force, so the grounded ice can flow faster."[16]

In sum, an ever-escalating tempo of climate change between now and 2050 will produce massive damage to the environment that sustains human life, with greater impact to come in subsequent decades. A November 2019 statement signed by eleven thousand scientists announced: "The climate crisis has arrived and is accelerating faster than most scientists expected. It is more severe than anticipated, threatening natural ecosystems and the fate of humanity." It added, "Especially worrisome are potential irreversible climate tipping points . . . that could lead to a catastrophic 'hothouse Earth,' well beyond the control of humans . . . potentially making large areas of Earth uninhabitable."[17] That same month, the UN's annual *Emissions Gap Report* concluded that "unless mitigation action and ambition are increased immediately and profoundly," global temperatures would likely rise by as much as 3.9°C at century's close. Just a year later, the UN Office of Disaster Risk Reduction reported that in the past 20 years, there had been a "a staggering rise in climate-related disasters" that caused 1.2 million deaths and $2.3 trillion in economic damage. If we "knowingly continue to sow the seeds of our own destruction," the UN warned, then we will make our planet "an uninhabitable hell for millions of people."[18]

The Impact of Climate Change on China

Even if China were to become the preeminent world power around 2030, the accelerating pace of climate change will likely curtail its hegemony within two or three decades. With world temperatures climbing toward an increase of 3.9°C by 2100, then, starting around 2070, unendurable heat waves would render densely populated areas of the country's north uninhabitable. Moreover, there is growing scientific evidence that by 2050, rising seas will inundate several major Chinese coastal cities, particularly the country's commercial hub at Shanghai.[19] As these problems gain intensity after midcentury, Beijing will likely be forced to retreat from its projection of global power to address urgent domestic concerns.

Back in 2013, the journal *Nature Climate Change* reported that rising seas would increase economic damages in 136 cities worldwide to $63 billion annually in 2050—which seemed relatively minimal given the enormous cost of the global urban infrastructure.[20] Four years later, however, scientists at the non-profit news organization Climate Central calculated that rising seas and storm surges could, by 2060 or 2070, flood areas inhabited by 275 million people worldwide, with 80 percent of them in Asia. While 5.2 million people would be affected in Osaka, and 8.4 million in Hong Kong, Shanghai is "the most vulnerable major city in the world to serious flooding." In that sprawling metropolis, 17.5 million people are likely to be displaced as most of the city "could eventually be submerged in water, including much of the downtown area."[21]

Advancing the date of this disaster by at least a decade, a 2019 report in the journal *Nature Communications* found that 150 million people worldwide are now living on land that will be below the high-tide line by 2050. Using artificial intelligence to correct past errors in measurements of urban elevations, which were "far too optimistic," the research tripled the estimates of global vulnerability to sea level rise. That data determined that the Vietnamese city of Saigon, for instance, "would disappear" by 2050 and that most of the nearby Mekong delta, home to 20 million people, would be completely inundated. Similarly, Bangkok would be "particularly imperiled," and Mumbai risks "being wiped out." But above all, those rising waters "threaten to consume the heart" of Shanghai and its surrounding cities, crippling one of China's main economic engines.[22] Dredged from sea and swamp in the fifteenth century, much of Shanghai will, in little more than 30 years, return to the waters from whence it came.

While rising waters threaten Shanghai's survival, increasing temperatures will devastate the North China Plain, a prime agricultural region between Beijing and Shanghai currently inhabited by four hundred million people, potentially making it the most lethal place on the planet. "This spot is going to be the hottest spot for deadly heat waves in the future," said Professor Elfatih Eltahir, a specialist on hydrology and climate at MIT. Between 2070 and 2100, he estimates, the region could face hundreds of periods of "extreme danger" when the combination of heat and humidity reaches a "wet bulb temperature" (WBT) of 31°C, and perhaps five lethal periods of 35° WBT (where a combination of heat and high humidity prevents the evaporation of sweat that cools the human body). After just six hours under the latter conditions, a healthy person at rest will die. Though almost unimaginable, that 35°C WBT was nearly reached during a 2015 heat wave in the southwest Iranian city of Bandar Mahshahr.[23]

Rather than becoming sudden and catastrophic, the devastating impact of climate change in North China is likely to be incremental and cumulative, escalating relentlessly with each passing decade.[24] If the "Chinese century" does indeed start around 2030, it is unlikely to last long, ending perhaps sometime around 2050, when the impact of global warming becomes unmanageable. With its main financial center at Shanghai flooded and its agricultural heartland baking in insufferable heat, China's days as a global power will be numbered.[25]

Beyond 2050, climate change, if not brought under some degree of control, threatens to create a new and eternally cataclysmic planet on which the very words "world order" may lose their normal meaning.

The Climate Change Cataclysm after 2050

Recent scientific research has provided ample evidence for the dire predictions about the world's environment after 2050. The key drivers will be the emerging feedback loops at both ends of the temperature spectrum. At the hotter end, in Africa, Australia, and the Amazon, warmer temperatures will spark forest fires, reducing tree cover and releasing carbon into the atmosphere. The combination of deforestation and rising temperatures is already pushing the Amazon close to a tipping point where this vast rain forest, the world's greatest carbon reservoir, will degrade into a dry savannah by 2040 or 2050. Increased CO_2 emissions, in turn, will help raise temperatures incrementally, fueling yet more fires and so creating a self-reinforcing feedback loop.[26]

The more serious and uncontrollable driver, however, will be found in the planet's polar regions. In the Arctic, ice is drama, but permafrost is death. The spectacle of polar ice sheets cascading into the sea is dramatic indeed, attracting scientists who can measure and model the breakup of those consistent structures of frozen water with some precision. But true mass death lies in the murky, mysterious permafrost—that sloppy stew of decayed matter and frozen water from ice ages past that covers 11.8 million square miles of the Northern Hemisphere, reaches depths of 2,300 feet below ground, and holds ample carbon and methane to melt the poles and inundate densely populated coastal plains worldwide. Warming Arctic temperatures, already rising at twice the global average, are melting the frozen permafrost that extends across a quarter of the Northern Hemisphere's land area. As successive swaths of permafrost that cover half of Canada and even more of Russia recede relentlessly toward the North Pole in 2050, 2100, and beyond, the thawing Arctic will release increasing amounts of previously trapped carbon and methane into the atmosphere.[27] That release, in turn, will raise Arctic temperatures further, melt more permafrost, and so on, year after year— forming a devastating feedback loop and potentially increasing greenhouse gases in the atmosphere beyond the capacity to compensate with increased tree planting elsewhere on the planet.

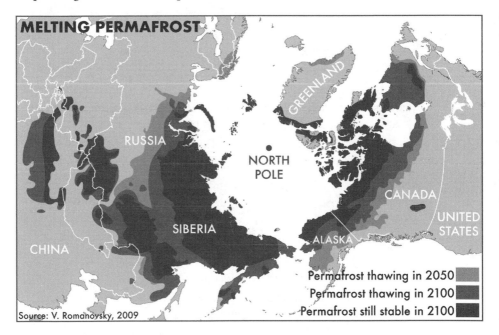

The latest scientific research suggests that this Arctic feedback loop is already accelerating climate change far more quickly than scientists once imagined, gaining a self-sustaining momentum that will soon move beyond humanity's capacity to control. There is a general agreement among the many thousands of climate researchers about the overall-troubling trend, but there are some differences in their dates and details. Reflecting the UN's need for a broad consensus, its IPCC offers generally more conservative predictions about the scale of change and so is more optimistic about the chances for re- mediation. Individual scientific teams, even when publishing in peer-reviewed journals, often follow the logic of their own research to more dire conclusions.

A UN climate panel report released in 2013 predicted, rather conservatively, a maximum sea rise of just 38.5 inches. But a more recent study done six years later—a "worst-case scenario" published by the National Academy of Sciences—projected an increase in global temperatures of 5°C by the end of the twenty-first century, accompanied by a sea level rise of as much as 5.8 feet, with "catastrophic" implications for low-lying areas world-wide. Under these more recent projections, an area of 690,000 square miles, three times the size of California, would be lost to the sea by the end of this century, displacing about 2.5 percent of the world's population. Not only would many small island nations become uninhabitable, but major cities like New York would also become inundated.[28]

Adding to this displacement, the earth's uninhabitable hot zones will grow from 1 percent of the earth's surface in 2020 to 20 percent by 2070, placing a third of the world population, or about 3.5 billion people, outside the narrow niche of temperatures that has sustained human life for the past six thousand years. In the vast Sahel region stretching across North Africa, for example, 65 percent of farmland has already been damaged by aridification, and many of the region's 150 million people will be displaced by century's end. In the densely populated plains of North India and North China, with a combined population of 800 million, heat waves will prove fatal for many of those without air conditioning. By 2070, a suitable climate for human life will be concentrated in a relatively narrow band stretching across North America and Eurasia (from 35 to 55 degrees north latitude), while a growing swath of unsuitable temperatures will cover the global South.[29]

The long-term prospect for the period from 2100 to 2300 is even more dismal. Drawing on some seven thousand scientific studies, in September 2019 the IPCC released the most definitive scientific consensus to date on the state of the world's oceans and frozen regions. By absorbing 90 percent of the heat trapped by CO_2 and methane in the atmosphere, the oceans are growing warmer, more acidic, and less oxygenated. If carbon emissions continue to rise, then the sustainable catch of fish could drop by a quarter at century's end, seriously depleting a resource that now provides 17 percent of humanity's animal protein.[30]

Climate change at the poles, according to this relatively conservative IPCC report, will have both an immediate and long-term impact on ocean levels worldwide. Most immediately, as ice sheets continue to melt in Greenland and Antarctica, rising oceans will make extreme sea-level events, like once-in-a-century storm surges and flooding, annual occurrences in many areas by 2050. Assuming that carbon-control measures were to actually meet the maximum 2°C target set by the Paris Agreement, then enough polar ice will thaw by the end of this century to cause the world's sea levels to rise by 11 to 23 inches. But if global warming grows beyond that, ocean levels could increase as much as 43 inches by century's end, depending on what happens to Antarctica's ice sheets. As greenhouse gas emissions and air temperatures continue to climb, seas could rise relentlessly by as much as 83 inches (nearly seven feet) in 2200 and 213 inches (nearly eighteen feet) by 2300.[31]

Scientists have learned to measure the melting of the great polar ice sheets with considerable accuracy, but their understanding of the more complex ecology of permafrost is still evolving. According to an April 2019 report in *Nature*, the vast zone of permanently frozen earth at the top of the world, covering about a quarter of the Northern Hemisphere, is a storehouse for about 1.6 trillion metric tons of carbon—twice the amount already in the atmosphere. Current models "assume that permafrost thaws gradually from the surface downwards," slowly releasing methane and CO_2 into the atmosphere. But frozen soil also "physically holds the landscape together," and so thawing rips the surface erratically, exposing ever-larger areas to the sun. Across the Arctic and Boreal regions, "permafrost is collapsing suddenly as pockets of ice within it melt," creating "unknown consequences for greenhouse-gas release." Around the Arctic Circle, there is already dramatic physical evidence of rapid change—including an increase in landslides and erosion in the mountains of Alaska's North Slope, thawing peatlands around Hudson Bay, the release of methane from thawed lakes in northern Sweden, and, most visibly, massive ground ice collapse in Northeast Siberia. Across that vast expanse of permafrost covering nearly 70 percent of Russia, one small Siberian town had temperatures that reached a historic 100°F (37.8°C) in June 2020—the highest ever recorded above the Arctic Circle—while several peninsulas on the Arctic Sea experienced methane eruptions that left enormous craters up to one hundred feet deep.[32]

While conventional models have predicted that such a slow, steady thaw will release 200 billion metric tons of carbon over the next three hundred years, the *Nature* report estimated that "abrupt permafrost thawing" could emit an additional 60 to 100 billion metric tons of carbon by 2300. Since rapid thawing produces more methane than gradual melting does, and methane has 25 times more heating power than CO_2, the "impacts of thawing permafrost on Earth's climate could be twice that expected from current models."[33] Adding a dangerous wild card, about seven hundred thousand square miles of Siberia also contain a form of methane-rich permafrost called yedoma, which forms a layer of ice 130 to 260 feet deep just beneath the region's thin ground cover of mossy peat. As rising temperatures melt this icy permafrost, expanding lakes, which now cover 30 percent of Siberia, will serve as conduits for the release of the methane, which will bubble up from their melting bottoms and escape into the atmosphere. By 2100, such northern waters could be emitting 100 to 200 million tons of methane every year, for an eventual total of some 50 billion tons, potentially raising the global annual release of this dangerous gas by 20 to 40 percent.[34]

Reinforcing the serious implications of that report, a December 2019 review by NOAA indicated that thawing permafrost was already releasing about 300 to 600 million tons of net carbon into the atmosphere annually—the equivalent to Japan's total carbon emissions. Of greater long-term import, the Arctic was already starting to pass the tipping point for an "accelerating feedback" that could triple the tonnage of permafrost carbon released annually by the end of this century.[35]

The IPCC's future scenarios assume that carbon emissions will rise fivefold from the 2015 level of 400 ppm to about 2,000 ppm by 2300, when humankind's impact on the environment will plateau. By then, such high levels of carbon concentration in the atmosphere would bring an "apocalyptic temperature rise" of about 9.0°C, creating a climate not seen since the Jurassic era.[36]

New World Order?

Given that Washington's world system and Beijing's emerging alternative are largely failing to limit carbon emissions, the international community will likely need a new form of collaboration to contain the damage. In the years following the Paris climate accord, the current world system—characterized by strong nation-states and weak global governance at the UN—has proven inadequate to the challenge of climate change. The 2019 Madrid climate summit failed to forge a collective agreement for emission reductions sufficient to cap global warming at 1.5°C, largely due to obstruction from the major emitters like Australia, Brazil, China, India, and the United States.[37]

Any world order, whether Washington's or Beijing's, that is based on primacy of the nation-state will probably prove incapable of coping with the political and economic crisis likely to arise from the appearance of some 275 million climate change refugees by 2060 or 2070.

After 2050, the international community will quite possibly face a growing contradiction, even a head-on collision, between the foundational principles of the current world order: national sovereignty and human rights. To mitigate the paramount sovereignty of the nation-state, the UN has, since its formation in 1945, created councils and conventions on human rights, refugees, international law, public health, and the global commons. While each of these bodies does important work in its sphere, none are up to the monumental task of coping with the turmoil of climate change. As long as nations have the sovereign right to seal their borders, the world will have no way of protecting the human rights of the 200 million climate change refugees anticipated by 2050 or the 275 million by 2070.

A Chinese hypernationalist world order is unlikely to prove effective at either the mobilization of a collective response to global warming or the creation of safe places for a growing influx of refugees. By 2050, if not earlier, the inability of individual nations, no matter how powerful, to cope with a crisis in the global commons should become blindingly apparent. If China were to turn inward to cope with its own climate crisis at midcentury, and the world were to face the spectacle of mass suffering by many millions of climate change refugees, the community of nations might well agree on the need for a new kind of collective response and an empowered form of global governance.

As the twenty-first century advances and the impacts of climate change grow more severe, the international community might finally change the balance between the key features that have defined world orders for the past five centuries—state sovereignty, human rights, and energy. To cope effectively with this crisis, the world would have to create an international system that privileged protection of the global commons and human rights over the inviolability of national sovereignty of the kind sanctioned by the current global order.

Such a supranational body or bodies would need sovereign authority over three critical areas—emissions controls, refugee resettlement, and environmental reconstruction. If the transition to renewable energy sources like solar, wind, and hydropower is still not complete by 2050, then this international body might well compel nations to curb emissions and adopt renewable energy. Whether under the auspices of the UN or a successor organization, a High Commissioner for Refugees would need the authority to supersede state sovereignty by requiring nations to help resettle such tidal flows of humanity. The future equivalents of the International Monetary Fund, the World Bank, and regional organizations like the Asian Development Bank could transfer resources from wealthy temperate countries to feed tropical communities decimated by climate change and fund major public works to remediate the environmental damage.

These massive programs would change the very idea of what constitutes a world order from the diffuse, almost amorphous ethos of the past five centuries into a concrete form of global governance. To exercise effective sovereignty over the global commons, the UN, should it take on this role, would require major but manageable reforms, notably an expansion of the Security Council and an abolition of the five permanent seats, held by the same nations since their victory in World War II, which enjoy the privilege of unilateral vetoes. At the very least, such a modernized body could include India (instead of Britain), Europe (instead of France), and rising powers from Asia, Africa, and Latin America, along with representation for smaller states through their regional associations—the African Union, Arab League, Association of Southeast Asian Nations, and the Organization of American States. Such a reformed body could also be given a mandate to override specific aspects of national sovereignty, which historically has never been an absolute. For the past five centuries, all world orders have punished violations of shared norms—whether papal excommunication in the Iberian age, the seizure of slave ships by imperial Britain, or UN Security Council sanctions in the current era. Just as the Security Council can now punish a nation that crosses international borders with armed force, so future global governance could sanction a state that releases greenhouse gases into the atmosphere or refuses to resettle climate change refugees. At present, no one can predict with any certainty whether such reforms will come soon enough to cap emissions and slow climate change, or arrive too late to accomplish anything but management of the endlessly escalating damage of uncontrollable feedback loops.

After more than two centuries of the promotion of state sovereignty over human rights—whether implicitly in the British and American world orders or explicitly under China's emerging global system—it might well be

time for a fundamental shift in the balance between these two core principles. A planet increasingly battered by climate change might well need an
empowered world order that can supersede national sovereignty to protect
the most fundamental and transcendent of all human rights: survival. While
the forms taken by state sovereignty have changed continuously over the
past five centuries, human rights have served as a constant touchstone for
progress through successive world orders, transcending all major forms of
government—autocratic, democratic, monarchical, and even imperial. The
environmental changes in the offing, however, are so profound that anything
less than the emergence of a new form of global governance—one capable
of protecting the planet and the human rights of all its inhabitants—in-
troduces a strong prospect of conflict and, in all likelihood, disaster of an
almost-unimaginable kind.

Unlike the catastrophes of epidemic disease and protracted warfare that
ended past world orders, climate change may not reach its conclusion in
foreseeable human time. The Black Death persisted for just four years in
its most intense phase and, if we count its recurring epidemics, another 90
years after that. The Napoleonic Wars lasted 20 years and World War II six
years. Instead of ending in 2050 or even 2100, climate change will, through
those emerging feedback loops, continue and likely escalate for at least two
more centuries before stabilizing with the formation of a very new kind of
climate. Absent some miraculous technology for the removal of carbon and
methane from the atmosphere, a far hotter climate will become a permanent feature of planet Earth. That changed climate will bring such cascading
consequences as aridification, drought, fire, flood, rising seas, and weather
extremes on a previously inconceivable scale—causing suffering for human
societies worldwide and incalculable disruption to any existing world order.

At some point after 2100, the planet will no doubt achieve a new ecological equilibrium in its own time. That balance may, however, only come
in a far-distant future beyond humanity's current capacity to imagine. For
now, the unfolding trajectory of the twenty-first century seems to augur both
cataclysmic climate change and the collapse of world orders.

Let me close on a personal note by apologizing, on behalf of my own
baby-boom generation, for leaving today's youth a climate crisis whose
costs will be painfully evident by 2050—when I am long dead and you
are middle-aged, raising your own children and struggling to survive in an

increasingly difficult environment. For you, I sincerely hope that the future will prove every word I have written in the paragraphs above to be utterly wrong. Unfortunately, the scientific evidence appears so strong that political engagement to constrain climate change and repair its human costs seems a far more prudent course of action for you to take. Good luck and God bless. You will need both.

Acknowledgments

I am particularly indebted to Tom Engelhardt, editor of the online journal *TomDispatch*, whose thoughtful questions over the phone one wintry February afternoon sparked reflections that allowed me to envision almost the entire argument for this book. And when the manuscript was done, the text benefited from a careful editorial review by both Tom and his co-editor for the Dispatch series, Nick Turse.

While I was recuperating from knee surgery and struggling to start this writing, colleagues at the Center for Southeast Asian Studies at University of Wisconsin–Madison kindly delivered plates of food to my front door—including Eunsook Jung, Jinda Moore, Tyrell Haberkorn, Mike and Marguerite Cullinane, Erlin Barnard, and Shelia Zamar.

As my ideas were taking form, numerous colleagues at the university, where I have taught for the past 30 years, provided the initial audiences for them, offering both a sympathetic hearing and useful suggestions. In the spring of 2019, a conference on Caribbean studies in honor of my history colleague Francisco Scarano allowed for their first formal presentation, particularly with regard to the Iberian age so central to the argument of this book. During the discussion that followed my paper, Anne Macpherson from SUNY Brockport asked a thoughtful question about my periodization of world orders that is now reflected in the text, while Herbert Klein of Columbia University gave a data-dense presentation on silver flows within the Spanish Empire that informed my analysis. That fall, the Center for Southeast Asian Studies allowed me to present a summary of my argument at its weekly Friday Forum lecture series, where, among many useful suggestions, Eunsook Jung asked a particularly provocative question about the comparative role of political elites in the decline of world orders.

During the long years that my thoughts on imperial history were taking form, I benefited greatly from conversations with students and colleagues at the University of Wisconsin. My partners in the earlier project "Empires in

Transition," Francisco Scarano and Courtney Johnson, shared insights into Latin America's colonial history. My fellow specialists in Southeast Asia—Katherine Bowie, Anne Hansen, Thongchai Winichakul, Mike Cullinane, Mary McCoy, Eunsook Jung, and Dan Doeppers—have deepened my understanding of that region's imperial history. Over the years, undergraduate and graduate students in the history department have invited me to supervise diverse projects that have introduced me to issues beyond my own narrow field—Anna Chotzen on human rights and poison gas in colonial Africa, Anthony Medrano on the geopolitics of the Pacific Ocean, Piotr Puchalski on interwar European imperialism in Africa, Tyler Lehrer on European trading companies in South Asia, and Samuel Bertsch on America's diplomatic agents in post-colonial Saigon.

Beyond my home university, the Association for Asian Studies (AAS) provided important professional support. Jeffrey Wasserstrom and his associate at the *Journal of Asian Studies*, Jennifer Munger, for instance, encouraged the analysis of US power in the Pacific for a roundtable in their journal that forms the foundation for chapter 5.

At the 2019 Bangkok conference of the AAS, where I first presented some of these findings, I am particularly grateful to my host, Lalita Hanwong of Kasetsart University; the conference chair, Anusorn Unno of Thammasat University; a Madison graduate, Yukti Mukdawijitra of Thammasat University, who first extended the invitation; my good friend, the past AAS president Katherine Bowie, for her thoughtful comments; Krisna Uk, a senior AAS adviser who organized a lively roundtable at that conference; my Madison colleague Anne Hansen, whose insights encouraged a post-conference visit to Angkor; a thoughtful paper on China's energy strategy by Christopher Len of the National University of Singapore; a helpful conversation on a river ferry in Bangkok with Sally Sargeson of the Australian National University about China's rural transformation; and countless attendees at the conference who did me the courtesy of a careful hearing.

While I was editing the book's final draft in early 2020, a former student at the University of Wisconsin, Bill Gibson, invited me to speak in the Human Rights Week assembly at Madison's East High School. Through their thoughtful questions about climate change and deep concern for the planet's future, those students compelled me to rewrite the concluding chapter with a greater sense of immediacy.

Once the manuscript was done, colleagues in Wisconsin's Department of History, Chris Hulshof and Ruth de Llobet, generously gave the entire text a close, careful reading, identifying lapses large and small. At the university's Cartography Lab, its director, Tanya Andersen, arranged for student cartographer Lily Houtman to draw the excellent maps that take readers across the globe. As my editors Tom Engelhardt and Nick Turse were reviewing the manuscript, Anthony Arnove arranged publication with Haymarket Books, giving this daunting project momentum that carried it to completion. When their work was done, the copyeditor, Sam Coleman Smith, and the proofreader, Dana Henricks, gave the work a final, careful review.

There are also some deeper debts. As a student at a small Connecticut boarding school, I had the good fortune to study English for two years with Robert Cluett, later a professor of English at York University, whose rigorous, inspired instruction taught me the craft of rendering complex issues into readable prose. Elsewhere, my sister Dace (known to the wider world as Lady Margarita Ground) listened carefully and responded critically to my ideas about Great Britain, where she resides, guided me about London to view imperial artifacts germane to this study, and gave the final manuscript a thoughtful reading. Throughout the period of writing and global circumnavigation that informed this study, my wife, Mary E. McCoy, questioned major and minor points, sharpened my analysis, and spared me various conceptual pitfalls. For all that, and much more, I am grateful to her beyond words.

Notes

Newspapers frequently cited have been identified by the following abbreviations:
NYT *New York Times*
WP *Washington Post*

Chapter 1: Empires and World Orders

1. Jonathan Watts, "The Environment in 2050," *Guardian*, 12/30/2019, https://www.theguardian.com/environment/2019/dec/30/environment-2050-flooded-cities-forced-migration-amazon-turning-savannah; Denise Lu and Christopher Flavelle, "Rising Seas Will Erase More Cities by 2050, New Research Shows," *NYT*, 10/29/2019, https://www.nytimes.com/interactive/2019/10/29/climate/coastal-cities-underwater.html; Tim McDonnell, "Climate Change Creates a New Migration Crisis for Bangladesh," *National Geographic*, 1/24/2019, https://www.nationalgeographic.com/environment/2019/01/climate-change-drives-migration-crisis-in-bangladesh-from-dhaka-sundabans.

2. Kanta Kumari Rigaud et al., *Groundswell* (2018), xix, 110–11, https://openknowledge.worldbank.org/handle/10986/29461.

3. Office of Coastal Management, National Oceanic and Atmosphere Administration, *Climate Change Predictions* (5/5/2021), https://coast.noaa.gov/states/fast-facts/climate-change.html; US Global Change Research Program, *Fourth National Climate Assessment*, vol. 2 (2018), 55–57, 73–75.

4. US Global Change Research Program, *Fourth National Climate Assessment*, vol. 2, 55–57, 73–75, 240–49, 412–14; Watts, "The Environment in 2050."

5. Intergovernmental Panel on Climate Change, "Summary for Policy Makers," *Climate Change 2014* (2014), 12, https://www.ipcc.ch/report/ar5/syr/; Matthew Collins et al., "Long-Term Climate Change," in Thomas F. Stocker et al., eds., *Climate Change 2013* (2013), 1031, 1058, https://www.ipcc.ch/site/assets/uploads/2017/09/WG1AR5_Frontmatter_FINAL.pdf.

6. Cal Fire, "2019 Incident Archive," https://www.fire.ca.gov/

incidents/2019/; Susie Cagle, "California's Fire Season Has Been Bad," *Guardian*, 11/1/2019, https://www.theguardian.com/us-news/2019/nov/01/california-wildfire-season-2019.

7. Reuters Staff, "Fires in Amazon Forest Rose 30% in 2019," *Reuters*, 1/8/2020, https://www.reuters.com/article/us-brazil-amazon-fires/fires-in-amazon-forest-rose-30-in-2019-idUSKBN1Z804V; Rhett A. Butler, "Amazon Deforestation Rises to 11 Year High in Brazil," *Mongabay*, 11/18/2019, https://news.mongabay.com/2019/11/amazon-deforestation-rises-to-11-year-high-in-brazil/.

8. Livia Albeck-Ripka et al., "'It's an Atomic Bomb,'" *NYT*, 1/4/2020, https://www.nytimes.com/2020/01/04/world/australia/fires-military.html; Jamie Tarabay, "Why These Australia Fires Are Like Nothing We've Seen Before," *NYT*, 1/21/2020, https://www.nytimes.com/2020/01/21/world/australia/fires-size-climate.html.

9. António Guterres, "Remarks at Opening Ceremony of UN Climate Change Conference COP25," 12/2/2019, https://www.un.org/sg/en/content/sg/speeches/2019-12-02/remarks-opening-ceremony-of-cop25.

10. Brady Dennis and Chico Harlan, "U.N. Climate Talks End with Hard Feelings, Few Results and New Doubts about Global Unity," *WP*, 12/15/2019, https://www.washingtonpost.com/climate-environment/un-climate-talks-end-with-hard-feelings-few-results-and-new-doubts-about-global-unity/2019/12/15/38918278-1ec7-11ea-b4c1-fd0d91b60d9e_story.html.

11. Angus Grigg and Angela Macdonald-Smith, "The Trade War Is Making China More Reliant on Australia," *Financial Review*, 8/15/2019, https://www.afr.com/companies/energy/the-trade-war-is-making-china-more-reliant-on-australia-20190814-p52gyn; Damien Cave, "Australia Wilts from Climate Change," *NYT*, 8/21/2018, https://www.nytimes.com/2018/08/21/world/australia/australia-climate-change-malcolm-turnbull.html/; Katharine Murphy, "Scott Morrison Brings Coal to Question Time," *Guardian*, 2/9/2017, https://www.theguardian.com/australia-news/2017/feb/09/scott-morrison-brings-coal-to-question-time-what-fresh-idiocy-is-this; Somini Sengupta, "Climate Change Policy Toppled Australia's Leader," *NYT*, 8/24/2018, https://www.nytimes.com/2018/08/24/climate/australia-climate-change.html; Matthew Brockett, "Australian PM Downplays Climate Change as Cause of Deadly Fires," *Bloomberg*, 12/22/2019, https://www.bloomberg.com/news/articles/2019-12-22/australian-pm-downplays-climate-change-as-cause-of-deadly-fires.

12. "Brazilian President Bolsonaro Blames Environmentalists for Amazon Fires," *Democracy Now!*, 8/22/2019, https://www.democracynow. org/2019/8/22/headlines/brazilian_president_bolsonaro_blames_ environmentalists_for_amazon_fires; Herton Escobar, "Brazilian Institute Head Fired after Clashing with Nation's President over Deforestation Data," *Science and Policy*, 8/4/2019, https://www.sciencemag.org/ news/2019/08/brazilian-institute-head-fired-after-clashing-nation- s-president-over-deforestation; Jon Lee Anderson, "At the U.N. Jair Bolsonaro Presents a Surreal Defense of His Amazon Policies," *New Yorker*, 9/24/2019, https://www.newyorker.com/news/daily-comment/ at-the-united-nations-jair-bolsonaro-presents-a-surreal-defense-of-his- amazon-policies.

13. Edward Wong, "Trump Has Called Climate Change a Chinese Hoax," *NYT*, 11/18/2016, https://www.nytimes.com/2016/11/19/ world/asia/china-trump-climate-change.html; "Trump on Climate Change Report," *BBC News*, 11/26/2018, https://www.bbc.com/ news/world-us-canada-46351940; Brady Dennis, "Trump Makes It Official," *WP*, 11/4/2019, https://www.washingtonpost.com/ climate-environment/2019/11/04/trump-makes-it-official-us-will- withdraw-paris-climate-accord/; Coral Davenport and Mark Landler, "Trump Administration Hardens Its Attack on Climate Science," *NYT*, 5/27/2019, https://www.nytimes.com/2019/05/27/us/politics/trump- climate-science.html.

14. Quint Forgey, "Trump Cautions Davos on Heeding 'Prophets of Doom' on Climate Change," *Politico*, 1/21/2020, https://www.politico.com/ news/2020/01/21/donald-trump-davos-climate-change-101327.

15. David E. Sanger and Maggie Astor, "Democratic Candidates Reject Trump's Foreign Policy, but Don't Agree on Theirs," *NYT*, 2/7/2020, https://www.nytimes.com//2020/02/07/us/politics/democratic- candidates-foreign-policy.html; Stephen Collinson, "What Happened during CNN's Climate Town Hall and What It Means for 2020," *CNN Politics*, 9/5/2019, https://www.cnn.com/2019/09/05/politics/ climate-town-hall-highlights/index.html; Catherine Garcia, "Alexandria Ocasio-Cortez Says It Was 'Horrifying' the Debate Didn't Have Any Climate Change Questions," *The Week*, 2/25/2020, https://theweek. com/speedreads/898187/alexandria-ocasiocortez-says-horrifying-debate- didnt-have-climate-change-questions-bernie-sanders-agrees; Emily Holden, "What Does the First Climate Question at a US Debate in 20 Years Reveal?," *Guardian*, 9/30/2020, https://www.theguardian.com/

us-news/2020/sep/30/presidential-debate-climate-crisis-question-trump-biden-analysis; Lisa Friedman, "A Debate Pledge to 'Transition' from Oil Puts Climate at Center of Campaign Finale," *NYT*, 10/23/2020, https://www.nytimes.com/2020/10/23/climate/biden-debate-oil.html.

16. Alfred W. McCoy, "Beyond Golden Shower Diplomacy," *TomDispatch*, 5/22/2018, http://www.tomdispatch.com/blog/176426/.

17. Nicholas Kristof, "Why 2018 Was the Best Year in Human History!" *NYT*, 1/5/2019, https://www.nytimes.com/2019/01/05/opinion/sunday/2018-progress-poverty-health.html; Max Roser and Esteban Oritz-Ospina, "Global Extreme Poverty," *Our World in Data,* 3/27/2017, https://ourworldindata.org/extreme-poverty.

18. Nicholas J. Bell and Muira McCammon, *Colloquium Report on Competing Visions of the Global Order and Status Report on the Global Order* (2018), 8, https://drive.google.com/file/d/1QVBxBCRU096eE6YozvsYNnbdKx6UZQ4K/view.

19. Daniel Deudney and G. John Ikenberry, "Liberal World," *Foreign Affairs* 97, no. 4 (2018), 16–24.

20. Richard N. Haass, "How a World Order Ends," *Foreign Affairs* 98, no. 1 (2019), 22–30.

21. "List of Empires," *Wikipedia*, https://en.wikipedia.org/wiki/List_of_empire.

22. David W. Dunlap, "A Section of the Berlin Wall Will Again Stand in Manhattan," *NYT*, 4/8/2015, https://www.nytimes.com/2015/04/09/nyregion/a-20-foot-section-of-the-berlin-wall-will-return-to-manhattan-this-summer.html.

23. "List of Empires," *Wikipedia.*

24. Harold D. Foster, "Assessing Disaster Magnitude," *Professional Geographer* 28, no. 3 (1976), 241–47.

25. Tom Phillips et al., "Beijing Rejects Tribunal's Ruling in South China Sea Case," *Guardian*, 7/12/2016, https://www.theguardian.com/world/2016/jul/12/philippines-wins-south-china-sea-case-against-china.

26. Rudyard Kipling, "Recessional," *A Choice of Kipling's Verse Made by T.S. Eliot* (1943); John Darwin, *Unfinished Empire* (2012), 30–32; A.W. Brian Simpson, *Human Rights and the End of Empire* (2001), 18–33.

27. Human Rights Watch, "China's Global Threat to Human Rights," *World Report 2020* (2020), https://www.hrw.org/world-report/2020/china-global-threat-to-human-rights.

28. Bartolomé Yun-Casalilla, *Iberian World Empires and Globalization of Europe 1415–1668* (2019), 445–49; Dr. Ruth de Llobet, personal

communication with author, 5/19/2020.

29. Andrew Glass, "Reagan Brands Soviet Union 'Evil Empire,' March 8, 1983," *Politico*, 3/8/2018, https://www.politico.com/story/2018/03/08/this-day-in-politics-march-8-1983-440258.

30. Chalmers Johnson, *The Sorrows of Empire* (2005); Andrew J. Bacevich, "New Rome, New Jerusalem," in Andrew J. Bacevich, ed., *The Imperial Tense* (2003); Andrew J. Bacevich, *American Empire* (2002); Charles S. Maier, *Among Empires* (2006); Jeet Heer, "Are We Witnessing the Fall of the American Empire?," *New Republic*, 3/7/2018, https://newrepublic.com/article/147319/witnessing-fall-american-empire; Ryan Cooper, "The American Empire Is Crumbling," *The Week*, 12/29/2017, https://theweek.com/articles/745597/american-empire-crumbling; Thomas J. Wright, *All Measures Short of War* (2017), 1–27, 158–71.

31. Jared Diamond, *Guns, Germs, and Steel* (1999), 360–63; Benjamin Foster, *The Age of Agade* (2016).

32. Niall Ferguson, *Colossus* (2004), 14–15; "List of Empires," *Wikipedia*.

33. Rein Taagepera, "Size and Duration of Empires," *Social Science History* 3, nos. 3/4 (1979), 115–38; John D. Durand, "Historical Estimates of World Population," *Population and Development Review* 3, no. 3 (1977), 253–96.

34. Johan Galtung et. al., "On the Decline and Fall of Empires" (1979), 5, https://www.transcend.org/galtung/papers/HSDR-GPID1.PDF.

35. Gerald A. Danzer, *An Atlas of World History* (2000), 46–47, 56–57; William Shepherd, *Historical Atlas* (1911), 53, 92.

36. D.K. Fieldhouse, *The Colonial Empires* (1982), 373.

37. John Francis Guilmartin Jr., *Gunpowder and Galleys* (1974), 221–52.

38. Paul Kennedy, "The Eagle Has Landed," *Financial Times*, 2/2/2002.

39. Eric Levitz, "The GOP Has No New Ideas Because Elderly Billionaires Own Its Brain," *New York Magazine*, 8/30/2018, http://nymag.com/intelligencer/2018/08/gop-ideas-billionaires-donors-tax-cuts-one-percent-paul-ryan.html; Benjamin I. Page et al., "What Billionaires Want," *Guardian*, 10/31/2018, https://www.theguardian.com/us-news/2018/oct/30/billionaire-stealth-politics-america-100-richest-what-they-want; Russell Berman, "A Guide to the Billionaires Bankrolling the GOP Candidates," *Atlantic*, 4/24/2015, https://www.theatlantic.com/politics/archive/2015/04/a-guide-to-the-billionaires-bankrolling-the-gop-candidates/391233/; Christine Mai-Duc and Jazmine Ulloa, "These Are the Billionaires Hoping to Influence Elections That Will Determine Control of Congress," *Los Angeles Times*, 11/5/2018, https://www.latimes.com/politics/

la-na-pol-midterm-election-billionaires-20181105-story.html.

40.   John R. Hale, *Lords of the Sea* (2010), 10–14, 70–74, 82–89.

41.   Ian Morris, "The Growth of Greek Cities in the First Millennium BC," *Princeton/Stanford Working Papers in Classics* (2005), 3, http://www.princeton.edu/~pswpc/pdfs/morris/120509.pdf.

42.   Errietta M.A. Bissa, *Governmental Intervention in Foreign Trade in Archaic and Classical Greece* (2009), 169–77; Alfonso Moreno, *Feeding Democracy* (2007), 32–33; Arthur de Graauw, "Merchant Ships," *Ancient Port—Ports Antiques* (2021), http://www.ancientportsantiques.com/ancient-ships/merchant-ships/.

43.   Hale, *Lords of the Sea*, 233–46, 308–18.

44.   Jeffrey Henderson, ed., *Plutarch Lives*, vol. 7 (1919), 477–511.

45.   Giles Laurén, *Caesar's Commentaries* (2012), chapters 1–29.

46.   Alfred Thayer Mahan, *Influence of Seapower upon History, 1660–1783* (1957); Holger H. Herwig, "The Failure of German Sea Power, 1914–1945," *International History Review* 10, no. 1 (1988), 68–105; Paul Kennedy, "The Influence and the Limitations of Sea Power," *International History Review* 10, no. 1 (1988), 2–17; Yôichi Hirama, "Japanese Naval Preparations for World War II," *Naval War College Review* 44, no. 2 (1991), 63–81.

47.   H.J. Mackinder, "The Geographical Pivot of History (1904)," *The Geographical Journal* 170, No. 4 (2004), 298–321.

48.   H.J. Mackinder, *Democratic Ideals and Reality* (1919), 185–89.

49.   B.W. Blouet, "Sir Halford Mackinder as British High Commissioner to South Russia, 1919–1920," *Geographical Journal* 142, no. 2 (1976), 228–36; Gerry Kearns, *Geopolitics and Empire* (2009), 202–10.

50.   Henning Heske, "Karl Haushofer," *Political Geography Quarterly* 6, no. 2 (1987), 135–44; Trevor J. Barnes and Christian Abrahamsson, "Tangled Complicities and Moral Struggles," *Journal of Historical Geography* 47 (2015), 64–73.

51.   Edmund A. Walsh, S.J., "The Mystery of Haushofer," *Life* 21, no. 12, 9/16/1945, 107–20; Barnes, "Tangled Complicities," 64–73; Arvid Brodersen, "Albrecht Haushofer 1903–1945," in Albrecht Haushofer, *Moabit Sonnets* (1978), sonnet 36, "My Father," 77–78.

52.   Zbigniew Brzezinski, *The Grand Chessboard* (1998); Daniel J. Sargent, *A Superpower Transformed* (2015), 170–73, 230–31.

53.   Brzezinski, *Grand Chessboard*, 38.

54.   Andrew Marshall, "Terror 'Blowback' Burns CIA," *Independent*, (10/23/2011), http://www.independent.co.uk/news/

terror-blowback-burns-cia-1182087.html; "Interview with Zbigniew Brzezinski," *Le Nouvel Observateur* (Paris), 1/15–21/1998, 76, http://www.globalresearch.ca/articles/BRZ110A.html; Brzezinski, *Grand Chessboard*, 38–39; Zbigniew Brzezinski, *Strategic Vision* (2013), 130–31.

55.   Brzezinski, *Grand Chessboard*, 35, 39.

Chapter 2: The Iberian Age

1.   "Naval Parade off Portugal," *Times* (London), 8/9/1960; G.M.M., "Prince Henry the Navigator," *Hispania* 43, no. 1 (1960), 118–19.

2.   Arthur Davies, "Prince Henry the Navigator," *Transactions and Papers (Institute of British Geographers)*, no. 35 (1964), 122–24; B.W. Diffie and G.D. Winius, *Foundations of the Portuguese Empire, 1415–1580* (1977), 78–81; C.R. Boxer, *The Portuguese Seaborne Empire, 1415–1825* (1969), 24–25.

3.   Gomes Eannes de Azurara, *The Chronicle of the Discovery and Conquest of Guinea*, vol. 1 (1896), 84–85.

4.   Diffie, *Foundations*, 113–22; W.G.L. Randles, "The Alleged Nautical School Founded in the Fifteenth Century at Sagres by Prince Henry of Portugal, Called the 'Navigator,'" *Imago Mundi* 45 (1993), 20–28; Edgar Prestage, "Prince Henry the Navigator," in Charles Herbermann et al., eds., *Catholic Encyclopedia*, vol. 7 (1910), 239–40.

5.   Gregorio Rosas Herrero, "América latina debe superar el 'desierto de la desunión,'" *Correo Económico* (México), 10/25/1982; Merry MacMasters, "Antonio de Montesinos," *El Nacional* (México), 10/11/1982; Isabel Zamorano, "JPL: Ante hegemonías que arruinan y avasallan, unidad," *Excélsior* (México), 10/13/1982; Fernando Meraz, "Imponente figura de 28 metros de alto de Fray Antón de Montesinos," *Excélsior*, 10/9/1982; Máximo Manuel Pérez, "Rendirán hoy tributo Fray Antón Montesinos," *Listín Diario* (Santo Domingo), 10/12/1982. The statue's sculptor was Antonio Castellanos, and his wife, Lavinia, kindly provided these newspaper articles.

6.   Anthony Pagden, "Introduction," in Bartolomé de Las Casas, *A Short Account of the Destruction of the Indies* (1992), xiii–xli; Frank Pons, *The Dominican Republic* (1995), 33–34.

7.   Bartolomé de Las Casas, *Historia de las Indias*, book 3 (1986), 13–14.

8.   J.H. Elliott, *Empires of the Atlantic World* (2006), 67–69, 98–99, 130–33; Pagden, "Introduction," in Las Casas, *Short Account*, xiii–xli; Mary Nona McGreal, ed., *Dominicans at Home in a Young Nation, 1786–1865*, vol. 1 (2001), chapter 1; Paul E. Hoffman, *A New Andalucia and a Way to the*

Orient (1990), 80–81; Alan Mikhail, *God's Shadow* (2020), 139–43.

9.   Elliott, *Empires*, 99–101.

10.   Roquinaldo Ferreira and Tatiana Seijas, "The Slave Trade to Latin America," in Alejandro de la Fuente and George Reid Andrews, eds., *Afro-Latin American Studies* (2018), 29–39; Elliott, *Empires*, 100.

11.   Marc Bloch, "Les 'inventions' Médiévales," *Annales d'histoire économique et sociale* 7, no. 36 (1935), 634–43; Astrid Kander et al., *Power to the People* (2013), 64–67.

12.   Kander, *Power*, 67–70, 75; Frederick Stokhuyzen, *The Dutch Windmill* (1962), 96–97.

13.   Sidney M. Greenfield, "Madeira and the Beginnings of New World Sugar Cane Cultivation and Plantation Slavery," *Annals of the New York Academy of Sciences* 292, no. 1 (1977), 536–52.

14.   Ole J. Benedictow, *The Black Death, 1346–1353* (2004), 382–83; Ole J. Benedictow, "The Black Death," *History Today* 55, no. 3 (2005), https://www.historytoday.com/archive/black-death-greatest-catastrophe-ever.

15.   J.D. Durand, "The Population Statistics of China, A.D. 2–1953," *Population Studies* 13, no. 3 (1960), 209–56; Lawrence G. Gundersen, "A Reassessment of the Decline of the Khmer Empire," *International Journal of Culture and History* 1, no. 1 (2015), 64.

16.   United States Census Bureau, "Historical Estimates of World Population," https://www.census.gov/data/tables/time-series/demo/international-programs/historical-est-worldpop.html.

17.   Jack Weatherford, *Genghis Khan and the Making of the Modern World* (2004), 81–217, 241–44; Giovanna Morelli et al., "*Yersinia Pestis* Genome Sequencing Identifies Patterns of Global Phylogenetic Diversity," *Nature Genetics* 42 (10/31/2010), 1140–43, https://www.nature.com/articles/ng.705; Nicholas Wade, "Europe's Plagues Came from China, Study Finds," *NYT*, 10/31/2010, https://www.nytimes.com/2010/11/01/health/01plague.html.

18.   John Kelly, *The Great Mortality* (2006), 43–48; Philip Ziegler, *The Black Death* (1969), 30–35; Andrew Lambert, *Seapower States* (2018), 114–22; Michele Fratianni and Franco Spinelli, "Italian City-States and Financial Evolution," *European Review of Economic History* 10, no. 3 (2006), 261–71; D.N. Ghosh, "Genesis of High Finance," *Economic and Political Weekly* 41, no. 7 (2006), 542–43.

19.   Robert S. Gottfried, *The Black Death* (1983), 23–30; Thomas H. McGovern, "The Demise of Norse Greenland," in William W. Fitzhugh and Elisabeth I. Ward, eds., *Vikings* (2000), 327–39.

20.   David Herlihy, *The Black Death and the Transformation of the West* (1997), 39–40.

21.   Gottfried, *Black Death*, xiii.

22.   Kelly, *Great Mortality*, xiii, xiv–xv, 8–11, 94–95, 110–11, 119, 150–51, 201, 215–26, 263, 281; Ziegler, *Black Death*, 50.

23.   Ziegler, *Black Death*, 40–63, 107–8, 113–16; Benedictow, *Black Death*, 77–90.

24.   Gottfried, *Black Death*, xvi, 8–9, 129–34; J.H. Elliott, *Imperial Spain, 1469–1716* (2002), 37; Randal Garza, *Understanding Plague* (2008), 7–10; Herlihy, *Black Death*, 17.

25.   Benedictow, *Black Death*, 382–83; Ziegler, *Black Death*, 232–51.

26.   Herlihy, *Black Death*, 40–57.

27.   Gottfried, *Black Death*, 16–18, 135–47.

28.   Weatherford, *Genghis Khan*, 241–54; William H. McNeill, *Plagues and Peoples* (1977), 168–75; Diffie, *Foundations*, 203; Adrian Goldsworthy, *How Rome Fell* (2009), 314–34.

29.   Kathryn Reyerson, "Identity in the Medieval Mediterranean World of Merchants and Pirates," *Mediterranean Studies* 20, no. 2 (2012), 129–46.

30.   Xavier Gil, "The Shaping of the Iberian Polities in the Late Fifteenth and Earlier Sixteenth Centuries," in Fernando Bouza et al., eds., *The Iberian World 1450–1820* (2020), 7–19.

31.   Eric R. Wolf, *Europe and the People without History* (2010), 38–44.

32.   Wolf, *Europe*, 44–50.

33.   Wolf, *Europe*, 56–58; Brendan M. Buckley et al. "Climate as a Contributing Factor in the Demise of Angkor, Cambodia," *Proceedings of the National Academy of Sciences* 107, no. 15 (2010), 6748–52.

34.   Wolf, *Europe*, 50–56.

35.   B.L. Turner II and Jeremy A. Sabloff, "Classic Period Collapse of the Central Maya Lowlands," *Proceedings of the National Academy of Sciences* 109, no. 35 (2012), 13908–14; Wolf, *Europe*, 58–72.

36.   "The Gokstad Ship," UiO Museum of Cultural History, 7/7/2016, https://www.khm.uio.no/english/visit-us/viking-ship-museum/exhibitions/gokstad/gokstad-ship.html; Beau Riffenburgh, *The Great Explorers and Their Journeys of Discovery* (2017), 7–11; Arne Emil Christensen, "Ships and Navigation," in Fitzhugh and Ward, *Vikings*, 86–97; Neil S. Price, "'Laid Waste, Plundered, and Burned,'" in Fitzhugh and Ward, *Vikings*, 116–26; Orri Vésteinsson, "The Archeology of Landnam," in Fitzhugh and Ward, *Vikings*, 164–74; Birgitta Linderoth Wallace, "The Viking Settlement at L'Anse aux Meadows," in Fitzhugh and Ward, *Vikings*, 208–16.

37.   Peter Bellwood, *Man's Conquest of the Pacific* (1979), 121, 123–24, 296–311, 329–77.

38.   Barbara Bennett Peterson, "The Ming Voyages of Cheng Ho (Zheng He), 1371–1433," *The Great Circle* 16, no. 1 (1994), 43–51; Tansen Sen, "The Formation of Chinese Maritime Networks to Southern Asia, 1200–1450," *Journal of Economic and Social History of the Orient* 46, no. 4 (2006), 421–53.

39.   Frances Gardiner Davenport, ed., *European Treaties Bearing on the History of the United States and Its Dependencies to 1648* (1917), 9, 56–79.

40.   "The Bull *Dudum Siquidem* of September 26, 1493," http://www. reformation.org/dudum-siquidem.html; Davenport, *European Treaties*, 20–26, 79–83.

41.   Davenport, *European Treaties*, 107–11, 118–68; Lawrence A. Coben, "The Events That Led to the Treaty of Tordesillas," *Terrae Incognitae* 47, no. 2 (2015), 148–51; Peter Borschberg, *Journal, Memorials and Letters of Cornelis Matelieff de Jonge* (2015), 8–10.

42.   Bartolomé Yun-Casalilla, *Iberian World Empires and Globalization of Europe 1415–1668* (2019), 16; Wolf, *Europe*, 110–12; Boxer, *Portuguese*, 4–5, 13, 56–57.

43.   Diffie, *Foundations*, 113–22; Randles, "The Alleged Nautical School," 20–28.

44.   Eric Axelson, "Prince Henry the Navigator and the Discovery of the Sea Route to India," *Geographical Journal* 127, no. 2 (1961), 146–47; M.N. Pearson, *The Portuguese in India* (1987), 16; António de Almeida Mendes, "Le Portugal et l'Atlantique," *Rives méditerranéennes* 53 (2016), 139–57; Francisco Rodríguez Mediano, "Iberia, North Africa, and the Mediterranean," in Bouza, *Iberian World*, 106–9.

45.   Cirilo Miguel Flórez, "Zacut," in Thomas Hockey et al., eds., *Biographical Encyclopedia of Astronomers* (2007), 1255–56.

46.   Axelson, "Prince Henry," 147–48.

47.   Filipe Castro, "Shipbuilding in Portugal in the Middle Ages," in Michel Balard and Christian Buchet, eds., *The Sea in History* (2017), 313–18; Diffie, *Foundations*, 118–19; Filipe Castro et al., "A Quantitative Look at Mediterranean Lateen- and Square-Rigged Ships (Part 1)," *International Journal of Nautical Archeology* 37, no. 2 (2008), 349–51; Vaclav Smil, *Energy Transitions* (2017), 62.

48.   Geoffrey Parker, "The Gunpowder Revolution 1300–1500," in Geoffrey Parker, ed., *Warfare* (1995), 106–10.

49.   Lambert, *Seapower States*, 124–26; John Francis Guilmartin Jr.,

Gunpowder and Galleys (1974), 86–88.

50. Guilmartin, *Gunpowder*, 159–63, 168–73, 199, 226–31.

51. C.R. Boxer, "Asian Potentates and European Artillery in the 16th–18th Centuries," *Journal of the Malaysian Branch of the Royal Asiatic Society* 38, no. 2 (1965), 156–72; Geoffrey Parker, "Ships of the Line 1500–1650," in Parker, ed., *Warfare*, 120–31; K.M. Mathew, *History of the Portuguese Navigation in India, 1492–1600* (1988), 174; J.N. Rodriguez and T. Devezas, *Portugal* (2009), 193, 260–64; Guilmartin, *Gunpowder*, 30–32.

52. Pearson, *Portuguese*, 57–58.

53. Carlo M. Cipolla, *Guns and Sails in the Early Phase of European Expansion 1400–1700* (1965), 80–81, 102–3; Guilmartin, *Gunpowder*, 62–63.

54. Diffie, *Foundations*, 57–73.

55. Boxer, *Portuguese*, 26; Diffie, *Foundations*, 67–69.

56. Davies, "Prince Henry," 122–24; Diffie, *Foundations*, 78–81; Boxer, *Portuguese*, 24–25.

57. Davies, "Prince Henry," 122–24; Diffie, *Foundations*, 90, 315; Boxer, *Portuguese*, 24–27.

58. Richard Raiswell, "Eugene IV, Papal Bulls of," in Junius Rodriguez, ed., *Historical Encyclopedia of World Slavery* (1997), 260–61; Davies, "Prince Henry," 122–24.

59. Jessalynn Bird et al., eds., *Crusade and Christendom* (2013), 124–29; Diana Hayes, "Reflections on Slavery," in Charles E. Curran, *Change in Official Catholic Moral Teachings* (2003), 65–75; José Eisenberg, "António Vieira and the Justification of Indian Slavery," *Luso-Brazilian Review* 40, no. 1 (2003), 89–95.

60. Boxer, *Portuguese*, 20–24; Davenport, *European Treaties*, 20–26.

61. Olivia Remie Constable, "Muslim Spain and Mediterranean Slavery," in Scott L. Waugh and Peter D. Diehl, eds., *Christendom and Its Discontents* (1996), 264–84; William Gervase Clarence-Smith, *Islam and the Abolition of Slavery* (2006), 223–26; Elliott, *Empires*, 106–8.

62. Wolf, *Europe*, 201–2; Clarence-Smith, *Islam*, 223–26.

63. Boxer, *Portuguese*, 22–25, 31; Wolf, *Europe*, 111; Pearson, *Portuguese*, 15; Mendes, "Le Portugal," 14–15.

64. Duarte Pacheco Pereira, *Esmeraldo de situ orbis* (1937), 88–89, 97–99, 110–12, 132, 134; Margaret T. Hodgen, *Early Anthropology in the Sixteenth and Seventeenth Centuries* (1964), 362.

65. Diffie, *Foundations*, 154–56; Boxer, *Portuguese*, 28–31.

66. Ivana Elbl, "Cross-Cultural Trade and Diplomacy," *Journal of World History* 3, no. 2 (1992), 165–204.

67. A.C. de C.M. Saunders, *A Social History of Black Slaves and Freedmen in Portugal, 1441–1555* (1982), 1–61; David Eltis, "The Volume and Structure of the Transatlantic Slave Trade," *William and Mary Quarterly* 58, no. 1 (2001), 17–46.

68. Alfred W. Crosby, *Ecological Imperialism* (1986), 77–78; Boxer, *Portuguese*, 88–89; Robert Garfield, "Three Islands of the Portuguese Atlantic," *Shima* 9, no. 2 (2015) 47–59; A.R. Disney, *A History of Portugal and the Portuguese Empire from Beginnings to 1807*, vol. 2 (2009), 79, 84–92, 110–15.

69. Sidney W. Mintz, *Sweetness and Power* (1985), chapters 1, 3.

70. Kander, *Power*, 42–47, 50–52, 88–99; Smil, *Energy*, 59–61.

71. Andreas Malm, *Fossil Capital* (2016), 166–67; Disney, *Portugal*, 250; Boxer, *Portuguese*, 103–4; Hilary McDonald Beckles and Andrew Downes, "The Economics of Transition to the Black Labor System in Barbados, 1630–1680," *Journal of Interdisciplinary History* 18, no. 2 (1987), 238–39; Edward Littleton, *The Groans of the Plantations* (1689), 18–20; Robert W. Fogel and Stanley L. Engerman, *Time on the Cross* (1974), 5, 209; Tomas Weiss, "Time on the Cross," *EH Net*, (11/15/2001), https://eh.net/book_reviews/time-on-the-cross-the-economics-of-american-negro-slavery/.

72. Axelson, "Prince Henry," 150–53; Diffie, *Foundations*, 156–62.

73. Kirti N. Chaudhuri, "The Portuguese Maritime Empire," *Portuguese Studies* 8 (1992), 57–70; Boxer, *Portuguese*, 44–45; Pearson, *Portuguese*, 29.

74. Diffie, *Foundations*, 175–86, 198–201; Boxer, *Portuguese*, 36–37.

75. Mathew, *History*, 173–75; Diffie, *Foundations*, 187–98, 223–25.

76. Parker, "Ships of the Line," 130–31; Mathew, *History*, 173–75.

77. H. Morse Stephens, *Rulers of India* (1892), 29–34; Roger Crowley, *Conquerors* (2015), 124–29.

78. Diffie, *Foundations*, 227–29; Stephens, *Rulers*, 33, 47–49.

79. Diffie, *Foundations*, 225, 259, 262; Pearson, *Portuguese*, 71–72.

80. Diffie, *Foundations*, 301–2, 311–20, 328, 408–16.

81. C.R. Boxer, *The Dutch Seaborne Empire 1600–1800* (1965), 237; Diffie, *Foundations*, 302, 313–16, 320–29.

82. Pearson, *Portuguese*, 22–23, 26–27, 52–53.

83. Diffie, *Foundations*, 227–30; Pearson, *Portuguese*, 25–26, 40–42.

84. K.S. Mathew, "Calicut, the International Emporium of Maritime Trade and the Portuguese during the Sixteenth Century," *Proceedings of the Indian History Congress* 67 (2006–2007), 251–57; Andreu Martínez d'Alòs-Moner, "Conquistadores, Mercenaries, and Missionaries," *Northeast*

African Studies 12, no. 1 (2012), 4–6; Diffie, *Foundations*, 230–39; Chaudhuri, "Portuguese Maritime Empire," 57–58.

85. Diffie, *Foundations*, 240–42.
86. Stephens, *Rulers*, 41–47.
87. Diffie, *Foundations*, 248–58; Boxer, *Portuguese*, 48–49.
88. Boxer, *Portuguese*, 40–41; Diffie, *Foundations*, 263–67.
89. Boxer, *Portuguese*, 40–41; Diffie, *Foundations*, 268–72; Mikhail, *God's Shadow*, 259–69.
90. Pearson, *Portuguese*, 44–45.
91. Giancarlo Casale, *The Ottoman Age of Exploration* (2010), 6–7, 49; Guilmartin, *Gunpowder*, 43–56; Mikhail, *God's Shadow*, 284–310, 343–52, 363–65.
92. d'Alòs-Moner, "Conquistadores," 11–12; Casale, *Ottoman*, 43, 53–63, 69–74, 80–83.
93. Diffie, *Foundations*, 414–18; d'Alòs-Moner, "Conquistadores," 1–28; Casale, *Ottoman*, 74–75, 111–16, 139–47; Guilmartin, *Gunpowder*, 100–3; Pearson, *Portuguese*, 62, 67.
94. Boxer, *Portuguese*, 58–59; Casale, *Ottoman*, 132–35, 139–47, 202–3; "Sokollu Mehmed Pasha," *Biyograpfya*, https://www.biyografya.com/biyografi/16739; Mikhail, *God's Shadow*, 318–20.
95. Casale, *Ottoman*, 119–39, 149–51, 152–55, 182–84.
96. Lambert, *Seapower States*, 219–26; Casale, *Ottoman*, 152–53; Boxer, *Portuguese*, 367–70.
97. Casale, *Ottoman*, 177–79, 182–85.
98. Pearson, *Portuguese*, 79–80.
99. Elliott, *Imperial Spain*, 13, 25; Guiseppe Marcocci, "Iberian Explorations," in Bouza, *Iberian World*, 284–85; Pedro Cardim et al., "The Political Constitution of Iberian Monarchies," in Bouza, *Iberian World*, 35–38; Yun-Casalilla, *Iberian*, 287.
100. Boxer, *Portuguese*, 30–31, 50–61, 157; Henry Kamen, *Empire* (2003), 287, 288–89, 294–97.
101. Elliott, *Imperial Spain*, 27–31, 36–41.
102. Gil, "Shaping," 22; Elliott, *Imperial Spain*, 15–43, 82–86, 92, 125–29; Yun-Casalilla, *Iberian*, 54.
103. Elliott, *Imperial Spain*, 45, 60–61, 101–2, 109, 122–23; Gil, "Shaping," 25.
104. Kamen, *Empire*, 41–46, 82–83, 85, 88–89; Elliott, *Imperial Spain*, 69–79, 101–2.
105. Elliott, *Imperial Spain*, 62–66, 114–15.
106. Winston A. Reynolds, "The Burning Ships of Hernán Cortés," *Hispania*

42, no. 3 (1959), 317–24; Kamen, *Empire*, 83, 99–104; Felix Hinz, "Spanish-Indian Encounters," in Robert Aldrich and Kirsten Mckenzie, eds., *The Routledge History of Western Empires* (2014), 18–22.

107.   Kamen, *Empire*, 83, 99–104; Hinz, "Spanish-Indian," 18–22.

108.   Gordon F. McEwan, *The Incas* (2008), 2–8, 112–33, 138–39; Kamen, *Empire*, 105–7.

109.   Hinz, "Spanish-Indian," 25–27; Jared Diamond, *Guns, Germs, and Steel* (1999), 67–81.

110.   Kamen, *Empire*, 105–19; Juan de Betanzos et al., *Narrative of the Incas* (1996), 180–81; Hinz, "Spanish-Indian," 27.

111.   Manuel Ballesteros-Gaibros, "Francisco Pizarro, Spanish Explorer," *Encyclopedia Britannica* (1/7/2021), https://www.britannica.com/biography/Francisco-Pizarro; Elliott, *Empires*, 132–33.

112.   Dennis O. Flynn and Arturo Giráldez, "Born with a 'Silver Spoon,'" *Journal of World History* 6, no. 2 (1995), 209; Wolf, *Europe*, 135–39; Jane Burbank and Frederick Cooper, *Empires in World History* (2010), 124.

113.   Wolf, *Europe*, 149–51; Stuart B. Schwartz, "Patterns of Conquest and Settlement of the Iberian Americas," in Bouza, *Iberian World*, 325–26, 334–35; Roquinaldo Ferreira and Pablo Miguel Sierra Silva, "Portugal, Spain, and the Transatlantic Slave Trade," in Bouza, *Iberian World*, 381–85.

114.   Kamen, *Empire*, 83; Wolf, *Europe*, 133–35; Toby Green, *The Rise of the Trans-Atlantic Slave Trade in Western Africa, 1300–1589* (2012), 185–89.

115.   Elliott, *Imperial Spain*, 71–76; Kamen, *Empire*, 83–84; Paul S. Vickery, "Bartolomé de Las Casas," *Mediterranean Studies* 9 (2000), 89–102; Pagden, "Introduction," xiii–xli.

116.   Enrique Dussel, "Bartolomé de Las Casas," *Encyclopedia Britannica* (1/4/2021), https://www.britannica.com/biography/Bartolome-de-Las-Casas; Elliott, *Empires*, 70–71; Yun-Casalilla, *Iberian*, 54–55; Eisenberg, "António Vieira," 90–91.

117.   Lewis Hanke, *All Mankind Is One* (1974), 6–22, 57–70.

118.   Robert A. Williams Jr., *The American Indian in Western Legal Thought* (1990), 97–108; Anthony Pagden, *The Burdens of Empire* (2015), 45–67; Anthony Pagden and Jeremy Lawrence, eds., *Francisco de Vitoria* (1991), xiii–xxvii, 225–26, 231–32, 249–51, 282–92; Antony Anghie, *Imperialism, Sovereignty and the Making of International Law* (2004), 13–31.

119.   Hanke, *All Mankind*, 6–22, 57–70; Henry Stevens and Fred W. Lucas, eds., *The New Laws of the Indies for the Good Treatment and Preservation of the Indians* (1893), lxxxvi–xciv; Elliott, *Empires*, 132–33.

120.   Hanke, *All Mankind*, 82–105; Brian Tierney, *The Idea of Natural Rights* (2001), 272–74; Anthony Pagden, *The Fall of Natural Man* (1982), 109–18.

121.   Las Casas, *Short Account*, 12–17, 27–30; Hanke, *All Mankind*, 113–22.

122.   Hanke, *All Mankind*, 113–22.

123.   Juan Comas, "Historical Reality and the Detractors of Father Las Casas," in Juan Friede and Benjamin Keen, eds., *Bartolomé de las Casas in History* (1971), 487–538.

124.   Hodgen, *Early Anthropology*, 361–64; Tierney, *Natural Rights*, 273–78; Pagden, *Natural Man*, 119–26; John L. Phelan, "The Apologetic History of Fray Bartolomé de las Casas," *Hispanic American Historical Review* 49, no. 1 (1969), 94–99.

125.   Pablo Miguel Sierra Silva, *Urban Slavery in Colonial Mexico Puebla de los Ángeles, 1531–1706* (2018), 35–42; Magnus Lundberg, *Unification and Conflict* (2002), 225–26.

126.   McNeil, *Plagues*, 177–92; Wolf, *Europe*, 133–35; Alfred W. Crosby, *The Columbian Exchange* (1972), 42–58; Yun-Casalilla, *Iberian*, 64, 149.

127.   Eltis, "Transatlantic Slave Trade," 17–46; Wolf, *Europe*, 195–201; Herbert S. Klein, *The Atlantic Slave Trade* (2010), 11, 99–100, 216–17.

128.   Timothy Brook, *Vermeer's Hat* (2008), 157–59, 160–61; Kamen, *Empire*, 285–91; Wolf, *Europe*, 138–39.

129.   Flynn, "Born," 201–21; Kamen, *Empire*, 210–21; Brook, *Vermeer's Hat*, 161–62, 170–79; Nicholas Cushner, *Spain in the Philippines* (1971), 135–36; William Lytle Schurz, *The Manila Galleon* (1939), 334–35; Herbert S. Klein and Sergio T. Serrano Hernández. "Was There a 17th Century Crisis in Spanish America?," *Journal of Iberian and Latin American Economic History* 37, no. 1 (2019), 46; Jan de Vries, "The Limits of Globalization in the Early Modern World," *Economic History Review* 63, no. 3 (2010), 730.

130.   "Coins of Latin America," *Encyclopedia Britannica*, https://www. britannica.com/topic/coin/Coins-of-Latin-America.

131.   Cardim, "Political Constitution," 38–39; G. Alvarez et al., "The Role of Inbreeding in the Extinction of a European Royal Dynasty," *PLoS ONE* 4, no. 4 (2009), 5174; Andrea Thompson, "Inbreeding," *Live Science*, 5/6/2021, https://www.livescience.com/3504-inbreeding-downfall-dynasty.html.

132.   José Javier Ruiz Ibáñez, "The Iberian Polities within Europe," in Bouza, *Iberian World*, 62–66; Yun-Casalilla, *Iberian*, 258–63.

133.   Kamen, *Empire*, 49–82; Wolf, *Europe*, 138–39; Parker, "Gunpowder

Revolution," 116–17; Burbank, *Empires*, 117, 128, 143–48.

134. Kamen, *Empire*, 91–93; Yun-Casalilla, *Iberian*, 162–63; Gerhard Geissler, *Europäische Dokumente aus fünf Jahrhunderten* (1939), 85.

135. Wolf, *Europe*, 138–39; Kamen, *Empire*, 91–93, 151–67, 192–93, 296; Guilmartin, *Gunpowder*, 109–12; Elliott, *Imperial Spain*, 249–56.

136. Boxer, *Portuguese*, 160–61; Kamen, *Empire*, 294–95.

137. Kamen, *Empire*, 70–77.

138. Kamen, *Empire*, 155–57.

139. Guilmartin, *Gunpowder*, 221–52; Kamen, *Empire*, 183–86; Lambert, *Seapower States*, 138–42.

140. Elliott, *Imperial Spain*, 241–42.

141. Kamen, *Empire*, 151–52; Andrew Pettegree, *Europe in the Sixteenth Century* (2002), 214.

142. Kamen, *Empire*, 77–78, 177; Philip Benedict, *Christ's Churches Purely Reformed* (2002), 174–88.

143. Kamen, *Empire*, 177–80, 190–91; Elliott, *Imperial Spain*, 262–63; Benedict, *Christ's Churches*, 189–92; Fletcher Pratt, *The Battles That Changed History* (1956), 151–69.

144. Kamen, *Empire*, 186–89, 190–91.

145. Violet Soen, "Reconquista and Reconciliation in the Dutch Revolt," *Journal of Early Modern History* 16, no. 1 (2012), 1–22; Kamen, *Empire*, 299–301; Elliott, *Imperial Spain*, 268–70; Earl J. Hamilton, "Imports of American Gold and Silver into Spain, 1503–1660," *Quarterly Journal of Economics* 43, no. 3 (1929), 436–72.

146. "The Union of Utrecht, January 23, 1579," http://www.constitution.org/cons/dutch/Union_Utrecht_1579.html.

147. Kamen, *Empire*, 299–301; Soen, "Reconquista," 9–22.

148. Kamen, *Empire*, 301–4; Elliott, *Imperial Spain*, 268–77; Jean-Frédéric Schaub, "The Union between Portugal and the Spanish Monarchy," in Bouza, *Iberian World*, 136.

149. Garrett Mattingly, *The Armada* (1959), 247; Kamen, *Empire*, 305–9; Parker, "Ships of the Line," 126–26; Jonathan I. Israel, *The Dutch Republic and the Hispanic World 1606–1661* (1982), 23.

150. Elliott, *Imperial Spain*, 285–89.

151. Wolf, *Europe*, 113–14; Elliott, *Imperial Spain*, 217–31, 292–300; Ruiz Ibáñez, "Iberian Polities," 74; Bartolomé Yun-Casalilla, "The Peninsular Economies and the Impact of Globalisation (ca. 1494–1700)," in Bouza, *Iberian World*, 197–201.

152. Israel, *Dutch Hispanic World*, 42–59, 412–23, 438–39.

153. William of Orange, *The Apologie of Prince William of Orange against the Proclamation of the King of Spaine* (1969), 53, 132; Benjamin Schmidt, "Hyper Imperialism," in René Koekkoek et al., eds., *The Dutch Empire between Ideas and Practices, 1600–2000* (2019), 67–88; Martine Julia van Ittersum, *Profit and Principle* (2006), 59–60, 69–71.

154. Benjamin Keen, "The Black Legend Revisited," *Hispanic American Historical Review* 49, no. 4 (1969), 703–19; Pierre Chaunu, "Las Casas et la première crise structurelle de la Colonisation Espagnole (1515–1523)," *Revue historique* 229, no. 1 (1963), 59–102; J.H. Elliott, *The Old World and The New, 1492–1650* (1970), 95–96; *Le miroir de la cruelle, et horrible tyrannie espagnole perpetrée au Pays Bas* (1620), 15–16, 19, 25, 30, 33, 50–51, 53, 57, 60; Van Ittersum, *Profit and Principle*, 71–77.

155. Steven B. Smith, "Hegel's Idea of a Critical Theory," *Political Theory* 15, no. 1 (1987), 99–126; G.W.F. Hegel, *The Philosophy of History* (1956), 30–31.

Chapter 3: Empires of Commerce and Capital

1. Peter Borschberg, "The Seizure of the Sta. Catarina Revisited," *Journal of Southeast Asian Studies* 33, no. 1 (2002), 31–62; Leonard Blussé, "Brief Encounter at Macao," *Modern Asian Studies* 22, no. 3 (1988), 647–64; Peter Borschberg, *Hugo Grotius, the Portuguese and Free Trade in the East Indies* (2011), 49–55, 114, 129, 194–95, 200–1, 203; "Jacob van Heemskerck," Rijksmuseum, https://www.rijksmuseum.nl/en/rijksstudio/historical-figures/jacob-van-heemskerck; Martine Julia van Ittersum, "Hugo Grotius in Context," *Asian Journal of Social Science* 31, no. 3 (2003), 511–48; Martine Julia van Ittersum, *Profit and Principle* (2006), 8–9, 35–40, 42, 56–67; Yasuaki Onuma, "Hugo Grotius, Dutch Statesman and Scholar," *Encyclopedia Britannica* (1/6/2020), https://www.britannica.com/biography/Hugo-Grotius.

2. Jan de Vries and Ad van der Woude, *The First Modern Economy* (1997), 83–84, 91, 127–29, 131–34, 137, 147–49, 151, 155; "Stock Market History / Historical Milestones / Amsterdam, 1602," TreeTop Asset Management, https://www.treetopam.com/behind-the-numbers/en/stock-market-history/historical-milestones/amsterdam-1602/.

3. James A. Welu, "The Sources and Development of Cartographic Ornamentation in the Netherlands," in David Woodward, ed., *Art and Cartography* (1987), 147–73.

4. Rex Wailes, "A Note on Windmills," in Bent Sorensen, ed., *Renewable Energy*, vol. 1 (2018), 81–86; De Vries, *First Modern Economy*, 296–303, 346–47; Frederick Stokhuyzen, *The Dutch Windmill* (1962), 14–19, 21,

24, 37, 49–54, 91, 96–97, 100; Vaclav Smil, *Energy Transitions* (2017), 63–64; "Houtzaagmolen (1593)," *Nationaal Archief* (Netherlands), https://web.archive.org/web/20110704055714/http://uitvindingen. nationaalarchief.nl/uitvinding/houtzaagmolen; Richard W. Unger, "Dutch Shipbuilding in the Golden Age," *History Today* 34, no. 1 (1981), 16–21.

5. Astrid Kander et al., *Power to the People* (2013), 69–70, 100, 193.

6. Philip Benedict, *Christ's Churches Purely Reformed* (2002), 174–79; Jonathan Israel, *The Dutch Republic* (1995), 79–84, 93–100; Nanne van der Zijpp, "Punishment of the Anabaptists in the Low Countries," *Global Anabaptist Mennonite Encyclopedia Online* (1959), https://gameo.org/index. php?title=Punishment_of_the_Anabaptists_in_the_Low_Countries.

7. Benjamin Schmidt, "Hyper Imperialism," in René Koekkoek et al., eds., *The Dutch Empire between Ideas and Practices, 1600–2000* (2019), 67–88.

8. C.R. Boxer, *The Dutch Seaborne Empire, 1600–1800* (1965), 21–23, 50; De Vries, *First Modern Economy*, 134, 139–41, 151.

9. Kerry Ward, *Networks of Empire* (2009), 21, 70–74; Gerrit J. Schutte, "Between Amsterdam and Batavia," *Kronos* 25 (1998–1999), 17–49; Jonathan I. Israel, *Democratic Enlightenment* (2011), 555–57; Guus Boone and Leendert Groenendijk, "The Dutch Calvinist Moral Offensive and the Colonial Training of Sailors and Tradesmen, 1595–1790," *Paedagogica Historica* 31, no. 1 (1995), 108–9; Charles H. Parker, "Converting Souls across Cultural Borders," *Journal of Global History* 8, no. 1 (2013), 50–71; Gert Oostiendie and Bert Paasman, "Dutch Attitudes towards Colonial Empires, Indigenous Cultures and Slaves," *Eighteenth-Century Studies* 31, no. 3 (1998), 349–55; De Vries, *First Modern Economy*, 475–76.

10. Boxer, *Dutch*, 6–7, 12–13, 20–21, 48–49; Eric Ketelaar, "Accountability Portrayed," *Archival Science* 14, no. 1 (2014), 69–93.

11. Markus Vink, *Encounters on the Opposite Coast* (2016), 118–19; Boxer, *Dutch*, 24–27, 50–51; Holden Furber, *Rival Empires of Trade in the Orient, 1600–1800* (1976), 132–33; D.K. Fieldhouse, *The Colonial Empires* (1982), 147–48; Timothy Brook, *Vermeer's Hat* (2008), 17–18; Peter Borschberg, *Journal, Memorials and Letters of Cornelis Matelieff de Jonge* (2015), 17–18; Ward, *Networks*, 34, 50–55.

12. Boxer, *Dutch*, 220–21; Geoffrey Parker, "Ships of the Line," in Geoffrey Parker, ed., *Warfare* (1995), 130–31.

13. Borschberg, "Seizure of the Sta. Catarina," 31–62; Boxer, *Dutch*, 28; C.R. Boxer, *The Portuguese Seaborne Empire, 1415–1825* (1969), 110–11;

Andrew Lambert, *Seapower States* (2018), 164–65.

14. Van Ittersum, "Hugo Grotius," 520–45; Van Ittersum, *Profit and Principle*, 1, 24–27, 50, 98; Peter Borschberg, "Hugo Grotius, East India Trade and the King of Johor," *Journal of Southeast Asian Studies* 30, no. 2 (1999), 225–48; James Brown Scott, *The Spanish Origin of International Law* (2000), xiii; Borschberg, *Hugo Grotius*, 1–5, 10–11, 61, 80, 107, 110–11, 122–23, 151–52, 159–64; Peter Borschberg, "Grotius, the Social Contract and Political Resistance," *International Law and Justice Working Papers* (2006–2007), 14–18, 48–49, 55.

15. Hugo Grotius, *The Freedom of the Seas* (1916), 1–2, 7–8, 11–13, 15–17, 45–46.

16. Borschberg, "Hugo Grotius," 230–48; Van Ittersum, "Hugo Grotius," 520–41.

17. Lambert, *Seapower States*, 164–65; Jacob F. Field, "Battle of Gibraltar," *Encyclopedia Britannica* (4/18/2021), https://www.britannica.com/event/Battle-of-Gibraltar-1607; Jonathan I. Israel, *The Dutch Republic and the Hispanic World, 1606–1661* (1982), 11–12.

18. Peter Limm, *The Dutch Revolt, 1559–1648* (2014), 65–67; Borschberg, *Journal*, 35–40.

19. Boxer, *Portuguese*, 109.

20. Boxer, *Dutch*, 23; Henry Kamen, *Empire* (2003), 314–19; Brook, *Vermeer's Hat*, 38–39; Bartolomé Yun-Casalilla, *Iberian World Empires and Globalization of Europe, 1415–1668* (2019), 351, 357, 363.

21. Michael Clodfelter, *Warfare and Armed Conflicts* (2017), 36–41; Geoffrey Parker, "Dynastic War, 1494–1660," in Parker, *Warfare*, 154–58; Carlo M. Cipolla, *Guns and Sails in the Early Phase of European Expansion, 1400–1700* (1965), 52–58.

22. Clodfelter, *Warfare*, 36–41.

23. Israel, *Dutch Hispanic World*, 96–97, 100–2, 106–9, 171, 182–83, 186–89, 250–65.

24. Israel, *Dutch Hispanic World*, 163–67, 170, 176–77; Diego Rodríguez de Silva y Velázquez, "The Surrender of Breda" (1635), Room 009A, Museo del Prado, viewed 11/25/1997, https://www.museodelprado.es/en/the-collection/art-work/the-surrender-of-breda/0cc7577a-51d9-44fd-b4d5-4dba8d9cb13a.

25. Parker, "Ships of the Line," 126; Boxer, *Portuguese*, 109–110.

26. Furber, *Rival Empires*, 34–38, 41–50; Borschberg, *Journal*, 44, 132–38.

27. Israel, *Dutch Hispanic World*, 277; Boxer, *Portuguese*, 106–11, 114–15.

28. Israel, *Dutch Republic*, 938–43; Boxer, *Portuguese*, 52–53, 57, 114–15;

Ward, *Networks*, 55–64; Jan de Vries, "The Limits of Globalization in the Early Modern World," *Economic History Review* 63, no. 3 (2010), 710–33; Jane Burbank and Frederick Cooper, *Empires in World History* (2010), 161; Om Prakash, "The Portuguese and the Dutch in Asian Maritime Trade," in Sushil Chaudhury and Michel Morineau, eds., *Merchants, Companies and Trade* (1999), 175–88.

29. Fieldhouse, *Colonial Empires*, 147–48.

30. Stuart B. Schwartz, "Looking for a New Brazil," in Michiel van Groesen, *The Legacy of Dutch Brazil* (2014), 42–46; Wim Klooster, "The Geopolitical Impact of Dutch Brazil on the Western Hemisphere," in Van Groesen, *Dutch Brazil*, 25–26, 33–40; Boxer, *Portuguese*, 111–13.

31. Brook, *Vermeer's Hat*, 132; Boxer, *Dutch*, 28–29; Kamen, *Empire*, 328–29; Schwartz, "Looking for a New Brazil," 46–52; Franz Binder and Norbert Schneeloch, "Dirck Dircksz," *Bulletin van het Rijksmuseum* 27 (1979), 7–29; Roquinaldo Ferreira and Tatiana Seijas, "The Slave Trade to Latin America," in Alejandro de la Fuente and George Reid Andrews, eds., *Afro-Latin American Studies* (2018), 37; De Vries, *First Modern Economy*, 467–81, 678.

32. Herbert S. Klein and Sergio T. Serrano Hernández, "Was There a 17th Century Crisis in Spanish America?," *Journal of Iberian and Latin American Economic History* 37, no. 1 (2019), 46, 64, 43–80; Boxer, *Dutch*, 23; Lambert, *Seapower States*, 166; Kamen, *Empire*, 403–6; De Vries, *First Modern Economy*, 83–91.

33. Boxer, *Dutch*, 28–29; Lambert, *Seapower States*, 165–66; Kamen, *Empire*, 398–99; J.H. Elliott, *Imperial Spain, 1469–1716* (2002), 340–49; Israel, *Dutch Hispanic World*, 266–70.

34. Elliott, *Imperial Spain*, 341–49.

35. Derek Croxton, "The Peace of Westphalia of 1648 and the Origins of Sovereignty," *International History Review* 21, no. 3 (1999), 569–91.

36. Boxer, *Dutch*, 28–29; Boxer, *Portuguese*, 119–27; Elliott, *Imperial Spain*, 353–57.

37. Boxer, *Portuguese*, 112–14.

38. Portrait of Catherine of Braganza, circa 1661, by or after Dirk Stoop (NPG 2563); Portrait of King Charles II, by John Michael Wright, circa 1660–1665 (NPG 531); Portrait of Nell Gwyn, attributed to Simon Verelst, circa 1670 (NPG L248), all viewed at Room 7, National Portrait Gallery, London, 7/20/2019, https://www.npg.org.uk/collections/search/portrait-list.php.

39. Pieter C. Emmer, "The Rise and Decline of the Dutch Atlantic,

1600–1800," in Gert Ootiendie and Jessica V. Roitmann, eds., *Dutch Atlantic Connections, 1680–1800* (2014), 339–56.

40. Israel, *Dutch Hispanic World*, 410, 412–13, 416–21, 437–40.

41. Croxton, "Peace of Westphalia," 569–91; Sebastian Schmidt, "To Order the Minds of Scholars," *International Studies Quarterly* 55, no. 3 (2011), 601–23; Henry Kissinger, *World Order* (2014), chapter 1; G. John Ikenberry, *Liberal Leviathan* (2011), 50–55.

42. Emmer, "Dutch Atlantic," 339; Israel, *Dutch Republic*, 547–64, 569–86.

43. Boxer, *Dutch*, 29, 35, 120–23, 319–20; Emmer, "Dutch Atlantic," 345–46; De Vries, *First Modern Economy*, 118–19, 142, 144.

44. Boxer, *Dutch*, 41–42; Portrait of Cornelis Tromp, by Peter Lely, National Maritime Museum, Greenwich, 1675 (BHC 3060), https://collections. rmg.co.uk/collections/objects/14533.html; *The "Gouden Leeuw" at the Battle of the Texel, 21 August 1673*, by William van de Velde, National Maritime Museum, Greenwich, 1687 (BHC 0315), https://collections. rmg.co.uk/collections/objects/11807.html; De Vries, *First Modern Economy*, 673–74.

45. John Seldcn, *Mare Clausum* (1663), 11, 171–72.

46. Lambert, *Seapower States*, 173–76, 185–86.

47. Parker, "Ships of the Line," 126–27; Lambert, *Seapower States*, 176–77; "Dutch Ship *De Zeven Provinciën* (1665)," *Wikipedia*, https:// en.wikipedia.org/wiki/Dutch_ship_De_Zeven_Provinciën_(1665).

48. Parker, "Ships of the Line," 127–28.

49. Israel, *Dutch Republic*, 776–806; Parker, "Ships of the Line," 127–28; S. Lindgrén and J. Neumann, "Great Historical Events That Were Significantly Affected by the Weather," *Bulletin of the American Meteorological Society* 64, no. 7 (1983), 770–78; "William III, King of England," *Encyclopedia Britannica*, vol. 28 (1911), 662–64.

50. Van de Velde, *"Gouden Leeuw"*; Israel, *Dutch Republic*, 797–814; Brook, *Vermeer's Hat*, 223.

51. Israel, *Dutch Republic*, 841–54; Jonathan Scott, *How the Old World Ended* (2019), 194–201; De Vries, *First Modern Economy*, 676–81.

52. Geoffrey Lock, "The 1689 Bill of Rights," *Political Studies* 37, no. 4 (1989), 540–61; Scott, *Old World Ended*, 203–4; "The Bill of Rights 1689," Parliament of the United Kingdom, https://www.parliament.uk/ about/living-heritage/evolutionofparliament/parliamentaryauthority/ revolution/collections1/collections-glorious-revolution/billofrights/.

53. Scott, *Old World Ended*, 201–10; Boxer, *Dutch*, 122–24; Israel, *Dutch Republic*, 852–54, 971; Emmer, "Dutch Atlantic," 344–45; De Vries, *First*

        Modern Economy, 127–28, 141, 155; François Crouzet, "The Second
        Hundred Years' War," *French History* 10, no. 4 (1996), 445–46.

54.   Parker, "Ships of the Line," 128–30.

55.   Nicholas Blake and Richard Lawrence, *The Illustrated Companion to Nelson's Navy* (2005), 64–79; Brian Lavery, *Nelson's Navy* (1989), 88–99; Michael Lewis, *England's Sea-Officers* (1939), 192–99.

56.   C.A. Bayly, *Imperial Meridian* (1989), 114–21.

57.   E. Lipson, *The Economic History of England*, vol. 2, *The Age of Mercantilism* (1943), 188.

58.   Philip J. Stern, *The Company-State* (2011), 12–13, 207–14.

59.   Ian Barrow, *The East India Company, 1600–1858* (2017), 19.

60.   William Dalrymple, *The Anarchy* (2019), 9, 12–15, 20–25, 63–65, 81–83; John Darwin, *Unfinished Empire* (2012), 54–55.

61.   Dalrymple, *Anarchy*, 48–49.

62.   J.F. Rees, "Historical Revision: XC—Mercantilism," *History* 24, no. 94 (1939), 129–35.

63.   Boxer, *Dutch*, 109–12, 211–12, 219; D.K. Bassett, "The 'Amboyna Massacre' of 1623," *Journal of Southeast Asian History* 1, no. 2 (1960), 1–19.

64.   Om Prakash, *The Dutch East India Company and the Economy of Bengal, 1630–1720* (1988), 145–57; Jan C. van Ours, "The Price Elasticity of Hard Drugs," *Journal of Political Economy* 103, no. 2 (1995), 261–79; Edilberto de Jesus, *The Tobacco Monopoly in the Philippines* (1980).

65.   Stern, *Company-State*, 196–97, 204–6; Fieldhouse, *Colonial Empires*, 151–52; John A. Lynn, "States in Conflict," in Parker, ed., *Warfare*, 178–85; Dalrymple, *Anarchy*, 31–48, 64–69, 240–42; Robert Travers, "Imperial Revolutions and Global Repercussions," in David Armitage and Sanjay Subrahmanyam, eds., *The Age of Revolutions in Global Context, c. 1760–1840* (2010), 146–47.

66.   Dalrymple, *Anarchy*, 139–40, 187–213.

67.   K.N. Chaudhuri, *The Trading World of Asia and the English East India Company 1660–1760* (1978), 19–21; Kaushik Roy, "Military Synthesis in South Asia," *Journal of Military History* 69, no. 3 (2005), 651–90; M.S. Naravane, *Battles of the Honourable East India Company* (2006), 76–77; Dalrymple, *Anarchy*, 207, 335–82.

68.   Sir John Strachey, *India, Its Administration and Progress* (1903), 133–42; J.F. Richards, "The Indian Empire and Peasant Production of Opium in the Nineteenth Century," *Modern Asian Studies* 15, no. 1 (1981), 59–82.

69.   Smil, *Energy*, 37–39, 100–101; R.F. Tylecote, *A History of Metallurgy*,

2nd ed. (1992), 122–25.

70. Eric R. Wolf, *Europe and the People without History* (2010), 204–31; Warren C. Whatley, "The Gun-Slave Hypothesis and the 18th Century British Slave Trade," *Explorations in Economic History* 67 (2018), 80–104; Herbert S. Klein, *The Atlantic Slave Trade* (2010), 59–60, 63–69, 105–6, 87–88, 119–23, 216–17.

71. Wolf, *Europe*, 195–201; William A. Pettigrew, *Freedom's Debt* (2018), 1–16; David Eltis, "The Volume and Structure of the Transatlantic Slave Trade," *William and Mary Quarterly* 58, no. 1 (2001), 17–46.

72. Wolf, *Europe*, 197–98; Pettigrew, *Freedom's Debt*, 1–16, 46–48, 104–5, 110–12, 115–17; Kenneth Morgan, *Edward Colston and Bristol* (1999), 1–18; Kenneth Morgan, "Colston, Edward (1636–1721)," *Oxford Dictionary of National Biography* (1/3/2008), https://www.oxforddnb.com/view/10.1093/ref:odnb/9780198614128.001.0001/odnb-9780198614128-e-5996.

73. Emmer, "Dutch Atlantic," 342–43; Schwartz, "Looking for a New Brazil," 48–49; Hilary McDonald Beckles and Andrew Downes, "The Economics of Transition to the Black Labor System in Barbados, 1630–1680," *Journal of Interdisciplinary History* 18, no. 2 (1987), 225–47; Dr. Karl Watson, "Slavery and Economy in Barbados," *History* (2/17/2011), https://www.bbc.co.uk/history/british/empire_seapower/barbados_01.shtml; J.H. Elliott, *Empires of the Atlantic World* (2006), 104–5.

74. R.B. Sheridan, "The Wealth of Jamaica in the Eighteenth Century," *Economic History Review* 18, no. 2 (1965), 292–311; Michael Ray, "Sir Henry Morgan," *Encyclopedia Britannica* (1/1/2021), https://www.britannica.com/biography/Henry-Morgan-Welsh-buccaneer; Lorraine Murray, "Port Royal," *Encyclopedia Britannica*, (5/11/2018), https://www.britannica.com/place/Port-Royal-Jamaica; Klein, *Atlantic Slave Trade*, 35.

75. Fieldhouse, *Colonial Empires*, 144–56; De Vries, "Limits of Globalization," 727–28; Israel, *Democratic Enlightenment*, 535–57.

76. Kamen, *Empire*, 439–42; Elliott, *Imperial Spain*, 361–62.

77. Kamen, *Empire*, 439–49; Lynn, "States in Conflict," 174–75; Clodfelter, *Warfare*, 70–75.

78. Kamen, *Empire*, 446–49; G.M. Trevelyan, *A Shortened History of England* (1942), 363; Boxer, *Portuguese*, 158–60; Israel, *Dutch Republic*, 968–75.

79. Clodfelter, *Warfare*, 82–89; Darwin, *Unfinished Empire*, 314–18; A.D. Francis, "The Campaign in Portugal, 1762," *Journal of the Society for Army Historical Research* 59, no. 237 (1981), 25–43.

80. Lynn, "States in Conflict," 182–85.

81. Clodfelter, *Warfare*, 85–89; Lynn, "States in Conflict," 174–85.

82. Josep M. Fradera, *The Imperial Nation* (2018), 17, 41, 50–51; Darwin, *Unfinished Empire*, 234–35.

83. Fradera, *Imperial Nation*, 53, 55, 57, 63, 73; Adam Hochschild, *Bury the Chains* (2005), 267.

84. Andrew Roberts, *Napoleon* (2014), xxxiv–xxxvi.

85. Stuart Woolf, "The Construction of a European World View in the Revolutionary-Napoleonic Years," *Past and Present* 137 (1992), 72–101.

86. Michael Sibalis, "The Napoleonic Police State," in Philip G. Dwyer, ed., *Napoleon and Europe* (2014), 79–94; Michael Broers, "Policing the Empire," in Dwyer, *Napoleon and Europe*, 153–68; Geoffrey Ellis, *The Napoleonic Empire* (2003), 26–27, 32–40, 48–58, 63–73.

87. Count Yorck von Wartenburg, *Napoleon as a General*, vol. 1 (1902), 38–39; Charles Esdaile, *Napoleon's Wars* (2008), 49–70; Travers, "Imperial Revolutions," 155–59; Darrell Dykstra, "The French Occupation of Egypt, 1798–1801," in M.W. Daly, ed., *The Cambridge History of Egypt*, vol. 2 (1998), 113–38; J. Christopher Herold, "Napoleon in Action," in Frank A. Kafker and James M. Laux, eds., *Napoleon and His Times* (1989), 22–36; Paul Strathern, *Napoleon in Egypt* (2007), 36; William Doyle, *The Oxford History of the French Revolution* (2003), 376–92.

88. J. Holland Rose, "Napoleon and Sea Power," *Cambridge Historical Journal* 1, no. 2 (1924), 138–57.

89. Michael A. Palmer, "Lord Nelson," *Naval War College Review* 41, no. 1 (1988), 105–16; Tom Pocock, "Horatio Nelson British Naval Commander," *Encyclopedia Britannica* (10/17/2019), https://www.britannica.com/biography/Horatio-Nelson/Victory-at-Trafalgar; N.A.M. Roger, "Nelson, Horatio, Viscount Nelson (1758–1805)," *Oxford Dictionary of National Biography* (5/21/2009), https://www.oxforddnb.com/view/10.1093/ref:odnb/9780198614128.001.0001/odnb-9780198614128-e-19877.

90. Palmer, "Lord Nelson," 105–16; A. Lambert, "'The Glory of England,'" *Great Circle* 28, no. 1 (2006), 3–12; Marianne Czisnik, "Admiral Nelson's Tactics at the Battle of Trafalgar," *History* 89, no. 4 (2004), 549–59; Lynn, "States in Conflict," 208–10; Darwin, *Unfinished Empire*, 24–25.

91. Fradera, *Imperial Nation*, 27–28, 30–31, 74–88; Hochschild, *Bury the Chains*, 258–61; Perry Viles, "The Slaving Interest in the Atlantic Ports, 1763–1792," *French Historical Studies* 7, no. 4 (1972), 529–43; Lynn Hunt, "The French Revolution in Global Context," in Armitage, *Age of Revolutions*, 26.

92. Hochschild, *Bury the Chains*, 256–58, 261, 268–79, 288–96; C.L.R. James, *The Black Jacobins* (1989), 90–93, 269–370; Philippe R. Girard, "'Liberté, Égalité, Esclavage,'" *French Colonial History* 6 (2005), 55–77.

93. Esdaile, *Napoleon's Wars*, 314–24, 418–28, 440–48, 479; Lynn, "States in Conflict," 204–5; Doyle, *French Revolution*, 356–60; Ellis, *Napoleonic Empire*, 57, 79, 85–87, 102–6, 123.

94. François Crouzet, "Wars, Blockade, and Economic Change in Europe, 1792–1815," *Journal of Economic History* 24, no. 4 (1964), 567–88; Lynn, "States in Conflict," 203–4.

95. Michael V. Leggiere, "From Berlin to Leipzig," *Journal of Military History* 67, no. 1 (2003), 41–44; Hans A. Schmitt, "Germany without Prussia," *German Studies Review* 6, no. 1 (1983), 9–39.

96. Leggiere, "From Berlin to Leipzig," 39–84; von Wartenburg, *Napoleon*, vol. 2, 318–69.

97. Esdaile, *Napoleon's Wars*, 532–65; Lynn, "States in Conflict," 208; Clodfelter, *Warfare*, 170–71; Crouzet, "Second Hundred Years' War," 432–50.

98. Henry A. Kissinger, "The Congress of Vienna," *World Politics* 8, no. 2 (1956), 264–80; Richard Langhorne, "Reflections on the Significance of the Congress of Vienna," *Review of International Studies* 12, no. 4 (1986), 313–24.

99. Kenneth Morgan, *Slavery and the British Empire* (2007), 174–75; T.C. Hansard, *The Parliamentary Debates from the Year 1803 to the Present Time*, vol. 32 (1816), 200–201, vol. 27 (1818), 232–34.

100. Immanuel Wallerstein, "The Congress of Vienna from 1763 to 1833," *Review (Fernand Braudel Center)* 36, no. 1 (2013), 1–24; Esdaile, *Napoleon's Wars*, 560–65; Bayly, *Imperial Meridian*, 3; Clodfelter, *Warfare*, 170–72.

101. Paul Gordon Lauren, *The Evolution of Human Rights* (2011), 74–75.

102. Boxer, *Dutch*, 101–5, 114.

Chapter 4: Britannia Rules the Waves

1. Dale T. Graden and Paulo Cesar Oliveira de Jesus, "The *Bella Miquelina* Affair," *Atlantic Studies* 13, no. 4 (2017), 196–215; Christopher Lloyd, *The Navy and the Slave Trade* (1968), 141–42; Siân Rees, *Sweet Water and Bitter* (2011), 260–61, 278–80; Herbert S. Klein, *The Atlantic Slave Trade* (2010), 139; "Our History," Wilson Sons, https://www.wilsonsons.com.br/en/grupo/our-history. In the 1840s, Bahia was still an alternate name for the city of Salvador, as seen in Henry S. Tanner, *New Universal*

Atlas (1846), 40, https://www.loc.gov/resource/g5400.br000011
/?r=-0.304,0,1.608,1.242,0.

2.   Graden, "The *Bella Miquelina* Affair," 197–202; Roquinaldo Ferreira
      and Tatiana Seijas, "The Slave Trade to Latin America," in Alejandro de
      la Fuente and George Reid Andrews, eds., *Afro-Latin American Studies*
      (2018), 38.

3.   Rudyard Kipling, "Recessional" (1897), in *A Choice of Kipling's Verse
      Made by T.S. Eliot* (1943), https://www.poetryfoundation.org/
      poems/46780/recessional.

4.   C.A. Bayly, *Imperial Meridian* (1989), 3, 16–17, 72–73, 102.

5.   Bayly, *Imperial Meridian*, 72–73, 104–5, 110–11, 121, 194–95; Vincent
      T. Harlow, *The Founding of the Second British Empire, 1763–1793*, vol. 1
      (1952), 4, 9.

6.   Michael D. Bordo et al., "Is Globalization Today Really Different than
      Globalization a Hundred Years Ago?," NBER Working Paper No. 7195,
      National Bureau of Economic Research (May 1999), https://eml.berkeley.
      edu/~eichengr/research/brooking.pdf; Martin Thomas and Andrew
      Thompson, "Empire and Globalisation," *International History Review* 36,
      no. 1 (2014), 142–70; Bayly, *Imperial Meridian*, 99.

7.   Jürgen Osterhammel, *The Transformation of the World* (2014), 651–52.

8.   Vaclav Smil, *Energy Transitions* (2017), 38–39, 43, 66–67, 101–3.

9.   On Barak, "Outsourcing," *International Journal of Middle East Studies* 47,
      no. 3 (2015), 425–45; Osterhammel, *Transformation*, 655.

10.   Ulbe Bosma and Roger Knight. "Global Factory and Local Field,"
      International Review of Social History 49, no. 1 (2004), 1–25; Richard
      B. Sheridan, "Changing Sugar Technology and the Labour Nexus in
      the British Caribbean, 1750–1900," *New West Indian Guide* 63, nos.
      1/2 (1989), 59–93; G. Roger Knight, *Sugar, Steam and Steel* (2014),
      11–31; O.H. Spate, "Beginnings of Industrialization in Burma," *Economic
      Geography* 17, no. 1 (1941), 75–92; Osterhammel, *Transformation*, 657;
      US Census Bureau, *Abstract of the Twelfth Census of the United States,
      1902* (1902), 330.

11.   Astrid Kander et al., *Power to the People* (2013), 176–79, 200–203;
      Agamemnon (1865), passenger/cargo vessel, National Maritime Museum
      (SLR0052), https://collections.rmg.co.uk/collections/objects/66013.
      html.

12.   J.M.W. Turner, *The Fighting Temeraire Tugged to Her Last Berth
      to Be Broken Up, 1838*, painting, National Gallery, London
      (NG-524), https://www.nationalgallery.org.uk/paintings/

joseph-mallord-william-turner-the-fighting-temeraire; J.M.W. Turner, *Rain, Steam, and Speed—The Great Western Railway*, painting, National Gallery (NG-538), https://www.nationalgallery.org.uk/paintings/joseph-mallord-william-turner-rain-steam-and-speed-the-great-western-railway. Both viewed at the National Gallery, London, 7/20/2019.

13. Andreas Malm, *Fossil Capital* (2016), 13; Kander, *Power*, 37; Paul J. Crutzen, "Geology of Mankind," *Nature* 415, no. 6867 (2002), 23; A.J. Stockwell, "Power, Authority, and Freedom," in P.J. Marshall, ed., *The Cambridge Illustrated History of the British Empire* (1996), 148–49; Svante Arrhenius, "On the Influence of Carbonic Acid in the Air upon the Temperature of the Ground," *London, Edinburgh and Dublin Philosophical Magazine and Journal of Science*, 5th ser., 41 (1896), 237–76; Rudy M. Baum Sr., "Future Calculation," *Distallations* (7/18/2016), https://www.sciencehistory.org/distillations/magazine/future-calculations.

14. David Steele, "Temple, Henry John, third Viscount Palmerston (1784–1865)," *Oxford Dictionary of National Biography* (5/21/2009), https://www.oxforddnb.com/view/10.1093/ref:odnb/9780198614128.001.0001/odnb-9780198614128-e-27112.

15. Timothy H. Parsons, *The British Imperial Century, 1815–1914* (2019), 22–28; John J. Mearsheimer, *The Tragedy of Great Power Politics* (2001), 220; Bayly, *Imperial Meridian*, 9.

16. Parsons, *British Imperial Century*, 28–34; Jane Burbank and Frederick Cooper, *Empires in World History* (2010), 288; John Darwin, *Unfinished Empire* (2012), 90, 390–94; O.P. Austin, *Colonial Administration, 1800–1900* (1903), 1199–1200, 1497.

17. Timothy H. Parsons, *The Second British Empire* (2014), 32; Darwin, *Unfinished Empire*, 182–85.

18. Smil, *Energy*, 43; Kander, *Power*, 256–58, 261–64; "Petroleum and Sea Power," American Oil and Gas Historical Society (6/28/2020), https://aoghs.org/petroleum-in-war/petroleum-and-sea-power/; Alexander Melamid, "The Geographical Pattern of Iranian Oil Development," *Economic Geography* 35, no. 3 (1959), 199–218; Erik J. Dahl, "Naval Innovation from Coal to Oil," *JFQ* (Winter 2000–2001), 50–56.

19. Smil, *Energy*, 50–53; Kander, *Power to the People*, 266–68, 304–5; J.F. Wilson, *Ferranti and the British Electrical Industry, 1864–1930* (1988), 36–37.

20. Mearsheimer, *Tragedy*, 220; Parsons, *Second British Empire*, 31; Kander, *Power*, 267.

21. Piers Brendon, *The Decline and Fall of the British Empire, 1781–1997* (2010), 61.

22. Alan Knight, "Britain and Latin America," in Andrew Porter, ed., *The Oxford History of the British Empire*, vol. 3 (1999), 135–36; Robert G. Albion, "Capital Movement and Transportation," *Journal of Economic History* 11, no. 4 (1951), 361–74; Parsons, *British Imperial*, 25; Darwin, *Unfinished Empire*, 87.

23. Adam Smith, *An Inquiry into the Nature and Causes of the Wealth of Nations* (1776), book 4, chapter 8, 145; Jonathan Israel, *Democratic Enlightenment* (2011), 237–41.

24. Bayly, *Imperial Meridian*, 151–52, 235–38, 246–47; David Fieldhouse, "For Richer, for Poorer," in Marshall, *Cambridge Illustrated History*, 108–9.

25. Sir John Strachey, *India, Its Administration and Progress* (1903), 133–42; Nancy Gardner Cassels, *Social Legislation of the East India Company* (2010), 303–15; J.F. Richards, "The Indian Empire and Peasant Production of Opium in the Nineteenth Century," *Modern Asian Studies* 15, no. 1 (1981), 66–76.

26. Michael Greenberg, *British Trade and the Opening of China 1800–42* (1951), 109–10.

27. Tan Chung, "The Britain-China-India Trade Triangle, 1771–1840," *Indian Economic and Social History Review* 11, no. 4 (1974), 411–31; Richards, "Indian Empire," 67–69.

28. Charles C. Stelle, "American Trade in Opium to China in the Nineteenth Century," *Pacific Historical Review* 9, no. 4 (1940), 427–42; Greenberg, *British Trade*, 127, 221; David Edward Owen, *British Opium Policy in China and India* (1934), 105–8, 113–45; Richards, "Indian Empire," 65; International Opium Commission, *Report of the International Opium Commission: Shanghai China, February 1 to February 26, 1909* (1909), 44–66.

29. Owen, *British Opium*, 146–89; Darwin, *Unfinished Empire*, 123.

30. Tan, "Trade Triangle," 426–27.

31. Robert C. Allen, "The Industrial Revolution in Miniature," *Journal of Economic History* 69, no. 4 (2009), 901–27; Eric R. Wolf, *Europe and the People without History* (2010), 273–74.

32. Smil, *Energy*, 13, 66–67.

33. Richard Brown, *Society and Economy in Modern Britain 1700–1850* (1991), 43–69; Thomas H. Marshall, *James Watt, 1736–1819* (1925), chapter 8.

34. Edward Baines, *History of the Cotton Manufacture in Great Britain* (1835), 199–207; H.B. Rodgers, "The Lancashire Cotton Industry in 1840," *Transactions and Papers (Institute of British Geographers)* 28 (1960), 135–53; Indrajit Ray, "Identifying the Woes of the Cotton Textile Industry in Bengal," *Economic History Review* 62, no. 4 (2009), 857–92; Wolf, *Europe*, 273–74; Brown, *Society*, 86; Theo Balderston, "The Economics of Abundance," *Economic History Review* 63, no. 3 (2010), 569–90; Malm, *Fossil Capital*, 56, 69–70, 75, 80, 150–51, 252.

35. Gene Dattel, "When Cotton Was King," *NYT*, 3/26/2011, https://opinionator.blogs.nytimes.com/2011/03/26/when-cotton-was-king/; R. Arthur Arnold, *The History of the Cotton Famine* (1865), 36–37; Wolf, *Europe*, 278–85; William J. Phalen, *The Consequences of Cotton in Antebellum America* (2014), 174–75; Brown, *Society*, 172–73; Ethan Davis, "An Administrative Trail of Tears," *American Journal of Legal History* 50, no. 1 (2008), 49–100.

36. Wolf, *Europe*, 282–84.

37. Robert W. Fogel and Stanley L. Engerman, *Time on the Cross* (1974), 5, 209; Tomas Weiss, "Time on the Cross," *EH Net*, 11/15/2001, https://web.archive.org/web/20111220190203/http://eh.net/node/2749; Alfred H. Conrad and John R. Meyer, "The Economics of Slavery in the Ante Bellum South," *Journal of Political Economy* 66, no. 2 (1958), 95–130; Richard Sutch, "The Profitability of Ante Bellum Slavery: Revisited," *Southern Economic Journal* 31, no. 4 (1965), 365–77; James D. Foust and Dale E. Swan, "Productivity and Profitability of Antebellum Slave Labor: A Micro-Approach," *Agricultural History* 44, no. 1 (1970), 39–62.

38. Guy Gugliotta, "New Estimate Raises Civil War Death Toll," *NYT*, 4/2/2012, https://www.nytimes.com/2012/04/03/science/civil-war-toll-up-by-20-percent-in-new-estimate.html.

39. Kenneth Morgan, *Slavery and the British Empire* (2007), 148–71; Adam Hochschild, *Bury the Chains* (2005), 72–78, 85–105, 306–8; Israel, *Democratic Enlightenment*, 229, 241; P. J. Marshall, "1783–1870," in Marshall, *Cambridge Illustrated History*, 44.

40. Lloyd, *Navy*, 67; W.E.F. Ward, *The Royal Navy and the Slavers* (1969), 43–44, 46–47, 62–63, 99–101, 127, 129–33, 138–51, 162–66.

41. Leslie Bethell, "The Mixed Commissions for the Suppression of the Transatlantic Slave Trade in the Nineteenth Century," *Journal of African History* 7, no. 1 (1966), 79–93; Morgan, *Slavery*, 158–59; Ward, *Royal Navy*, 182; Padriaic X. Scanlan, *Freedom's Debtors* (2017), 3, 102–7, 169–70; Lloyd, *Navy*, 79–81; Royal Naval Museum, "Chasing

Freedom Information Sheet," http://www.royalnavalmuseum.org/ visit_see_victory_cfexhibition_infosheet.htm; Marcel van der Linden, "Introduction," in Marcel van der Linden, ed., *Humanitarian Intervention and Changing Labor Relations* (2011), 13; Christopher Leslie Brown, "The Abolition of the Slave Trade," in Gad Heuman and Trevor Burnard, eds., *The Routledge History of Slavery* (2011), 287–92; Rees, *Sweet Water*, 308; Klein, *Atlantic Slave Trade*, 194–95.

42.   Donald L. Canney, *Africa Squadron* (2006), 117, 215–16, 233–34; Ward, *Royal Navy*, 222; Ron Soodalter, "The Limits of Lincoln's Mercy," *NYT*, 2/23/2012, https://opinionator.blogs.nytimes.com/2012/02/23/the-limits-of-lincolns-mercy/; "The Execution of Gordon," *NYT,* 2/22/1862, https://www.nytimes.com/1862/02/22/archives/the-execution-of-gordon-scenes-incident-to-his-last-moments-attempt.html.

43.   Morgan, *Slavery*, 172–89.

44.   Seymour Drescher, *Abolition* (2009), 248–66; Morgan, *Slavery*, 127–45, 188–92, 197–98; Hochschild, *Bury the Chains*, 337–43.

45.   Brown, "Abolition," 287–92; Howard Hazen Wilson, "Some Principal Aspects of British Efforts to Crush the African Slave Trade, 1807–1929," *American Journal of International Law* 44, no. 3 (1950), 516–20; Lloyd, *Navy*, 139–48; Ward, *Royal Navy*, 205–19; Rees, *Sweet Water*, 295–308; Ferreira and Seijas, "Slave Trade," 39–40; Klein, *Atlantic Slave Trade*, 195; Roquinaldo Ferreira and Pablo Miguel Sierra Silva, "Portugal, Spain, and the Transatlantic Slave Trade," in Fernando Bouza et al., eds., *The Iberian World 1450–1820* (2020), 384.

46.   Richard B. Allen, "Suppressing a Nefarious Traffic," *William and Mary Quarterly* 66, no. 4 (2009), 873–94; Matthew S. Hopper, "East Africa and the End of the Indian Ocean Slave Trade," *Journal of African Development* 13, no. 1 (2011), 39–65.

47.   Hopper, "East Africa," 39–65; Wilson, "Some Principal," 520–23; Lloyd, *Navy*, 278.

48.   Philip J. Stern, *The Company-State* (2011), 207–14; Brendon, *Decline*, 98–99, 125–33.

49.   William Dalrymple, *The Last Mughal* (2008), 186–87, 394–402; Brendon, *Decline*, 133–40.

50.   David Cannadine, *Victorious Century* (2017), 375–76, 381; Brendon, *Decline*, 234–39; Darwin, *Unfinished Empire*, 204–5.

51.   Benedict William Ginsburg, "Steamship Lines," *Encyclopedia Britannica*, vol. 25 (1911), 850–60; Thomas, "Empire," 146.

52.   John Ambrose Fleming, "Telegraph," *Encyclopedia Britannica*, vol. 26

(1911), 510–41.

53.   Hugh Munro Ross, "Railways," *Encyclopedia Britannica*, vol. 22 (1911), 819–22.

54.   Niall Ferguson, *Empire* (2002), 201–4; Michael Lisle-Williams, "Merchant Banking Dynasties in the English Class Structure," *British Journal of Sociology* 35, no. 3 (1984), 333–62.

55.   Cannadine, *Victorious Century*, 193–94, 250–51, 257–60, 388–89, 491–93.

56.   Barbara Freese, *Coal* (2003), 99–101, 167–68; Cannadine, *Victorious Century*, 260–62, 274–82, 299, 491–93; Kander, *Power*, 61, 191.

57.   Fred T. Jane, *Jane's Fighting Ships* (1900), 68–70; Clark G. Reynolds, *Navies in History* (1998), 104–20.

58.   T.A. Heathcote, "The Army of British India," in David Chandler, ed., *The Oxford History of the British Army* (1994), 379; *World Almanac and Encyclopedia 1899* (1899), 342.

59.   Marshall, "1870–1918," in Marshall, *Cambridge Illustrated History*, 59–61, 64–67; Peter T. Marsh, "Chamberlain, Joseph [Joe] (1836–1914)," *Oxford Dictionary of National Biography* (10/3/2013), https://www.oxforddnb.com/view/10.1093/ref:odnb/9780198614128.001.0001/odnb-9780198614128-e-32350.

60.   Angus Maddison, *The World Economy* (2001), 97; Austin, *Colonial Administration,* 1497; D.K. Fieldhouse, *The Colonial Empires* (1982), 373; Rein Taagepera, "Expansion and Contraction Patterns of Large Polities," *International Studies Quarterly* 41, no. 3 (1997), 501–2; Darwin, *Unfinished Empire*, 11–12, 86–88; Parsons, *Second British Empire*, 11–13, 40–41.

61.   Antony Anghie, *Imperialism, Sovereignty and the Making of International Law* (2004), 58–60, 69, 83–84, 90–97; "General Act of the Berlin Conference on West Africa, 26 February 1885," *South African History Online*, https://www.sahistory.org.za/archive/general-act-berlin-conference-west-africa-26-february-1885.

62.   Caroli Linnaei, *Systema Naturae* (1748), Quadrupedia Anthropomorpha, 3; Stephen Jay Gould, "The Geometer of Race," *Discover* 15, no. 11 (1994), 64–69.

63.   Brendon, *Decline*, 149–52; Stephen Jay Gould, "The Great Physiologist of Heidelberg—Friedrich Tiedemann," *Natural History* 108, no. 6 (J1999), 26–36; Marshall, "Imperial Britain," in Marshall, *Cambridge Illustrated History*, 333; Stephen Jay Gould, *The Mismeasure of Man* (1996), 104–51, 176–263; Photograph of the Royal College of Surgeons, 1941, *The*

Last Tasmanian (produced by Tom Haydon, 1978); Doreen Carvajal, "Museums Confront the Skeletons in Their Closets," *NYT*, 5/24/2013, https://www.nytimes.com/2013/05/25/arts/design/museums-move-to-return-human-remains-to-indigenous-peoples.html; Emily S. Renschler and Janet Monge, "The Samuel George Morton Cranial Collection," *Expedition* 50, no. 3 (2008), 30-38 .

64. Charles Darwin, *Journal of Researches into the Natural History and Geology of the Countries Visited during the Voyage of H.M.S. Beagle round the World* (1845), 435; Tony Barta, "Mr. Darwin's Shooters," *Patterns of Prejudice* 39, no. 2 (2005), 116–37.

65. Gould, *Mismeasure*, 142–48; Parsons, *Second British Empire*, 8–9; Stockwell, "Power," 173.

66. Richard B. Woodbury and Nathalie F.S. Woodbury, "The Rise and Fall of the Bureau of American Ethnology," *Journal of the Southwest* 41, no. 3 (1999), 283–96; Nancy J. Parezo, "A 'Special Olympics,'" in Susan Brownell, ed., *The 1904 Anthropology Days and Olympic Games* (2008), 59–126; Mark Dyreson, "The 'Physical Value' of Races and Nations," in Brownell, *1904 Anthropology Days*, 127–55; W.J. McGee, "Report of the Department of Anthropology to Frederick J.V. Skiff, Director, Universal Exposition of 1904, Division of Exhibits," 5/10/1905, file series 3, subseries 11, Louisiana Purchase Exposition Collection, State Historical Society of Missouri, St. Louis.

67. Robert W. Rydell, *All the World's a Fair* (1987), 154–83; "The Evolution of the Filipino, as Shown in the Philippine Exhibit, World's Fair, St. Louis, U.S.A.," *World's Fair Bulletin* 5, no. 8 (1904), 53, https://dl.mospace.umsystem.edu/mu/islandora/object/mu:356701/datastream/JPG/view.

68. Jerry D. Moore, *Visions of Culture* (2009), 33–46.

69. Adam Hochschild, *King Leopold's Ghost* (1998), 21–32; Brendon, *Decline*, 159–62; "Sir Henry Morton Stanley," *Encyclopedia Britannica*, vol. 25 (1911), 778–81.

70. Brendon, *Decline*, 162–66; "Stanley," 778–81; Hochschild, *King*, 47–57.

71. "Stanley," 778–81; Hochschild, *King*, 47–72, 75–84; G. Macharia Munene, "The United States and the Berlin Conference on the Partition of Africa 1884–1885," *Transafrican Journal of History* 19 (1990), 73–79; G.N. Uzoigwe, "Reflections on the Berlin West Africa Conference, 1884–1885," *Journal of the Historical Society of Nigeria* 12, nos. 3/4 (1984), 12–14.

72. Hochschild, *King*, 84–87; Uzoigwe, "Reflections," 9–22; Charles H. Alexandrowicz, "The Juridical Expression of the Sacred Trust of

Civilization," *American Journal of International Law* 65, no. 1 (1971), 149–59; Cathal M. Doyle, *Indigenous Peoples, Title to Territory, Rights and Resources* (2014), 46–68.

73. Mark I. Choate, "New Dynamics and New Imperial Powers, 1876–1905," in Robert Aldrich and Kirsten Mckenzie, eds., *The Routledge History of Western Empires* (2014), 121–22, 126–27; Hochschild, *King*, 86–87.

74. Hochschild, *King*, 118–19, 123–25, 127, 137, 145, 148.

75. Adam Hochschild, "In the Heart of Darkness," *New York Review of Books* 52, no. 15 (10/6/2005), 39–42; Hochschild, *King*, 158–66, 232–33.

76. Antoine Mioche, "De Livingstone à Lavigerie," *Cahier Charles V* 46 (2009), 203–39; Samantha Travis, "Turning Points in Transnational Anti-Slavery Activism" (MA thesis, Tufts University, 2017), 44–78; Catherine Ann Cline, "The Church and the Movement for Congo Reform," *Church History* 32, no. 1 (1963), 46–56; David M. Gordon, "Slavery and Redemption in the Catholic Missions of the Upper Congo, 1878–1909," *Slavery and Abolition* 38, no. 3 (2017), 577–600; François Renault, *Cardinal Lavigerie* (1994), 367–85; "In Plurimis," Libreria Editrice Vaticana, http://www.vatican.va/content/leo-xiii/en/encyclicals/documents/hf_l-xiii_enc_05051888_in-plurimis.html; Paul Gordon Lauren, *The Evolution of Human Rights* (2011), 53.

77. Hochschild, *King*, 195–220, 235–52, 270–72; Cline, "Church," 48–49; Lauren, *Evolution*, 83–85.

78. Cline, "Church," 53–54; Arthur Vermeersch, *La Question Congolaise* (1906), 30–39, 47–54, 92–93, 142–92, 327–68.

79. Julia Seibert, "More Continuity Than Change?," in Marcel M. Linden and Magaly Rodriguez Garcia, eds., *On Coerced Labor* (2016), 369–86; Sven Van Melkebeke, "Coerced Coffee Cultivation and Rural Agency," in Linden, *Humanitarian*, 185–207.

80. Hochschild, *King*, 257–59, 279–83; Marlous van Waijenburg, "Financing the African Colonial State," *Journal of Economic History* 78, no. 1 (2018), 40–80.

81. Pim de Zwart and Jan Luiten van Zanden, "Labor, Wages, and Living Standards in Java, 1680–1914," *Journal of Economic History* 19, no. 3 (2015), 215–34; Van Waijenburg, "Financing," 40–80; Clifford Geertz, *Agricultural Involution* (1963), 52–53.

82. Linden, "Introduction," 30–32; Alec Gordon, "Contract Labour in Rubber Plantations," *Economic and Political Weekly* 36, no. 10 (2001), 847–60; Martin J. Murray, "'White Gold' or 'White Blood'?," *Journal of Peasant Studies* 19, nos. 3/4 (1992), 41–67; Pierre Brocheux, "Le

prolétariat des plantations d'hévéas au Vietnam Méridional," *Le Mouvement Social* 90 (1975), 55–86; Rana Behal and Prabhu Mohapatra, "'Tea Money versus Human Life,'" *Journal of Peasant Studies* 19, nos. 3/4 (1992), 142–72.

83. Burbank, *Empires*, 316.

84. Benjamin Madley, "From Africa to Auschwitz," *European History Quarterly* 35, no. 3 (July 2005), 429–64; Jürgen Zimmerer, "Colonialism and the Holocaust," in A. Dirk Moses, ed., *Genocide and Settler Society* (2004), 49–76.

85. Brendon, *Decline*, 144–45; Ferguson, *Empire*, 211; Darwin, *Unfinished Empire*, 136–44.

86. Ferguson, *Empire*, 238–39; Brendon, *Decline*, 146–47, 171–72, 178–83; J.G. Darwin, "Baring, Evelyn, First Earl of Cromer (1841–1917)," *Oxford Dictionary of National Biography* (1/3/2008), https://www.oxforddnb.com/view/10.1093/ref:odnb/9780198614128.001.0001/odnb-9780198614128-e-30583; Marshall, "1870–1918," 74; Fieldhouse, "For Richer," 115; Darwin, *Unfinished Empire*, 144–47.

87. Shula Marks and Stanley Trapido, "Rhodes, Cecil John (1853–1902)," *Oxford Dictionary of National Biography* (10/3/2013), https://www.oxforddnb.com/view/10.1093/ref:odnb/9780198614128.001.0001/odnb-9780198614128-e-35731.

88. Ferguson, *Empire*, 186–88, 190–92; Michael Clodfelter, *Warfare and Armed Conflicts* (2017), 208–9; Marks and Trapido, "Rhodes, Cecil John"; Marshall, "1870–1918," 73–74.

89. Keith Nelson, "Kitchener, Horatio Herbert, Earl Kitchener of Khartoum (1850–1916)," *Oxford Dictionary of National Biography* (1/6/2011), https://www.oxforddnb.com/view/10.1093/ref:odnb/9780198614128.001.0001/odnb-9780198614128-e-34341.

90. Brendon, *Decline*, 207–10; Ferguson, *Empire*, 221–26; Clodfelter, *Warfare*, 203.

91. Brendon, *Decline*, 191–93; Ferguson, *Empire*, 226–36; Marks and Trapido, "Rhodes, Cecil John."

92. Brendon, *Decline*, 222–31; Clodfelter, *Warfare*, 210–12.

93. Ferguson, *Empire*, 229–36; Brendon, *Decline*, 228–30; Parsons, *Second British Empire*, 32.

94. Lauren, *Evolution*, 121.

95. Anna Chotzen, "Beyond Bounds," *Humanity* 5, no. 1 (2014), 33–54; C.R. Pennell, *A Country with a Government and a Flag* (1986), 83–89, 196–218; Clodfelter, *Warfare*, 354.

96. Andrew Stewart, *The First Victory* (2016), 12–13; Clodfelter, *Warfare*, 355.

97. Marshall, "1870–1918," 52–56.

98. Williamson A. Murray, "Towards World War, 1871–1914," in Parker, *Warfare*, 256–60; Holger H. Herwig, "The German Reaction to the Dreadnought Revolution," *International History Review* 13, no. 2 (1991), 273–83.

99. Paul G. Halpern, "Fisher, John Arbuthnot, First Baron Fisher (1841–1920)," *Oxford Dictionary of National Biography* (9/23/2010), https://www.oxforddnb.com/view/10.1093/ref:odnb/9780198614128.001.0001/odnb-9780198614128-e-33143; Herwig, "German Reaction," 277–83; Darwin, *Unfinished Empire*, 328–29.

100. C. Paul Vincent, *The Politics of Hunger* (1985), 141; Clodfelter, *Warfare*, 423–34; Williamson A. Murray, "The West at War, 1914–18," in Parker, *Warfare*, 282–83; Holger H. Herwig, "The Failure of German Sea Power, 1914–1945," *International History Review* 10, no. 1 (1988), 82–85, 103.

101. Clodfelter, *Warfare*, 423–34; Murray, "The West at War, 1914–18," 387–423; Eugene Rogan, *The Fall of the Ottomans* (2015), 79–90.

102. Parsons, *Second British Empire*, 54–55; Clodfelter, *Warfare*, 430–32.

103. Giselher Wirsing et al., *The War in Maps 1939–40* (1941), 8–19, 54–57.

104. Arthur B. Ferguson, "The AAF in the Battle of the Atlantic," in Wesley Frank Craven and James Lea Cate, eds., *The Army Air Forces in World War II*, vol. 1 (1983), 514–53; Williamson A. Murray, "The World in Conflict, 1919–41," in Parker, *Warfare*, 310–11; Williamson A. Murray, "The World at War, 1941–45," in Parker, *Warfare*, 324–25; "Major British and Dominion Warship Losses in World War 2," Naval History Home Page, National Museum of the Royal Navy, http://www.naval-history.net/WW2aBritishLosses10tables.htm.

105. Vincent O'Hara and Enrico Cernuschi, "The Other Ultra," *Naval War College Review* 66, no. 3 (2013), 117–138; Melamid, "Geographical Pattern," 201, 213; Danny M. Johnson, "The Persian Gulf Command and the Lend-Lease Mission to the Soviet Union during World War II," *On Point* 20, no. 2 (2014), 6–13; Darwin, *Unfinished Empire*, 338–39.

106. Clodfelter, *Warfare*, 472–73.

107. Paul Gordon Lauren, "Human Rights in History," *Diplomatic History* 2, no. 3 (1978), 257–78; Lauren, *Evolution*, 102–7, 116–29; Andrew J. Crozier, "The Establishment of the Mandates System 1919–25," *Journal of Contemporary History* 14, no. 3 (1979), 483–513; Kendrick

A. Clements, *The Presidency of Woodrow Wilson* (1992), 172–202; Anghie, *Imperialism*, 136–56; James Brown Scott, *The Spanish Origin of International Law* (2000), 286–87; Becky Little, "How Woodrow Wilson Tried to Reverse Black American Progress," *History.com*, (7/12/2020), https://www.history.com/news/woodrow-wilson-racial-segregation-jim-crow-ku-klux-klan; John Milton Cooper Jr. "Wilson and Race," *Princeton Alumni Weekly*, 12/2/2015, https://paw.princeton.edu/article/wilson-and-race-historians-perspective.

108.　Mark Mazower, *Hitler's Empire* (2008), 576–88.

109.　Henry J. Gwiazda II, "The Nazi Racial War," *Polish Review* 59, no. 4 (2014), 45–72; Burbank, *Empires*, 404–6.

110.　Gwiazda, "Nazi Racial War," 45–72; Burbank, *Empires*, 404–6; Michael Berenbaum, "Holocaust," *Encyclopedia Britannica* (9/10/2020), https://www.britannica.com/event/Holocaust; "Introduction to the Holocaust," US Holocaust Memorial Museum (3/12/2018), https://encyclopedia.ushmm.org/content/en/article/introduction-to-the-holocaust.

111.　Louise Young, *Japan's Total Empire* (1998), 95–101, 147–49, 321–34, 362–73; A.J. Grajdanzev, "Japan's Co-Prosperity Sphere," *Pacific Affairs* 16, no. 3 (1943), 311–28.

112.　Paul Gordon Lauren, "First Principles of Racial Equality," *Human Rights Quarterly* 5, no. 1 (1983), 1–26.

113.　Gwiazda, "Nazi Racial War," 45–72; Mazower, *Hitler's Empire*, 2–8, 181–222, 298–312, 576–97; Berenbaum, "Holocaust."

114.　Clodfelter, *Warfare*, 526–29.

115.　Darwin, *Unfinished Empire*, 340, 351–52; Clodfelter, *Warfare*, 526–28; Geir Lundestad, "Empire by Invitation?," *Journal of Peace Research* 23, no. 3 (1986), 263–77; Parsons, *Second British Empire*, 116–17.

116.　Stewart Patrick, *Best Laid Plans* (2009), 299–300; Office of Public Affairs, "Bagby, Philip Haxal," *Biographic Register of the Department of State: April 1, 1949* (1949), 29.

117.　Patrick, *Best Laid Plans*, 200–201, 297–318, 330–31; Parsons, *Second British Empire*, 145–46.

118.　Bob Moore, "Dutch Decolonization," in Martin Thomas et al., eds., *Crises of Empire* (2008), 244–93; Christopher Bayly and Tim Harper, *Forgotten Wars* (2007), 193.

119.　Clodfelter, *Warfare*, 611–16.

120.　Anthony Clayton, *The Wars of French Decolonization* (1994), 79–87.

121.　Alistair Horne, *A Savage War of Peace* (2006), 28–43, 60–65.

122.　Horne, *Savage War*, 3–20, 349–72, 415–60, 480–504; Clodfelter,

Warfare, 548–51.

123. Brendon, *Decline*, 605; Parsons, *Second British Empire*, 115–18, 168; Bayly and Harper, *Forgotten Wars*, 95–98; Christopher Bayly and Tim Harper, *Forgotten Armies* (2004), 240–44.

124. Ian Talbot and Gurharpal Singh, *The Partition of India* (2009), 1–24; Parsons, *Second British Empire*, 120–21; P.J. Marshall, "1918 to the 1960s," in Marshall, *Cambridge Illustrated History*, 94, 98–100; Tapan Ryachaudhuri, "British Rule in India," in Marshall, *Cambridge Illustrated History*, 362–63; Burbank, *Empires*, 311.

125. Stanley A. Wolpert, *Shameful Flight* (2006), 1–11, 130–45, 163; Larry Collins and Dominique Lapierre, *Freedom at Midnight* (1997), 72; Bayly and Harper, *Forgotten Wars*, 284–301.

126. Parsons, *Second British Empire*, 123, 179, 185; Toyin Falola, "Africa," in Marshall, *Cambridge Illustrated History*, 348; Bayly and Harper, *Forgotten Wars*, 98–100, 408–9, 470–96.

127. Parsons, *Second British Empire*, 132, 138–40; Fieldhouse, "For Richer," 112–13; Darwin, *Unfinished Empire*, 356–57; Bayly and Harper, *Forgotten Wars*, 408–9.

128. John Darwin, "The Geopolitics of Decolonization," in Alfred W. McCoy et al., eds., *Endless Empire* (2012), 197–99; Darwin, *Unfinished Empire*, 342–43, 361–63.

129. Brendon, *Decline*, 551–74; Parsons, *Second British Empire*, 42, 79–81, 138–40, 154, 165–67, 177–78, 183–84, 186; W.T.W. Morgan, "The 'White Highlands' of Kenya," *Geographical Journal* 129, no. 2 (1963), 140–55; Ian Cobain and Peter Walker, "Secret Memo Gave Guidelines on Abuse of Mau Mau in 1950s," *Guardian*, 4/11/2011, https://www.theguardian.com/world/2011/apr/11/mau-mau-high-court-foreign-office-documents; Anthony Clayton, "Baring, (Charles) Evelyn, First Baron Howick of Glendale (1903–1973)," *Oxford Dictionary of National Biography* (9/28/2006), https://www.oxforddnb.com/view/10.1093/ref:odnb/9780198614128.001.0001/odnb-9780198614128-e-30789.

130. Brendon, *Decline*, 504.

131. Darwin, *Unfinished Empire*, 396.

132. Ferguson, *Empire*, 295–96.

133. Anthony Gorst and Lewis Johnman, *The Suez Crisis* (1997), 27–35, 38–39.

134. Ervand Abrahamian, *The Coup* (2013), 11–17, 74–79, 207–11; Brendon, *Decline*, 480–86, 491, 495–96.

135. D.R. Thorpe, *Eden* (2004), chapters 1, 3; D.R. Thorpe, "Eden (Robert) Anthony, First Earl of Avon (1897–1977)," *Oxford Dictionary of National*

Biography (5/19/2011), https://www.oxforddnb.com/view/10.1093/ref:odnb/9780198614128.001.0001/odnb-9780198614128-e-31060.

136. Alden Whitman, "Anthony Eden Is Dead at 79," *NYT*, 1/15/1977, https://www.nytimes.com/1977/01/15/archives/anthony-eden-is-dead-at-79-anthony-eden-although-typecast-for.html.

137. Brendon, *Decline*, 494–95.

138. Whitman, "Anthony Eden"; Cahal Milmo, "Churchill and Eden," *Independent*, 2/4/2008, http://www.independent.co.uk/news/uk/politics/churchill-and-eden-their-struggle-777683.html.

139. Gorst, *Suez Crisis*, 40–44.

140. Roger Hardy, "How Suez Made Nasser an Arab Icon," *BBC One Minute World News*, 7/25/2006, http://news.bbc.co.uk/2/hi/middle_east/5204490.stm; "Egypt, the Counterpuncher," *Time*, 8/27/1956.

141. Stephen Dorril, *MI6* (2002), 613; Gorst, *Suez Crisis*, 46–47; Andrew Roth, "Sir Anthony Nutting Obituary," *Guardian*, 2/25/1999, https://www.theguardian.com/news/1999/feb/26/guardianobituaries1.

142. Keith Kyle, *Suez* (2011) 138–39, 148–51, 218–19; Peter Wright, *Spycatcher* (1987), 84–85, 160–61; "Suez—The Missing Dimension," *Archive Hour*, BBC Radio 4, October 28, 2006, 20:02–21:00, https://www.nlpwessex.org/docs/BBCSuez.htm#MissingDimension.

143. David A. Nichols, *Eisenhower 1956* (2011), 170–75, 188–204; Kyle, *Suez*, 314–31, 589–91; Ian Black, "A Painful Lesson in Diplomacy," *Guardian*, 10/30/2006, https://www.theguardian.com/world/2006/oct/31/worlddispatch.egypt; Ian Black, "Secrets and Lies at the Heart of Britain's Middle Eastern Folly," *Guardian*, 7/11/2006, https://www.theguardian.com/uk/2006/jul/11/egypt.past.

144. Martin Bowman, *Cold War Jet Combat* (2016), 156–67; Kyle, *Suez*, 382–84.

145. Clodfelter, *Warfare*, 573; Nichols, *Eisenhower 1956*, 213.

146. Gorst, *Suez Crisis*, 126–33; Kyle, *Suez*, 464–71; Brendon, *Decline*, 499; Geoffrey Warner "Review Article," *International Affairs* 67, no. 2 (1991), 309–10; Thorpe, "Eden"; Darwin, *Unfinished Empire*, 361.

147. Derek Brown, "Suez and the End of Empire," *Guardian*, 3/14/2001, https://www.theguardian.com/politics/2001/mar/14/past.education1; James M. Boughton, "Was Suez in 1956 the First Financial Crisis of the Twenty-First Century?," *Finance and Development* 38, no. 3 (2001), http://www.imf.org/external/pubs/ft/fandd/2001/09/boughton.htm; Gorst, *Suez Crisis*, 137–46.

148. Kyle, *Suez*, 467–68; Wright, *Spycatcher*, 160–61.

149. Kyle, *Suez*, 518–19, 532–34; Laurie Milner, "The Suez Crisis," *BBC History*, 3/3/2011, http://www.bbc.co.uk/history/british/modern/suez_01.shtml; H.G.C. Matthew, "Macmillan, (Maurice) Harold, First Earl of Stockton (1894–1986)," *Oxford Dictionary of National Biography* (1/6/2011), https://www.oxforddnb.com/view/10.1093/ref:odnb/9780198614128.001.0001/odnb-9780198614128-e-40185.

150. Kyle, *Suez*, 488–92; "Suez Crisis: British, French Rush Warships to Area," *Universal International News*, 1956, https://www.youtube.com/watch?v=4qA0Ffbljt8; Brendon, *Decline*, 499.

151. Warner, "Review Article," 316; Parsons, *Second British Empire*, 87.

152. Parsons, *Second British Empire,* 145–46, 171–72, 184–86; Darwin, *Unfinished Empire*, 378–80.

153. H.J. Mackinder, "The Geographical Pivot of History (1904)," *Geographical Journal* 170, no. 4 (2004), 309-11; H.J. Mackinder, *Democratic Ideals and Reality* (1919), 67.

154. Clodfelter, *Warfare*, 430, 527; World Health Organization, "Ten Things You Need to Know about Pandemic Influenza (Update of 14 October 2005)," *Weekly Epidemiological Record* 80, nos. 49/50 (12/9/2005), 428–31; "Worldwide Deaths in World War II," National World War II Museum, https://www.nationalww2museum.org/students-teachers/student-resources/research-starters/research-starters-worldwide-deaths-world-war.

155. Smil, *Energy*, 20, 152; Nicola Jones, "How the World Passed a Carbon Threshold and Why It Matters," *Yale Environment 360* (1/26/2017), https://e360.yale.edu/features/how-the-world-passed-a-carbon-threshold-400ppm-and-why-it-matters; Chris Mooney, "Earth's Atmosphere Just Crossed Another Troubling Climate Change Threshold," *WP*, 5/3/2018, https://www.washingtonpost.com/news/energy-environment/wp/2018/05/03/earths-atmosphere-just-crossed-another-troubling-climate-change-threshold/; Hannah Ritchie and Max Roser, "Co2 and Greenhouse Gas Emissions," *Our World in Data*, (2019), https://ourworldindata.org/co2-and-other-greenhouse-gas-emissions#how-have-global-co2-emissions-changed-over-time.

Chapter 5: Pax Americana

1.   "Theodore Roosevelt's Speech to the Great White Fleet, February 1909," Theodore Roosevelt Center, http://www.theodorerooseveltcenter.org/Research/Digital-Library/Record.aspx?libID=o283081.

2.   Michael J. Crawford, "Overview," in Michael J. Crawford, ed., *The World*

Cruise of the Great White Fleet, (2008), 2–3.

3. Eleanor Roosevelt, "The Struggle for Human Rights," 9/28/1948, https:// erpapers.columbian.gwu.edu/struggle-human-rights-1948.

4. "Mrs. Roosevelt Scored," *NYT*, 10/25/1948, https://www.nytimes. com/1948/10/25/archives/mrs-roosevelt-scored-soviet-organ-holds-her-antirussian-and.html; John Kenton, "Human Rights Declaration Adopted by U.N. Assembly," *NYT*, 12/11/1948, https://www.nytimes. com/1948/12/11/archives/human-rights-declaration-adopted-by-un-assembly-un-votes-accord-on.html.

5. Kenton, "Human Rights"; Richard N. Gardner, "Eleanor Roosevelt's Legacy," *NYT*, 12/10/1988, https://www.nytimes.com/1988/12/10/ opinion/eleanor-roosevelt-s-legacy-human-rights.html.

6. Daniel J. Sargent, *A Superpower Transformed* (2015), 68–99, 198–228.

7. Philip C. Jessup, *Elihu Root* (1938).

8. Richard W. Leopold, *Elihu Root and the Conservative Tradition* (1954), 12–19.

9. Warren Zimmermann, *First Great Triumphs* (2002), 129–31, 134–42.

10. Stephen Skowronek, *Building a New American State* (1982), 26, 45–56; Walter Isaacson and Evan Thomas, *The Wise Men* (1986), 179–80.

11. Zimmermann, *First Great Triumphs*, 148, 411–12, 417; Leopold, *Elihu Root*, 24–46.

12. William J. Johnston, "The Pan-American Conference and the Cuban Crisis," *NYT*, 9/23/1906, https://timesmachine.nytimes.com/ timesmachine/1906/09/23/101799110.html?pageNumber=36; Leopold, *Elihu Root*, 53–69; Frederick W. Marks, *Velvet on Iron* (1979), 203; Jessup, *Elihu Root, vol. 1, 1845–1909*, 474–92; Vredespaleis, "Verede Door Recht," https://www.vredespaleis.nl/; Stephen Barcroft, "The Hague Peace Conference of 1899," *Irish Studies in International Affairs* 3, no. 1 (1989), 55–68; David D. Caron, "War and International Adjudication," *American Journal of International Law* 94, no. 1 (2000), 4–30; George H. Aldrich, and Christine M. Chinkin, "A Century of Achievement and Unfinished Work," *American Journal of International Law* 94, no. 1 (2000), 90–98.

13. Leopold, *Elihu Root*, 67, 161–64; "Elihu Root—Biographical," Nobel Prize official website, http://www.nobelprize.org/nobel_prizes/peace/ laureates/1912/root-bio.html.

14. Courtney Johnson, "Understanding the American Empire," in Alfred W. McCoy and Francisco Scarano, eds., *Colonial Crucible* (2009), 175–90; "Dr. Paul S. Reinsch Dies in Shanghai," *NYT*, 1/26/1923, https:// timesmachine.nytimes.com/timesmachine/1923/01/26/105843680.

html?pageNumber=17; Jessup, *Elihu Root, vol. 2, 1905–1937*, 416–17, 486–93.

15.   Caron, "War," 13, 30.
16.   David Milne, *Worldmaking* (2015), 22–52.
17.   Alfred Thayer Mahan, *Influence of Seapower upon History, 1660–1783* (1957), 71–72.
18.   H.W. Brands, *T.R.* (1997), 236–38.
19.   James A. Field Jr., "American Imperialism," *American Historical Review* 83, no. 3 (1978), 652–53; Milne, *Worldmaking*, 32–33.
20.   John J. Mearsheimer, *The Tragedy of Great Power Politics* (2001), 220.
21.   George W. Baer, *One Hundred Years of Sea Power* (1994), 21–22, 30–33; Mike McKinley, "Narrative," in Crawford, *World Cruise*, 34–35.
22.   A.T. Mahan, *The Interest of America in Sea Power, Present and Future* (1898), 12–13, 59–104.
23.   Victor Bulmer-Thomas, *Empire in Retreat* (2018), 103–7, 121, 133–35.
24.   David McCullough, *The Path between the Seas* (1977), 381, 442, 496–98, 530–31, 537, 546–49.
25.   Bulmer-Thomas, *Empire in Retreat*, 107–25.
26.   Alfred Thayer Mahan, "The United States Looking Outward," *Atlantic Monthly* (December 1890), http://www.theatlantic.com/magazine/ archive/1890/12/the-united-states-looking-outward/306348/.
27.   James C. Thompson et al., *Sentimental Imperialists* (1982), 103–4, 111, 136; Brands, *T.R.*, 238, 308–9, 325–29.
28.   Michael Clodfelter, *Warfare and Armed Conflicts* (2017), 240–41.
29.   Joseph R. Morgan et al., "Pacific Ocean," *Encyclopedia Britannica* (1/28/2021), https://www.britannica.com/place/Pacific-Ocean.
30.   William E. Berry Jr., "American Military Bases in the Philippines, Base Negotiations, and Philippine-American Relations" (PhD dissertation, Cornell University, 1981), 21–25.
31.   Thompson, *Sentimental Imperialists*, 140–43; Berry, "American Military Bases in the Philippines," 27–28.
32.   Louis Morton, "War Plan Orange," *World Politics* 11, no. 2 (1959), 221–25.
33.   Morton, "War Plan Orange," 227–31; H.P. Wilmott, *Empires in the Balance* (1982), 108–9.
34.   Morton, "War Plan Orange," 231.
35.   David F. Schmitz, *Henry L. Stimson* (2001), 1–12; Isaacson, *Wise Men*, 180–83.
36.   Memorandum from Robert A. Lovett to Secretary of War Henry

L. Stimson, March 10, 1941, US National Archives and Records Administration, RG 107, Stimson "Safe File," box 1.

37. Michael S. Sherry, *The Rise of American Air Power* (1987), 103–8.

38. Berry, "American Military," 80–81.

39. Henry L. Stimson, "Diary," 10/21/1941, Yale University Archives, 149–50.

40. Stimson, "Diary," 12/31/1941, 160.

41. Peter Calvocoressi et al., *Total War*, vol. 2 (1989), 940–1013; Daniel Yergin, *The Prize* (2009), 291–300.

42. Calvocoressi, *Total War*, 953–55.

43. Calvocoressi, *Total War*, 940–59; Yergin, *The Prize*, 309–10; Clodfelter, *Warfare*, 523–29.

44. Louis Morton, *The Fall of the Philippines* (1953), 77–144; Calvocoressi, *Total War*, 978–98; Winston Churchill, *The Hinge of Fate* (1951), 43.

45. Calvocoressi, *Total War*, 975–1013.

46. Kramer J. Rohfleisch, "Drawing the Battle Line in the Pacific," in Wesley Frank Craven and James Lea Cate, eds., *The Army Air Forces in World War II*, vol. 1 (1983), 427–70; Paul S. Dull, *A Battle History of the Imperial Japanese Navy* (1978), 151–79.

47. James A. Knortz, *The Strategic Leadership of Chester W. Nimitz* (2012), 4–18, https://apps.dtic.mil/dtic/tr/fulltext/u2/a561569.pdf.

48. David C. Evans and Mark R. Peattie, *Kaigun* (2012), 24–25, 134–35, 139–40, 514–16.

49. Clay Blair Jr., *Silent Victory* (1975), 17–18, 359–60, 474–75, 486–93, 551–54, 609–12, 816–19; Yergin, *The Prize*, 337–46; Clodfelter, *Warfare*, 523–24.

50. William W. Ralph, "Improvised Destruction," *War in History* 13, no. 4 (2006), 495–522; Sherry, *Air Power*, 264–82, 311–15; Clodfelter, *Warfare*, 525.

51. Ralph, "Improvised Destruction," 517–22; Clodfelter, *Warfare*, 525–26.

52. Clodfelter, *Warfare*, 523–34.

53. Stewart Patrick, *The Best Laid Plans* (2009), 199–200.

54. Letter from Major General Thomas T. Handy, Assistant Chief of Staff, Operations Division, War Department General Staff to Secretary of War, 11/81943, US National Archives and Records Administration, RG 107, Box 11, Entry 74-A, Secretary of War "Safe File," July 1940 – September 1945.

55. Theodore Friend, *Between Two Empires* (1965), 235–37; Stephen Rosskamm Shalom, *The United States and the Philippines* (1981), 59–60.

56. Stimson, "Diary," 4/17/1945, 46–47.

57. William E. Berry Jr., *U.S. Bases in the Philippines* (1989), 32–37, 47–57.

58. North Atlantic Treaty Organization, "The Atlantic Charter, August 14, 1941," NATO, https://www.nato.int/cps/en/natohq/official_texts_16912.htm; Paul Gordon Lauren, "First Principles of Racial Equality," *Human Rights Quarterly* 5, no. 1 (1983), 3–4.

59. Lauren, "First Principles," 5.

60. Clodfelter, *Warfare*, 526–29.

61. Sargent, *Superpower*, 15; "US Military by the Numbers," National World War II Museum, https://www.nationalww2museum.org/students-teachers/student-resources/research-starters/research-starters-us-military-numbers; "US Ship Force Levels: 1886–present," Naval History and Heritage Command, https://www.history.navy.mil/research/histories/ship-histories/us-ship-force-levels.html; "Airplanes on Hand in AAF, By Major Type: Jul 1939 to Aug 1945," Army Air Forces Statistical Digest—World War II, table 83, https://www.ibiblio.org/hyperwar/AAF/StatDigest/aafsd-3.html.

62. Patrick, *Best Laid Plans*, x–xiii.

63. Paul Gordon Lauren, *The Evolution of Human Rights* (2011), 160–64.

64. Lauren, *Evolution*, 172–89.

65. United Nations, *Charter of the United Nations and Statute of the International Court of Justice* (1945), http://www.un.org/en/sections/un-charter/un-charter-full-text/.

66. Lauren, *Evolution*, 187–89.

67. Lauren, *Evolution*, 213–14; David Sloss, "How International Human Rights Transformed the U.S. Constitution," *Santa Clara Law Digital Commons* (2015), 16–25; Mark Philip Bradley, *The World Reimagined* (2016), 86–91, 93–95, 99–112.

68. G. John Ikenberry, "State Power and the Institutional Bargain," in Rosemary Foot et al., *US Hegemony and International Organizations* (2003), 49–56.

69. William I. Hitchcock, "The Marshall Plan and the Creation of the West," in Melvyn P. Leffler and Odd Arne Westad, eds., *The Cambridge History of the Cold War*, vol. 1 (2010), 154–76.

70. Nicholas Kristof, "Why 2017 May Be the Best Year Ever," *NYT*, 1/21/2017, https://www.nytimes.com/2017/01/21/opinion/sunday/why-2017-may-be-the-best-year-ever.html; World Bank Group, *Piecing Together the Poverty Puzzle* (2019), 1–4, 22–24, https://openknowledge.worldbank.org/bitstream/handle/10986/30418/9781464813306.pdf; World Bank, "Nearly Half the World Lives on Less than $5.50 a Day" (10/17/2018),

https://www.worldbank.org/en/news/press-release/2018/10/17/nearly-half-the-world-lives-on-less-than-550-a-day.

71. Raymond Bonner, *Waltzing with a Dictator* (1987), 33; Christopher Simpson, *Science of Coercion* (1994), 3-14; Alfred W. McCoy, *Torture and Impunity* (2012), 16-113; Alfred W. McCoy, "Land Reform as Counter-Revolution," *Bulletin of Concerned Asia Scholars*, 3, no. 1 (1971), 14-49.

72. Bruce Cumings, *Dominion from Sea to Sea* (2009), 305–8, 420–28.

73. Alfred W. McCoy, *In the Shadows of the American Century* (2017), 52–55.

74. Sargent, *Superpower*, 17–19, 108–16; Livia Chitu et al., "When Did the Dollar Overtake Sterling as the Leading International Currency? Evidence from the Bond Markets," NBER Working Paper No. 18097, National Bureau of Economic Research (May 2012), https://www.nber.org/system/files/working_papers/w18097/w18097.pdf.

75. Cumings, *Dominion*, 393, 420–21.

76. Paul F. Braim, *The Will to Win* (2001), 5–7; Lawrence S. Wittner, *American Intervention in Greece, 1943–1949* (1982), 235–53; Svetozar Rajak, "The Cold War in the Balkans, 1945–1956," in Leffler, *Cold War*, vol. 2, 198–220. Robert B. Bruce, "Tethered Eagle," *Army History* 82 (2012), 6–29; William D. Harris Jr., *Instilling Aggressiveness* (2013), 67–100.

77. "Van Fleet Awardees," Korea Society, https://www.koreasociety.org/special-events/van-fleet-award.

78. Stephen E. Ambrose, *Eisenhower*, vol. 1 (1983), chapters 1, 2, 9; Stephen E. Ambrose, *Eisenhower: Soldier and President* (1990), 60–72.

79. Elliott V. Converse III, *History of Acquisition in the Department of Defense*, vol. 1 (2012), 457–64, 490–500, 522–30.

80. Office of Management and Budget, The White House, "Table 9.7 - Summary of Outlays for the Conduct of Research and Development: 1949–2021," *Historical Tables*, https://www.whitehouse.gov/omb/historical-tables/.

81. Michael J. Muolo, *Space Handbook*, vol. 1 (1998), 18.

82. Barry R. Posen, "Command of the Commons," *International Security* 28, no. 1 (2003), 8–9.

83. John Darwin, *After Tamerlane* (2009), 470; Milne, *Worldmaking*, 277–82.

84. Darwin, *After Tamerlane*, 470–71; "U.S. Has 300 Bases on Foreign Soil," *Chicago Daily Tribune*, 9/11/1954; Walter Trohan, "U.S. Strategy Tied to World Air Superiority," *Chicago Daily Tribune*, 2/14/1955.

85. Sargent, *Superpower*, 131–61, 287–89; Bulmer-Thomas, *Empire in Retreat*, 193–210.

86.   Vaclav Smil, *Energy Transitions* (2017), 116–24; Astrid Kander et al.,
      Power to the People (2013), 291–98; Jean-Paul Rodrigue, *The Geography of
      Transport Systems* (2017), 132–33; "Oil: Crude and Petroleum Products
      Explained," US Energy Information Administration (5/29/2019),
      https://www.eia.gov/energyexplained/oil-and-petroleum-products/
      imports-and-exports.php; Hannah Ritchie and Max Roser, "CO2 and
      Greenhouse Gas Emissions: Annual CO2 emissions by world region,"
      Our World in Data (2019), https://ourworldindata.org/co2-and-
      other-greenhouse-gas-emissions; David S. Painter, "Oil and the American
      Century," *Journal of American History* 99, no. 1 (2012), 24–39.

87.   Simon Bromley, "The United States and the Control of World Oil,"
      Government and Opposition 40, no. 2 (2005), 225–55; Joyce Dargay et
      al., "Vehicle Ownership and Income Growth, Worldwide: 1960–2030,"
      Energy Journal 28, no. 4 (2007), 143–70; Hannah Ritchie and Max Roser,
      Table: Global fossil fuel consumption, "Fossil Fuels," *Our World in Data*
      (2019), https://ourworldindata.org/fossil-fuels#citation; International
      Organization of Motor Vehicle Manufacturers, "World Vehicles in Use:
      All Vehicles," *Motorization Rate 2015—Worldwide*, http://www.oica.net/
      category/vehicles-in-use/; Painter, "Oil and the American Century," 33–36.

88.   Ronald Robinson, "Non-European Foundations of European
      Imperialism," in Roger Owen and Robert Sutcliffe, eds., *Studies in
      the Theory of Imperialism* (1972), 128–48; Brett Reilly, "Cold War
      Transition," in McCoy, *Colonial Crucible*, 344–59.

89.   McCoy, *Shadows*, 61–79.

90.   David F. Rudgers, "The Origins of Covert Action," *Journal of
      Contemporary History* 35, no. 2 (2000), 253–59; Tim Weiner, *Legacy of
      Ashes* (2008), 624–25.

91.   Weiner, *Legacy of Ashes*, 29–31, 48–54; Daniele Ganser, *NATO's
      Secret Armies* (2005), 1–37, 63–83, 84–102; Daniele Ganser, "Beyond
      Democratic Checks and Balances," in Eric Wilson, ed., *Government of the
      Shadows* (2009), 256–75.

92.   Dov H. Levin, "Partisan Electoral Interventions by the Great Powers,"
      Conflict Management and Peace Science 36, no. 1 (2016), 88–106;
      Chalmers Johnson et al., "The CIA and Japanese Politics," *Asian
      Perspective* 24, no. 4 (2000), 79–103.

93.   Robert Kagan, *The World America Made* (2012), 23–24; Weiner, *Legacy of
      Ashes*, 29–30, 39–40, 44–54, 61–70, 84–87, 92–105, 157, 133–40, 142,
      187–89, 321–23, 717; Samuel P. Huntington, *The Third Wave* (1991),
      16–21.

94.   Madeline G. Kalb, "The C.I.A. and Lumumba," *NYT*, 8/2/1981, https://www.nytimes.com/1981/08/02/magazine/the-cia-and-lumumba.html; Ed Pilkington, "Suleimani Killing the Latest in a Long Grim Line of US Assassination Efforts," *Guardian*, 1/4/2020, https://www.theguardian.com/us-news/2020/jan/04/us-political-assassinations-history-iran-suleimani; Nicholas M. Horrock, "C.I.A. Is Reported to Have Helped in Trujillo Death," *NYT*, 6/13/1975, https://www.nytimes.com/1975/06/13/archives/cia-is-reported-to-have-helped-in-trujillo-death-material-support.html.

95.   Weiner, *Legacy of Ashes*, 32–33, 40–41, 628–29; Bulmer-Thomas, *Empire in Retreat*, 151–56.

96.   Mark Gasiorowski, "The 1953 Coup D'etat in Iran," *International Journal of Middle East Studies* 19, no. 3 (1987), 261–86; Mostafa T. Zahrani, "The Coup That Changed the Middle East," *World Policy Journal* 19, no. 2 (2002), 93–99; Stephen Schlesinger and Stephen Kinzer, *Bitter Fruit* (1982), 227–55; Piero Gleijeses, "Ships in the Night," *Journal of Latin American Studies* 27, no. 1 (1995), 1–42; Milne, *Worldmaking*, 293–95, 307–9.

97.   Richard A. Bitzinger, *Assessing the Conventional Balance in Europe, 1945–1975*, RAND Corporation (1989), 7, https://www.rand.org/content/dam/rand/pubs/notes/2007/N2859.pdf.

98.   Mike Bowker, "Brezhnev and Superpower Relations," in Edwin Bacon and Mark Sandle, eds., *Brezhnev Reconsidered* (2002), 95.

99.   Weiner, *Legacy of Ashes*, 48–54, 87.

100.   A.J. Langguth, "Torture's Teachers," *NYT*, 6/11/1979, https://www.nytimes.com/1979/06/11/archives/tortures-teachers.html; Alfred W. McCoy, *A Question of Torture* (2006), 60–108.

101.   John Ranelagh, *The Agency* (1986), 649–50.

102.   Amnesty International, *Amnesty International Briefing: Iran* (1976), 9.

103.   Reza Baraheni, "The Savak Documents," *The Nation* (2/23/1980), 198–202; James Risen, "How a Plot Convulsed Iran in '53 (and in '79)," *NYT*, 4/16/2000, https://www.nytimes.com/2000/04/16/world/secrets-history-cia-iran-special-report-plot-convulsed-iran-53-79.html.

104.   Walter LaFeber, *Inevitable Revolutions* (1993), 113–27, 166–72, 255–60; Duilia Mora Turner, "Violent Crime in Post–Civil War Guatemala," *Naval Postgraduate School* (2015), 1, 14–15; Anna Belinda Sandoval Girón, "Taking Matters into One's Hands," *Urban Anthropology and Studies of Cultural Systems and World Economic Development* 36, no. 4 (2007), 357–79.

105. Weiner, *Legacy of Ashes*, 207.

106. Andrew F. Krepinevich Jr., *The Army and Vietnam* (1986), 228–29; Ralph W. McGehee, *Deadly Deceits* (1983), 156; Clodfelter, *Warfare*, 700–3; Victor Marchetti and John D. Marks, *The CIA and the Cult of Intelligence* (1974), 246; Seymour M. Hersh, "Moving Targets," *New Yorker*, 12/7/2003, https://www.newyorker.com/magazine/2003/12/15/moving-targets; Felix Belair Jr., "U.S. Aide Defends Pacification Program in Vietnam Despite Killings of Civilians," *NYT*, 7/20/1971, https://www.nytimes.com/1971/07/20/archives/us-aide-defends-pacification-program-in-vietnam-despite-killings-of.html.

107. Ronald H. Spector, "The Vietnam War, 1954–1975," *Encyclopedia Britannica* (11/1/2019), https://www.britannica.com/event/Vietnam-War; McGehee, *Deadly Deceits*, 156.

108. Chris Hilton, *Shadow Play* (2003), 1 hr 19 mins, http://www.cultureunplugged.com/documentary/watch-online/play/52240/Shadow-Play; Vincent Bevins, "The 'Liberal World Order' Was Built with Blood," *NYT*, 5/29/2020, https://www.nytimes.com/2020/05/29/opinion/sunday/united-states-cold-war.html.

109. Sargent, *Superpower*, 48–67.

110. Sargent, *Superpower*, 30–31, 100–30, 161, 193–94, 240–50.

111. Norrie MacQueen, "Elusive Settlement," in Oliver Furley and Roy May, eds., *Ending Africa's War* (2006), 147; Lydia Polgreen, "Angolans Come Home to 'Negative Peace,'" *NYT*, 7/30/2003, https://www.nytimes.com/2003/07/30/world/angolans-come-home-to-negative-peace.html; "Tazara," *Railways Africa* 4 (2016), 6-13, https://issuu.com/railwaysafrica/docs/ra_4-2016_final/15; Davide Rampe, "Bush Pledges Angola Rebel Aid," *NYT* 1/12/1989, https://www.nytimes.com/1989/01/12/world/bush-pledges-angola-rebel-aid.html; Piero Gleijeses, "Moscow's Proxy? Cuba and Africa 1975–1988," *Journal of Cold War Studies* 8, no. 2 (2006), 3-51.

112. Peter Popham, "Taliban Is a 'Monster Hatched by the US,'" *Independent*, 4/21/2014, https://www.independent.co.uk/news/world/asia/taliban-is-a-monster-hatched-by-the-us-9272787.html; John Pilger, "The Colder War," *Counterpunch*, 1/31/2002, https://www.counterpunch.org/2002/01/31/the-colder-war/.

113. Charles G. Cogan, "Partners in Time," *World Policy Journal* 10, no. 2 (1993), 73–83; Central Intelligence Agency, Directorate of Intelligence, *The Costs of Soviet Involvement in Afghanistan* (1987), 5–7, https://www.cia.gov/readingroom/docs/CIA-RDP89T00296R000100040006-9.

pdf; Robert Pear, "Arming Afghan Guerrillas," *NYT*, 4/18/1988, https://timesmachine.nytimes.com/timesmachine/1988/04/18/821888.html?pageNumber=1; Serge Schmemann, "Gorbachev Says U.S. Arms Note Is Not Adequate," *NYT*, 2/26/1986, https://www.nytimes.com/1986/02/26/world/gorbachev-says-us-arms-note-is-not-adequate.html.

114.   McCoy, *Shadows*, 94–96.

115.   Tacitus, *Dialogus Agricola Germania* (1914), 219–21.

116.   Defense Secretary's Commission, *Base Realignments and Closures* (1988), 15; US Department of the Air Force, *United States Air Force Statistical Digest, FY 1998* (1999), 92; US General Accounting Office, *Navy Aircraft Carriers* (1998), 4.

117.   Office of Management and Budget, The White House, "Table 3.1: Outlays by Superfunction and Function: 1940–2025," *Historical Tables*, https://www.whitehouse.gov/omb/historical-tables/.

118.   US Secretary of Defense James Mattis, *Summary of the 2018 National Defense Strategy of the United States of America* (2018), 3, https://dod.defense.gov/Portals/1/Documents/pubs/2018-National-Defense-Strategy-Summary.pdf.

119.   Zbigniew Brzezinski, *The Grand Chessboard* (1998), 35, 39.

120.   Jeff Himmelman, "A Game of Shark and Minnow," *NYT*, 10/27/2013, http://www.nytimes.com/newsgraphics/2013/10/27/south-china-sea/index.html.

121.   Eric Heginbotham et al., *The U.S.-China Military Scorecard, Forces, Geography and the Evolving Balance of Power, 1996–2017*, RAND Corporation (2015), 36, https://www.rand.org/pubs/research_reports/RR392.html.

122.   Bulmer-Thomas, *Empire in Retreat*, 219–24; Farah Stockman, "The W.T.O. Is Having a Midlife Crisis," *NYT*, 12/17/2020, https://www.nytimes.com/2020/12/17/opinion/wto-trade-biden.html; Henry Veltmeyer, "Liberalisation and Structural Adjustment in Latin America," *Economic and Political Weekly* 28, no. 39 (1993), 2080–86; E. Borensztein and J. Ostrym, *Economic Reform and Structural Adjustment in East European Industry* (1994); Gavin Williams, "Why Structural Adjustment Is Necessary and Why It Doesn't Work," *Review of African Political Economy* 21, no. 60 (1994), 214–25; James Peck, *Ideal Illusions* (2010), 193–206.

123.   Nick Routley, "Mapped: The World's Network of Undersea Cables," *Business Insider*, 8/26/2017, https://www.businessinsider.com/

map-the-worlds-network-of-undersea-cables-2017-8/commerce-on-business-insider; "UCS Satellite Database," *Union of Concerned Scientists*, 1/1/ 2021, https://www.ucsusa.org/resources/satellite-database.

124. Richard Haass, "Present at the Disruption," *Foreign Policy* 99, no. 5 (2020), 24–34.

125. United Nations International Drug Control Programme, *Afghanistan: Annual Opium Poppy Survey 2001* (2001), iii, 11, 15–17, https://www.unodc.org/pdf/publications/report_2001-10-16_1.pdf; United Nations Office of Drugs and Crime, *World Drug Report 2018: Executive Summary* (2018), 8, https://www.unodc.org/wdr2018/prelaunch/WDR18_Booklet_1_EXSUM.pdf; Special Inspector General for Afghan Reconstruction, *Quarterly Report to the United States Congress* (2019), 49, 200–1, https://www.sigar.mil/pdf/quarterlyreports/2019-10-30qr.pdf; "Text: Bush Announces Strikes Against Taliban," *WP*, 10/7/2001, https://www.washingtonpost.com/wp-srv/nation/specials/attacked/transcripts/bushaddress_100801.htm; Brian Knowlton, "Rumsfeld Rejects Plan To Allow Mullah Omar 'To Live in Dignity'," *NYT*, 12/7/2001, https://www.nytimes.com/2001/12/07/news/rumsfeld-rejects-planto-allow-mullah-omar-to-live-in-dignity-taliban.html.

126. Amy Belasco, *The Cost of Iraq, Afghanistan, and Other Global War on Terror Operations Since 9/11* (2014), 10–11, 17, https://fas.org/sgp/crs/natsec/RL33110.pdf.

127. Joseph Goldstein, "Taliban Make Gains across 3 Provinces in Afghanistan," *NYT*, 7/28/2015, http://www.nytimes.com/2015/07/29/world/asia/taliban-make-gains-across-3-provinces-in-afghanistan.html.

128. Mathew Rosenberg, "Obama Is Rethinking Pullout in Afghanistan, Officials Say," *NYT*, 10/14/2015, https://www.nytimes.com/2015/10/14/world/asia/obama-is-rethinking-pullout-in-afghanistan-officials-say.html; Rod Nordland and Joseph Goldstein, "Afghan Taliban's Reach Is Widest Since 2001, U.N. Says," *NYT*, 10/11/2015, https://www.nytimes.com/2015/10/12/world/asia/afghanistan-taliban-united-nations.html; Mujib Mashal, "Taliban and U.S. Strike Deal to Withdraw American Troops from Afghanistan," *NYT*, 2/29/2020, https://www.nytimes.com/2020/02/29/world/asia/us-taliban-deal.html; Mujib Mashal, "How the Taliban Outlasted a Superpower," *NYT*, 5/26/2020, https://www.nytimes.com/2020/05/26/world/asia/taliban-afghanistan-war.html; David E. Sanger and Michael D. Shear, "Biden saying, it is 'time to end America's longest war,' declares troops will be out of Afghanistan by Sept. 11," *NYT*, 4/14/2021, https://

www.nytimes.com/2021/04/14/us/biden-afghanistan-troops.html; Carter Malkasian, "The Taliban Are Ready to Exploit America's Exit," *Foreign Affairs*, 4/14/2021, https://www.foreignaffairs.com/articles/ afghanistan/2021-04-14/taliban-are-ready-exploit-americas-exit?.

129. Craig Whitlock, "At War with the Truth," *WP*, 12/9/2019, https:// www.washingtonpost.com/graphics/2019/investigations/afghanistan- papers/afghanistan-war-confidential-documents/; "U.S. Costs To Date for the War in Afghanistan, 2001-2021," *Costs of War* (2021), https:// watson.brown.edu/costsofwar/figures/2021/human-and-budgetary- costs-date-us-war-afghanistan-2001-2021; Luis Martinez, et al., "As US troops prepare to pull out, a look at the war in Afghanistan by the numbers," *ABC News*, 4/13/2021, https://abcnews.go.com/Politics/ us-troops-prepare-pull-war-afghanistan-numbers/story?id=77050902.

130. James P. Pfiffner, "U.S. Blunders in Iraq," *Intelligence and National Security* 25, no. 1 (2010), 76–85; James Dobbins et al., *Occupying Iraq* (2009), xv, xxvi; Joel D. Rayburn and Frank K. Sobchak, *The U.S. Army in the Iraq War*, vol. 1 (2019), 140–44; Michael Gordon and Bernard E. Trainor, *Cobra II* (2006), 475–83.

131. Pfiffner, "U.S. Blunders," 80–85; Rayburn, *Iraq War*, vol. 1, 141–42, 272–73; "Letter from L. Paul Bremer to George W. Bush, May 22, 2003," *NYT*, 5/22/2003, https://archive.nytimes.com/www.nytimes.com/ref/ washington/04bremer-text1.html.

132. Rayburn, *Iraq War*, vol. 1, 125, 177, 235–37, 239–40, 264–65, 290, 300, 507; Joel D. Rayburn and Frank K. Sobchak, *The U.S. Army in the Iraq War*, vol. 2 (2019), 615; Gregg Zoroya, "How the IED Changed the U.S. Military," *USA Today*, 12/18/2013, https://www.usatoday. com/story/news/nation/2013/12/18/ied-10-years-blast-wounds- amputations/3803017/; Evan Thomas, "Iraq: Can American Military Stop Deadly IEDs?," *Newsweek*, 8/15/2007, https://www.newsweek.com/ iraq-can-american-military-stop-deadly-ieds-99133.

133. Alfred W. McCoy, *Torture and Impunity* (2012), 16–51; Alfred W. McCoy, "How to Read the Senate Report on CIA Torture," *History News Network*, 12/21/2014, http://historynewsnetwork.org/article/157950.

134. Robert Fisk, "Secrets of the Morgue," *Independent*, 9/20/2015, https:// www.independent.co.uk/voices/commentators/fisk/secrets-of-the- morgue-baghdads-body-count-503223.html; Alissa J. Rubin and Stephen Farrell, "Awakening Councils by Region," *NYT*, 12/22/2007, https://www.nytimes.com/2007/12/22/world/middleeast/23awake- graphic.html; Mirian Berger, "Invader, Allies, Occupiers, Guests," *WP*,

1/11/2020, https://www.washingtonpost.com/world/2020/01/11/ invaders-allies-occupiers-guests-brief-history-us-military-involvement- iraq/; "Iraq's Sectarian War: James Steele; America's Mystery Man in Iraq," *Guardian / BBC Arabic* (2013), 51 mins, https://www.youtube.com/ watch?v=_ca1HsC6MH0.

135. Liz Sly and Louisa Loveluck, "The Caliphate Is No More," *WP*, 3/23/2019, https://www.washingtonpost.com/world/ the-islamic-states-caliphate-has-been-defeated-us-backed-forces- say/2019/03/23/04263d74-36f8-11e9-8375-e3dcf6b68558_story. html; Berger, "Invader, Allies, Occupiers, Guests"; Tim Arango et al., "The Iran Cables," *NYT*, 11/19/2019, https://www.nytimes.com/ interactive/2019/11/18/world/middleeast/iran-iraq-spy-cables.html.

136. Rayburn, *Iraq War*, vol. 2, 639–41.

137. McCoy, *Shadows,* 178; US Special Operations Command, *USSOCOM Fact Book 2015* (2014), 12, https://www.socom.mil/FactBook/2015%20 Fact%20Book.pdf; Nick Turse, "American Special Operations Forces Have a Very Funny Definition of Success," *The Nation*, 10/26/2015, https://www.thenation.com/article/american-special-operations-forces- have-a-very-funny-definition-of-success/.

138. Micah Zenko and Emma Welch, "Where the Drones Are," *Foreign Policy*, 5/29/2012, http://foreignpolicy.com/2012/05/29/ where-the-drones-are/.

139. Andrew Cockburn, *Kill Chain* (2016), 252–53.

140. Herbert Docena, *'At the Door of All the East'* (2007), 7, 22–23, 45–51, 71, 91–106; Bulmer-Thomas, *Empire in Retreat*, 234–35.

141. Bryan Clark et al., *Restoring American Seapower* (2017), 43–46, https:// csbaonline.org/uploads/documents/CSBA6224-Fleet_Architecture_ Study_WEB.pdf.

142. James C. Hsiung, "The Aftermath of China's Accession to the World Trade Organization," *Independent Review* 8, no. 1 (2003), 87–89, http:// www.independent.org/pdf/tir/tir_08_1_6_hsiung.pdf.

143. Neil C. Hughes, "A Trade War with China?," *Foreign Affairs* 84, no. 4, (2005), 94–106.

144. US National Intelligence Council, *Global Trends 2030* (2012), i–iii, 105, http://www.dni.gov/files/documents/GlobalTrends_2030.pdf.

145. Bulmer-Thomas, *Empire in Retreat*, 278–79; Mike Patton, "U.S. Role in Global Economy Declines Nearly 50%," *Forbes*, 2/29/2016, https://www. forbes.com/sites/mikepatton/2016/02/29/u-s-role-in-global-economy- declines-nearly-50/; PricewaterhouseCoopers, *The World in 2050* (2015),

1–3, https://www.pwc.com/gx/en/issues/economy/the-world-in-2050.html.

146. James McBride and Andrew Chatzky, "Is 'Made in China 2025' a Threat to Global Trade?," *Council on Foreign Relations*, 5/13/2019, https://www.cfr.org/backgrounder/made-china-2025-threat-global-trade.

147. World Intellectual Property Organization, *World Intellectual Property Indicators 2015* (2015), 6, https://www.wipo.int/edocs/pubdocs/en/wipo_pub_941_2015.pdf.

148. World Intellectual Property Organization, *World Intellectual Property Indicators 2017* (2017), 29, https://www.wipo.int/edocs/pubdocs/en/wipo_pub_941_2017.pdf.

149. Ashlee Vance, "China Wrests Supercomputer Title from U.S.," *NYT*, 10/28/2010, https://www.nytimes.com/2010/10/28/technology/28compute.html.

150. Steve Lohr, "Move Over China," *NYT*, 6/8/2018, https://www.nytimes.com/2018/06/08/technology/supercomputer-china-us.html.

151. OECD, Programme for International Student Assessment (*PISA*), "Results from PISA 2012: United States," http://www.oecd.org/pisa/keyfindings/PISA-2012-results-US.pdf.

152. OECD, *PISA 2015: PISA Results in Focus* (2015), 5, https://www.oecd.org/pisa/pisa-2015-results-in-focus.pdf; OECD, "Snapshot of Students' Performance in Reading, Mathematics and Science," *PISA 2018 Results* (2018), https://www.oecd.org/pisa/PISA-results_ENGLISH.png.

153. Christopher J. Neely, "Chinese Foreign Exchange Reserves and the U.S. Economy," Federal Reserve Bank of St. Louis, *Economic Synopses*, no. 9 (2016), https://research.stlouisfed.org/publications/economic-synopses/2016/05/06/chinese-foreign-exchange-reserves-and-the-u-s-economy/; World Bank, *China Economic Update* (June 2015), 3–4, https://www.worldbank.org/content/dam/Worldbank/document/EAP/China/ceu_06_15_en.pdf.

154. "Remarks by President Obama to the Australian Parliament," Office of the Press Secretary, White House, 11/17/2011, https://www.whitehouse.gov/the-press-office/2011/11/17/remarks-president-obama-australian-parliament.

155. Jeffrey Goldberg, "The Obama Doctrine," *The Atlantic* (April 2016), http://www.theatlantic.com/magazine/archive/2016/04/the-obama-doctrine/471525/.

156. Office of the Press Secretary, "Obama Administration Finalizes Historic 54.5 MPG Fuel Efficiency Standards," White House, 8/28/2012, https://obamawhitehouse.archives.gov/the-press-office/2012/08/28/

obama-administration-finalizes-historic-545-MPG-fuel-efficiency-standard; Marianne Lavelle, "2016: Obama's Climate Legacy Marked by Triumphs and Lost Opportunities," *Inside Climate News*, 12/26/2016, https://insideclimatenews.org/news/23122016/obama-climate-change-legacy-trump-policies; Smil, *Energy*, 123–24; US Energy Information Administration, "Table 1.1. Net Generation by Energy Source: Total (All Sectors), 2010–April 2020," *Electric Power Monthly* (6/24/2020), https://www.eia.gov/electricity/monthly/epm_table_grapher.php?t=epmt_1_01.

157. Lavelle, "2016"; "Overview of U.S. Petroleum Production, Imports, Exports, and Consumption," Bureau of Transportation Statistics, US Department of Transportation, https://www.bts.gov/content/overview-us-petroleum-production-imports-exports-and-consumption-million-barrels-day; "Oil: Crude and Petroleum Products Explained," US Energy Information Administration (4/14/2021), https://www.eia.gov/energyexplained/index.php?page=oil_use; Robert Rapier, "How Much Oil Do We Import from the Middle East?," *Forbes*, 1/7/2020, https://www.forbes.com/sites/rrapier/2020/01/07/how-much-oil-do-we-import-from-the-middle-east/#74cce8fb21c6.

158. Australia Centre on China in the World, "Australia and the American 'Pivot to Asia,'" The Australia-China Story (2015), http://aus.thechinastory.org/archive/australia-and-the-american-pivot-to-asia/.

159. "Editorial: Jeju Naval Base," *Korea Herald*, 2/29/2016, http://www.koreaherald.com/view.php?ud=20160229001123; Andrew Salmon, "S. Korea Base Tests U.S., Chinese Interests," *Washington Times*, 10/5/2011, http://www.washingtontimes.com/news/2011/oct/5/us-base-tests-dueling-interests-in-s-korea/; Javier C. Hernandez and Floyd Whaley, "Philippine Supreme Court Approves Return of U.S. Troops," NYT, 1/12/2016, https://www.nytimes.com/2016/01/13/world/asia/philippines-us-military.html.

160. Vince Scappatura, "The US 'Pivot to Asia,' the China Specter and the Australian-American Alliance," *Asia-Pacific Journal* 12, issue 36, no. 3 (2014), https://apjjf.org/2014/12/36/Vince-Scappatura/4178/article.html.

161. "Remarks by Secretary Hagel at the IISS Asia Security Summit, Shangri-La Hotel, Singapore," 6/01/2013, https://content.govdelivery.com/accounts/USDOD/bulletins/7d7ac2.

162. Liu Zhun, "Vying for Influence Dilutes Obama's African Visit," *Global Times*, 7/27/2015, http://www.globaltimes.cn/content/933987.shtml.

163. Bulmer-Thomas, *Empire in Retreat*, 344–45; Peter Baker, "Obama, on China's Turf, Presents U.S. as a Better Partner for Africa," *NYT*,

7/29/2015, https://www.nytimes.com/2015/07/30/world/africa/obama-on-chinas-turf-presents-us-as-a-better-partner-for-africa.html.

164. Kevin Granville, "The Trans-Pacific Partnership Trade Deal Explained," *NYT*, 5/11/2015, http://www.nytimes.com/2015/05/12/business/unpacking-the-trans-pacific-partnership-trade-deal.html.

165. Alan Rappeport, "Elizabeth Warren Knocks Obama over Trade Deal Transparency," *NYT*, 4/22/2015, http://www.nytimes.com/politics/first-draft/2015/04/22/elizabeth-warren-knocks-obama-over-trade-deal-transparency/.

166. Jonathan Weisman, "Trade Authority Bill Wins Final Approval in Senate," *NYT*, 6/24/2015, http://www.nytimes.com/2015/06/25/business/trade-pact-senate-vote-obama.html.

167. International Monetary Fund, "Report for Selected Country Groups and Subjects," *World Economic Outlook*, 7/24/2014, https://www.imf.org/en/Publications/WEO/weo-database/2014/April; European Commission, "EU Position in World Trade," 2/9/2019, http://ec.europa.eu/trade/policy/eu-position-in-world-trade; Economist Intelligence Unit, *Foresight 2020* (2006), 8–9, http://graphics.eiu.com/files/ad_pdfs/eiuForesight2020_WP.pdf.

168. Andrew Walker, "TTIP," *BBC News*, 5/13/2015, http://www.bbc.com/news/business-32691589.

169. Philip Blenkinsop, "Trump Victory Could Spell Defeat for EU–U.S. Trade Deal," *Reuters*, 11/9/2016, https://www.reuters.com/article/us-usa-election-trade-eu-idUSKBN1342TF.

170. Gordon Lubold, "Has the White House Bungled a Historic Africa Summit?," *Foreign Policy*, 7/9/2014, http://foreignpolicy.com/2014/07/09/has-the-white-house-bungled-a-historic-africa-summit/.

171. Baker, "Obama, on China's Turf."

172. Sylvie Lanteaume, "US Wants to Reduce Presence in Africa, Warns Top Officer," *AFP*, 1/13/2020, https://news.yahoo.com/us-wants-reduce-presence-africa-warns-top-officer-160719391.html; John Ford, "The Pivot to Asia Was Obama's Biggest Mistake," *The Diplomat*, 1/21/2017, https://thediplomat.com/2017/01/the-pivot-to-asia-was-obamas-biggest-mistake/.

173. Peter S. Goodman, "More Wealth, More Jobs, but Not for Everyone," *NYT*, 9/28/2016, https://www.nytimes.com/2016/09/29/business/economy/more-wealth-more-jobs-but-not-for-everyone-what-fuels-the-backlash-on-trade.html.

174. Bulmer-Thomas, *Empire in Retreat*, 260–61; Binyamin Appelbaum,

"A Little-Noticed Fact about Trade," *NYT*, 10/30/2016, https://www.nytimes.com/2016/10/31/upshot/a-little-noticed-fact-about-trade-its-no-longer-rising.html.

175. John B. Judis, *The Populist Explosion* (2016), 131–53; Jan-Werner Müller, *What Is Populism?* (2016), 7–40.

176. Peter Baker, "Trump Abandons Trans-Pacific Partnership," *NYT*, 1/23/2017, https://www.nytimes.com/2017/01/23/us/politics/tpp-trump-trade-nafta.html.

177. Michael D. Shear, "Trump Will Withdraw U.S. from Paris Climate Agreement," *NYT*, 9/13/2020, https://www.nytimes.com/2017/06/01/climate/trump-paris-climate-agreement.html; Michael D. Shear and Coral Davenport, "In Visiting a Charred California, Trump Confronts a Scientific Reality He Denies," *NYT*, 9/14/2020, https://www.nytimes.com/2020/09/13/us/politics/california-fires-trump-climate-change.html.

178. Smil, *Energy*, 20, 152; Nicola Jones, "How the World Passed a Carbon Threshold and Why It Matters," *Yale Environment 360*, 1/26/2017, https://e360.yale.edu/features/how-the-world-passed-a-carbon-threshold-400ppm-and-why-it-matters.

179. Julie Pace and Jonathan Lemire, "Trump Scolds Fellow NATO Leaders," *AP News*, 5/26/2017, https://www.apnews.com/2ed02c1ee7c64061a2bf146bfb0a4b2c.

180. Oliver Holmes and Tom Phillips, "Trump Attacks Countries 'Cheating' America at Apec Summit," *Guardian*, 11/10/2017, https://www.theguardian.com/us-news/2017/nov/10/trump-attacks-countries-cheating-america-at-apec-summit.

181. "Remarks by President Trump at APEC CEO Summit, Danang, Vietnam, November 10, 2017," *U.S. Mission to ASEAN*, https://asean.usmission.gov/remarks-president-trump-apec-ceo-summit-da-nang-vietnam/.

182. "Full Text of Chinese President Xi's Address at APEC CEO Summit," *Xinhuanet*, 11/11/2017, http://www.xinhuanet.com/english/2017-11/11/c_136743492.htm.

183. Alexandra Stevenson and Motoko Rich, "Trans-Pacific Trade Partners Are Moving On, Without the U.S.," *NYT*, 11/11/2017, https://www.nytimes.com/2017/11/11/business/trump-tpp-trade.html.

184. David D. Kirkpatrick, "In Snub to U.S., Russia and Egypt Move Toward Deal on Air Bases," *NYT*, 11/30/2017, https://www.nytimes.com/2017/11/30/world/middleeast/russia-egypt-air-bases.html.

185. Jane Perlez, "In China, Aung San Suu Kyi Finds a Warm Welcome (and No Talk of Rohingya)," *NYT*, 11/30/2017, https://www.nytimes.

com/2017/11/30/world/asia/china-myanmar-aid-sanctions.html.

186. Jane Perlez and Damien Cave, "As China Rises, Australia Asks Itself: Can It Rely on America?," *NYT*, 12/3/2017, https://www.nytimes. com/2017/12/03/world/australia/australia-us-china-alliances.html.

187. Melissa Eddy, "In Era of Trump, Germany Seeks a Stronger Role Abroad," *NYT*, 12/5/2017, https://www.nytimes.com/2017/12/05/world/ europe/germany-trump-sigmar-gabriel.html.

188. Jean Kirby, "Mexican President Enrique Peña Nieto Goes Ahead and Cancels That Meeting with Donald Trump," *New York Magazine*, 1/26/2017, http://nymag.com/daily/intelligencer/2017/01/mexican -president-cancels-that-meeting-with-trump.html; Stephen Castle, "Trump's Tweets Manage a Rare Feat," *NYT*, 11/30/2017, https://www .nytimes.com/2017/11/30/world/europe/trump-tweets-uk-visit.html; Missy Ryan et al., "Piling on pressure over safe havens, U.S. suspends military aid to Pakistan," *WP*, 1/4/2018, https://www.washingtonpost.com/ world/national-security/feud-between-us-and-pakistan-flares-up-after- trumps-lies-and-deceit-tweet/2018/01/04/7cb457b8-f08a-11e7-97bf- bba379b809ab_story.html.

189. Mark Landler, "Trump Threatens to End American Aid," *NYT*, 12/20/2017, https://www.nytimes.com/2017/12/20/world/middleeast/ trump-threatens-to-end-american-aid-were-watching-those-votes-at- the-un.html; Tracy Wilkinson and Noga Tarnopolsky, "U.N. Votes Overwhelmingly to Condemn U.S. Decision to Recognize Jerusalem Despite Trump's Threats," *Los Angeles Times*, 12/21/2017, http://latimes. com/nation/la-fg-un-jerusalem-vote-20171221-story.html.

190. Gallup, "Rating World Leaders: 2018; The U.S. vs. Germany, China and Russia," https://www.politico.com/f/?id=00000161-0647-da3c- a371-867f6acc0001.

191. Fareed Zakaria, "The Decline of U.S. Influence Is the Great Global Story of Our Age," *WP*, 12/28/2017, https://www.washingtonpost. com/opinions/global-opinions/the-decline-of-us-influence-is-the-great- global-story-of-our-times/2017/12/28/bfe48262-ebf6-11e7-9f92- 10a2203f6c8d_story.html.

192. Mark Landler, "Trump Abandons Iran Nuclear Deal He Long Scorned," *NYT*, 5/8/2018, https://www.nytimes.com/2018/05/08/world/ middleeast/trump-iran-nuclear-deal.html; "Quadrilateral security dialogue," *Times of India*, 11/12/2017, https://timesofindia.indiatimes. com/india/quadrilateral-security-dialogue-india-australia-japan-us-hold- talks-on-indo-pacific-cooperation/articleshow/61616602.cms.

193. Jeremy Diamond, "Trump Opens NATO Summit with Blistering Criticism of Germany, Labels Allies 'Delinquent,'" CNN Politics, 7/11/2018, https://www.cnn.com/2018/07/10/politics/donald-trump-nato-summit-2018/index.html.

194. Eileen Sullivan, "Trump Questions the Core of NATO: Mutual Defense, Including Montenegro," *NYT*, 7/18/2018, https://www.nytimes.com/2018/07/18/world/europe/trump-nato-self-defense-montenegro.html.

195. Tom Newton Dunn, "Exclusive Interview with President Trump," *Sun* (London), 7/13/2018, https://www.thesun.co.uk/news/6766531/trump-may-brexit-us-deal-off/.

196. Editorial Board, "Russia Attacks America's Election System," *NYT*, 8/1/2018, https://www.nytimes.com/2018/08/01/opinion/editorials/russia-election-meddling-trump-putin.html.

197. John W. Schoen, "Japanese Prime Minister Shinzo Abe Faces Pressure to Join Trade War against the US," *CNBC*, 6/7/2018, https://www.cnbc.com/2018/06/07/abe-faces-pressure-to-join-trade-war-against-the-u-s.html; Robin Harding, "Japan Plays It Cool on Response to US Steel Tariffs," *Financial Times*, 4/4/2018, https://www.ft.com/content/c7fc9ae0-37e4-11e8-8b98-2f31af407cc8; Reuters, "Pompeo Announces $113 Million in New US Initiatives in 'Indo-Pacific,'" *CNBC*, 7/30/2018, https://www.cnbc.com/2018/07/30/pompeo-to-announce-initiatives-focusing-on-digital-economy-energy-an.html.

198. Damian Paletta and Joel Achenbach, "Trump Accuses Canadian Leader of Being 'Dishonest' and 'Weak,'" *WP*, 6/10/2018, https://www.washingtonpost.com/politics/trump-attacks-canada-to-show-north-korea-hes-strong-aide-says/2018/06/10/afc16c0c-6cba-11e8-bd50-b80389a4e569_story.html; Reuters, "Trump Claims North Korea Is 'No Longer a Nuclear Threat,'" *CNBC*, 6/13/2018, https://www.cnbc.com/2018/06/13/trump-says-north-korea-no-longer-a-nuclear-threat.html.

199. Ellen Nakashima and Joby Warrick, "U.S. Spy Agencies: North Korea Is Working on New Missiles," *WP*, 7/30/2018, https://www.washingtonpost.com/world/national-security/us-spy-agencies-north-korea-is-working-on-new-missiles/2018/07/30/b3542696-940d-11e8-a679-b09212fb69c2_story.html.

200. Editorial Board, "North Korea's Complaint," *Wall Street Journal*, 8/5/2018, https://www.wsj.com/articles/north-koreas-complaint-1533501905.

201. David E. Sanger and Edward Wong, "How the Trump–Kim Summit Failed," *NYT*, 3/2/2019, https://www.nytimes.com/2019/03/02/world/asia/trump-kim-jong-un-summit.html; Choe Sang-Hun, "North

Korea Launches 2 Projectiles," *NYT*, 8/15/2019, https://www.nytimes. com/2019/08/15/world/asia/north-korea-missile-tests.html; Editorial Board, "Mr. Trump's Lose-Lose Proposition in Korea," *NYT*, 11/21/2019, https://www.nytimes.com/2019/11/21/opinion/trump-korea.html.

202. Thom Shanker and David E. Sanger, "Privacy May Be a Victim in Cyberdefense Plan," *NYT*, 6/12/2009, https://www.nytimes. com/2009/06/13/us/politics/13cyber.html; David E. Sanger, "Obama Order Sped Up Wave of Cyberattacks against Iran," *NYT*, 6/1/2012, https://www.nytimes.com/2012/06/01/world/middleeast/obama-ordered-wave-of-cyberattacks-against-iran.html; James Glanz and Andrew W. Lehren, "N.S.A. Spied on Allies, Aid Groups and Businesses," *NYT*, 12/20/2013, https://www.nytimes.com/2013/12/21/world/nsa-dragnet-included-allies-aid-groups-and-business-elite.html.

203. US Senate, 116th Congress, 1st Session, *Report of the Select Committee on Intelligence, United States Senate on Russian Active Measures Campaigns and Interference in the 2016 U.S. Election*, vol. 2, *Russia's Use of Social Media with Additional Views* (2020), 1–22, https://www.intelligence. senate.gov/sites/default/files/documents/Report_Volume2.pdf.

204. Greg Miller and Ellen Nakashima, "Wikileaks Says It Has Obtained a Trove of CIA Hacking Tools," *WP*, 3/7/2017, https://www. washingtonpost.com/world/national-security/wikileaks-says-it-has-obtained-trove-of-cia-hacking-tools/2017/03/07/c8c50c5c-0345-11e7-b1e9-a05d3c21f7cf_story.html; Ellen Nakashima and Shane Harris, "Elite CIA Unit That Developed Hacking Tools Failed to Secure Its Own Systems, Allowing Massive Leak, an Internal Report Found," *WP*, 6/16/2020, https://www.washingtonpost.com/ national-security/elite-cia-unit-that-developed-hacking-tools-failed-to-secure-its-own-systems-allowing-massive-leak-an-internal-report-found/2020/06/15/502e3456-ae9d-11ea-8f56-63f38c990077_story. html; David E. Sanger et al., "Scope of Russian Hacking Becomes Clear," *NYT*, 12/14/2020, https://www.nytimes.com/2020/12/14/us/politics/ russia-hack-nsa-homeland-security-pentagon.html.

205. Paul-Martin Foss, "Trade War with China Continues to Escalate," *Red Tea News*, 9/19/2018, http://redtea.com/america-now/ trade-war-with-china-continues-to-escalate/.

206. Ana Swanson and Keith Bradsher, "Trump Officials Praise Gains from China Deal, but They Come at a Cost," *NYT*, 12/15/2019, https://www. nytimes.com/2019/12/15/business/economy/us-china-trade-deal.html; Ana Swanson and Alan Rappeport, "Trump Signs China Trade Deal,

Putting Economic Conflict on Pause," *NYT*, 1/15/2020, https://www.nytimes.com/2020/01/15/business/economy/china-trade-deal.html.

207. Matina Stevis-Gridneff and Lara Jakes, "World Leaders Join to Pledge $8 Billion for Vaccine as U.S. Goes It Alone," *NYT*, 5/4/2020, https://www.nytimes.com/2020/05/04/world/europe/eu-coronavirus-vaccine.html; Hope Yen, "AP Fact Check: Trump's Move to Quit WHO Cites Flawed Facts," *AP News*, 6/1/2020, https://apnews.com/article/united-nations-donald-trump-us-news-ap-top-news-virus-outbreak-e9fe85641b9 3d447dfd529095c2640c4; "Covid-19 Coronavirus Pandemic: Reported Cases and Deaths by Country, Territory, or Conveyance," *Worldometer*, 1/20/2021, https://www.worldometers.info/coronavirus; Avie Schneider, "40.8 million Out of Work in The Past 10 Weeks—26% of Labor Force," *NPR*, 5/28/2020, https://www.npr.org/sections/coronavirus-live-updates/2020/05/28/863120102/40-8-million-out-of-work-in-the-past-10-weeks; Centre for Economics and Business Research, *World Economic League Table 2021* (London), 70–71, https://cebr.com/wp-content/uploads/2020/12/WELT-2021-final-23.12.pdf; Steven Lee Myers et al., "Power, Patriotism and 1.4 Billion People," *NYT*, 2/5/2021, https://www.nytimes.com/2021/02/05/world/asia/china-covid-economy.html; Keith Bradsher, "With Covid-19 Under Control, China's Economy Surges Ahead," *NYT*, 10/18/2020, https://www.nytimes.com/2020/10/18/business/china-economy-covid.html; Jeanna Smialek, "Fed Chair Says Economic Recovery May 'Stretch' through End of 2021," *NYT*, 5/17/2020, https://www.nytimes.com/2020/05/17/business/economy/fed-powell-economic-recovery.html.

208. Monika Pronczuk and Mihir Zaveri, "Statue of Leopold II, Belgian King Who Brutalized Congo, Is Removed in Antwerp," *NYT*, 6/9/2020, https://www.nytimes.com/2020/06/09/world/europe/king-leopold-statue-antwerp.html; Meryl Kornfield et al., "Huge Peaceful Protests Mark Anti-racism Demonstrations around the Globe," *WP*, 6/6/2020, https://www.washingtonpost.com/health/huge-peaceful-protests-mark-anti-racism-demonstrations-around-the-globe/2020/06/06/da2b9bd0-a817-11ea-bb20-ebf0921f3bbd_story.html; Michael Levenson, "Protesters Topple Statue of Jefferson Davis on Richmond's Monument Avenue," *NYT*, 6/11/2020, https://www.nytimes.com/2020/06/11/us/Jefferson-Davis-Statue-Richmond.html; Lateshia Beachum et al., "Christopher Columbus Statues Toppled in Minnesota, Beheaded in Boston, Attacked in Richmond," *WP*, 6/10/2020, https://www.washingtonpost.com/history/2020/06/10/

christopher-columbus-statue-beheaded-boston-richmond/; Michael Wines, "'Looting' Comment from Trump Dates Back to Racial Unrest of the 1960s," *NYT*, 5/29/2020, https://www.nytimes.com/2020/05/29/us/looting-starts-shooting-starts.html.

209.   Mark Berman et al., "Protests Spread over Police Shootings," *WP*, 6/8/2020, https://www.washingtonpost.com/investigations/protests-spread-over-police-shootings-police-promised-reforms-every-year-they-still-shoot-nearly-1000-people/2020/06/08/5c204f0c-a67c-11ea-b473-04905b1af82b_story.html; Steven Raphael and Michael A. Stoll, *Why Are So Many Americans in Prison?* (2013), 4–13; David Brooks, "How to Do Reparations Right," *NYT*, 6/4/2020, https://www.nytimes.com/2020/06/04/opinion/united-states-reparations.html; Condoleezza Rice, "This Moment Cries Out for Us to Confront Race in America," *WP*, 6/4/2020, https://www.washingtonpost.com/opinions/2020/06/04/condoleezza-rice-moment-confront-race-america/.

210.   Stephen Erlanger, "Embattled at Home, Trump Finds Himself Isolated Abroad, Too," *NYT*, 6/2/2020, https://www.nytimes.com/2020/06/02/world/europe/trump-merkel-allies.html; Haass, "Present at the Disruption."

211.   Maggie Haberman, "Trump Told Crowd 'You Will Never Take Back Our Country with Weakness,'" *NYT*, 1/6/2021, https://www.nytimes.com/2021/01/06/us/politics/trump-speech-capitol.html; Lisa Lerer, "Marooned at Mar-a-Lago, Trump Still Has Iron Grip on Republicans," *NYT*, 5/8/2021, https://www.nytimes.com/2021/05/08/us/politics/trump-republicans-liz-cheney.html.

212.   Keith Bradsher and Ana Swanson, "China-Led Trade Pact Is Signed, in Challenge to the U.S.," *NYT*, 11/15/2020, https://www.nytimes.com/2020/11/15/business/china-trade-rcep.html; Robin Emmott and John Irish, "After Trump, Europe Aims to Show Biden It Can Fight for Itself," *Reuters*, 11/27/2020, https://www.reuters.com/article/usa-election-eu-defence/after-trump-europe-aims-to-show-biden-it-can-fight-for-itself-idINKBN27X0WX; Tom McTague, "Joe Biden Won't Fix America's Relationships," *The Atlantic*, 11/8/2020, https://www.theatlantic.com/international/archive/2020/11/joe-biden-america-world/617016/; "Transition Highlights," *NYT*, 11/25/2020, https://www.nytimes.com/live/2020/11/24/us/joe-biden-trump; Michael Crowley and Steven Erlanger, "Biden's Plan to Link Arms with Europe against Russia and China Isn't So Simple," *NYT*, 2/18/2021, https://www.nytimes.com/2021/02/18/us/politics/biden-europe-russia-china.html.

213. Brzezinski, *Grand Chessboard*, 35, 39.

214. Smil, *Energy,* 200–201; Yessenia Funes, "Denmark Sets New Record for Wind Energy, Putting Us All to Shame," *Gizmodo,* 1/2/2020, https://earther.gizmodo.com/denmark-sets-new-record-for-wind-energy-putting-us-all-1840777389; "Renewable Energy's Share of German Power Mix Rose to 46% Last Year: Research Group," *Reuters,* 1/3/2020, https://www.reuters.com/article/us-germany-power-outputmix/renewable-energys-share-of-german-power-mix-rose-to-46-last-year-research-group-idUSKBN1Z21K1; US Energy Information Administration, "What Is U.S. Electricity Generation by Energy Source?," 2/27/2020, https://www.eia.gov/tools/faqs/faq.php?id=427&t=3; BP, "China's Energy Market in 2018," *Statistical Review 2019,* https://www.bp.com/content/dam/bp/business-sites/en/global/corporate/pdfs/energy-economics/statistical-review/bp-stats-review-2019-china-insights.pdf; Clifford Krauss, "U.S. and European Oil Giants Go Different Ways on Climate Change," *NYT,* 9/21/2020, https://www.nytimes.com/2020/09/21/business/energy-environment/oil-climate-change-us-europe.html.

215. Andreas Malm, *Fossil Capital* (2016), 3, 328–29, 353; International Energy Administration, "Global CO2 emissions in 2019 / Energy related CO2 emissions, 1990–2019," 2/11/2020, https://www.iea.org/articles/global-co2-emissions-in-2019; Zeke Hausfather, "Analysis: Global CO2 Emissions Set to Rise 2% in 2017 after Three-Year 'Plateau,'" *Global Carbon Project,* 11/13/2017, https://www.carbonbrief.org/analysis-global-co2-emissions-set-to-rise-2-percent-in-2017-following-three-year-plateau.

Chapter 6: Beijing's World System

1. Xi Jinping, "Promote Friendship between Our People and Work Together to Build a Bright Future," Nazarbayev University, Astana, Kazakhstan, 9/7/2013, https://www.fmprc.gov.cn/mfa_eng/wjdt_665385/zyjh_665391/t1078088.shtml.

2. Jane Perlez and Yufan Huang, "Behind China's $1 Trillion Plan to Shake Up the Economic Order," *NYT,* 5/13/2017, https://www.nytimes.com/2017/05/13/business/china-railway-one-belt-one-road-1-trillion-plan.html.

3. H.J. Mackinder, "The Geographical Pivot of History (1904)," *Geographical Journal* 170, no. 4 (2004), 298–321.

4. Christopher J. Neely, "Chinese Foreign Exchange Reserves, Policy Choices and the U.S. Economy" (2017), 1, 31, Federal Reserve Bank of St. Louis, https://files.stlouisfed.org/files/htdocs/wp/2017/2017-001.

pdf; Neta C. Crawford, "United States Budgetary Costs and Obligations of Post-9/11 Wars through FY 2020: $6.4 Trillion," (2019), 1–3, https://watson.brown.edu/costsofwar/figures/2019/budgetary-costs-post-911-wars-through-fy2020-64-trillion; Kurt M. Campbell and Ely Ratner, "The China Reckoning," *Foreign Affairs* 97, no. 2 (2018), 60–70; H.R. McMaster, *Battlegrounds* (2020), 130.

5. World Bank, "Nearly Half the World Lives on Less than $5.50 a Day," 10/17/2018, https://www.worldbank.org/en/news/press-release/2018/10/17/nearly-half-the-world-lives-on-less-than-550-a-day.

6. Sally Sargeson, "The Demise of China's Peasantry as a Class," *Asia-Pacific Journal* 14, Issue 13, no. 1 (2016), 1–23.

7. Wayne M. Morrison, *China's Economic Rise* (2019), 5, 11–12, https://fas.org/sgp/crs/row/RL33534.pdf; National Bureau of Statistics of China, "Table 3.1 Gross Domestic Product," *Chinese Statistical Yearbook 2018* (2019), http://www.stats.gov.cn/tjsj/ndsj/2018/indexeh.htm.

8. Xiangming Chen and Tomas de'Medici, "Research Note—The 'Instant City' Coming of Age," *Urban Geography* 31, no. 8 (2009), 1141–47; Thomas Hout and Pankaj Ghemawat, "China vs the World," *Harvard Business Review* (December 2010), https://hbr.org/2010/12/china-vs-the-world-whose-technology-is-it.

9. Liyan Chen et al., "Alibaba Claims Title for Largest Global IPO Ever with Extra Share Sales," *Forbes*, 9/22/2014, https://www.forbes.com/sites/ryanmac/2014/09/22/alibaba-claims-title-for-largest-global-ipo-ever-with-extra-share-sales/#5303ae028dcc; Kevin Fitchard, "Huawei Knocks Off Ericsson as World's Biggest Telecom Vendor," *Gigaom*, 7/24/2012, https://gigaom.com/2012/07/24/huawei-knocks-off-ericsson-as-worlds-biggest-telecom-vendor/.

10. Jane Perlez, "'China Creates a World Bank of Its Own, and the U.S. Balks," *NYT*, 12/4/2015, https://www.nytimes.com/2015/12/05/business/international/china-creates-an-asian-bank-as-the-us-stands-aloof.html; Saadat Hassan, "OBOR," *IRAS: Institute for Iran-Eurasia Studies*, 5/14/2017, http://www.iras.ir/en/doc/article/3171/obor-infrastructure-investment-connectivity.

11. "Full Text of President Xi's Speech at Opening of Belt and Road Forum," *Xinhuanet*, 5/14/2017, http://www.xinhuanet.com/english/2017-05/14/c_136282982.htm.

12. François de Soyres et al., "Common Transport Infrastructure," World Bank Policy Research Working Paper 8801 (2019), 3–5, http://documents1.worldbank.org/curated/en/879031554144957551/pdf/.

13. Brook Larmer, "What the World's Emptiest International Airport Says about China's Influence," *NYT*, 9/13/2017, https://www.nytimes.com/2017/09/13/magazine/what-the-worlds-emptiest-international-airport-says-about-chinas-influence.html; Alexandra Stevenson and Cao Li, "China's Plan to Win Friends and Influence Includes Ski Slopes and Spas," *NYT*, 8/1/2018, https://www.nytimes.com/2018/08/01/business/china-belt-and-road.html; Brook Larmer, "Is China the World's New Colonial Power?," *NYT*, 5/2/2017, https://www.nytimes.com/2017/05/02/magazine/is-china-the-worlds-new-colonial-power.html.

14. Jason Horowitz and Liz Alderman, "Chastised by E.U., a Resentful Greece Embraces China's Cash and Interests," *NYT*, 8/26/2017, https://www.nytimes.com/2017/08/26/world/europe/greece-china-piraeus-alexis-tsipras.html; Bloomberg News, "IMF Aims to Nudge Xi's Silk Road Plan Away from Spending Splurge," *American Journal of Transportation*, 4/12/2018, https://www.ajot.com/news/imf-aims-to-nudge-xis-silk-road-plan-away-from-spending-splurge; "Will China's Belt and Road Initiative Outdo the Marshall Plan?," *The Economist*, 3/8/2018, https://www.economist.com/finance-and-economics/2018/03/08/will-chinas-belt-and-road-initiative-outdo-the-marshall-plan; Simon Shen, "How China's 'Belt and Road' Compares to the Marshall Plan," *The Diplomat*, 2/6/2016, https://thediplomat.com/2016/02/how-chinas-belt-and-road-compares-to-the-marshall-plan/; Saeed Shah and Jeremy Page, "China Readies $46 Billion for Pakistan Trade Route," *Wall Street Journal*, 4/16/2015, https://www.wsj.com/articles/china-to-unveil-billions-of-dollars-in-pakistan-investment-1429214705.

15. Raushan Nurshayeva and Shamil Zhumatov, "Update 3—China's Hu Boosts Energy Ties with Central Asia," *Reuters*, 12/12/2009, https://www.reuters.com/article/china-kazakhstan/update-3-chinas-hu-boosts-energy-ties-with-central-asia-idUKGEE5BB01D20091212; Demir Azizov, "Construction of Third Branch of Uzbekistan–China Gas Pipeline Completed," *Trend News Agency*, 12/23/2014, http://en.trend.az/casia/uzbekistan/2346917.html.

16. Vaclav Smil, *Energy Transitions* (2017), 134–39, 157; Reuters Staff, "Update 1—China 2015 Coal Output Drops 3.5 pct on Soft Demand, Pollution Curbs," *Reuters*, 1/18/2016, https://www.reuters.com/article/china-economy-output-coal-idUSL3N1531CD.

17. Jean-Paul Rodrigue, "Length of the Interstate Highway System and of the Chinese Expressway System, 1959–2017," *Geography of Transport Systems* (2020), https://transportgeography.org/?page_id=1869.

18.   Monika, "China's Automobile Population Totals 250 Million Units by June 2019," *Gasgoo*, 7/4/2019, http://autonews.gasgoo.com/china_news/70016117.html; I. Wagner, "Number of Vehicles in Operation in the United States between 1st quarter 2017 and 1st quarter 2019," *Statistica*, 7/24/2019, https://www.statista.com/statistics/859950/vehicles-in-operation-by-quarter-united-states/; M. Muntean et al., *Fossil CO2 Emissions of All World Countries—2018 Report* (2018), https://op.europa.eu/en/publication-detail/-/publication/41811494-f131-11e8-9982-01aa75ed71a1/language-en; Paul Gao, Arthur Wang et al., "Winning the Race," *McKinsey China Auto CEO Quarterly* (December 2019), 14, https://www.mckinsey.com/~/media/mckinsey/industries/automotive%20and%20assembly/our%20insights/winning%20the%20race%20chinas%20auto%20market%20shifts%20gears/winning-the-race-chinas-auto-market-shifts-gears.ashx.

19.   Richard Nunno, "Fact Sheet: High Speed Rail Development Worldwide," *Environmental and Energy Study Institute*, 7/19/2018, https://www.eesi.org/papers/view/fact-sheet-high-speed-rail-development-worldwide; Gerald Olivier, "Chinese High-Speed," *International Railway Journal*, 2/18/2015, https://www.railjournal.com/in_depth/chinese-high-speed-an-evaluation-of-traffic; Keith Bradsher, "Hauling New Treasure along the Silk Road," *NYT*, 7/20/2013, https://www.nytimes.com/2013/07/21/business/global/hauling-new-treasure-along-the-silk-road.html, Jean-Paul Rodrigue, *The Geography of Transport Systems* (2017), 167.

20.   Thodsapol Hongtong and Kornchanok Raksaseri, "From Bangkok to Beijing," *Bangkok Post*, 7/7/2019.

21.   Jane Perlez, "China Retools Vast Global Building Push Criticized as Bloated and Predatory," *NYT*, 4/25/2019, https://www.nytimes.com/2019/04/25/business/china-belt-and-road-infrastructure.html.

22.   Keith Johnson, "Why Is China Buying Up Europe's Ports?," *Foreign Policy*, 2/2/2018, https://foreignpolicy.com/2018/02/02/why-is-china-buying-up-europes-ports/; Maria Abi-Habib, "How China Got Sri Lanka to Cough Up a Port," *NYT*, 6/25/2018, https://www.nytimes.com/2018/06/25/world/asia/china-sri-lanka-port.html; Joanna Kakissis, "Chinese Firms Now Hold Stakes in over a Dozen European Ports," *NPR*, 10/9/2018, https://www.npr.org/2018/10/09/642587456/chinese-firms-now-hold-stakes-in-over-a-dozen-european-ports.

23.   Jason Horowitz and Steven Erlanger, "Italy Gives Xi, and China's Vast Infrastructure Project, a Royal Welcome," *NYT*, 3/22/2019, https://www.nytimes.com/2019/03/22/world/europe/italy-china-xi-road.html.

24. Reuters Staff, "China Unveils Vision for 'Polar Silk Road' across Arctic," *Reuters*, 1/26/2018, https://www.reuters.com/article/us-china-arctic/china-unveils-vision-for-polar-silk-road-across-arctic-idUSKBN1FF0J8.

25. Peter Baker, "Obama, on China's Turf, Presents U.S. as a Better Partner for Africa," *NYT*, 7/29/2015, https://www.nytimes.com/2015/07/30/world/africa/obama-on-chinas-turf-presents-us-as-a-better-partner-for-africa.html.

26. Ernesto Londoño, "From a Space Station in Argentina, China Expands Its Reach in Latin America," *NYT*, 7/28/2018, https://www.nytimes.com/2018/07/28/world/americas/china-latin-america.html.

27. Perlez, "China Retools Vast Global Building Push"; Jonathan Watts, "Belt and Road Summit Puts Spotlight on Chinese Coal Funding," *Guardian*, 4/25/2019, https://www.theguardian.com/world/2019/apr/25/belt-and-road-summit-puts-spotlight-on-chinese-coal-funding; Keith Bradsher, "China Renews Its 'Belt and Road' Push for Global Sway," *NYT*, 1/15/2020, https://www.nytimes.com/2020/01/15/business/china-belt-and-road.html.

28. Christine Lagarde, "BRI 2.0," 4/26/2019, International Monetary Fund, https://www.imf.org/en/News/Articles/2019/04/25/sp042619-stronger-frameworks-in-the-new-phase-of-belt-and-road.

29. Manoj Joshi, "With BRI 2.0, Xi Jinping Pledges to Step Up China's Game," *Observer Research Foundation* (4/29/2019), https://www.orfonline.org/research/bri-xi-jinping-pledges-step-up-chinas-game-50343/; Bradsher, "China Renews."

30. Deborah Brautigam, "Is China the World's Loan Shark?," *NYT*, 4/26/2019, https://www.nytimes.com/2019/04/26/opinion/china-belt-road-initiative.html.

31. David Pilling and James Politi, "US Senate Passes $60bn Foreign Development Bill," *Financial Times*, 10/3/2018, https://www.ft.com/content/14400aa2-c743-11e8-ba8f-ee390057b8c9; Bhavan Jaipragas, "Trump Strikes a Blow in US–China Struggle with Build Act to Contain Xi's Belt and Road," *South China Morning Post*, 10/20/2018, https://www.scmp.com/week-asia/geopolitics/article/2169441/trump-strikes-blow-us-china-struggle-build-act-contain-xis.

32. Molly Ball, "Peter Navarro Used to Be a Democrat," *Time*, 8/3/2018, http://time.com/5375727/peter-navarro/; Josh Rogin, "How Peter Navarro Got His Groove Back," *WP*, 2/27/2018, https://www.washingtonpost.com/news/josh-rogin/wp/2018/02/27/how-peter-navarro-got-his-groove-back/.

33. Ball, "Peter Navarro."

34. Peter Navarro, *San Diego Confidential* (1998), 110–11, 198–99, 210–11.

35. Peter Navarro, *The Coming China Wars* (2006), xii–xix; Peter Navarro and Greg Autry, *Death by China* (2011), 1–11, 122–26, 137–50, 151–68.

36. Peter Navarro, *Crouching Tiger* (2015), 54–55, 56–61.

37. Navarro, *Crouching Tiger*, 187–93.

38. Navarro, *Crouching Tiger*, 194–201.

39. Ball, "Peter Navarro"; Navarro, *Crouching Tiger*, 256–60.

40. Thomas Franck, "Trump Doubles Down," *CNBC*, 3/2/2018, https:// www.cnbc.com/2018/03/02/trump-trade-wars-are-good-and-easy-to-win.html.

41. Don Lee, "Trump Announces Plans for Heavy Tariffs on Steel and Aluminum Imports, Inviting a Trade War with China," *Los Angeles Times*, 3/1/2018, http://www.latimes.com/business/la-fi-trump-steel-tariffs-20180301-story.html; Kevin Breuninger and Kayla Tausche, "Trump Slaps China with Tariffs on Up to $60 Billion in Imports,'" *CNBC*, 3/22/2018, https://www.cnbc.com/2018/03/22/trump-moves-to-slap-china-with-50-billion-in-tariffs-over-intellectual-property-theft.html.

42. Raymond Zhong, "China Strikes Back at Trump's Tariffs, but Its Consumers Worry," *NYT*, 7/6/2018, https://www.nytimes.com/2018/07/06/business/china-trump-trade-war-tariffs.html.

43. Jim Tankersley and Keith Bradsher, "Trump Hits China with Tariffs on $200 Billion in Goods, Escalating Trade War," *NYT*, 9/17/2018, https://www.nytimes.com/2018/09/17/us/politics/trump-china-tariffs-trade.html; Sylvan Lane, "Fed Chief Lays Out Risks of Trade War," *The Hill*, 7/17/2018, http://thehill.com/policy/finance/397470-fed-chief-lays-out-risks-of-trade-war.

44. Paul-Martin Foss, "Trade War with China Continues to Escalate," *Red Tea News*, 9/19/2018, http://redtea.com/america-now/trade-war-with-china-continues-to-escalate/.

45. Mikio Sugeno, "China Is Trying to Steal Our Future: Navarro," *Nikkei Asian Review*, 12/22/2018, https://asia.nikkei.com/Editor-s-Picks/Interview/China-is-trying-to-steal-our-future-Navarro.

46. Cassell Bryan-Low et al., "Hobbling Huawei," *Reuters*, 5/21/2019, https://www.reuters.com/investigates/special-report/huawei-usa-campaign/; Fareed Zakaria, "The New China Scare," *Foreign Affairs* 99, no. 1 (2020), 52–69; McMaster, *Battlegrounds*, 130–33, 141–44, 400–401, 405–6.

47. "Huawei's Founder Ren Zhengfei," Huawei (1/15/2019), https://www.

huawei.com/en/facts/voices-of-huawei/interview-with-ren-zhengfei; Thomas Seal, "Huawei Sales Rebound Despite U.S. Efforts to Halt Great Deal," *Bloomberg*, 7/13/2020, https://www.bloomberg.com/news/articles/2020-07-13/huawei-sales-rebound-despite-u-s-efforts-to-halt-gear-deals; Dan Sabbagh, "What Is Huawei and Why Is Its Role in UK's 5G so Controversial," *Guardian*, 7/13/2020, https://www.theguardian.com/technology/2020/jul/13/what-is-huawei-and-why-role-in-uk-5g-so-controversial; Dilip Hiro, "Who's Century Is It?," *TomDispatch*, 8/18/2020, http://www.tomdispatch.com/blog/176742/.

48.   John Bolton, *The Room Where It Happened* (2020), 300–301, 311; Peter Baker and Keith Bradsher, "Trump and Xi Agree to Restart Trade Talks, Avoiding Escalation in Tariff War," *NYT*, 6/29/2019, https://www.nytimes.com/2019/06/29/world/asia/g20-trump-xi-trade-talks.html; Gabriel Sherman, "'Make Sure I Win,'" *Vanity Fair*, 6/18/2020, https://www.vanityfair.com/news/2020/06/boltons-unredacted-book-shows-trump-trying-to-hide; Ana Swanson and Alan Rappeport, "With Trade Talks Looming, U.S. and China Move to Relax Tensions," *NYT*, 9/12/2019, https://www.nytimes.com/2019/09/12/us/politics/trump-china-trade.html.

49.   Ana Swanson, "As Trump Escalates Trade War, U.S. and China Move Further Apart with No End in Sight," *NYT*, 9/1/2019, https://www.nytimes.com/2019/09/01/world/asia/trump-trade-war-china.html; Yun Li, "Trump Says US Will Impose 10% Tariffs on Another $300 Billion of Chinese Goods Starting Sept. 1," *CNBC*, 9/1/2019, https://www.cnbc.com/2019/08/01/trump-says-us-will-impose-10percent-tariffs-on-300-billion-of-chinese-goods-starting-september-1.html.

50.   Jim Tankersley, "In Delaying Tariffs, Trump Faces Up to Economic Reality," *NYT*, 8/14/2019, https://www.nytimes.com/2019/08/14/us/politics/china-tariffs-donald-trump.html; Philip Rucker et al., "Trump, Banking on Strong Economy to Win Reelection, Frets over a Possible Downturn," *WP*, 8/15/2019, https://www.washingtonpost.com/politics/trump-banking-on-strong-economy-to-win-reelection-frets-over-a-possible-downturn/2019/08/15/04a85352-bf67-11e9-b873-63ace636af08_story.html.

51.   Peter Navarro interviewed by Stuart Varney, *Fox Business News*, 8/14/2019, https://www.youtube.com/watch?v=7j0xuYKZO4g; Ana Swanson and Matt Phillips, "Markets Soar on News of China Talks, but Hopes for Progress Are Low," *NYT*, 9/5/2019, https://www.nytimes.com/2019/09/05/business/markets-trump-china-trade.html.

52. Joe McDonald, "China Announces Tariff Hike on $75 Billion of US Products," *ABC News*, 8/23/2019, https://abcnews.go.com/International/wireStory/china-announces-tariff-hike-75-billion-us-products-65145696.

53. Peter S. Goodman, "Trump Can Battle China or Expand the Economy," *NYT*, 8/26/2019, https://www.nytimes.com/2019/08/26/business/economy/trump-china-trade-war.html; Alan Rappeport, "Farmers' Frustration with Trump Grows as U.S. Escalates China Fight," *NYT*, 8/27/2019, https://www.nytimes.com/2019/08/27/us/politics/trump-farmers-china-trade.html; Swanson, "As Trump Escalates Trade War."

54. Keith Bradsher, "China's Hard-Liners Win a Round in Trump's Trade Deal," *NYT*, 12/14/2019, https://www.nytimes.com/2019/12/14/business/china-trade-hardliners.html; Paul Wiseman, "A Look at Trump's Trade Wars," *Wisconsin State Journal*, 11/1/2020; Alan Rappeport, "Trump's Supporters See U.S. Victory in China Trade Deal," *NYT*, 1/14/2020, https://www.nytimes.com/2020/01/14/us/politics/trump-china-trade-deal.html; Ryan Hass and Abraham Denmark, "More Pain Than Gain," *Brookings*, 8/7/2020, https://www.brookings.edu/blog/order-from-chaos/2020/08/07/more-pain-than-gain-how-the-us-china-trade-war-hurt-america/.

55. Peter S. Goodman, "The Global Economy Was Improving," *NYT*, 5/15/2019, https://www.nytimes.com/2019/05/15/business/us-china-trade-war-economy.html; Winston Mok, "Trump Wants US Businesses to Cut All Ties with China," *South China Morning Post*, 9/11/2019, https://www.scmp.com/comment/opinion/article/3026384/trump-wants-us-businesses-cut-all-ties-china-why-thats-lose-lose; Policy Planning Staff, Office of the Secretary of State, *The Elements of the China Challenge* (2020), 1, 7, https://www.state.gov/wp-content/uploads/2020/11/20-02832-Elements-of-China-Challenge-508.pdf.

56. Keith Bradsher, "China Needs New Place to Sell Its Mountains of Stuff," *NYT*, 7/26/2019, https://www.nytimes.com/2019/07/26/business/china-trade-war-us-rcep.html; Keith Bradsher and Ana Swanson, "China-Led Trade Pact Is Signed, in Challenge to the U.S.," *NYT*, 11/15/2020, https://www.nytimes.com/2020/11/15/business/china-trade-rcep.html; Tim McDonald, "What Is the Regional Comprehensive Economic Partnership?," *BBC News*, 11/16/2020, https://www.bbc.com/news/business-54899254; Jack Ewing and Steven Lee Myers, "China and E.U. Leaders Strike Investment Deal, but Political Hurdles Await," *NYT*, 12/30/2020, https://www.nytimes.com/2020/12/30/business/china-eu-investment-deal.html; Steven Lee Myers, "With Concessions and Deals,

China's Leader Tries to Box Out Biden," *NYT*, 1/3/2021, https://www.nytimes.com/2021/01/03/world/asia/china-eu-investment-biden.html.

57. Ronald O'Rourke, *China Naval Modernization* (2016), 8, https://news.usni.org/wp-content/uploads/2016/06/RL33153.pdf.

58. Eric Heginbotham et al., *The U.S.-China Military Scorecard, Forces, Geography and the Evolving Balance of Power, 1996–2017*, RAND Corporation (2015), xix, xxx–xxxii, https://www.rand.org/pubs/research_reports/RR392.html.

59. "Pakistan and China Boost Security at Gwadar Port," *Maritime Executive*, 12/15/2016, https://www.maritime-executive.com/article/pakistan-boosts-maritime-security-at-gwadar-port.

60. PTI, "Chinese Navy Ships to Be Deployed at Gwadar," *Times of India*, 11/25/2016, https://timesofindia.indiatimes.com/world/pakistan/Chinese-navy-ships-to-be-deployed-at-Gwadar-Pak-navy-official/articleshow/55622674.cms.

61. Behram Baloch, "China Hands Over Two Ships to Pakistan for Maritime Security," *Dawn*, 1/15/2017, https://www.dawn.com/news/1308491; ANI, "China's Second Overseas Naval Base to Be in Pakistan?," *New Indian Express*, 1/9/2018, http://www.newindianexpress.com/world/2018/jan/09/chinas-second-overseas-naval-base-to-be-in-pakistan-1748554.html.

62. "China Opens First Overseas Military Base," *VOA*, 11/3/2017, https://www.voanews.com/a/china-overseas-military-base/4099717.html.

63. Simon Mundy, "China-Backed Port Sparks Sri Lanka Sovereignty Fears," *Financial Times*, 10/23/2017, https://www.ft.com/content/f8262d56-a6a0-11e7-ab55-27219df83c97.

64. Asia Maritime Transparency Initiative, "South China Sea Energy Exploration and Development," https://amti.csis.org/south-china-sea-energy-exploration-and-development; Christopher Bodeen, "Looming Collapse of Fisheries in the South China Sea?," *Navy Times*, 5/20/2019, https://www.navytimes.com/news/your-navy/2019/05/20/looming-collapse-of-fisheries-in-the-south-china-sea.

65. Hans M. Kristensen, "China SSBN Fleet Getting Ready—But for What?," *Federation of American Scientists Strategic Security Blog*, 5/25/2014, https://fas.org/blogs/security/2014/04/chinassbnfleet/.

66. Derek Watkins, "What China Has Been Building in the South China Sea," *NYT*, 10/27/2015, https://www.nytimes.com/interactive/2015/07/30/world/asia/what-china-has-been-building-in-the-south-china-sea.html; "Occupation and Island Building," Asia Maritime Transparency Initiative,

http://amti.csis.org/island-tracker/.

67.   Michael Forsythe and Jane Perlez, "South China Sea Buildup Brings Beijing
Closer to Realizing Control," *NYT*, 3/8/2016, https://www.nytimes.
com/2016/03/09/world/asia/south-china-sea-militarization.html; Thomas
J. Wright, *All Measures Short of War* (2017), 81; Ben Westcott, "South
China Sea," *CNN*, 3/29/2017, https://www.cnn.com/2017/03/28/asia/
south-china-sea-islands-aircraft-hangars/index.html.

68.   Cid Standifer, "Updated," *USNI News*,
5/29/2017, https://news.usni.org/2017/05/29/
brief-history-us-freedom-navigation-operations-south-china-sea.

69.   Floyd Whaley, "Eye on China, U.S. and Philippines Ramp Up Military
Alliance," *NYT*, 4/12/2016, https://www.nytimes.com/2016/04/13/
world/asia/philippines-south-china-sea-ash-carter.html; AP, "US,
Philippines Sign Military Deal to Counter Chinese Aggression,"
Australian, 4/28/2014, https://www.theaustralian.com.au/news/world/
us-philippines-sign-military-deal-to-counter-chinese-aggression/news-sto
ry/43e9cac698180b35662e4c0db7db66c0.

70.   "Philippines Reopens Subic Bay as Military Base to Cover South China
Sea," *Guardian*, 7/15/2015, https://www.theguardian.com/world/2015/
jul/16/philippines-reopens-subic-bay-as-military-base-to-cover-south-
china-sea; Ralph Jennings, "US Navy Edges Back to Subic Bay in
Philippines—under New Rules," *Christian Science Monitor*, 11/12/2015,
http://www.csmonitor.com/World/Asia-Pacific/2015/1112/
US-Navy-edges-back-to-Subic-Bay-in-Philippines-under-new-rules.

71.   Keith Bradsher, "Philippine Leader Sounds Alarm on China," *NYT*,
2/4/2014, https://www.nytimes.com/2014/02/05/world/asia/
philippine-leader-urges-international-help-in-resisting-chinas-sea-
claims.html; Michaela Del Callar, "DFA: China Boats Blocking
PHL Vessels from Panatag Shoal," *GMA News Online*, 7/18/2012,
http://www.gmanetwork.com/news/story/265889/news/nation/
dfa-china-boats-blocking-phl-vessels-from-panatag-shoal.

72.   Permanent Court of Arbitration, "Award," *In the Matter of the South
China Sea Arbitration before an Arbitral Tribunal Constituted under
Annex VII to the 1982 United Nations Convention on the Law of the
Sea between the Republic of the Philippines and the People's Republic of
China*, 7/12/2016, 68–77, 116–17, http://www.pcacases.com/pcadocs/
PH-CN%20-%2020160712%20-%20Award.pdf; Zhiguo Gao and Bing
Bing Jia, "The Nine-Dash Line in the South China Sea," *American Journal
of International Law* 107, no. 1 (2013), 103–4; Jane Perlez, "Tribunal

Rejects Beijing's Claims in South China Sea," *NYT*, 7/12/2016, https://www.nytimes.com/2016/07/13/world/asia/south-china-sea-hague-ruling-philippines.html.

73. Wright, *All Measures Short of War*, 82–83.

74. Kyle Mizokami, "China's Second Aircraft Carrier Is Its Most Crucial Yet," *Popular Mechanics*, 12/11/2017, https://www.popularmechanics.com/military/navy-ships/a14408704/chinas-second-aircraft-carrier-is-its-most-crucial-yet/.

75. Kyle Mizokami, "China's Next Aircraft Carrier Will Be a Major Leap Forward," *Popular Mechanics*, 1/19/2018, https://www.popularmechanics.com/military/navy-ships/a15392390/chinas-next-aircraft-carrier-002/; H.I. Sutton, "Power Projection," *Forbes*, 12/3/2019, https://www.forbes.com/sites/hisutton/2019/12/03/super-power-projection-work-to-start-on-chinas-4th-aircraft-carrier/#72d44fe65d38.

76. Simon Denyer, "By 2030, South China Sea Will Be 'Virtually a Chinese Lake,' Study Warns," *WP*, 1/20/2016, https://www.washingtonpost.com/news/worldviews/wp/2016/01/20/by-2030-south-china-sea-will-be-virtually-a-chinese-lake-u-s-study-warns/; Michael Forsythe, "Possible Radar Suggests Beijing Wants 'Effective Control' in South China Sea," *NYT*, 2/23/2016, https://www.nytimes.com/2016/02/24/world/asia/china-south-china-sea-radar.html.

77. Congressional Research Service, *China Naval Modernization* (2021), 32, https://fas.org/sgp/crs/row/RL33153.pdf.

78. O'Rourke, *China Naval Modernization*, 16–18; Kyle Mizokami, "China Will Soon Have More Submarines Than America," *Popular Mechanics*, 12/14/2020, https://www.popularmechanics.com/military/navy-ships/a34965433/us-vs-china-navy-submarines/.

79. O'Rourke, *China Naval Modernization*, i–ii, 95–104.

80. Jeffrey Lin and Peter W. Singer, "China's Hypersonic Aircraft Would Fly from Beijing to New York in Two Hours," *Popular Science*, 2/26/2018, https://www.popsci.com/china-hypersonic-double-wing-aircraft-i-plane.

81. Office of the Secretary of Defense, *Military and Security Developments Involving the People's Republic of China, 2010* (2010), i, 1–3, 7, 25–37, https://archive.defense.gov/pubs/pdfs/2010_CMPR_Final.pdf; Thom Shanker, "Pentagon Cites Concerns in China Military Growth," *NYT*, 8/16/2010, https://www.nytimes.com/2010/08/17/world/asia/17military.html; Reuters Staff, "China Launches New Global Positioning Satellite," *Reuters*, 7/31/2010, http://www.reuters.com/article/idUSTRE67005R20100801; Steven Lee Myers, "China Will

Answer 'Heavenly Question': Can It Land on Mars?," *NYT*, 7/22/20, https://www.nytimes.com/2020/07/22/science/china-mars-mission.html.

82. William J. Broad and David E. Sanger, "China Tests Anti-Satellite Weapon, Unnerving U.S.," *NYT*, 1/18/2007, https://www.nytimes.com/2007/01/18/world/asia/18cnd-china.html; Marc Kaufman and Dafna Linzer, "China Criticized for Anti-Satellite Missile Test," *WP*, 1/19/2007, https://www.washingtonpost.com/archive/politics/2007/01/19/china-criticized-for-anti-satellite-missile-test-span-classbankheaddestruction-of-an-aging-satellite-illustrates-vulnerability-of-us-space-assetsspan/ae3462c4-c2d9-422b-bc17-dc040458fe64/.

83. David C. Gompert et al., *War with China* (2016), iii–iv.

84. David B. Larter, "US Navy to Add 46 Ships in Next Five Years, but 355 Ships Won't Come for a Long Time," *Defense News*, 2/12/2018, https://www.defensenews.com/smr/federal-budget/2018/02/13/us-navy-to-add-46-ships-in-five-years-but-355-ships-is-well-over-the-horizon/.

85. Ankit Panda, "Straight from the US State Department," *The Diplomat*, 3/14/2017, https://thediplomat.com/2017/03/straight-from-the-us-state-department-the-pivot-to-asia-is-over/; Demetri Sevastopulo, "Trump Gives Glimpse of 'Indo-Pacific' Strategy to Counter China," *Financial Times*, 11/10/2017, https://www.ft.com/content/e6d17fd6-c623-11e7-a1d2-6786f39ef675.

86. John M. Richardson, "A Design for Maintaining Maritime Superiority," *Naval War College Review* 69, no. 2 (2016), 13.

87. US Department of the Navy, *The Future Navy*, 5/17/2017, https://admin.govexec.com/media/gbc/docs/pdfs_edit/futurenavyfinal.pdf.

88. T.S. Rowden, *Surface Force Strategy*, US Navy (2017), 1–2, https://media.defense.gov/2020/May/18/2002302052/-1/-1/1/SURFACEFORCESTRATEGY-RETURNTOSEACONTROL.PDF.

89. "About USINDOPACOM," United States Indo-Pacific Command, https://www.pacom.mil/About-USINDOPACOM/.

90. Michael E. Hutchens et al., "Joint Concept for Access and Maneuver in the Global Commons," *Joint Force Quarterly* 84 (2017), 134–36, https://ndupress.ndu.edu/Portals/68/Documents/jfq/jfq-84/jfq-84_134-139_Hutchens-et-al.pdf.

91. O'Rourke, *China Naval Modernization*, i–ii, 95–104; Department of Defense, *Military and Security Developments Involving the People's Republic of China* (2020), i–xii, https://media.defense.gov/2020/Sep/01/2002488689/-1/-1/1/2020-DOD-CHINA-MILITARY-

POWER-REPORT-FINAL.PDF.

92. Graham Allison, "The New Spheres of Influence," *Foreign Affairs* 99, no. 2 (2020), 30-40.

93. Zbigniew Brzezinski, *The Grand Chessboard* (1998), 35, 39.

94. "China Says Uighur Detention Centers Fight Terrorism, Rejects UN Criticism," *Reuters*, 11/6/2018, https://www.pri.org/stories/2018-11-06/china-says-uighur-detention-centers-fight-terrorism-rejects-un-criticism; Austin Ramzy and Chris Buckley, "'Show Absolutely No Mercy': Inside China's Mass Detentions," *NYT*, 11/17/2019, https://static01.nyt.com/images/2019/11/17/nytfrontpage/scan.pdf.

95. Human Rights Watch, "China's Global Threat to Human Rights," *World Report 2020* (2020), https://www.hrw.org/world-report/2020/china-global-threat-to-human-rights.

96. Ji Guoxing, "SLOC Security in the Asia Pacific," Center Occasional Papers, Asia-Pacific Center for Security Studies (2000), http://apcss.org/Publications/Ocasional%20Papers/OPSloc.htm; Robert D. Kaplan, "The South China Sea Will Be the Battleground of the Future," *Business Insider*, 2/6/2016, http://www.businessinsider.com/why-the-south-china-sea-is-so-crucial-2015-2.

97. U. Rashid Sumaila and William W.L. Cheung, *Boom or Bust* (2015), 1–3; John W. McManus et al., "Toward Establishing a Spratly Islands International Marine Peace Park," *Ocean Development and International Law* 41, no. 3 (2010), 273.

98. Richard Weitz, "The SCO and NATO Compared," *China-US Focus*, 8/30/2018, https://www.chinausfocus.com/peace-security/the-sco-and-nato-compared.

99. S.R., "Why China Is Creating a New 'World Bank' for Asia," *The Economist*, 11/11/2014, https://www.economist.com/the-economist-explains/2014/11/11/why-china-is-creating-a-new-world-bank-for-asia.

100. David Tweed, "China's New Silk Road," *Bloomberg*, 4/15/2019, https://www.bloomberg.com/quicktake/china-s-silk-road; "Embracing the BRI Ecosystem in 2018," *Deloitte Insights*, 2/13/2018, https://www2.deloitte.com/insights/us/en/economy/asia-pacific/china-belt-and-road-initiative.html.

101. Li Congjun, " Toward a New World Media Order," *Wall Street Journal*, 6/1/2011, https://www.wsj.com/articles/SB10001424052748704816604576335563624853594; Reporters without Borders, *China's Pursuit of a New World Media Order* (2019), 3, 9–10, https://rsf.org/sites/default/files/en_rapport_chine_web_final.pdf; James M. Dorsey,

"How Illiberals & Autocrats Unite to Craft a New World Media Order," *Counter Currents*, 4/12/2019, https://countercurrents.org/2019/04/illiberals-and-autocrats-unite-to-craft-a-new-world-media-order/.

102. Joya Chatterji, "From Subjecthood to Citizenship in South Asia," in Alfred W. McCoy et al., eds., *Endless Empire* (2012), 317.

103. Victoria de Grazia, *Irresistible Empire* (2006), 18–75; James Peck, *Ideal Illusions* (2010), 26–38, 41–44.

104. Ethan Epstein, "How China Infiltrated U.S. Classrooms," *Politico Magazine*, 1/17/2018, https://www.politico.com/magazine/story/2018/01/16/how-china-infiltrated-us-classrooms-216327; US Senate, Permanent Subcommittee on Investigations, *China's Impact on the U.S. Education System* (2019), 1–4, 76–77, https://www.hsgac.senate.gov/imo/media/doc/PSI%20Report%20China%27s%20Impact%20on%20the%20US%20Education%20System.pdf; Rachelle Peterson, "Confucian Institutes in the US That Are Closing" (2019), National Assocation of Scholars, https://www.nas.org/storage/app/media/Reports/Outsourced%20to%20China/confucius-institutes-that-closed-updated-june-3-2019.pdf; Andreas Fulda, "Chinese Propaganda Has No Place on Campus," *Foreign Policy*, 10/15/2019, https://foreignpolicy.com/2019/10/15/confucius-institute-chinese-propaganda-campus-communist-party-censorship/.

105. Permanent Court of Arbitration, *South China Sea*; Perlez, "Tribunal Rejects"; Gao, "Nine-Dash Line," 103–4.

106. Perlez, "Tribunal Rejects"; Tom Phillips et al., "Beijing Rejects Tribunal's Ruling in South China Sea Case," *Guardian*, 7/12/2016, https://www.theguardian.com/world/2016/jul/12/philippines-wins-south-china-sea-case-against-china.

107. António Guterres, "Remarks at Opening Ceremony of UN Climate Change Conference COP25," 12/2/2019, https://www.un.org/sg/en/content/sg/speeches/2019-12-02/remarks-opening-ceremony-of-cop25; Associated Press, "U.N. Chief Warns of 'Point of No Return' on Climate Change," NBC News, 12/2/2019, https://www.nbcnews.com/news/world/u-n-chief-warns-point-no-return-climate-change-n1093956.

108. Sabrina Shankman, "Rapidly Warming Mediterranean Headed for Desertification, Study Warns," *Inside Climate News*, 10/27/2016, https://insideclimatenews.org/news/27102016/global-warming-mediterranean-region-desertification-drought-climate-change; "Climate Change," United Nations, https://www.un.org/en/sections/issues-depth/climate-change/.

109. Colin P. Kelley et al., "Climate Change and Implications of the Recent

Syrian Drought," *Proceedings of the National Academy of Sciences* 112, no. 11 (2015), 3241–46, https://www.pnas.org/content/112/11/3241.

110. "Migrant Crisis," BBC News, 3/4/2016, https://www.bbc.com/news/ world-europe-34131911; Steven Erlanger, "Facing Migrant Crisis, E.U. Makes a Dubious Deal with Turkey," *NYT*, 3/10/2016, https://www. nytimes.com/2016/03/11/world/europe/europe-turkey-erdogan-refugees-migrants.html; Samya Kullab and Nabil Al-Jurani, "Record Heat, Politics Inflame Iraq's Electricity Shortages," *WP*, 8/4/2020, https:// www.washingtonpost.com/business/record-temperatures-pending-deals-inflame-iraqs-power-woes/2020/08/04/c5fc051c-d618-11ea-a788-2ce86cc81129_story.html.

111. Lauren Markham, "How Climate Change Is Pushing Central American Migrants to the US," *Guardian*, 4/6/2019, https://www.theguardian. com/commentisfree/2019/apr/06/us-mexico-immigration-climate-change-migration; Jonathan Blitzer, "How Climate Change Is Fueling the U.S. Border Crisis," *New Yorker*, 4/3/2019, https://www.newyorker.com/ news/dispatch/how-climate-change-is-fuelling-the-us-border-crisis.

112. Blitzer, "Climate Change."

113. Kirk Semple, "Central American Farmers Head to the U.S., Fleeing Climate Change," *NYT*, 4/13/2019, https://www.nytimes. com/2019/04/13/world/americas/coffee-climate-change-migration.html.

114. Blitzer, "Climate Change"; Monique O. Madan, "U.S. to Slash More than $500 Million in Aid to El Salvador, Guatemala and Honduras," *Miami Herald*, 3/30/2019, https://www.miamiherald.com/news/local/ immigration/article228647089.html; Abrahm Lustgarten, "The Great Climate Migration," *NYT*, 7/23/2020, https://www.nytimes.com/ interactive/2020/07/23/magazine/climate-migration.html; Michael D. Shear and Thomas Gibbons-Neff, "Trump Sending 5,200 Troops to the Border in an Election-Season Response to Migrants," *NYT*, 10/29/2018, https://www.nytimes.com/2018/10/29/us/politics/border-security-troops-trump.html.

115. Kanta Kumari Rigaud et al., *Groundswell* (2018), xix–xxvi, https:// openknowledge.worldbank.org/handle/10986/29461; Lustgarten, "Great Climate Migration"; Institute for Economics and Peace, *Global Peace Index 2020* (2020), 3, 71; Markham, "How Climate Change Is Pushing Central American Migrants to the US."

116. Daniel R. Coats, *Worldwide Threat Assessment of the US Intelligence Community*, Office of the Director of National Intelligence (2019), 23, https://www.dni.gov/files/ODNI/documents/2019-ATA-SFR---SSCI.pdf.

117. Douglas Lute and Nicholas Burns, *NATO at Seventy*, Belfer Center for Science and International Affairs (2019), 13, 34, 40, https://www.belfercenter.org/NATO70; Tim Arango, "Turkish Dam Project Threatens to Submerge Thousands of Years of History," *NYT*, 9/1/2016, https://www.nytimes.com/2016/09/02/world/europe/turkey-hasankeyf-ilisu-dam.html; Alexandra Marvar, "Turkey's Other Weapon against the Kurds: Water," *The Nation*, 11/11/19, https://www.thenation.com/article/archive/turkey-syria-iraq-kurds/.

118. Chris Matthews, "Fortune 5," *Fortune*, 10/5/2014, https://fortune.com/2014/10/05/most-powerful-economic-empires-of-all-time/; Office of the Under Secretary of Defense, *National Defense Budget Estimates for FY 2000* (1999), 1–16, https://comptroller.defense.gov/Portals/45/Documents/defbudget/Docs/fy2000_greenbook.pdf; Office of the Under Secretary of Defense, *National Defense Budget Estimates for FY 2020* (2019), 1–4, https://comptroller.defense.gov/Portals/45/Documents/defbudget/fy2020/FY20_Green_Book.pdf; H. Plecher, "United States' Share of Global Gross Domestic Product (GDP) Adjusted for Purchasing Power Parity (PPP) from 2014 to 2025" *Statistica* (1/6/2021), https://www.statista.com/statistics/270267/united-states-share-of-global-gross-domestic-product-gdp.

119. US Global Change Research Program, *Fourth National Climate Assessment*, vol. 2 (2018), 29, 36, 64, 413, 1349; Rebecca Lindsey, "Climate Change: Global Sea Level," *NOAA Climate. gov*, 8/14/2020, https://www.climate.gov/news-features/understanding-climate/climate-change-global-sea-level.

120. Michael T. Klare, "When the Climate Replaces Our Forever Wars," *The Nation*, 12/11/2019, https://www.thenation.com/article/when-the-climate-replaces-our-forever-wars/.

121. Jonathan Vespa, "The U.S. Joins Other Countries with Large Aging Populations," *U.S. Bureau of Census* (2018), https://www.census.gov/library/stories/2018/03/graying-america.html.

122. Robert Fogel, "Forecasting the Cost of U.S. Health Care in 2040," *Journal of Policy Modeling* 31, no. 4 (2009), 482–88; Congressional Budget Office, *The 2019 Long-Term Budget Outlook* (2019), 19–20, 53–57, https://www.cbo.gov/system/files/2019-06/55331-LTBO-2.pdf.

123. Rigaud, *Groundswell*, 99–107.

124. US National Intelligence Council, *Global Trends 2030* (2012), i–iii, 105, http://www.dni.gov/files/documents/GlobalTrends_2030.pdf; PricewaterhouseCoopers, *The World in 2050* (2015), 1–3, https://

www.pwc.com/gx/en/issues/the-economy/assets/world-in-2050-february-2015.pdf.

125.   Erin Duffin, "Military Expenditure as Percentage of Gross Domestic Product (GDP) in Highest Spending Countries 2018," *Statista* (2020), https://www.statista.com/statistics/266892/military-expenditure-as-percentage-of-gdp-in-highest-spending-countries/; Nicholas Kristof, "This Is How a War with China Could Begin," *NYT*, 9/4/2019, https://www.nytimes.com/2019/09/04/opinion/china-taiwan-war.html; Kevin Rudd, "Short of War," *Foreign Affairs* 100, no. 2 (2021), 58-72; David Pierson and Michelle Yun, "The most important company you've never heard of is being dragged into the U.S.-China rivalry," *Los Angeles Times*, 12/17/2020, https://www.latimes.com/world-nation/story/2020-12-17/taiwan-chips-tsmc-china-us; "The most dangerous place on Earth," *The Economist*, 5/1/2021, https://www.economist.com/leaders/2021/05/01/the-most-dangerous-place-on-earth?utm_campaign=the-economist-today.

126.   Åshild Kolås, "Tibetan Nationalism: The Politics of Religion," *Journal of Peace Research* 33, no. 1 (1996), 51–66.

127.   Jiang Shigong, "Empire and World Order," *Reading the China Dream* (April 2019), https://www.readingthechinadream.com/jiang-shigong-empire-and-world-order.html; Ryan Mitchell, "Chinese Receptions of Carl Schmitt Since 1929," *Journal of Law and International Affairs* 8, no. 1 (2020), 181–263; Chris Buckley, "'Clean Up this Mess,'" *NYT*, 8/2/2020, https://www.nytimes.com/2020/08/02/world/asia/china-hong-kong-national-security-law.html.

128.   Steven Lee Myers, "A Blue Sky in Beijing?," *NYT*, 1/11/2018, https://www.nytimes.com/2018/01/11/world/asia/pollution-beijing-declines.html; Michael Wines, "China Admits Problems with Three Gorges Dam," *NYT*, 5/19/2011, https://www.nytimes.com/2011/05/20/world/asia/20gorges.html; Andrew Jacobs, "China's Appetite Pushes Fisheries to the Brink," *NYT*, 4/30/2017, https://www.nytimes.com/2017/04/30/world/asia/chinas-appetite-pushes-fisheries-to-the-brink.html.

129.   Yanzhong Huang, "Why China's Good Environmental Policies Have Gone Wrong," *NYT*, 1/14/2018, https://www.nytimes.com/2018/01/14/opinion/china-environmental-policies-wrong.html; Steven Lee Myers, "Xi Sets 40-Year Target in Ambitious Pledge on Carbon Neutrality," *NYT*, 9/24/2020, https://blendle.com/i/the-new-york-times/xi-sets-40-year-target-in-ambitious-pledge-on-carbon-neutrality/bnl-newyorktimes-20200924-11_1; Zhang Chun, "Can China Meet Its 2017 Air Quality Goals," *China Dialogue*, 1/25/2017, https://chinadialogue.

net/en/pollution/9574-can-china-meet-its-2-17-air-quality-goals/.

130. Scott Moore and Michelle Melton, "China's Pivot on Climate Change and National Security," *Lawfare Institute*, 4/2/2019, https://www.lawfareblog.com/chinas-pivot-climate-change-and-national-security; Christine Shearer et al., "Out of Step," *Global Energy Monitor* (November 2019), https://endcoal.org/global-coal-plant-tracker/reports/out-of-step/; Stephanie Yang, "In Tougher Times, China Falls Back on Coal," *Wall Street Journal*, 12/23/2019, https://www.wsj.com/articles/in-tougher-times-china-falls-back-on-coal-11577115096; Stuart Lau, "COP25 summit," *South China Morning Post*, 12/12/2019, https://www.scmp.com/news/china/diplomacy/article/3041711/cop25-summit-china-leads-four-nation-attack-over-imbalances-un; Somini Sengupta, "U.N. Climate Talks End with Few Commitments and a 'Lost' Opportunity," *NYT*, 12/15/2019, https://www.nytimes.com/2019/12/15/climate/cop25-un-climate-talks-madrid.html; Bradsher, "China Renews"; Muntean, *Fossil CO2 emissions*; Andrew S. Erickson and Gabriel Collins, "Competition with China Can Save the Planet," *Foreign Affairs* 100, no. 3 (2021), 136-49; Reuters Staff, "China generated over half world's coal-fired power in 2020," *Reuters*, 3/28/2021, https://www.reuters.com/article/us-climate-change-china-coal/china-generated-over-half-worlds-coal-fired-power-in-2020-study-idUSKBN2BK0PZ."

131. Steven Mufson, "U.S. Greenhouse Gas Emissions Fell Slightly in 2019," *WP*, 1/7/2020, https://www.washingtonpost.com/climate-environment/us-greenhouse-gas-emissions-fell-slightly-in-2019/2020/01/06/568f0a82-309e-11ea-a053-dc6d944ba776_story.html; Nadja Popovich and Brad Plumer, "What Trump's Environmental Rollbacks Mean for Global Warming," *NYT*, 9/17/2020, https://www.nytimes.com/interactive/2020/09/17/climate/emissions-trump-rollbacks-deregulation.html.

132. Hannah Ritchie and Max Roser, "Annual CO2 Emissions, by World Region," *Our World in Data* (August 2020), https://ourworldindata.org/co2-and-other-greenhouse-gas-emissions; M. Crippa, et al., *Fossil CO2 emissions of all world countries—2020 Report* (2020), https://edgar.jrc.ec.europa.eu/report_2020#emissions_table.

133. Intergovernmental Panel on Climate Change, *Global Warming of 1.5°C* (2019), 14, 34, https://www.ipcc.ch/sr15/chapter/spm/; Ren21, *Renewables 2020* (2020), 32, https://www.ren21.net/reports/global-status-report/.

134. Megpin Ge and Johannes Friedrich, "World Greenhouse Gas Emissions: 2016 (Sector/End Use/Gas)," *4 Charts Explain Greenhouse Gas Emissions*

by Countries and Sectors, World Resources Institute (2/3/2020), https://www.wri.org/resources/data-visualizations/world-greenhouse-gas-emissions-2016; Hannah Ritchie and Max Roser, "Sector by Sector: Where Do Global Greenhouse Gas Emissions Come From," *Our World in Data*, https://ourworldindata.org/emissions-by-sector.

135.　Brad Plumer, "To Cut Emissions to Zero, U.S. Needs to Make Big Changes in Next 10 Years," *NYT*, 12/15/2020, https://www.nytimes.com/2020/12/15/climate/america-next-decade-climate.html; Corinne Purtill, "How Climate Policy Will Change in 2021," *NYT*, 12/14/2020, https://www.nytimes.com/2020/12/14/business/dealbook/climate-policy-debate.html; Chen Zhou et al., "Greater Committed Warming after Accounting for the Pattern Effect," *Nature Climate Change* 11 (1/4/2021), 132–6, https://www.nature.com/articles/s41558-020-00955-x; Seth Borenstein, "Study: Warming Already Baked in Will Blow Past Climate Goals," *AP News*, 1/4/2021, https://apnews.com/article/climate-climate-change-pollution-3f226aed9c58e36c69e7342b104d48bf; Brad Plumer and Nadja Popovich, "The U.S. Has a New Climate Goal," *NYT*, 4/22/2021, https://www.nytimes.com/interactive/2021/04/22/climate/new-climate-pledge.html.

136.　Smil, *Energy*, 156–57, 227–28, 232–33.

Chapter 7: Climate Change in the Twenty-First Century

1.　"Changes in the Carbon Cycle," Earth Observatory, NASA (6/16/2011), https://earthobservatory.nasa.gov/features/CarbonCycle/page4.php.

2.　"Changes in the Carbon Cycle."

3.　"The Greenhouse Effect?," University Corporation for Atmospheric Research (2011), https://scied.ucar.edu/longcontent/greenhouse-effect.

4.　Eugene Linden, "How Scientists Got Climate Change So Wrong," *NYT*, 11/8/2019, https://www.nytimes.com/2019/11/08/opinion/sunday/science-climate-change.html; Article 2, United Nations Framework Convention on Climate Change (1992), https://unfccc.int/files/essential_background/background_publications_htmlpdf/application/pdf/conveng.pdf.

5.　Linden, "How Scientists Got Climate Change So Wrong"; National Research Council, *Abrupt Climate Change* (2002), 10, https://www.nap.edu/read/10136/chapter/1; UN Framework Convention on Climate Change, *Report of the Conference of the Parties on its Third Session, Held at Kyoto from 1 to 11 December 1997* (1998), https://unfccc.int/resource/docs/cop3/07a01.pdf; John D. Sutter and Joshua Berlinger,

"Obama Climate Agreement 'Best Chance We Have' to Save the Planet," *CNN*, 12/14/2015, http://www.cnn.com/2015/12/12/world/global-climate-change-conference-vote/; United Nations Development Programme and United Nations Framework Convention on Climate Change, *The Heat Is On* (2019), 4–9, https://unfccc.int/news/the-heat-is-on-taking-stock-of-global-climate-ambition.

6. Coral Davenport, "Major Climate Report Describes a Strong Risk of Crisis as Early as 2040," *NYT*, 10/7/2018, https://www.nytimes.com/2018/10/07/climate/ipcc-climate-report-2040.html; H. Pletcher, "Global Gross Domestic Product (GDP) at Current Prices from 2014 to 2024 (in Billion Dollars)," *Statista* (6/3/2020), https://www.statista.com/statistics/268750/global-gross-domestic-product-gdp; David Wallace-Wells, "Time to Panic," *NYT*, 2/16/2019, https://www.nytimes.com/2019/02/16/opinion/sunday/fear-panic-climate-change-warming.html; Intergovernmental Panel on Climate Change, *Global Warming of 1.5°C* (2019), 177, https://www.ipcc.ch/sr15/chapter/spm/.

7. UN Development Programme, *The Heat Is On*, 6–9; Brad Plumer, "5 Global Trends Shaping Our Climate Future," *NYT*, 11/12/2019, https://www.nytimes.com/2019/11/12/climate/energy-trends-climate-change.html; Yaryna Serkez, "Our World in 20 Years," *NYT*, 1/28/2021, https://www.nytimes.com/interactive/2021/01/28/opinion/climate-change-risks-by-country.html.

8. Marcelo de Souza, Associated Press, "More About the Amazon Wildfires," *Wisconsin State Journal*, 8/28/2019; Kendra Pierre-Louis, "Amazon, Siberia, Indonesia: A World of Fire," *NYT*, 8/28/2019, https://www.nytimes.com/2019/08/28/climate/fire-amazon-africa-siberia-worldwide.html; Julie Turkewitz, "The Amazon Is on Fire. So Is Central Africa," *NYT*, 8/27/2019, https://www.nytimes.com/2019/08/27/world/africa/congo-angola-rainforest-fires.html; Somini Sengupta, "How Europe Turned into a Perfect Landscape for Wildfires," *NYT*, 2/5/2020, https://www.nytimes.com/2020/02/05/climate/forests-europe-climate-changed.html.

9. Livia Albeck-Ripka et al., "'It's an Atomic Bomb,'" *NYT*, 1/4/2020, https://www.nytimes.com/2020/01/04/world/australia/fires-military.html; Shonal Ganguly and Steve McMorran, Associated Press, "Fire Threats Intensify in Australia," *Wisconsin State Journal*, 1/5/2020; Damien Cave, "Australia's Witnesses to Fire's Fury Are Desperate to Avoid a Sequel," *NYT*, 9/14/2020, https://www.nytimes.com/2020/09/14/world/australia/bush-fires-preventive-burns.html.

10. Maria Magdalena Arréllaga et al., "Brazil's Fires Burn World's Largest

Tropical Wetlands at 'Unprecedented' Scale," *NYT*, 9/4/2020, https://www.nytimes.com/2020/09/04/world/americas/brazil-wetlands-fires-pantanal.html; Holly Yan et al., "California Set New Record for Land Torched by Wildfires," *CNN*, 9/6/2020, https://www.cnn.com/2020/09/05/us/california-mammoth-pool-reservoir-camp-fire/index.html; "Why California Is Experiencing Its Worst Fires on Record," *The Economist*, 8/26/2020, https://www.economist.com/united-states/2020/08/26/why-california-is-experiencing-its-worst-fires-on-record; Thomas Fuller and Sarah Mervosh, "'You Couldn't See Anything,'" *NYT*, 9/8/2020, https://www.nytimes.com/2020/09/08/us/california-wildfires-helicopter-rescue.html; Bill Morlin and Mike Baker, "Wildfires Bring New Devastation across the West," *NYT*, 9/9/2020, https://www.nytimes.com/2020/09/09/us/fires-washington-california-oregon-malden.html; Jack Healy et al., "A Line of Fire South of Portland and a Yearslong Recovery Ahead," *NYT*, 9/11/2020, https://www.nytimes.com/2020/09/11/us/fires-oregon-california-washington.html; Jason Wilson et al., "Dozens Missing in Oregon as Historic Fires Devastate Western US," *Guardian*, 9/11/2020, https://www.theguardian.com/world/2020/sep/11/oregon-fires-california-washington-deaths-wildfires; Associated Press, "Wildfires Set Record," *NYT*, 10/5/2020; Charlie Brennan and Rick Rojas, "Colorado Wildfire Grows into Largest in State History," *NYT*, 10/18/2020, https://www.nytimes.com/2020/10/18/us/colorado-wildfires-cameron-peak.html.

11. Somini Sengupta, "Extreme Weather Displaced a Record 7 Million People in First Half of 2019," *NYT*, 9/12/2019, https://www.nytimes.com/2019/09/12/climate/extreme-weather-displacement.html; Henry Fountain and Nadja Popovich, "2019 Was the Second-Hottest Year Ever, Closing Out the Warmest Decade," *NYT*, 1/15/2020, https://www.nytimes.com/interactive/2020/01/15/climate/hottest-year-2019.html.

12. Kendra Pierre-Louis, "Ocean Warming Is Accelerating Faster than Thought, New Research Finds," *NYT*, 1/10/2019, https://www.nytimes.com/2019/01/10/climate/ocean-warming-climate-change.html.

13. Chris Mooney and John Muyskens, "Dangerous New Hot Zones Are Spreading around the World," *WP*, 9/11/2019, https://www.washingtonpost.com/graphics/2019/national/climate-environment/climate-change-world/.

14. Durwood J. Zaelke and Paul Bledsoe, "Our Future Depends on the Arctic," *NYT*, 12/14/2019, https://www.nytimes.com/2019/12/14/opinion/sunday/climate-change-arctic.html; D. Perovich et al., "Sea

Ice," *2019 Arctic Report Card*, NOAA Arctic Program (2019), https://arctic.noaa.gov/Report-Card/Report-Card-2019/ArtMID/7916/ArticleID/841/Sea-Ice; Kristina Pistone, et al., "Radiative Heating of an Ice-Free Arctic Ocean," *Geophysical Research Letters* 46, no. 13 (6/20/2019), 7474–80, https://agupubs.onlinelibrary.wiley.com/doi/abs/10.1029/2019GL082914.

15.   Nicholas R. Golledge et al., "Global Environmental Consequences of Twenty-First-Century Ice-Sheet Melt," *Nature*, vol. 566 (2/6/2019), 65–72, https://www.nature.com/articles/s41586-019-0889-9; Justin Gillis and Kenneth Chang, "Scientists Warn of Rising Oceans from Polar Melt," *NYT*, 5/12/2014, https://www.nytimes.com/2014/05/13/science/earth/collapse-of-parts-of-west-antarctica-ice-sheet-has-begun-scientists-say.html; Chris Mooney, "Two Major Antarctic Glaciers Are Tearing Loose from Their Restraints, Scientists Say," *WP*, 9/14/2020, https://www.washingtonpost.com/climate-environment/2020/09/14/glaciers-breaking-antarctica-pine-island-thwaites; Stef Lhermitte et al., "Damage Accelerates Ice Sheet Instability and Mass Loss in Amundsen Sea Embayment," *Proceedings of the National Academy of Sciences*, 9/14/2020, https://www.pnas.org/content/early/2020/09/08/1912890117.

16.   UCI/JPL, "Antarctica Losing Six Times More Ice Mass Annually Now than 40 Years Ago," *Landsat Science*, 1/28/2019, https://landsat.gsfc.nasa.gov/article/antarctica-losing-six-times-more-ice-mass-annually-now-than-40-years-ago/; Eric Rignot et al., "Four Decades of Antarctic Ice Sheet Mass Balance from 1979–2017," *Proceedings of the National Academy of Sciences* 116, no. 4 (1/22/2019), https://www.pnas.org/content/116/4/1095; Brandon Specktor, "New Satellite Maps Show Dire State of Ice Melt in Antarctica and Greenland," *Live Science*, 5/5/2020, https://www.livescience.com/antarctica-greenland-ice-loss-map-nasa.html. The data in the map titled "Antarctica's Melting Ice Sheets" is based on a map published in Ben Smith et al., "Pervasive Ice Sheet Mass Loss Reflects Competing Ocean and Atmospheric Processes," *Science* 368, issue 6496 (6/12/2020), https://science.sciencemag.org/content/368/6496/1239/tab-article-info.

17.   William J. Ripple et al., "World Scientists' Warning of a Climate Emergency," *BioScience* 70, issue 1 (11/5/2019), https://academic.oup.com/bioscience/advance-article/doi/10.1093/biosci/biz088/5610806.

18.   UN Environment Programme, *Emissions Gap Report 2019* (2019), xiii–xxv, 1, 27, https://wedocs.unep.org/bitstream/handle/20.500.11822/30797/EGR2019.pdf; UN Office of Disaster Risk

Reduction, *Human Costs of Disasters* (2020), 3–7, https://www.undrr.
org/publication/human-cost-disasters-2000-2019.

19.   Damian Carrington, "Unsurvivable Heatwaves Could Strike
       Heart of China by End of Century," *Guardian*, 7/31/2018,
       https://www.theguardian.com/environment/2018/jul/31/
       chinas-most-populous-area-could-be-uninhabitable-by-end-of-century.

20.   Stephanie Hallegatte et al., "Future Flood Losses in Major Coastal Cities,"
       Nature Climate Change 3 (2013), 802–6, https://www.nature.com/
       articles/nclimate1979.

21.   Josh Holder et al., "The Three-Degree World," *Guardian*, 11/3/2017,
       https://www.theguardian.com/cities/ng-interactive/2017/nov/03/three-
       degree-world-cities-drowned-global-warming; Michael Kimmelman,
       "Rising Waters Threaten China's Rising Cities," *NYT*, 4/7/2017, https://
       www.nytimes.com/interactive/2017/04/07/world/asia/climate-change-
       china.html; Jeff Tollefson, "How Hot Will Earth Get by 2100?," *Nature
       News Feature*, 4/22/2020, https://www.nature.com/articles/d41586-020-
       01125-x; Matther Collins et al., "Long-Term Climate Change," in Thomas
       F. Stocker et al., eds., *Climate Change 2013* (2013), 1037, https://www.
       ipcc.ch/site/assets/uploads/2017/09/WG1AR5_Frontmatter_FINAL.
       pdf.

22.   Denise Lu and Christopher Flavelle, "Rising Seas Will Erase More Cities
       by 2050, New Research Shows," *NYT*, 10/29/2019, https://www.
       nytimes.com/interactive/2019/10/29/climate/coastal-cities-underwater.
       html; Scott A. Kulp and Benjamin H. Strauss, "New Elevation Data
       Triple Estimates of Global Vulnerability to Sea-Level Rise and Coastal
       Flooding," *Nature Communications* 10, no. 4844 (2019), https://www.
       nature.com/articles/s41467-019-12808-z.

23.   Carrington, "Unsurvivable Heatwaves"; S. Kang and E.A.B. Eltahir,
       "North China Plain Threatened by Deadly Heatwaves Due to Climate
       Change and Irrigation," *Nature Communication* 9, no. 2894 (2018),
       https://www.nature.com/articles/s41467-018-05252-y.

24.   Kimmelman, "Rising Waters."

25.   "The Chinese Century Is Well Under Way," *The Economist*, 10/27/2018,
       https://www.economist.com/graphic-detail/2018/10/27/
       the-chinese-century-is-well-under-way.

26.   Thomas E. Lovejoy and Carlos Nobre, "Amazon Tipping Point," *Science
       Advances* 5, no. 12 (2019), https://advances.sciencemag.org/content/5/12/
       eaba2949; Bruno Carvalho and Carlos Nobre, "We're Turning the
       Amazon into a Savannah," *NYT*, 10/2/2020, https://www.nytimes.

com/2020/10/02/opinion/amazon-rainforest-climate-change.html.

27. "Fast Facts about Permafrost," Center for Permafrost, University of
    Copenhagen, https://cenperm.ku.dk/facts-about-permafrost/; Canadian
    Cryosphere Watch, "Current Permafrost in Canada" (6/11/2017),
    https://ccin.ca/ccw/permafrost/current; Canadian Cryosphere Watch,
    "Future of Permafrost in Canada" (6/11/2017), https://ccin.ca/
    ccw/permafrost/future; Vladimir E. Romanovsky et al., "Permafrost
    Thermal State in the Polar Northern Hemisphere during International
    Polar Year 2007–2009," *Permafrost and Periglacial Processes* 21 (2010),
    106–16, https://onlinelibrary-wiley-com.ezproxy.library.wisc.edu/doi/
    pdfdirect/10.1002/ppp.689. The Canadian Cryosphere Watch site
    ("Future of Permafrost in Canada") contains a publicly accessible version
    of Vladimir E. Romanovsky's 2009 map "The Future Permafrost Thaw
    across the Circumpolar Arctic," which was reproduced in a *Scientific
    American* article (Katey Walter Anthony, "Methane," December 2009, 70)
    and is the basis for the "Melting Permafrost" map in this chapter.

28. Jonathan L. Bamber et al., "Ice Sheet Contributions to Future Sea-Level
    Rise from Structured Expert Judgment," *Proceedings of the National
    Academy of Sciences* 116, no. 23 (6/4/2019), 11195–200, https://www.
    pnas.org/content/early/2019/05/14/1817205116; Sareena Dayaram,
    "Sea Levels May Rise Much Faster than Previously Predicted, Swamping
    Coastal Cities Such as Shanghai, Study Finds," *CNN*, 5/21/2019, https://
    www.cnn.com/2019/05/21/health/climate-change-sea-levels-scn-intl/
    index.html.

29. Abrahm Lustgarten, "The Great Climate Migration," *NYT*, 7/23/2020,
    https://www.nytimes.com/interactive/2020/07/23/magazine/climate-
    migration.html; Chi Xu et al., "Future of the Human Climate Niche,"
    Proceedings of the National Academy of Sciences 117, no. 21 (5/26/2020),
    11350–55, https://www.pnas.org/content/117/21/11350/tab-article-
    info; Eun-Soon Im et al., "Deadly Heat Waves Projected in the Densely
    Populated Agricultural Regions of South Asia," *Science Advances* 3, no. 8
    (8/2/2017), https://advances.sciencemag.org/content/3/8/e1603322;
    Dilip Kumar, "River Ganges," *Aquatic Ecosystem Health and Management*
    20, nos. 1/2 (2017), 8–20, https://www.tandfonline.com/doi/full/10.108
    0/14634988.2017.1304129.

30. Brad Plumer, "The World's Oceans Are in Danger, Major Climate Report
    Warns," *NYT*, 9/25/2019, https://www.nytimes.com/2019/09/25/
    climate/climate-change-oceans-united-nations.html; Intergovernmental
    Panel on Climate Change, "IPCC Press Release," 9/25/2019, https://

www.ipcc.ch/site/assets/uploads/sites/3/2019/09/SROCC_
PressRelease_EN.pdf; Intergovernmental Panel on Climate Change,
*IPCC Special Report on the Ocean and Cryosphere in a Changing Climate:
Summary for Policy Makers* (9/24/2019), 22–23, https://www.ipcc.ch/
site/assets/uploads/sites/3/2019/11/03_SROCC_SPM_FINAL.pdf.

31. Plumer, "The World's Oceans Are in Danger"; IPCC, "Press Release,"
     9/25/2019; IPCC, *Special Report*, 6–7, 20.

32. Merritt R. Turetsky et al., "Permafrost Collapse Is Accelerating Carbon
     Release," *Nature* 569 (4/30/2019), 32–34, https://www.nature.
     com/articles/d41586-019-01313-4; Anton Troianovski, "A Historic
     Heat Wave Roasts Siberia," *NYT*, 6/25/2020, https://www.nytimes.
     com/2020/06/25/world/europe/siberia-heat-wave-climate-change.
     html; Andrew Kramer, "Land in Russia's Arctic Blows 'Like a Bottle of
     Champagne,'" *NYT*, 9/5/2020, https://www.nytimes.com/2020/09/05/
     world/europe/russia-arctic-eruptions.html.

33. Turetsky, "Permafrost Collapse."

34. Katey Walter Anthony, "Arctic Climate Threat—Methane from Thawing
     Permafrost," *Scientific American* (December 2009), 69–75, https://
     www.scientificamerican.com/article/methane-a-menace-surfaces/; K.M.
     Walter et al., "Methane Bubbling from Siberian Thaw Lakes as a Positive
     Feedback to Climate Warming," *Nature* 443 (2006), 71–75, https://www.
     nature.com/articles/nature05040.

35. T. Schuur, "Permafrost and the Global Carbon Cycle," *2019 Arctic Report
     Card*, NOAA Arctic Program (2019), https://arctic.noaa.gov/Report-
     Card/Report-Card-2019/ArtMID/7916/ArticleID/844/Permafrost-
     and-the-Global-Carbon-Cycle; Brian Resnick, "Scientists Feared
     Unstoppable Emissions from Melting Permafrost," *Vox*, 12/12/2019,
     https://www.vox.com/energy-and-environment/2019/12/12/21011445/
     permafrost-melting-arctic-report-card-noaa; IPCC, *Special Report*, 24.

36. Nicola Jones, "How the World Passed a Carbon Threshold and Why It
     Matters," *Yale Environment 360* (1/26/2017), https://e360.yale.edu/
     features/how-the-world-passed-a-carbon-threshold-400ppm-and-
     why-it-matters.

37. Somini Sengupta, "U.N. Climate Talks End with Few Commitments
     and a 'Lost' Opportunity," *NYT*, 12/15/2019, https://www.nytimes.
     com/2019/12/15/climate/cop25-un-climate-talks-madrid.html.

Index

Page numbers in *italic* refer to illustrations. "Passim" (literally "scattered") indicates intermittent discussion of a topic over a cluster of pages.

About the Author

Alfred McCoy holds the Harrington Chair in History at the University of Wisconsin–Madison. His 2009 book Policing America's Empire wonthe Kahin Prize from the Association for Asian Studies. In 2012, Yale University awarded him the Wilbur Cross Medal for work as "one of the world's leading historians of Southeast Asia and an expert on international political surveillance."

About Haymarket Books

Haymarket Books is a radical, independent, nonprofit book publisher based in Chicago.

Our mission is to publish books that contribute to struggles for social and economic justice. We strive to make our books a vibrant and organic part of social movements and the education and development of a critical, engaged, international left.

We take inspiration and courage from our namesakes, the Haymarket martyrs, who gave their lives fighting for a better world. Their 1886 struggle for the eight-hour day—which gave us May Day, the international workers' holiday—reminds workers around the world that ordinary people can organize and struggle for their own liberation. These struggles continue today across the globe—struggles against oppression, exploitation, poverty, and war.

Since our founding in 2001, Haymarket Books has published more than five hundred titles. Radically independent, we seek to drive a wedge into the risk-averse world of corporate book publishing. Our authors include Noam Chomsky, Arundhati Roy, Rebecca Solnit, Angela Y. Davis, Howard Zinn, Amy Goodman, Wallace Shawn, Mike Davis, Winona LaDuke, Ilan Pappé, Richard Wolff, Dave Zirin, Keeanga-Yamahtta Taylor, Nick Turse, Dahr Jamail, David Barsamian, Elizabeth Laird, Amira Hass, Mark Steel, Avi Lewis, Naomi Klein, and Neil Davidson. We are also the trade publishers of the acclaimed Historical Materialism Book Series and of Dispatch Books.